For All We Have and Are

For All We Have and Are

Regina and the Experience of the Great War

James M. Pitsula

UNIVERSITY OF MANITOBA PRESS

© 2008 James M. Pitsula

University of Manitoba Press
Winnipeg, Manitoba Canada R3T 2M5
www.umanitoba.ca/uofmpress

Printed in Canada.

All rights reserved. No part of this publication may be reproduced or transmitted in any form or by any means, or stored in a database and retrieval system, without the prior written permission of the University of Manitoba Press, or, in the case of photocopying or any other reprographic copying, a licence from ACCESS COPYRIGHT (Canadian Copyright Licencing Agency) 6 Adelaide Street East, Suite 901, Toronto, Ontario M5C 1H6, www.accesscopyright.ca.

Cover and interior design: Doowah Design

Cover photograph: Unveiling of the Regina cenotaph, 11 November, 1926. (Saskatchewan Archives Board)

Library and Archives Canada Cataloguing in Publication

Pitsula, James M. (James Michael), 1950-
For all we have and are : Regina and the experience of the great war / James M. Pitsula.
Includes bibliographical references and index.
ISBN 978-0-88755-708-8 (pbk.).--ISBN 978-0-88755-185-7 (bound)
1. World War, 1914-1918--Saskatchewan--Regina. 2. Regina (Sask.)--History.
I. Title.
FC3546.4.P58 2008   940.3'712445   C2008-902256-4

The University of Manitoba Press gratefully acknowledges the financial support for its publication program provided by the Government of Canada through the Book Publishing Industry Development Program (BPIDP), the Canada Council for the Arts, the Manitoba Arts Council, and the Manitoba Department of Culture, Heritage, Tourism and Sport.

Support for the publication of this book has also been provided by the Humanities Research Institute, University of Regina.

Table of Contents

Introduction	1
Chapter 1: War Comes to Regina	21
Chapter 2: The First Year	45
Chapter 3: Brave New World	69
Chapter 4: The Battle over Schools	95
Chapter 5: The Preacher and the Premier	113
Chapter 6: News from the Front	131
Chapter 7: The Twenty-Eighth Battalion	157
Chapter 8: The End of Voluntarism	173
Chapter 9: The Economy and the Rural Myth	195
Chapter 10: Religion and Social Reform	213
Chapter 11: Returned Soldiers	233
Chapter 12: Victory	249
Epilogue: Crown of Thorns	265
Notes	283
Bibliography	339
Index	355

Photographs appear between pages 172 and 173.

Photo credits:
The photographs in this book are reproduced courtesy of the Saskatchewan Archives Board (SAB) and the Major Gordon F. Goddard collection (GG).

For Michael Pitsula,
RCAF, 1943-1945

Introduction

WHEN DID CANADA BECOME A NATION? SOME SAY 1 JULY 1867, WHEN Ontario, Quebec, Nova Scotia, and New Brunswick came together in Confederation to form the Dominion of Canada. Others suggest the statute of Westminster in 1931, when Canada was given the right to control its own foreign policy. Still others wonder whether, even today, we are fully a nation. Charles Stacey gave one of the best responses to the question in an address to the Canadian Historical Association in 1967. He said that "among the deep experiences of the Canadian people one stands out. In many ways the First World War was the most important event in Canadian history.... It came on the country without warning; at midsummer of 1914 nobody thought that the Little Town in the sunshine that Stephen Leacock had described two years before was to be plunged into that maelstrom, along with a thousand other Canadian communities great and small."[1] Regina was one such little town, and this book is the story of how it experienced the Great War.[2]

With a population of 30,213 in 1911, Regina contributed 6500 men to the Canadian Expeditionary Force.³ Many came from the surrounding farms, towns, and villages to enlist in the city because they could not do so in their home communities. Conversely, men from Regina enlisted in Winnipeg, Toronto, and other cities, where they had family ties or happened to be residing, for example, as university students, when the war broke out. Their departure was keenly felt. In May 1918 the Salisbury chapter of the Imperial Order Daughters of the Empire (IODE) held a supper party at the Legislative Building to honour women of Regina and district who had at least three men in their immediate family (three sons or a husband and two sons) in khaki. A total of 155 mothers fit the description. One Regina mother had seven boys, six of whom had enlisted. Another with nine sons had five of them overseas.⁴

Those at home followed the course of the war with close attention. Families who received letters from the front submitted them to the newspaper, and hundreds were published, giving readers an intimate (if censored) glimpse of life in the trenches. There was the usual bravado—soldiers boasted of how they could hardly wait to get into action and have a go at the Germans—but there were also admissions of fear and anxiety. Men worried about how they would perform when they first went into battle; they described horrific scenes of death and destruction, and, in some cases, expressed deep longing to have done with it and come home as soon as possible.

Wounded men began to return to Regina as early as 1915. In the fall of 1916, a veterans' organization was formed in the city. The chasm between home front and battlefront was not always as wide as one might expect. Those at home knew, dimly at least, what their loved ones were going through. They understood something of the courage, agony, and sacrifice of the Canadian soldier. Grief, at times, was overwhelming. News reached the city in October 1916 that thirty-four-year-old A. Frank Mantle, Deputy Minister of Agriculture, had been killed at the front. He was a man of such ability and character that it had been said of him that one day he might be premier. When word of his death reached the Legislative Building in Regina, the staff at first kept on working, but as the news sank in, employees were seen weeping at their desks. Everyone was sent home for the remainder of the day.[5]

Regina women mobilized to support the Patriotic Fund (to help soldiers' wives, children, and other dependents), the Red Cross, Belgian Relief Fund, and other wartime charities. They sponsored concerts, teas, dances, and raffles, and stood on street corners holding collection boxes and "tagging" those who made a twenty-five-cent donation. They sewed, knit, and rolled bandages. Scanning casualty lists, they hoped not to find what they were looking for. Each time a draft of troops left, an enthusiastic crowd gathered at the train station to see them off. A crowd was there again when the trains came back, carrying the wounded heroes. On each anniversary of the declaration of the war, Reginans marched in a parade, rededicating themselves to the cause. When victory finally came on 11 November 1918, joy was unrestrained.

Regina's war was in many respects a microcosm of Saskatchewan's war. The city identified itself closely with the province of which it was capital city. Its fortunes were tied to agriculture, and the urban-rural split of later years had not yet emerged. Regina lived, as did Saskatchewan, by the motto "In Wheat We Trust."[6] As capital city, it was the place where the wartime political dramas played out—the granting of votes to women, the implementation of prohibition, and the banning of foreign languages from the schools. Regina mirrored the province in another way, too. The proportion of "foreigners" (those not born under the British flag) in the city in 1911 was about 30.6 percent. For the province as a whole, it was about 49 percent.[7] Thus, Regina knew firsthand the ethnic tensions exacerbated by the war. In this, as in other respects, Regina was Saskatchewan distilled.

The British Canadian and the "Foreigner"

Canada did not declare war against Germany in 1914; we were included in and bound by Britain's declaration of war. As a colony, we did not have the constitutional authority to make the decision. That being said, it is not correct to say that Canada went to war "just because Britain told us to." Many Canadians, especially those of British heritage, were emotionally attached to the empire. It was part of their identity, and they saw no contradiction in being both British and Canadian. For them, a Canadian was a British type of North American, their patriotism a hybrid of imperialism and nationalism.[8] They were British, but "British in their own way."[9]

There was also an ideological dimension to the war. Germany in 1914 was not the liberal democracy it later became. The kaiser had absolute power. He did not have to listen to his parliament (*Reichstag*), which had a purely advisory function. Parliament was not supreme, as it was in Britain and Canada. Further, Germany was widely perceived as a bully and disturber of international peace. It invaded Belgium despite having signed a treaty to respect Belgian neutrality, a clear breach of international law. If Britain allowed Germany to get away with it, "might" would have triumphed over "right." To this extent, World War I had an ideological underpinning. It was fought for democracy, human rights, freedom, and the rule of law, the same justification that was used for World War II, the Cold War, and now the war in Afghanistan.

World War I was also what Jay Winter calls a "cultural mobilization."[10] Germany challenged British civilization and all it stood for, its ideals, values, and codes of conduct. It came down, in the end, to a fight for a way of life. Ian Miller, in his study of wartime Toronto, puts it this way: "Torontonians were committed, body and soul, to defeating Germany. They believed that everything the Empire stood for was being tested in the great conflict. Citizens understood that they were fighting for more than territorial or political gain. They were fighting for the very future of the civilization they had created."[11] They fought, in Rudyard Kipling's words, for "all we have and are."[12]

Although not everybody in Regina or Saskatchewan was British, Anglo-Saxon Protestants were firmly in the driver's seat. They controlled the government (except at the local level where the non-British were sometimes elected to municipal councils and school boards), the judiciary, professions, education, businesses and financial institutions, daily newspapers, the Grain Growers' Association, trade unions, and most women's groups and social reform organizations. The non-British, for the most part, did the heavy, manual work. They ploughed the fields, built the railways, cut the timber, mined the coal, and dug the ditches for water and sewer lines. Economic prosperity depended on their backbreaking labour. As Angus McLaren writes, "most realized that Canada needed immigrants to do the hard, dirty work of building a country, but they worried about the sort of country that would result."[13]

The "foreigner," notwithstanding his lowly status, had a powerful weapon. He could vote. An immigrant had only to live in Canada for three years to be eligible for naturalization, which conferred status as a British subject.[14] In Saskatchewan, the Liberal Party assiduously courted him, which partly explains why it held uninterrupted power from 1905 to 1929. Jim Calder, the Liberal Party boss, got to the heart of the matter in 1908: "There is not a Dominion or local Constituency in Saskatchewan in which there is not a very heavy German vote, and as the majority of them have been voting Liberal in the past it is very important indeed that they should be kept thoroughly posted regarding the political questions of the day."[15] The Liberals in 1907 put up the money for a German-language newspaper, *Der Courier*, which was published in Regina. The paper posed the question: "Why are most German-Canadians Liberal?" The reason, it said, was simple: "The Liberal party is for the farmer, the working man. In addition, the Tories are always prone to British jingoism—'Old England,' while we are the 'foreigners' ... Tories espouse English, not Canadian interests, and if they, with their pro-British policies can arouse anti-German feelings, why, they think 'so much the better.'"[16] The Liberals also subsidized newspapers for Icelanders, Norwegians, Swedes, Ukrainians, Hungarians, and Jews,[17] leaving nothing to chance in the quest for Liberal votes.

It is a mistake to read today's multiculturalism policy into early twentieth-century politics. The British of the day, as Philip Buckner rightly points out, were not "cultural relativists."[18] They believed in the superiority of British civilization and they expected the "foreigner" to conform to it. That is what they meant by "Canadianization." There was no real difference between Liberals and Conservatives in this respect. They differed only as to tactics. The Liberals favoured a soft, gradualist approach; the Conservatives came across as shrill and coercive. But they were in agreement as to the essential features of the British-Canadian society they wanted to build in Saskatchewan.

Thousands of Britons left Saskatchewan to fight in the trenches, while "foreigners" stayed home and sold wheat at record prices. The British were getting killed; the "foreigners" were getting rich. School inspector and future premier J.T.M. Anderson worried in 1918: "When the vastness of this immigrant tide that has almost unceasingly set towards our Dominion during the past ten years is considered, we may well ask whether this in-sweeping immigration can be Canadianized."[19] The conflict centred on the public school, which was seen as the primary instrument of assimilation. Before the war, the School Act allowed non-English-language instruction in the last hour of the school day. In 1918 the right was taken away and an English-only policy enforced.[20] The measure was symbolic as much as it was substantive. It showed the "foreigner" who was boss. The victory for British civilization won on the battlefields of Europe was not to be squandered in the schoolrooms of Saskatchewan.

As it turned out, there was an unexpected development in the politics of conflicting national identities. The war proved to be a "coming-of-age" event for Canada.[21] The remarkable feats of the Canadian Corps (in battle after battle, they defeated the Germans and, as Charles Stacey says, the Germans "are not really easy people to beat")[22] fostered a Canada-oriented, as distinct from a Britain-oriented, Canadian nationalism. When Canadians mentioned "the national anthem" in 1914, they referred invariably to "God Save the King." "O Canada" was sung at concerts and public gatherings, but it was not accorded, either legally or by popular consent, the status of anthem. The Regina *Leader* published an article (reprinted from the Victoria *Colonist*) in August 1917, which suggested a shift in public attitude. "God Save the King" was no longer a fully satisfactory expression of national sentiment:

To be sure we have the National Anthem, and everybody knows that and sings it with a will. But just now we want something more, something more intimate; more directly appealing to us as Canadians.... For the old order of things is passing away; what was enough for us in the past is no longer. We shall always sing 'God Save the King' with unflinchable loyalty, but we want something more than that to express all that is in our hearts, and that is growing stronger the older we grow and the better we appreciate our status as Canadians.[23]

During the war, Canadians added a new verse to "God Save the King":

God save our noble men,
Send them back home again,
God save our men.
Turn Thou their Hearts to Thee,
Fighting to keep us free,
God grant them victory,
Our much loved men.[24]

The Great War Veterans' Association at their national convention in August 1918 made a slight change to the order of proceedings at their meetings. They voted to sing one verse of "O Canada" before they sang "God Save the King."[25] The intention was not to discard the old anthem. It was still a part of the program, but it no longer fully expressed what the veterans felt about their national identity. Canada was still British, but not as British as it had been before the war.

The Rural Myth

For Regina and Saskatchewan, the war reinforced the rural myth. The term "myth" is used here in the sense of a dominant cultural narrative, as Richard Hofstadter writes, "that so effectively embodies men's values that it profoundly influences their way of perceiving reality and hence their behavior."[26] The Saskatchewan rural myth arose from the rapid expansion of the wheat economy in the years preceding the war.[27] The population of the Prairie provinces increased from 420,000 in 1900 to 1,700,000 in 1916.[28] Homesteaders poured in, railways were built, towns sprang up, and Saskatchewan became the third-most populous province in the Dominion

7

(647,835 in 1916).²⁹ Elizabeth Mitchell, a Scottish travel writer, captured the ebullient spirit: "All along the railway across three provinces, in those pre-1914 days, new towns were bursting from the empty prairie like the grass and flowers after the thaw. The air was full of youth and confidence. The citizens were so proud of their towns, partly no doubt from the profit motive, partly from sheer exuberance. It was a refreshing atmosphere to breathe."³⁰ Walter Scott, the first premier of Saskatchewan, matter-of-factly observed that "a young man of fair intelligence and industrious habits can scarcely fail to reach an independent position before he has passed middle life."³¹

The prairie farmer was not a self-sufficient pioneer. From the outset, he was engaged in commercial agriculture, producing a large surplus of grain and using the proceeds to purchase manufactured goods. He bought "farm implements, hardware goods, wagons, harnesses, lumber and other supplies." He needed banking services and "consumer goods that he could not produce himself: clothing and staple foodstuffs."³² In other words, he needed a town. Towns in turn required central distribution centres "to receive large volumes of manufactured goods from the East which could be shipped to the towns in smaller quantities." Five such centres emerged in the Prairie West before the war—Winnipeg, Regina, Saskatoon, Edmonton, and Calgary—setting the pattern of urban development that continues to this day. Here were established grain terminals, stockyards, warehouses, wholesale houses and rail yards, banks, office buildings, not to mention "teachers, doctors, lawyers, entertainers, barbers, cooks, launderers, policemen, engineers, accountants, prostitutes, saloon keepers, and clergymen."³³

Regina made its living as a service and distribution centre for the surrounding agricultural hinterland. First settled in 1882, it acquired a townsite in 1883, when it was designated North West Mounted Police headquarters and seat of government for the Northwest Territories. In 1903 it was incorporated as a city, and it became capital of the newly formed province of Saskatchewan in 1905. As homesteaders entered the region, Regina's population leapt from 2249 in 1901 to 30,213 in 1911. Eight lines of railway track radiated from its centre, including the Canadian Pacific Railway, the

Canadian Northern Railway, and the Grand Trunk Pacific. By 1913, thirty-three passenger trains arrived and departed daily.[34] Wholesale goods were shipped out to an estimated 250 towns and villages in an area with a population of about 400,000.[35]

The big money was in real estate, "the Great Goddess of the Western town whom Saskatchewan and all the world worshippeth."[36] The formula was "to purchase vacant land, divide it into lots, advertise the surrounding country as suitable arable land, and grow rich by selling the town lots."[37] Extensive subdivisions were laid out that existed only in the imagination of the speculator-cum-gambler. With an area of 1942 acres in 1883, Regina quadrupled its size in 1911 by adding 6458 acres. It did not have to acquire additional land until the 1950s.[38] Seven of Regina's ten aldermen in 1913 were involved in the real estate business.[39] If you had money to invest, you were a fool not to be buying and selling land in the feverish boom that preceded the war.

The buoyant mood found expression in the construction of the Legislative Building, which formally opened in October 1912. A magnificent edifice, it dominated the small, straggling city of modest homes, wooden sidewalks, and unpaved streets. The elegant, classical dome could be seen for miles around. When the architect selected red brick to cover the exterior walls, Premier Walter Scott felt compelled to intervene. He did not think that red brick did justice to the province, whose lofty aspirations the building was meant to symbolize. No, it had to be Tyndall limestone for the exterior, and, for the inside, thirty-four different types of marble.[40] Scott predicted that the population of Saskatchewan would soon be "running into the tens of millions."[41] (One hundred years later, it is slightly over one million.)

The heady ambitions of the day were centred on agriculture. As the Regina *Leader* stated in 1917:

> Nobody in this Province will be found to question the truth of the assertion that the growth, development and prosperity of our cities, towns and villages is based on our agricultural development and the rural prosperity of the Province. The city and town dweller follows the ups and downs of the growing crop throughout the summer with almost as deep an anxiety as does

the farmer himself. And rightly so, because if the crop fails the farmers suffer, but so, too, does the business man, the workingman, and all those who live in the cities and towns.[42]

Provincial Treasurer Charles Dunning admitted in 1920, only half-sheepishly, that he had no accurate statistics of the manufacturing output of the province.[43] It was so inconsequential as to be hardly worth mentioning.

The annual convention of the Saskatchewan Grain Growers' Association (SGGA), which in 1917 had 1100 locals and 30,000 members,[44] constituted a shadow parliament for the province. Politicians ignored it at their peril. Premier Walter Scott appointed two former members of the SGGA executive to his cabinet: W.R. Motherwell, Minister of Agriculture in 1905, and George Langley, Minister of Municipal Affairs, in 1912.[45] Langley continued as a director of the SGGA, even while serving as minister. William Martin, who succeeded Scott as premier in October 1916, made Charles Dunning, who was SGGA vice-president and manager of the Saskatchewan Cooperative Elevator Company, provincial Treasurer, further strengthening the relationship between the farmers' organization and the government.

The *Leader* called the SGGA "the largest, best organized and undoubtedly most influential secular organization in the Province of Saskatchewan."[46] The SGGA secretary, F.W. Green, deemed it "God's great engine of Democracy."[47] One Sunday each year was designated "Grain Growers' Sunday." Pulpits offered up praise for the honest tillers of the soil and their unsurpassed contribution to the welfare of the province. "In the everyday, workaday world, through their many locals, district conventions and great annual gatherings, the Saskatchewan Grain Growers are steadily endeavoring to raise the standard in all things affecting the lives of our people," enthused the *Leader*. "In this work the church may well bid it Godspeed."[48] The rural myth gave the farmer special status. On him the success of the province depended.

The myth had another ingredient, which increased its potency. The farmer waged a constant struggle against early frosts, blinding blizzards, too much water, too little water, tornadoes, hail, grasshoppers, and other natural disasters. Such trials and tribulations had to be borne. Nothing could be done about them. Not so the burdens imposed by central Canadian manufacturers, railways, banks, and grain companies, who, together with their political friends in Ottawa, plotted against the farmer. Known collectively as the "Big Interests," they were the farmer's nemesis, his evil foil. As Russel Nye writes, the agenda of the big business corporation went something like this: "*Order of Business*: bankrupt farmers, form new monopoly, rig market, fix prices; *Resolutions passed*: raise interest rates, lower farm prices, instruct business through interlocking directorates to raise prices on all goods sold to farmers, order newspapers to support regular party candidates, allot money to 'educate' legislatures, declare dividend, adjourn."[49] The war against the Big Interests was the "salt and savor" of Saskatchewan politics.[50]

Discontent centred on the protective tariff, put in place by John A. Macdonald in 1879 for the benefit of the business elites of central Canada. It imposed an average 30 percent tariff on imported manufactured goods, raising prices for farmers, and shielding Ontario and Quebec industry from outside competition.[51] Farmers, meanwhile, had to sell on the open market, putting their product up against the best the world had to offer. They had no allies in Ottawa to cut them a sweet deal. To this was added a litany of grievances concerning freight costs, grain-handling procedures, and interest rates. The injustice of it all made the blood boil.

Prime Minister Wilfrid Laurier, in the 1911 federal election, promised free trade in natural products with the United States and a reduced tariff on a limited list of manufactured goods. The Big Interests threw their support to the Tories led by Robert Borden, who won the election. The main beneficiaries at the provincial level were the Liberals, who based their 1912 Saskatchewan election campaign on opposition to the protective tariff, the Big Interests, and their federal Tory friends. As one prominent Liberal remarked, "You have only to go out into any part of the Province—ask the man on the street—and ask what is going to be the chief question of the campaign, and you will receive this answer: Reciprocity or the question of markets."[52] Scott swept the province, winning forty-six out of fifty-four seats and 57 percent of the popular vote.[53] The rural myth was not entirely spontaneous; rather, it was deliberately whipped up to serve partisan political advantage.

World War I confirmed and consolidated the myth. The federal government asked farmers to grow as much wheat as possible to feed the soldiers and hungry civilian allies. They responded with patriotic enthusiasm, doubling their acreages. The value of Saskatchewan agricultural production soared as a result of the war. Industrial production, by contrast, was modest. Regina was not awarded any contracts for munitions production, while the entire Prairie West received only 0.67 percent of the more than $1 billion worth of munitions work allocated by the Imperial Munitions Board.[54] The basic structure of pre-war economic development—staple production in the west and manufacturing in central Canada—was perpetuated. The war did nothing to develop industry on the Prairies; it failed utterly to diversify the economy.

The war also deepened popular antagonism against the Big Interests. The manufacturers, who were already protected by the tariff, now benefited from war contracts. They made exorbitant profits on the production of shells, guns, wagons, uniforms, boots, and other commodities. It was the same old tune in a different key. With Tory friends in high places, the Big Interests got both the tariff and the munitions contracts they wanted. Meanwhile, the cost of living rose to unprecedented levels, and Canadians died by the thousands in the trenches. This was democracy? This was what we were fighting for? The *Leader* declared in October 1917 that Canada was fighting two wars.[55] One was against Germany and the other against the Big Interests. Both enemies crushed the people, trampled democracy, and imposed a ruthless tyranny. Both had to be defeated.

The rural myth expressed itself in yet another way. Acute farm labour shortages made it necessary for Reginans and other urban-dwellers to plough the furrow and gather in the sheaves. Emergency calls went out to able-bodied men and women. High school and senior elementary students were excused from writing final examinations if they signed up as "Soldiers of the Soil." Business and professional men were asked to forego their summer vacations for the higher duty of milking cows. Even those who stayed in the city did not escape the barrage of rural propaganda. Homeowners were instructed to grow vegetables in their backyards and cultivate vacant lots. There was no excuse for not growing food. Every potato was a bullet, and every gardener's blister an honourable wound.

The Social Gospel

World War I was a shock to the progressive mind. The upward march of mankind to enlightenment and prosperity was suddenly arrested and reversed. The response was to turn calamity into opportunity, to give the war apocalyptic significance, making it "the war to end war."[56] Progressivism in Canada was heavily inflected with the social gospel, the Protestant movement to reform society in accordance with Christian principles.[57] Rev. J.S. Woodsworth in May 1913 preached a sermon at Metropolitan Methodist Church in Regina on the theme, "Thy Kingdom come, as in Heaven, so in Regina and Moose Jaw, Saskatoon and Winnipeg." For too long, he said, the church "had spent its time telling people how to die and how to get into Heaven, away from this wicked world. I am glad that the new thought is how to live so that Heaven may be brought to earth. We are learning that religion is not a form, not a creed, but a life."[58]

The social gospel turned the war into a holy crusade. Germany was demonized, made to represent the ultimate evil that the social gospel was trying to get rid of. Rev. Samuel D. Chown, general superintendent of the Methodist Church in Canada, declared in September 1914: "We are persuaded that this war is just, honorable and necessary for the defence of the principle of righteousness and the freedom of our Empire in all its parts. We believe it to be a world struggle for liberty against military despotism which, if successful, would make our life not worth living."[59] Rev. Robert Milliken, a Methodist minister in Regina, was even more direct. He characterized the war as "only another step in the age-long conflict between the Christ and the anti-Christ, so that those responding to the call of the country are really responding to the call of God.... So that any one denying the call or failing to help in any way that lies in his power is in reality denying Christ."⁶⁰

Saskatchewan liked to think of itself as the "banner province," leading the Dominion on the path of social reform. Scott, a printer by trade, sympathized with organized labour. A 1908 Liberal election poster read: "Vote for Scott and Boost the Union Label."⁶¹ The government introduced a fair-wage clause in government contracts, workmen's compensation, and laws to regulate working conditions for women and children. The Liberal Party advertised itself as the friend of the common man and an enemy of the Big Interests, running in 1917 on the slogan, "Vote Liberal and so secure that in the future, as in the past, the party representing the masses, and not the classes, shall govern the province."⁶²

The Saskatchewan government was willing to intervene in the workings of the free market to achieve goals deemed in the public interest. It subsidized the farmer-owned Saskatchewan Cooperative Elevator Company,⁶³ paying 85 percent of the upfront cost of new grain elevators.⁶⁴ It bought out the Bell Telephone Company and established a provincial Department of Telephones to deliver long-distance service.⁶⁵ Local service was left to municipal and cooperative enterprise. Although not socialist, the government was more than willing to help citizens who were willing to help themselves, even if it meant going against laissez-faire principles.

The war did not sidetrack progressive tendencies, but rather boosted them. It was a time of personal sacrifice for the good of the nation. The soldier's service on the battlefield compelled commensurate sacrifice at home. The prohibition movement, which had sputtered before the war, now rode an irresistible wave to success. By December 1916, the entire province was dry, at least officially. Similarly, the women's suffrage movement, which had plodded along before 1914, achieved its goal in 1916 with almost no controversy. Towards the end of the war, the Saskatchewan Social Service Council put forward a "win-the-war platform" that called for a massive expansion of the role of government, including nationalization of war industries and transportation, price controls, a minimum wage, public health, and child welfare.

Progressivism built on and reinforced the anti-big business mindset of the province. Greedy capitalists, it was charged, flouted the biblical golden rule, maximizing profits at the expense of toiling humanity. The 1918 national conference of the Methodist Church, with only four dissenting votes, passed a resolution that called for "nothing less than a transference of the whole economic life from a basis of competition and profits to one of cooperation and service." Private property and the free market stood condemned. "A new system of production and service for human needs rather than for private profit" was to replace it.[66]

The largely Protestant social gospel viewed doubtfully the hordes of Catholic immigrants from central and eastern Europe. The illiteracy and customs of Ukrainians confirmed the belief that "Catholicism negated individual freedom and fostered superstition and ignorance."[67] Father George T. Daly, rector of Holy Rosary Cathedral in Regina, noted of Protestant missionaries: "With the preconceived idea that their [referring to the Ukrainians] religion with its ritual, language and traditions, is the greatest obstacle to their nationalization and to its inherent benefits, these agents are multiplying their efforts to wean new Canadians from the faith of their fathers." He cited the 1918 report of the Methodist Missionary Society: "Many of these Ruthenian [i.e., Ukrainian] people are ignorant and degraded; and under the sinister influence of their priests are resolved to resist all Canadianizing influences."[68] A good Canadian was a British Protestant Canadian, or so said the social gospel.

Interlocking themes came together to shape Regina's war experience. The increase in agricultural production confirmed the belief that agriculture was destiny. Profiteering on munitions contracts intensified opposition to the Big Interests. The soldier's heroism was held up as the model for the sacrifices at home required to build a better Canada. British Protestants made the school the front-line defence of the English language and British civilization. In each case, Saskatchewan read homegrown concerns into the war being fought overseas. The latter was a screen onto which the province projected its domestic anxieties. Conversely, the war against Germany reverberated back to the home front, making social reform and Canadianization even more urgent than they had been before the fighting started.

Regina before the War

Regina before the war had the usual amenities of a modest-sized Prairie town. There were two hospitals, the General and the Grey Nuns', plus a small isolation hospital for quarantine cases. The Collegiate Institute (a fancy name for a high school) had an enrolment in 1913 of 237 boys and 234 girls. The educational establishment also included public schools (3030 pupils), separate schools (628 pupils), a normal school for teacher training, Methodist Regina College, a Roman Catholic boarding school for girls, and three business colleges.[69] A fine downtown edifice housed the Regina Public Library, which had two smaller branches, one in the northwest part of the city and the other in the east end. At the latter, the librarian spoke German, the first language of most of the clientele.

Churches abounded. Regina had no fewer than five Presbyterian congregations (total seating capacity 2600 with average morning attendance of 1480 and average evening attendance of 2390); seven Anglican churches (seating capacity 1310 with morning attendance 920 and evening attendance 985), and four Methodist churches (seating capacity 2250 and average attendance 2170). There were also five Baptist churches and missions, a Reformed Presbyterian church, Salvation Army barracks, two Lutheran churches, a Roman Catholic cathedral and German Catholic church, a Rumanian Greek Orthodox church, a Jewish synagogue, and several small sects. The YMCA enrolled 1000 members and the YWCA 800. Both offered physical training, Bible study, educational classes, and social opportunities for the "better class of young men and women."[70]

There were a number of city parks and recreational sports leagues for hockey, football (soccer), rugby football, baseball, cricket, boxing, curling, and bowling. On the shores of Wascana Lake (not really a lake, more like a pond) in front of the Legislative Building were a boathouse and bathing hut. Every schoolyard had an outdoor skating rink in winter, and there were two indoor rinks, which became roller rinks in summer. There were five theatres, where avid fans took in vaudeville performances and the latest moving pictures starring Charlie Chaplin and Mary Pickford. Everybody went to the movies, from government officials and college teachers to "European immigrants and Chinamen." On Saturday nights, there were always lineups. Rev. J.S. Woodworth, who conducted a "social survey" of Regina in 1913 for the Methodist and Presbyterian churches, judged the films "fairly good" on the whole, though some were "positively indecent" and others too "American, Wild West, slushy, and cheap."[71] He suggested that the city government take over the movie houses and turn them into a "People's University."[72] That, at least, would have eliminated the Saturday night lineups.

Woodsworth was even more exercised by Regina's ten barrooms, six liquor stores, and two social clubs where liquor was sold. The bars were closed for the Sabbath (from seven o'clock Saturday night until seven o'clock on Monday morning),[73] but during the week they were open from early morning until 10:30 p.m. There were also fourteen poolrooms and eighty pool tables (Woodsworth actually counted them), and three dance halls, all in the east end. "Ordinary rules of etiquette," Woodsworth sniffed, were not observed. Girls came to the dances unaccompanied and introductions were "not necessary."[74] Wordsworth detected little "immorality," but "much coarseness." Quarrelling and fighting were common, and policemen had to be called in to settle disputes.

At any given hour of the day, it was estimated that about 115 men were sitting in one or other of the east-end barrooms. One of Woodsworth's investigators noticed lights on at one bar on Saturday night, even though it was past closing time. When he knocked on the door, the lights were immediately extinguished. Inquiries at one of the dance halls revealed that it had a five-piece orchestra composed of family members of the proprietor. A fifty-cent entry free was charged for male patrons, but women were admitted free. A young man said: "I like this better than to lie on my dirty bed all the time. The room where I am staying drives me mad; I am not satisfied with these people with whom I live, and my job is hard in the day-time, so

I am very willing to spend my fifty cents twice a week because I have here an hour of life."[75]

Regina's non-English-speaking population was largely concentrated in the east end in an area known as Germantown, a working-class district of small houses and shacks. Overcrowding was severe, and sanitation left much to be desired. A five-room house was found to contain a man, his wife, and fourteen boarders. In another dwelling, four rooms accommodated a married couple and six boarders, not to mention a number of chickens, which roamed freely through the house.[76] Each family was permitted to keep one cow, and many did. According to a city bylaw, manure had to be deposited in a tight box with a close-fitting cover. Streets and lanes were mostly unpaved, and very few homes had indoor plumbing.[77] Water lines extended only to Winnipeg Street, which left half of Germantown without service. In any case, over 60 percent of the homes were too poorly constructed to allow for water and sewer hook-ups.[78]

Not that everybody in Germantown was poor. The district boasted thirty-one fruit and grocery stores, seventeen clothing and boot stores, five second-hand shops, five butcher shops, five laundries, eight barber shops (some with pool rooms), six restaurants, five licensed hotels, seven pool rooms, and three dance halls.[79] An ethnically diverse community of Germans, Ukrainians, Rumanians, Bulgarians, and Russians, with sprinklings of British, Belgians, Danes, Finns, French, Greeks, Dutch, Icelandic, Italians, Norwegians, Swedes, Chinese, Syrians, and Turks, it generally supported the Liberal Party, who were perceived as hospitable to immigrants. A well-known Liberal owned a liquor store, and the chairman of the local Liberal committee was proprietor of a licensed hotel.[80] Needless to say, liquor flowed freely at election time. A local Liberal boss, who arrived in Regina with $400 to his name, amassed a fortune of over $100,000 (the equivalent of $1,870,000 today) in just four years.[81]

The inner life of Germantown was largely a mystery to the rest of the population. Not much information appeared in the local press, apart from lurid accounts of knife fights and other incidents that ended up in police court.

The *Leader* was the dominant newspaper with a circulation in December 1917 of 21,887. Of these, 13,475 were sold in the city and the rest in outlying towns and rural areas.[82] Assuming five readers for every copy sold, the paper reached 100,000 people daily.[83] It was a good newspaper—comprehensive, thoughtful, and well written—but relentlessly Liberal. Walter Scott had owned it until 1905, and W.F. Kerr, editor during the war years, was the premier's friend and business partner. Kerr ran for office in the 1930s and was appointed to the Liberal cabinet. The *Leader* benefited financially from its political connections, receiving $90,379 in provincial government printing contracts from 1911 to 1912 alone (about $1,690,000 today).[84] It was a Liberal paper for a Liberal town. Regina had elected nothing but Liberals to the provincial legislature since 1905 and to Ottawa since 1900.

The Conservative paper lacked the financial security and stability of the *Leader*. First it was the *Evening Province and Standard*, then the *Evening Province* (from 14 February 1916) and finally the *Daily Post* (from 19 October 1916). Denied access to government patronage, it eked out a hand-to-mouth existence. The layout was sometimes amateurish, and there were occasional typographical errors in the headlines. Articles were not always well researched, and editorials tended to be skimpy. But at least it was an alternative to incessant Liberal proselytizing, and, by its very existence, kept its rival on its toes. However, in the run-up to the June 1917 provincial election, the *Post* threw in the towel and gave its support to William Martin and the Liberals. Now it, too, received a few crumbs from the government patronage table.[85]

The *Leader*, like all newspapers in Canada, was subject to federal government wartime censorship regulations, put in place to keep sensitive information from the enemy and to maintain public morale. According to Jeffrey Keshen, "the Dominion's jingoistic press did not encourage diversity of opinion, but rather fed off an imperialistic dogma that many historians have asserted held considerable sway in pre-war Canada."[86] On the other hand, the press could not ignore or show contempt for the views of its readers if it wanted to sell newspapers. Even papers with an axe to grind inadvertently shed light on the opinions of dissenters. During the 1916 recruiting crisis, for example, the *Leader* quoted what it considered to be the lame excuses of those who refused to enlist. The quotes were meant to embarrass the "slackers," but they also revealed what they were thinking, even if it did not conform to official patriotism. Read critically, newspapers are a rich source of information for what people in the community were thinking and doing. What rolled off the presses largely corresponded to what was happening on the street.

* * *

Regina before the war was a new, vibrant frontier city. Scarcely more than 10 percent of the population had been born in Saskatchewan. "Real Estate, Wheat and Party Spoils" were the dominant interests. The economy was driven by agriculture, the Liberal Party ruled the roost, and fortunes were amassed in quick turnovers of city lots. Anglo-Saxons may have looked down on "foreigners," but in one sense they were not all that different. Everyone was on the make, pushing to make the most of their opportunities and build a new society in the "Last, Best West." The parties of the "smart set" at Wascana Country Club, said Rev. Woodsworth, "rival[ed] in coarseness those of East End dance halls."[87]

The speculative land bubble burst in 1913, and a serious economic recession set in. Building construction projects ground to a halt, and unemployed workers begged for food and shelter. The fragility of the boom was now exposed. There had been too much greed, too much of the spirit of "getting something for nothing," moralists said. Nothing comes easily; man must live by the sweat of his brow. Sacrifice and service were what counted, not self-aggrandizement and materialism. If that was the moral lesson of the recession, it was about to be mightily reinforced.

Chapter 1

War Comes to Regina

WORLD WAR I BEGAN IN THE BALKANS. WITH THE COLLAPSE OF THE Ottoman Empire, Serbia expelled the Turks and established itself as an independent state. Neighbouring Bosnia, where many ethnic Serbs lived, fell under the rule of the Austro-Hungarian Empire. Serbia set out to unify the Slavs of the region, and, to that end, embarked on a secret campaign of terror against the Austro-Hungarian authorities. On 28 June 1914, in Sarajevo, Bosnia, nineteen-year-old Gavrilo Princep, assisted by Serbian military intelligence, shot and killed Archduke Francis Ferdinand, heir to the throne of Austria-Hungary. Vienna sought revenge, but felt constrained by Serbia's friendship with Russia, which, like Serbia, was Slav in population and Greek Orthodox in religion. If Austria-Hungary were to punish Serbia too harshly, Russia was likely to intervene, escalating the crisis from local dispute to major war.

Austria-Hungary turned to Germany, her principal ally, for advice. This was a crucial turning point, for, if Germany had counselled restraint, the crisis might have been averted. Instead, Kaiser Wilhelm II gave Austria-Hungary carte blanche, signalling that Germany was ready for war. Austria-Hungary made extreme demands, which, if accepted, would have destroyed the independence and integrity of the Serb state. Serbia refused to comply, whereupon Austria-Hungary declared war on Serbia. Russia ordered the mobilization of its army, but stopped short of declaring war. Germany warned that if Russia did not halt the mobilization, it would be attacked. Russia ignored the ultimatum, with the result that Germany declared war on Russia (August 1) and France (August 3), Russia's main ally.

Germany now faced the dilemma of a two-front war. Its strategy was to knock out France as quickly as possible, and then deal with Russia, which was slower to mobilize. To achieve swift victory over France, the German army invaded Belgium, whose border was less heavily fortified than the Franco-German frontier. This contravened the treaty Germany had signed in 1839 to respect Belgian neutrality. The Belgians put up a determined, if futile, resistance, incurring severe casualties among both soldiers and civilians. Britain, a signatory of the 1839 treaty, felt duty-bound to uphold its terms. Fearing a German-dominated Europe, the British declared war on Germany on 4 August 1914. An expeditionary force crossed the channel to assist the beleaguered French, who fell back before the invading forces in hurried, though orderly, retreat. The Allies made a stand at the river Marne, not far from Paris, and stopped the German advance. The latter retreated northward and dug in. The Allies did likewise, eventually establishing a line of trenches and barbed wire that stretched from the English Channel to the Swiss border. Thus was launched a war of attrition that lasted more than four years and took over nine million combatant lives.[1]

Patriotism at the Outbreak of War

The residents of Regina followed these distant events with close attention. In late July and early August 1914, crowds gathered daily at the *Leader* building (Hamilton Street north of Twelfth Avenue) to hear the latest news coming in over the wires. Bulletins were posted on a large board in front of the building, and urgent dispatches were read out over a megaphone. The crowd on 3 August surged to an estimated 2000. People milled around, chatting nervously, and discussed various scenarios. A joker relieved the tension by inquiring in a loud voice as to the movements of the Swiss navy. A few youngsters climbed to the top of the building across the street to get a better view. The policeman on duty ordered them to come down, but they just laughed at him. His dignity affronted, the constable found a ladder and climbed up; however, as soon as he reached the roof, the crowd below removed the ladder. He begged them to put the ladder back, and they finally relented, but only after he showed some humility. He was given "three hearty British cheers" and allowed to go about his business.[2]

The next evening, 4 August 1914, there were close to 3000 people outside the *Leader*. Shortly after nine o'clock, the fateful news arrived. Britain was at war with Germany. The crowd erupted in a mighty roar and sang "God Save the King." "A band, get us a band!" someone shouted, and, within minutes, the Boy Scout band appeared on the scene. They marched up and down the street, playing "Rule Britannia," "Soldiers of the King," and "The Maple Leaf Forever." The thoroughfares were clogged, impassable to automobiles, except for one that managed to get through. It carried "a great grim-jawed white bulldog," the pugnacious emblem of Britain, and "was greeted with delighted cheers as a good omen during the coming events."[3]

Such scenes of jubilation occurred in towns and cities all across Canada, even in the province of Quebec, where loyalty to the British Empire was weakest.[4] In Montreal, mixed crowds of French and English marched down the streets "carrying French and British Flags, singing songs such as the Marseillaise and Rule Britannia." In Quebec City, "English and French and Irish paraded together in an outburst of combined patriotism."[5] For a brief moment, the entire country was united in the "almost carnival gaiety" that greeted the outbreak of World War I.[6]

In Regina the celebrations continued all through the night and into the early hours of the morning. Tables were set up at the downtown headquarters of the Ninety-Fifth Rifles, at the northeast corner of Scarth Street and Twelfth Avenue, and recruits rushed to enlist. From the YMCA just down the street, young men in gym togs marched out four abreast, arms stretched out across one another's shoulders.[7] At the *Leader*, impromptu orators held forth. A patriot declared that he wished he were already in England so that he could get into the fighting right away. Another, described as "a gentleman of Danish descent," said that it was the duty of all Canadians, not just those from Britain, to defend the flag that gave them their rights and freedom. Bud Protich, a Serb employed as a translator at the police court, announced his intention to enlist out of gratitude for Britain's having come to the aid of his native land.[8] There was only one sour note. A Britisher and veteran of the Boer War remarked that by the next day the German flag would be flying over Regina. An angry mob chased him down the street, threatening to beat him up. He dove into the Dairy Lunch building and escaped through the back door. The next morning he returned to retrieve his automobile, which he had been forced to abandon in the melee.[9]

A few days later, an Englishman, who was described as light-haired and "Germanic" in appearance, was quietly reading bulletins on the *Leader* board. A band suddenly struck up "God Save the King." Absorbed in his reading, the man neglected to take off his hat. The person standing next to him took offence at the apparent snub and knocked off his hat. The Englishman demanded an explanation, but before one could be given, a third man interjected, "He's a German." A good deal of pushing and shoving ensued, and the man whose patriotism had been challenged was slapped in the face. When he tried to walk away, his path was blocked. He made a run for the police station, where he was given sanctuary until the crowd dispersed.[10]

According to the 1911 census, 31 percent of the Regina population were "foreign born," that is, not born under the British flag, and many came from countries with which Canada was now at war.[11] Two days before the war broke out, a *Leader* reporter toured Germantown, where he found residents quietly smoking and talking on their verandas. Austria-Hungary did not recognize the naturalization procedure whereby immigrants with three years' residence in Canada were accorded status as British subjects. Consequently, from Vienna's point of view, reservists in the Austro-Hungarian army, whether naturalized or not, still had a legal obligation to their homeland. If they ignored the military call-up, they risked penalties, such as denial of permission to re-enter Austria-Hungary to visit family. Even so, the *Leader* found little support among the "Austrians" for the land of their birth. One said: "I am a Canadian. I own my home and lot. I have property worth $20,000. Why should I go back and help bolster up a government that never did anything for a poor man?"[12]

Regina police stationed extra men in Germantown to guard against outbreaks of violence. As it turned out, there were no serious incidents, apart from a botched attempt to set fire to the house of a printer at *Der Courier*, the local German newspaper.[13] The *Leader* appealed for sympathy for "those in our midst who cannot forget their homeland is Germany or Austria, men who while loyal enough to the land of their adoption cannot forget the land of their birth and of their forefathers."[14] Walter Murray, president of the University of Saskatchewan, said that tolerance of minority rights was "the British way." The feelings of Canadians of German or Austro-Hungarian origin deserved consideration, and they in turn must have regard for those whose sympathies belonged "just as naturally" with Britain and her allies. He hoped that Saskatchewan, with its diverse population, would adopt the motto, "Bear and forbear."[15] Premier Scott, at the beginning of the war, had feared an outbreak of racial strife. When it failed to materialize, he was greatly relieved and congratulated the citizens of the province, British and non-British alike, for the restrained manner in which they had conducted themselves.[16]

The first Sunday following the declaration of war, the churches of the city rang with patriotic sermons. Rev. S.J. Farmer of First Baptist Church pronounced Britain entirely in the right and Germany just as completely in the wrong, saying "if he saw a big boy [Germany] bullying the small boy on the street [Belgium], he would feel very much like taking off his coat and assisting the little fellow."[17] He said that there would be no peace in the world until the German navy was utterly destroyed, a statement that elicited a burst of applause from the congregation. Bishop Harding of the Anglican diocese of Qu'Appelle saw the war as a clash between civilization and barbarism. He thought that "great principles would be violated were Britain to witness treaties disregarded, and the clock of civilization would be put back hundreds of years were she to allow herself to be a party to acts of faithlessness in international affairs."[18] Rev. Harry T. Lewis, minister at Metropolitan Methodist Church, invoked the manly ideal, portraying the call to battle as a "man's call." Canada did God's will because her soldiers fought "with the strength and the courage and virility of young manhood" and with words of scripture ringing in their hearts and minds.[19] Rev. Father Derling at Holy Rosary Catholic Cathedral was more subdued, asking merely that the congregation pray for the success of British arms. At St. Mary's, where German Catholics worshipped, the war was not even mentioned in the homily. The only reference came in the intercessory prayers, which included a petition for the restoration of peace.[20] Britishness, though not wholly a Protestant phenomenon, had a Protestant accent. Catholics did not always embrace it with the same ardour.[21]

Politicians eagerly made known their support for the war. Liberal cabinet minister George Bell proclaimed that Canada stood shoulder to shoulder with the British Empire, while Conservative MLA F.C. Tate orated: "We have sunk our differences today in this province ... in order that the world may know that in the face of a menace from without, we are as one people—that the lion's cubs are as ready to take their part in the great conflict for the maintenance of British freedom, for the maintenance of the rights of the small nations and for the cause of international good faith, as is the lion."[22] George Langley, Minister of Municipal Affairs, said that he had nothing against the German people as such. For years he had admired their intellectual and industrial accomplishments. The difficulty lay with their system of government, which was based on a "principle entirely opposed to our own" and depended on the "endorsement of autocracy in its most flagrant form."[23] Liberal MLA and future Saskatchewan premier J.G. Gardiner, in his maiden speech before the House, confessed his high regard for the German race, if only because "they had given England a line of sovereigns in which Queen Victoria was one." He predicted that victory, when it came, would not be interpreted as a victory "over the German people, but for them, for our victory will mean the downfall, not of their race, but of the causes of the oppression of their race."[24] Germany would be freed of the evils of militarism and the dictatorship of one who was "substantially a lunatic."[25]

Lieutenant-Governor George W. Brown borrowed from the language of chivalry, saying that Britain had been obliged to fight in order to "keep her escutcheon clean." The British Empire would have been bereft of honour had it stood idly by, while Germany trampled treaty obligations and laid waste Belgium. "Unless the people of Britain, the people of Canada, the people of Saskatchewan were willing to give of the flower of their manhood to vindicate the cause of freedom and international good faith," he averred, "they would be unworthy of the race from which they sprang."[26] Premier Walter Scott struck a slightly different tone. While agreeing that Canada must do her part or suffer "everlasting disgrace," he saw deep tragedy in what was about to unfold. War was "the blackest of all crimes." Of the three great disasters that could befall the human race—war, pestilence, and famine—it was the worst, because it led inevitably to the other two. Yet Scott fully supported Canada's participation. It was our duty, he asserted, to maintain the traditions of the British people and uphold the honour of the flag: "When we have emerged from this great trial, we shall appreciate more than we have ever done before the privileges of British citizenship."[27]

The legislature approved the spending of $750,000 for patriotic purposes, including a gift of 1500 horses for the British army.[28] Married civil servants with families received full pay during their military service; married men without families received 60 percent pay; and single men no salary, but were promised reinstatement in their jobs when they returned.[29] The

City of Regina made similar arrangements, though not quite as generous. Married men and single men with dependents received half pay, and single men without dependents quarter pay.[30] Later, when civic finances came under pressure, benefits were cut back,[31] but all City of Regina employees were assured "positions equally good as the ones they vacated, though the actual positions vacated could not be guaranteed, upon their return from Active Service."[32]

Recruits Rush to the Colours

Canada was ill-prepared to fight a major war. The permanent force numbered only about 3000, while the 77,000 men in the part-time militia had received only rudimentary training, most of it at annual summer camps of a few weeks' duration.[33] Minister of Militia and Defence Sam Hughes sent out telegrams on 6 August 1914 to 226 militia colonels across the country, asking them to sign up men for the first contingent.[34] They were to be concentrated at Valcartier camp, located sixteen miles northwest of Quebec City, for preliminary training prior to being dispatched overseas. Infantrymen had to be at least five feet, three inches tall with a minimum chest measurement of thirty-three and a half inches. Gunners were slightly bigger, at least five feet, seven inches and a chest of thirty-four and a half inches. The age limit was eighteen to forty-five, though it was widely disregarded by younger men eager not to miss the "great adventure." Married men required the consent of their spouse before signing up.[35]

Avid Regina volunteers overwhelmed the local militia units—the Ninety-Fifth Saskatchewan Rifles, Twenty-Sixth Battery Canadian Field Artillery, Sixteenth Light Horse, Third Field Troop Civil Engineers, and Corps of Guides. An out-of-town unit, the Legion of Frontiersmen (later merged with Princess Patricia's Canadian Light Infantry), opened a recruiting office at the Alexandra Hotel on Hamilton Street, a stone's throw from Union Station. They advertised for "dare-devils" and men "ready to fight from the drop of a hat."[36] In two days they garnered fifty-seven recruits, mostly "cowboys or roughriders."[37] On Saturday, 15 August 1914, a military camp opened at the Regina exhibition grounds, occupied initially by 300 officers and men.[38] The city council provided 400 cots and voted $1000 for field comforts,[39] while local businesses pitched in with supplies (including bars of soap from the Young Tom Soap Company). The YMCA set up a reading room and installed a piano.[40] The drill sergeant reported that the men were "keen as mustard," "vastly improved in marksmanship," and possessed of "the best soldierly qualities."[41]

The city organized a send-off for the men on 20 August 1914 at the Roller and Ice Skating Rink (roller skating in summer, ice skating in winter), which was located downtown at the corner of Rose Street and Twelfth. Almost 2000 spectators were on hand. The program began with the introduction of John McKinnon, a veteran of the Crimean War (1853 to 1856), a living embodiment of the military tradition of the British Empire, and, as such, an inspiration for the young troops about to go to war. The audience cheered him to the echo and sang "For He's a Jolly Good Fellow." Lieutenant-Governor George W. Brown, on behalf of the province, bid the soldiers Godspeed: "We send you knowing that whatever befalls you will be true to this great province. While we all must feel that this occasion is in many ways a sad one, we rejoice at the loyal response to the call to arms, in the knowledge that you are willing to die if need be in defence of the cause which you are to defend."[42]

Three days later, on a bright Sunday afternoon, the first contingent of 500 men departed from Regina. Union Station was packed with friends and family. Onlookers climbed to the roof of the main building and freight sheds. Bands played, ladies fluttered their handkerchiefs, and men threw their hats in the air. Soldiers leaned out of every rail car window, waving and singing. As the trains glided out of the station, the "crowds gave vent to cheer after cheer." Their shouts mingled with those of the soldiers, and "even when the trains were a considerable distance away, they could be seen hanging to the cars and frantically waving their caps, while the strains of well known airs were wafted back to the crowd."[43]

As soon as the first group had left, the various militia units in the city resumed recruiting to restore their numbers to full strength. The *Leader* warned that Canada had a hard fight ahead of her, and it was incumbent on young men to fill the gaps left by the departed men.[44] Fresh recruits were kept busy learning the rudiments of drill and rifle shooting. One Sunday, after church parade, the Ninety-Fifth marched out to the rifle ranges about three and a half miles east of the city. They spent the morning skirmishing, and in the afternoon advanced in formation on the Grand Trunk Pacific Railway water tower. Part of the regiment was held back in reserve, while the rest moved forward stealthily to take up positions on the firing line. By means of silent signals, word was sent back to the reserves to advance in a series of rushes, while the remainder of the company provided rifle-fire cover (imaginary, since the rifles had been left behind at the barracks). The bugle sounded, and in no time at all the water tower was captured.[45]

The effects of the 1913 recession were still being felt, and jobs were hard to come by. The crops had been light, especially in the western sections of the province, leaving harvest labourers idle. The orders for the mobilization of the second contingent were unaccountably delayed, which meant that recruits could not be formally sworn in and put on the payroll. In the meantime, they had to eke out a meagre existence, many of them surviving on handouts from recruiting officers. Others applied for aid to the Bureau of Public Welfare, the civic relief agency that assisted the unemployed and down-and-out.[46] It was a disgrace, wrote an irate citizen, that "these men who offer their lives that our cause may be upheld and our honor vindicated should in our midst, at our very doors, go unfed and uncared for."[47] A number of patriotic-spirited citizens offered them work digging gardens, the pitchforks having been supplied by Peart Brothers hardware store.[48]

At last, on 21 October 1914, the mobilization orders came through. The men now had a roof over their head (even if it was canvas) and three square meals a day. Regina's quota for the second contingent was 252 men. The rest had to wait a while longer before being allowed to go overseas. Among those enrolled were 5 Americans, 63 Canadians, 144 English, 1 French Canadian,

5 Irish, 2 Russian, 1 New Zealander, 30 Scots, 1 South African, and 4 Welsh. Only sixty-four, or about one-quarter of the total, had been born in Canada. This was typical of enlistment patterns in the early stages of the war. Fully 60 percent of the 30,000 men in the First Division were British-born,[49] reflecting the fact that transplanted Britons, whose ties to the Old Country were still fresh, felt most keenly the desire to defend the land of their birth. Moreover, as recent immigrants, they were less likely to have family responsibilities or businesses to look after in Canada. Others were British reservists with experience in previous imperial wars. When the call came, they felt a duty to respond.

Regina's second contingent included 45 farmers, 41 labourers, 81 skilled workers (bricklayer, boilermaker, barber, butcher, carpenter, cook, electrician, engineer, plumber, plasterer, shoemaker, tinsmith, teamster, tailor, etc.), 72 white-collar workers (accountants, clerks, salesmen, merchants), 1 lawyer, 4 law students, 8 students, and 1 veterinary surgeon.[50] Thirty-four percent were "middle class," that is, white-collar workers, businessmen, professionals, and students. About 18 percent were farmers, 16 percent unskilled labourers, and 32 percent skilled workers. Recruiting cut a wide swath through all segments of society. It was not just the working class who provided the cannon fodder.

When the men left Regina on 31 October 1914, the mood was slightly different from what it had been at the departure of the first group. The seriousness of the war had begun to sink in. Marching to the Grand Trunk Pacific Railway depot (Regina had two train stations, Union Station on South Railway Street and the Grand Trunk Station on Sixteenth Avenue near Albert Street), the soldiers shouted out in unison, "Are we downhearted?" immediately answering with a loud "No!" Occasionally, along the line of the march, "one caught sight of a flushed girlish face in the long file of volunteers, or a father or mother walking bravely along with a stalwart son, on their faces a mingling of sorrow and pride."[51] At the station the band played the popular new war song "It's a Long, Long Way to Tipperary." Already, it was sufficiently familiar for the crowd to join in the refrain.[52]

The men boarded the cars, poking their heads out the windows and prolonging last-minute conversations. At precisely 11:00 p.m., the train pulled out amid resounding cheers and to the strains of "God Be with You Till We Meet Again."[53]

Unlike the first contingent, the second did not gather at Valcartier. Instead, infantry battalions were assembled in various centres across Canada, where they received preliminary training. When that was completed, they travelled overseas, retaining the battalion formations that had been established. This differed from the first contingent, in which groups of men from various militia units were broken up at Valcartier and placed in battalions of which they had not previously been part. Regina's men were dispersed in a number of different formations so that it was impossible to identify a Regina battalion as such. The city could not "take ownership" of a unit and follow its exploits through the course of the war.

This changed with the second contingent. The Department of Militia and Defence abandoned the centralized Valcartier approach in favour of a militia-regiment-based structure. The men from Regina recruited through the Ninety-Fifth Rifles went to Winnipeg, where they formed the core of the Twenty-Eighth Infantry Battalion under the command of Regina lawyer Lieutenant-Colonel J.F.L. Embury. The battalion retained its identity throughout the war. It was never broken up to reinforce other units. Although it suffered many casualties, and the repeated infusions of reinforcements were not necessarily from Regina (though many were), the Twenty-Eighth never lost its connection with the city. When the war ended, the commanding officer insisted that the battalion be demobilized in Regina. Today, it is perpetuated in the Regina Royal Rifles.

Along with Embury were eight other officers from the city, including Lieutenant A.G. "Tiny" Styles, son of W.G. Styles, president of the Regina Board of Trade. Tiny (the nickname belied his size) played for the Regina football team, which won Western Canadian Rugby Football Union championships in 1912 and 1913. The team was scheduled to defend its title in Winnipeg on 31 October 1914, the very day the troops were to leave

Regina. Styles obtained permission to travel a day early so that he could play in the championship game before joining the Twenty-Eighth Battalion in Winnipeg. Football fans gathered at the train station to give the rugby players a rousing send-off, not unlike the send-off the soldiers were given the following day. Styles and his teammates successfully defended the title by a score of twenty to twelve. Tommy Murphy took a knee between the eyes and was knocked unconscious, while Stan Milne played the game in a daze after taking a blow to the head.[54] Styles escaped without injury, spared for combat on another field of battle.

Business and professional men in the city who were too old to go overseas volunteered for the Home Guard. Although Regina was under no immediate threat, these patriotic gentlemen were eager to prepare themselves to "be able to act for defensive purposes in the case of an emergency."[55] By the end of October 1914, 120 men drilled on Tuesday and Thursday evenings and practised rifle shooting Saturday afternoons.[56] Many were veterans of the Home Guard that had been set up at the time of the Northwest Rebellion in 1885. Herbert W. Taylor berated those who were not inclined to offer their services in defence of the city. "It makes me ashamed," he wrote, "to see so many young men in this city taking no interest in fitting themselves to fight well, in defence of Canada and the great British Empire to which we belong." A shoot on the ranges on a Saturday afternoon, he advised, was far superior to attendance at a football match, and "a march out on the prairie on Sunday starting at ten o'clock [did not] interfere with a 'good sleep in,' nor with church in the evening." As for the shirkers, "the girls will know what to think of and say to them."[57] "Girls," too, were shouldering rifles. Close to fifty young women, led by Captain James McAra of the Ninety-Fifth Rifles, assembled in the basement of the McAra Bros. and Wallace building, where they spent the evenings improving their shot.[58]

War news was eagerly sought. The Regina Public Library displayed a large map showing the battle lines and kept a scrapbook in the reading room with the latest clippings.[59] The *Leader's* daily circulation jumped to 20,106 in November 1914, an increase of 6658 over the same month in the previous year.⁶⁰ Regina dentist (and later mayor) Walter D. Cowan, riding the streetcar in September 1914, asked a fellow passenger, whose nose was buried in the newspaper, for the latest news. Cowan was quite shocked when the man replied that he was reading the sports page first.⁶¹ For some people, the constant war talk was too much. An advertisement for the Regina Steam Laundry announced in October 1914: "We Don't Talk War … It doesn't interest us as much as pleasing our customers."⁶²

By December 1914, Regina theatres offered film footage taken at the front. Ads promised to lay bare the "grim reality of war" and give viewers "a thrill and a deeper understanding of what the present war really means." Patrons were assured that nothing "distasteful" would be shown. In one scene, a British soldier was hit and fell to the ground. Stretcher-bearers appeared instantly and whisked him away to a waiting motor ambulance, leaving the impression that he had not been seriously hurt and would soon be back on his feet again.⁶³ Moving pictures were not alone in taking up war themes. An ad appeared in the *Leader* for baritone Edward Hamilton's just-released gramophone recording of "Highlanders! Fix Bayonets!" On the reverse side, Herbert Stuart gave a rendition of "The Soldiers of the King."⁶⁴

The Glasgow House (also known as the R.H. Williams and Sons department store) at the corner of Hamilton Street and Eleventh presented a window display depicting Canadian troops crossing the Atlantic. The blades of double-handed saws formed the bodies of the ships, and shovel handles represented the ships' guns. Red lights flashed from the boats, simulating the firing of broadsides. On the transport deck stood miniature toy soldiers in military red, while cash boxes placed amidships served as the men's quarters and cabins. Around the ships, on a sea of blue cloth, tipped with cotton-batten white foam, ranged models of submarines and destroyers. At the back of the display a large painting illustrated a naval battle, surmounted by a portrait of King George V. To the left, Lord Nelson bade farewell to adoring crowds, and, on the right, he triumphed at the Battle of Trafalgar.⁶⁵ Shoppers bustling along Hamilton Street were often seen gathered around the window admiring the scene.

Gender, Class, and Ethnicity

In the fall of 1914, as men joined the colours, women, too, found ways to express their patriotism. As soon as the war broke out, the national Imperial Order Daughters of the Empire launched a fundraising campaign to equip a hospital ship.[66] The Regina chapters of the IODE joined in, as did the Local Council of Women, Women's Christian Temperance Union (WCTU), Alexandra Club (a local charity organization that supported the General Hospital and Children's Aid Society), and the Daughters and Maids of England.[67] Mrs. H.M. Hillman, president of the Hebrew Ladies Benevolent Society, declared:

> We have become Canadians despite the fact that most of us are foreign born, and when in this hour of trouble the Daughters of the Empire at large, whether organized or not, are doing their utmost for their country, we shall shirk no duty, and we shall be found among the first to offer not only our sons for the defence of the great empire, but will do all we can to cooperate with others for the complete success of the men who have been chosen to fight for us at the front.[68]

Mrs. Walter Scott, wife of the premier, helped organize a Hospital Fund tag day on 15 August 1914. The city was divided into twelve districts, each under the supervision of two captains and assisted by several girls. They stood on street corners and pinned miniature Union Jacks on the lapels of those who gave a donation. Receipts were $1177,[69] which went toward the nearly $3500 contributed locally for the hospital ship.[70]

A Regina branch of the Red Cross was organized on 16 September 1914.[71] At the downtown headquarters, in space donated by the Northwestern Electric Company,[72] women rolled bandages and collected sheets, pillow-slips, pajamas, and socks.[73] The Belgian Relief Fund got underway at about the same time. Horse-drawn rigs, decked out with British and Belgian flags, made the rounds of the city, picking up gifts of boots and second-hand clothing.[74] On a designated Saturday, the Forget chapter of the IODE took over as the sales staff at the Glasgow House department store, a share of the proceeds being dedicated to Belgian relief. Mrs. William M. Martin, wife of

Regina's Liberal Member of Parliament (and later premier), supervised the operation. The tea room was decorated with "grape vines and peach trees lit with many miniature electric globes." The waitresses were costumed as Belgian peasants. Mr. Mee sang "By the Side of the Zuyder Zee" in the uniform he had worn in the Boer War. Net proceeds were $616.10.[75]

Patriotic concerts were ubiquitous in the early days of the war. They were usually held Sunday evening, since it was the only day the theatres were not in use for moving pictures or vaudeville performances. The Ministerial Association, representing the clergy of the city, frowned on the concerts because they desecrated the Sabbath and drew people away from church services.[76] To overcome the clergy's objections, concert promoters delayed the start time to 8:30 p.m., which allowed audience members to attend church before taking in the concert. They promised also that only music of a "sacred character" would be performed.

A special concert, more elaborate than most, was held on 22 December 1914, under the patronage of the lieutenant-governor, the premier, and other notables. It featured a series of elaborate tableaux. The first depicted "the mental struggle of a young man, torn between opposite attractions of society and home sports and his duty to the flag." In the second, the anguished youth made his decision and joined the army. The third tableau, titled "Faithful Unto Death," drew the loudest applause. It showed a horse (a real one borrowed from the Mounted Police) standing patiently on the battlefield at the side of the "stilled form of its master." In the next scene, a handful of soldiers valiantly defended a field gun from enemy capture. Finally, a group of young ladies, each in the national costume of one of the Allies, paraded across the stage. Britannia, tall and proud, entered with a flourish, commanding enthusiastic cheers and applause.[77]

There were many war charities in need of funds—the Red Cross, Belgian Relief, and later Polish Relief and Serbian Relief—but closer to home, no cause was more compelling than assistance for the wives, children, and other dependents of soldiers serving overseas. At the farewell ceremony for the first contingent in August 1914, Premier Scott had promised the men that their families would be well looked after.[78] Although soldiers received remuneration, in most cases it was not sufficient to support families bereft of their breadwinner. The soldier's allowance was one dollar a day plus a field allowance of ten cents, with extra pay for officers according to rank.[79] The men could assign up to four-fifths of this amount to be paid out to their dependents, but were under no obligation to do so.[80] In addition to assigned pay, the government gave a "separation allowance" to families of soldiers in the amount of twenty dollars a month for the wife of a private, twenty-five dollars for a sergeant's wife, and so on up the scale to a maximum of sixty dollars a month for the wife of a lieutenant-colonel.[81] Even when combined, assigned pay and the separation allowance were not enough to support a family, except for "a very small family free of costly crises,"[82] such as medical expenses.

To fill the need, the Canadian Patriotic Fund was inaugurated on 18 August 1914, a national organization with numerous branches across the country. Money collected at the local level was sent to headquarters in Ottawa, and branches drew on the central fund to assist soldiers' families in accordance with an agreed-upon payment scale.[83] In this way, the burden was spread out evenly across the country. Lieutenant-Governor Brown was president of the Saskatchewan Patriotic Fund, with Royal North West Mounted Police (RNWMP) commissioner A.B. Perry and University of Saskatchewan president Walter Murray serving as vice-presidents. The provincial government provided free office space in the Legislative Building and covered administrative costs, including the salary of provincial Canadian Patriotic Fund secretary Thomas M. Bee.[84]

The Regina branch was organized on 14 September 1914. It emphasized that the fund was not a charity, but rather a debt owed to the soldier. As the *Leader* put it, "No matter how great may be the sacrifice made by those at home, it will at best be small in comparison with the sacrifice made by the men who have given up their employment, said good-bye to those nearest and dearest to them, and have offered their lives as a gift and sacrifice to the Empire, and the great cause for which the Empire has staked its very existence."[85] Members of the RNWMP in Regina, from the highest-ranking officer to the lowest, pledged one day's pay per month to the fund,[86] and provincial cabinet ministers gave 10 percent of their salaries. Civil servants were asked to contribute according to a set formula. Those earning $3000 or more per year were supposed to give 7 to 10 percent; those earning $1800 to $3000, 5 to 7 percent; $1200 to $1800, 3 to 5 percent; and under $1200, "such percentage as the contributor feels should be given."[87] The amount was deducted from the individual's paycheque. In theory, the contributions were voluntary, but in practice it was very hard to refuse the request for a donation, just as it was almost impossible to snub the Red Cross lady's collection box.

The Regina Patriotic Fund committee conducted a whirlwind fundraising campaign in the third week of September 1914. All sectors of the community participated—from the law society to the retail merchants' association to sports clubs.[88] Labour unions joined, too, suggesting that, for the time being at least, class conflict was suspended in a united war effort. Just a few days before the start of the war, on 1 August 1914, socialist Alfred Budden of Winnipeg had addressed a large gathering at the Regina labour hall on the topic "War—for What?" For two and a half hours, he expounded the theme that war was "merely a method of getting the workers of one country to slaughter those who lived under a different flag in order to prevent the overthrow of the capitalist system."[89] The onset of war drowned such opinions in a sea of patriotism. At a meeting of the printers' union on 8 August 1914, president J.D. Noonan heaped praise on the six members of the local who had already heeded the call of duty. The union agreed to pay the dues of the absent men in order to protect their benefits and seniority rights while they were away.[90] The Street and Electric Railway employees put on a "smoker" to honour members of the union who had joined the colours. It had to be held at midnight, since that was the only time when everybody was off duty and able to attend.[91] By the middle of October fully one-eleventh of the union's 100 or so members had donned khaki. Those who stayed at home contributed $247 a month to the Patriotic Fund, which averaged $2.54 per member.[92]

The outbreak of war brought Regina together, crossing barriers of class and gender. Less easily overcome were the ethnic differences. Naturalization, prior to 1914, required only the submission of an affidavit, establishing that the immigrant had lived in Canada for three years. When an adult male was naturalized, so, too, were his wife and underage children. The federal government in May 1914 tightened up the procedure. It was now necessary to demonstrate an "adequate knowledge" of English or French and to have lived in Canada for five years. Also, the secretary of state had "absolute discretionary powers to withhold naturalization from persons not deemed conducive to the 'public good.'"[93] This was but a foretaste of the hardened attitude to the "foreigner" that came with the war.

According to the "patterns of prejudice"[94] of the day, preference was given to ethnic groups who seemed closest to being British. Scandinavians and those from northwestern Europe came first, then central and eastern Europeans, and last Jews, Asians, and blacks.[95] During the war, Germans were temporarily demoted from "hardworking Germans" to "militaristic Huns."[96] Those from Austria-Hungary were known as "Austrians,"[97] a handy umbrella term that covered a diversity of groups including Hungarians, Czechs, Croats, Poles, Austrians, Slovenes, and Ukrainians, who had little in common other than that they had come to Canada bearing Austro-Hungarian passports. Turkey and Bulgaria were fighting on the enemy side; Rumania and Serbia were with the Allies. Close to half a million people in Canada (out of 7.5 million) were born in or traced their ancestry to enemy countries.[98] Of these, an estimated 80,000 to 120,000 had not been naturalized[99] and were labelled "enemy aliens": "enemy" because they came from enemy countries and "alien" because they were not naturalized.

By a federal government proclamation of 15 August 1914, immigrants of German or Austro-Hungarian nationality who "quietly pursue[d] their ordinary avocations" were allowed "to continue to enjoy the protection of the law and be accorded the respect and consideration due to peaceful and law-abiding citizens." They were not to be "arrested, detained or interfered with, unless there is reasonable ground to believe that they are engaged in espionage, or engaging or attempting to engage in acts of a hostile nature, or are giving or attempting to give information to the enemy, or unless they otherwise contravene any law, order in council or proclamation."[100] A further order-in-council on 28 October 1914 issued under the authority of the War Measures Act provided for the appointment of civilian registrars across Canada to register all enemy aliens according to "name, age, nationality, place of residence, occupation, desire or intention to leave Canada, intention of military service and next of kin." Those who registered had to "report monthly and carry special internal travel documents and identification cards." Registration was compulsory, and those who neglected to do so were liable for internment as prisoners of war.[101]

The federal government set up an internment operations branch within the Department of Justice, supervising a total of twenty-four detention stations and internment camps across Canada.[102] The camp nearest Regina was at Brandon, Manitoba. Internees over the course of the war numbered 8579 men, 81 women, and 156 children. Only 3138 of these were reservists eligible for military service in their home countries.[103] By ethnic category, 2009 were Germans, 5954 Austro-Hungarians (mostly Ukrainian), 205 Turks, 99 Bulgarians, and 312 classified as miscellaneous.[104] The grounds for internment were vague, allowing officials considerable discretionary authority. Apart from failure to register or to report monthly once having registered, enemy aliens could be interned if they acted in a "suspicious" manner.[105] Persons were incarcerated for using "seditious" or "intemperate" language, for "being found hiding or destitute in a freight car," and for being considered "unreliable," "of shiftless character," or "undesirable."[106]

It did not help when Bishop Nykyta Budka, head of the Ukrainian Catholic Church in Canada,[107] issued a pastoral letter on 27 July 1914 calling upon Ukrainians who still had military reservist obligations in Austria to return home. "Perhaps," he wrote, "we will have to defend Galicia from seizure by Russia with its appetite for Ruthenians."[108] The pastoral letter was singularly ill-timed. Although Canada was not yet at war with Germany (August 4) or Austria-Hungary (August 12), Budka's statement was regarded as disloyal, if not treasonous. He quickly acted to repair the damage, promulgating a second letter on 6 August, which cancelled the 27 July statement and exhorted Ukrainian Catholics to perform their duty to Canada.[109] Nonetheless, an air of suspicion hung over the bishop, and, by extension, the members of his church. Twice he was hauled up before courts on charges of disloyalty and sedition, and twice he was exonerated.[110]

Most of the interned Ukrainians were unskilled labourers who had been laid off in the 1913 recession. They were imprisoned because they were destitute, not because they were disloyal. Municipalities were loath to devote tax dollars to poor relief, especially for those who were not British subjects,[111] and the internment camp became the welfare agency of last resort. Inmates were put to work building roads, clearing land, and cutting wood.[112] They worked on construction projects at Banff, Jasper, and other national parks. Ironically, men who were not considered good enough to be Canadians built national assets in which we all can now take pride.[113]

By the beginning of December 1914, some 200 enemy aliens were registered at the Regina police station, of whom five were interned at Brandon. In each case, the reason given for detention was unemployment, not disloyalty or treason.[114] When a policeman visited the Nicholak home in north Regina, he found nothing to eat but a loaf of bread and a few pounds of flour. Although Mrs. Nicholak was taking in washing to support her three children, her husband failed to give "a satisfactory account" of himself and was considered incurably lazy. Unfortunately, Mrs. Nicholak had fallen ill, and the family was in dire straits. On the advice of the policeman, the husband was taken to the internment camp, and she and the children placed in care of the Bureau of Public Welfare.[115]

The number of enemy aliens registered at Regina rose to 800 by the end of December, with more names being added daily. Most were classified as "Galicians"[116] or "Roumanians," but there were also sixty Germans and three Turks. According to Inspector Belcher of the Regina police force, who had been appointed registrar for the district, enemy aliens had savings on the average of seventy dollars, and most had stored up enough food to last through the winter. He noted with interest that only twenty families entrusted their money to a bank; most preferred to keep it under the mattress.[117]

When Belcher detected a slowdown in enemy alien registration around Christmas time, he dispatched Constable Dickie to Germantown. The latter came across a party of five Galicians and asked them whether they had registered. They replied that it was Christmas, and they were celebrating. "Well, how long does it last?" inquired the constable. "Maybe one week, maybe two," came the answer. Dickie hauled them off to the police station, where they were committed to the internment camp at Brandon. Inspector Belcher was of the opinion that many alien enemies laboured under a dangerous delusion. "They do not seem to understand," he said, "that they are all prisoners, subject to internment, if the authorities think fit, because of the state of war that exists between their own country and this."[118] The roundups continued, and by mid-January 1915 the number registered in Regina had increased to 1200.[119]

Der Courier, Regina's German-language newspaper, repeatedly and emphatically avowed its loyalty to Canada. "Canada is our second home," it said on 12 August 1914, "our adopted Fatherland. When we became citizens we swore an oath of loyalty to the king and it is unthinkable that we should consider breaking it."[120] The paper carried a special notice on its front page for several months running, pledging allegiance to the Crown and reaffirming the loyalty of the German-Canadian Association of Saskatchewan.[121] A.B. Perry, RNWMP commissioner, was not so sure. In a confidential letter to Premier Scott in October 1914, he wrote suspiciously: "The attitude of the Germans in Saskatchewan is very uncertain. So far we have ascertained that most of the Germans here are in sympathy with their native land, but I have not got any trace of any active exhibition of this sympathy."[122]

A group of men and boys roamed through Germantown on 6 August 1914, throwing stones and dirt at homes and damaging fences. Later that fall, a German family was conversing in front of city hall, when a woman, unknown to them, walked up and slapped one of the men in the face. She demanded they speak the King's English.[123] Germans found it prudent to pretend they could not speak their native language, and others anglicized their names to conceal their identity. Koch became Cook, Mueller became Miller, and Jauch became Young.[124] According to one Germantown resident, those who were interned had only themselves to blame because they "couldn't keep their big mouths shut when they should."[125]

Across the border in North Dakota, German Americans gave vent to anti-British sentiments. The Fargo *Courier-News* advised readers not to believe the stories about alleged German atrocities in Belgium. They were all lies and propaganda. The Bismarck *Der Staats-Anzeiger* exulted in German military victories, while the Fargo *Forum* commented that Germany was guilty of nothing more than "making more rapid advance in commerce than any of her rivals."[126] All this changed when the United States entered the war in April 1917, but for the time being, the forty-ninth parallel made all the difference in differentiating patriotism from treason.

* * *

Christmas 1914 marked the end of the first five months of the war. The initial wave of enthusiasm had subsided, and the predictions for a swift victory set aside. It was acknowledged that the Germans were doing better than expected. Although the enemy had failed in its initial assault, it was firmly entrenched in northern France and Belgium. Not a single Allied soldier stood on German soil. On the Eastern Front, the German army won a major victory at Tannenburg, forcing the Russians to abandon East Prussia. Thousands of Canadian soldiers had crossed the Atlantic, but had yet to see major action. It remained an open question as to how they would perform in their first taste of battle.

"Can anything good come out of the war?" pondered the *Leader* on Christmas Eve 1914. "Yes," was the cautious answer. Already, some benefits were perceived. The war had "aroused in the hearts and minds of all our people a deeper sense of responsibility to one another, to our Dominion and Empire, and to mankind at large." It had "awakened many from a life of ease and selfishness to a grim realization of the real significance of life....

Men who had never soiled their hands before are now proud to dig ditches on the firing line; women are found sewing and knitting like poor factory girls." Selflessness and sacrifice were valued as never before. Thousands of Canadians went about their daily lives in a spirit of quiet heroism. The war had exposed the pettiness of party politics, bringing former enemies together to work for a common cause. It taught that man was his brother's keeper and liberty a precious gift. "In support of these great foundation principles," the *Leader* earnestly observed, "men are laying down their lives, women are giving up their loved ones, and nations are pouring out treasure like water." The British Empire had not sought war. It fought only because decency and honour required it. Now the battle was waged "in the hope and belief that we are making final and successful war on War, and that never again will the world be cursed by armed conflict among men."[127]

The weather in Regina on New Year's Day 1915 was surprisingly mild. The cold snap of several weeks suddenly broke, and the residents of the city took full advantage. They were out in full force at church services in the morning, and large numbers boarded the Red Line streetcar to attend the lieutenant-governor's annual levee at Government House. Hundreds more flocked to the skating rinks or glided through the streets on horse-drawn sleighs. The movie houses were busy, while at the YMCA the medical doctors challenged the retail merchants to a game of indoor baseball. Only a few revellers had to be detained at the police station for having "indulged too freely in tanglefoot."[128] It was a sparkling, peaceful New Year's Day on the Prairies. The war seemed far away.

Chapter 2

The First Year

IN 1915 REGINA HAD ITS FIRST REAL TASTE OF WAR. ON THE HOME FRONT, the recession that had begun in 1913 lingered, and unemployment was severe, worse than the previous winter because workers' savings were now almost completely exhausted. Non-English-speaking labourers staged a protest in April 1915, demanding "work or bread," all the while avowing their loyalty to the land of their adoption. That same month, the Battle of Second Ypres was fought, the first major action for the First Canadian Division. In Regina sorrow at the loss of loved ones mingled with pride in what the soldiers had accomplished. Inexperienced troops, seeing battle for the first time, had proved themselves the equal of any fighting formation on the Western Front. Reginans rededicated themselves to the war effort and the ideals for which it was being fought.

The Hard Winter of 1914 to 1915

The depth of the economic recession was evident in the collapse of building permits, which fell from $8,047,309 in 1912 to $4,018,350 in 1913 to $1,765,875 in 1914.[1] During the pre-war boom, the city had borrowed heavily to pay for roads, sidewalks, and other infrastructure, amassing a total debt in 1913 of $7,553,607.[2] Interest payments still had to be met, notwithstanding the steep decline in revenue.[3] In the spring of 1914, the city cut back on sewer and water construction and postponed the building of a new fire hall. The outbreak of war temporarily shut down capital markets, making a bad situation even worse. All but essential public works projects were cancelled, and work stopped on the construction of the police station.[4] The business elite of the city drafted prominent lawyer James Balfour to deal with the crisis. He ran for mayor in December 1914 and was duly elected on a platform promising to put the finances of the city in order. Balfour was the classic "city father." Apart from his business acumen (his clients included the local branch of the Bank of Montreal), he had served as elder of Knox Presbyterian Church, president of the YMCA, city councillor, and member of the collegiate board and the board of Regina General Hospital.[5]

Following his election, Balfour outlined his priorities. He intended to practise "the most rigid economy consistent with efficient administration,"[6] but he was also mindful of the unemployment crisis. Even in the best of times, construction was a seasonal occupation. Bricklayers worked at most seven months of the year, carpenters perhaps eight.[7] Tradesmen normally saved up enough money during the summer to carry them through the winter, but with the collapse of building activity in 1913, there was little opportunity to earn or save, and many families bordered on starvation.[8] In addition, unskilled labourers, laid off from their jobs in railroad construction and the resource industries, began drifting into the city in search of food and shelter.[9]

Mayor Balfour convened a meeting of civic leaders at city hall in early January 1915 to discuss the situation. John Balfour, the secretary of the Bureau of Public Welfare (and the mayor's brother), reported that the Bureau had spent $2900 on poor relief in November 1914 and $3600 in December. An estimated 450 Regina families were on the dole,[10] half of them British and half non-British.[11] There was every prospect that the number needing help in January would be much higher. Poor relief, though a municipal responsibility, was too big for the city to handle, and an approach was made to the provincial government. The cabinet responded sympathetically, offering interest-free loans to all the cities in the province. Regina's share was $21,000, spread over three months, most of which was used to buy food and fuel.[12] In addition, the city established a Labour Bureau to act as a liaison between the unemployed and those who wanted to hire them, if any such existed. The unemployed workmen asked for "work not charity," because they saw charity as demeaning and unmanly. On the first day of the Labour Bureau's operations, 319 men signed up. By the end of the week, there were 700 names on the register.[13]

The Ministerial Association organized 575 volunteers[14] from the various churches to conduct a door-to-door canvass, asking householders whether they had any odd jobs that needed doing.[15] No job was considered too small or trivial—emptying ashes, housecleaning, painting, calsomining basements, hauling away refuse, digging gardens—all were eagerly accepted.[16] The canvassers filled out a card for each job and then handed the cards in to the Labour Bureau at city hall. It was agreed to pay the city scale of wages, so as not to arouse the opposition of the labour unions.[17] As it turned out, very few jobs were offered. Quite the opposite, many householders said they were unemployed and asked the canvassers to put their names on the list of those needing work.[18]

The Bureau of Public Welfare doled out its stingy relief. Each morning the unemployed showed up at the office on Hamilton Street. An official stood on the platform in front of the building and bawled out: "British born first." If work was available, it was provided. Next came naturalized immigrants, and, last of all, those who were not British subjects.[19] The Bureau also operated a second-hand clothing depot with a cobbler on the premises to repair old shoes. By arrangement with the Yale shoe store, the purchaser of new footwear received a coupon for a fifty-cent donation to the Bureau, provided he turned in his old shoes for distribution to the poor.[20]

Homeless transients slept at the Bureau of Public Welfare shelter located in the old Salvation Army hall on Broad Street south of Tenth Avenue. Hearing rumours of substandard conditions, the Trades and Labor Council conducted a surprise inspection in February 1915. Their worst fears were confirmed. Thirty-three men were crowded into a space thirty-nine feet by twenty-one feet. The lavatory was in the same room as the bunks, separated only by a small partition and ventilating into the larger area. The stench was almost unbearable. Lodgers received a breakfast of two slices of bread and jam with tea. If they sawed half a cord of wood, they were eligible for a second meal of bread and soup.[21] The Trades and Labor Council condemned the shelter as "not only a blemish on our fair city, but a menace to public health"[22] and demanded an investigation.[23] John Balfour, Bureau secretary, replied that the shelter was not a hotel. If the men were too comfortable, they would hang around the city instead of looking for work.[24] The shelter was open only in the winter months. By the time the provincial sanitary inspector had made his report, the warm weather had returned and it was scheduled to close.

With the coming of spring, the unemployed eagerly anticipated the resumption of city public works. Food supplies were depleted and savings non-existent. It came as a shock, therefore, when city council delayed the opening of the construction season. A protest meeting at the Rumanian Hall on Sunday, 25 April 1915, drew more than 700 people. One hundred more waited outside the doors, unable to get in. The meeting lasted five hours, since all the speeches had to be translated into seven languages: English, Rumanian, Russian, Polish, Austrian (i.e., Ukrainian), German, and Serbian. The Regina police kept a close watch on the proceedings, and there was no violence. The speakers professed their loyalty to Canada, emphasizing again and again that all they wanted was work and a chance to feed their families.

Many had been unemployed for months and were reduced to one meal per day. A burly Ukrainian told of his daily tramp in search of work and the disappointment in the face of his "woman" when he returned home empty-handed. Another hinted that he might be forced to steal to get food. "But that is not good," he quickly added. He continued:

> I may do it once, twice, three times. Then policeman catch me. He knows I am poor and out of work, but he must take me or he will be fired and out of work himself. So they take me to court, and send me away to jail for two, three year maybe. That not so bad for me, because I get plenty to eat. But I have a woman and three children—one just so high. What will become of them? She go out and work maybe for a while and then no job. Another man come along with 50 or 60 dollar in the pocket and maybe she go with him. She have to live somehow. I go back to my woman, but she is with another man and I have nothing so she does not want me. Neither do I want her when I see she has another man. So instead of being an honest man I am only a vagrant, down and out, and the police watch me and follow me. No, we do not want to steal.

As he concluded, the audience cheered and stamped their feet. "Work, let us work!" they shouted.[25]

Alderman Lewis Rounding was the only member of city council to attend the meeting. (Shortly afterward, he joined the Sixty-Eighth Battalion and died in England on 16 May 1916.[26]) He explained that the City was short of money. Financial markets were tight, and it was almost impossible to sell debentures. Nonetheless, he encouraged the workers to take their demands directly to city hall. A petition was drawn up, which read in part:

> We, the undersigned petitioners most humbly ask your honorable body to find some way out of the difficulties in which a large percentage of Regina citizens find themselves at the present time through lack of work. We who have been assembled today to discuss the situation are poor but loyal citizens and are near starvation together with our families. We think it is only right that steps for relief be taken by your honorable body at once…. We do not ask for charity, but most earnestly desire to see that ample work is provided which would enable us to buy food and prevent starvation.[27]

Mayor James Balfour was able to arrange a million-dollar loan from the Bank of Montreal, and, while most of the money was used to retire treasury bills, $293,159 was allocated for public works, $145,111 of which was spent on labourers' wages. The work was rationed so that each worker received two or three days' employment per week. Balfour warned the men not to become dependent on make-work projects. He said that water and sewer line construction would terminate on 1 August, at which point labourers were expected to go out to the harvest fields.[28]

Conventional wisdom held that the cure for unemployment was to get men "back on the land."[29] Premier Scott moved a resolution, which the legislative assembly passed unanimously, urging that "joint action should be taken by the Federal Government and the several Provincial Governments towards the end that unemployed workmen who have had agricultural experience may become producers of agricultural produce."[30] L.T. McDonald, secretary of the Regina Board of Trade, grumbled that "a certain class of men" did not want to go out to the farms. They seemed to think the city owed them a living. Such men were not "real Canadians."[31] Charles Dunning, manager of the Saskatchewan Cooperative Elevator Company and soon to be provincial treasurer, was of the opinion that unemployment was the result of overpopulation of the cities and depletion of the rural areas. The remedy was to promote farming and rural life as the preferred mode of living.[32]

Moreover, according to the rural myth, agriculture was "the mainspring of national greatness and the moulder of national and personal character."[33] "There is some power about the land," editorialized the *Farmer's Advocate and Home Journal Advocate*, "that elevates, morally and emotionally, if not intellectually."[34] The farm taught hard work, honesty, resourcefulness, perseverance, and frugality. It instilled a spirit of independence and self-worth. Not so the ways of the city, with its shams and deceits, its "vanities and baubles," its "vulgarians of every stripe," "debauched prostitutes," "gamesters, loafers and speculators."[35]

The fact remained, as the Regina Trades and Labor Council pointed out, that not everyone wanted to be a farmer or was qualified to be one. Some men were not physically strong. Others lacked the necessary capital or skills.[36] The wages of a farm labourer were meagre, not nearly enough to support a wife and family. Hours were long, and the working conditions could be brutal. According to the *Leader*'s labour columnist, a Regina man and his wife went out to work on a farm on a Thursday and returned to the city the following Monday. "The living conditions," the man complained, "were far from desirable, and we didn't get enough to eat, so we thought it better to run our chances of starving in the city than to work on a farm and still starve."[37] "Back to the land" was not the cure-all it was touted to be.[38]

John Balfour attributed 75 percent of the poverty in Regina to "lack of character."[39] He thought that the majority of those who applied to the Bureau had no one but themselves to blame for their predicament. They wasted too much money on picture shows and were too lazy to grow vegetable gardens.[40] Rev. Hugh Dobson, the Methodist minister who had been the driving force behind the house-to-house job canvass, blamed the "system" rather than the individual.[41] Unemployment, he said, was "the result of community indifference manifested in our inadequate systems by which we control land tenure, labor exchange and wealth."[42] The remedy was a national network of government-run Labour Bureaus and a comprehensive public insurance program to cushion the impact of temporary joblessness. The shift from individual to social solutions was typical of the social gospel movement, which, as we shall see, gained ground in Regina and Saskatchewan during the war.[43]

Dobson predicted that the economic crisis from 1914 to 1915 was but a foretaste of things to come. Unemployment, he felt sure, would be much worse in 1916. However, when spring returned to the Prairies, the recession lifted and job prospects improved. The Regina Board of Trade reported hopefully in March that the economy was "adjust[ing] itself."[44] In July the Robert Simpson Company announced plans to build a large mail-order house.[45] August brought expectations of a bumper crop, and for once the hopes were not disappointed. The wheat crop of 224.3 million bushels was the largest ever, and the average yield of 25.1 bushels per acre set a record.[46]

Regina and district experienced a severe labour shortage in the fall of 1915. Men who had enlisted and were already in training received a month's leave to help with the harvest. They earned double pay, collecting both their military allowance and the wage of a farm labourer. The City of Regina street-cleaning department released half of its men from their regular jobs to work in the harvest fields.[47] A disgruntled farmer stood outside an employment agency on South Railway Street in Regina, complaining that farm hands were turning down job offers at $3.50 a day and board. He paced the street for two hours, unable to convince "strong, healthy-looking loafers" to work for him.[48]

As the farm economy prospered, Regina bounced back. The City put up for auction 8000 lots in October 1915. Purchased by speculators in the pre-war land boom, they had fallen into tax arrears.[49] The lowest price the City was willing to accept for them was the unpaid taxes on the property. Buyers at auction did not obtain clear title to the lots until two years after the sale, during which time the original owner had the opportunity to redeem the property, on condition that he paid the full amount of tax arrears plus 10 percent interest on the purchase price.[50] As the day of the auction approached, tardy taxpayers and land company agents scrambled to pay the taxes they owed. "Well, Regina is certainly not broke," mused city assessor R.J. Westgate. An estimated $50,000 in tax arrears was paid in a single day. Many erstwhile speculators who had been claiming bankruptcy or that taxes were an impossible burden, suddenly produced "wads that would choke a horse" and wrote out "cheques with more figures on than would have been admitted possible when discussing their financial condition previously."[51]

Nonetheless, real estate values continued well below the levels they had attained at the height of the boom. In November 1916 lots in desirable parts of the city were selling for $3 apiece.[52] A group of real estate firms came up with an original marketing scheme. They put up eighty lots for sale at 50 percent less than 1914 prices. Buyers were given a lottery ticket on "a thoroughly modern house," which the winner received as a bonus prize together with the lot he had purchased.[53] Even after the October 1915 tax sale, $74,000 was still owed in 1914 property taxes.[54] Building permits for 1915 amounted to only $463,865, which was about one-fourth the value for 1914 and one-twentieth the 1912 figure.[55]

Although the effects of the land bust lingered, jobs were plentiful. John Balfour reported in November 1915 that "practically every able-bodied man can find work. We have lots of odd jobs, and are forced at times to send out cripples and women to do the lighter of these jobs. Several times women have gone out to beat carpets and do housecleaning."[56] Poor relief was disbursed only for those unable to support themselves because of illness, age, or physical incapacity. With money in their pockets, customers returned to the movie houses. "Business is better than it has been before," said D.W. Fisher, manager of the Rose Theatre. "October returns are in advance of September, and we expect business will materially improve."[57] "Business has been very good," smiled J.K.R. Williams, co-owner of the Glasgow House department store. "Although we have not touched the record of 1913, we are quite satisfied with the volume of sales during the last season." W.G.F. Scythes of the Scythes Piano Company was delighted to see "a very noticeable increase in sales over a corresponding period last year," while Mr. Paulson of Mason and Risch Piano Company reported, "business is at least 40 per cent in excess of last year."[58] If farmers were buying pianos, it was a clear sign that the recession was over.

In the Trenches

While economic conditions rallied at home, the news overseas turned grim. April 1915 saw the "baptism by fire" of Canadian troops at the Battle of Second Ypres. Raw recruits were transformed into battle-hardened soldiers. For Regina boys, like William Scanlan, city editor of the *Leader*, the road to Ypres was filled with adventure. He left the city in September 1914 with bands playing and crowds cheering. "How much we appreciate[d] it [the send-off] I cannot tell you," he wrote. "I am sure all of us had somewhat dreaded the hour of departure, but the citizens turned out and gave us such a hearty farewell and voiced such earnest expressions of goodwill and well wishes for success and speedy return that we managed to keep down the lump in the throat which at times almost choked."[59] All along the route to Valcartier, crowds gathered to cheer the men. The mayor of Indian Head gave a patriotic speech and presented a purse of money. At Fort William (now Thunder Bay) the residents turned out en masse. The recruits got off the train at Sudbury and paraded through the streets to the strains of "John Peel," which, apparently, was the only tune the local band knew how to play. Even in Quebec, the reception was warm. Women showered the soldiers with bouquets of flowers, and men handed out cigars.[60]

At last the train arrived at Valcartier, where, after a hasty breakfast, the men marched into camp and were greeted with shouts of "Well done 16th," "You soldier brat, you'll never get fat," and other more scurrilous verses. Tents were pitched, and the troops fell into the daily routine: reveille at 5:30 a.m.; kit inspection at 6:00; breakfast at 6:15; parade at 7:00, followed by practice at the rifle ranges. Scanlan and his mates were outfitted in standard issue: "peaked cap with a bronzed maple-leaf badge, a tight-fitting khaki serge tunic with stand-up collar and seven brass buttons, matching serge trousers, brown boots and puttees—long woolen strips bound around the ankle and up the calf almost to the knee."[61] Their kit included "a razor, shaving brush, hair brush, boot brush, and toothbrush; a mess tin; two hand towels; woolen gloves, and a 'cap comforter' that resembled a toque and could be rolled down over the face, with a hole for the eyes and nose."[62] And each soldier received a Canadian-manufactured Ross rifle and bayonet.

Scanlan marvelled at the beauty of the countryside:

> The sun invariably rises in a mist like a yellow ball of fire and disappears behind the Western hills in a soft haze. To the northeast is a range of hills with one or two rather high peaks in the distance. Nearer, the rising ground is covered with spruce, away to the north the valley widens and turns and over to the northwest is the highest peak of all, about three miles as the crow flies.... During the daytime the hills have a far away blue look and a sight to delight the eye may be seen in the soft light through the blue film of smoke arising from our camp fires.[63]

At day's end, men clustered in small groups around campfires, telling stories and singing familiar tunes. In one corner, Scanlan heard "Soon We'll Be in London Town" and, from a nearby tent, "Wrap Me Up in My Old Stable Jacket." In the distance, somebody plunked at a banjo. Old soldiers swapped stories, the ribbons on their chests glinting in the firelight. Down Canteen Alley, vendors advertised their wares: "A whole hog and a biscuit for ten cents"; "Here meester, mutton pie." "Pop" sold for ten cents a bottle, and a package of cigarettes for fifteen cents (only ten cents in Regina).[64] No alcohol was allowed in camp, but soldiers on leave had access to the bars and taverns of nearby Quebec City.[65] After the sun went down and the bugler sounded the last post, the camp fell silent. One by one, candles were snuffed out, and voices died away.[66]

The first contingent in training at Valcartier comprised seventeen infantry battalions (each with about 1000 men), ten field-artillery batteries, four ammunition columns, and four field companies of engineers—30,617 men in total.[67] In addition to the troops, there were 7697 horses, 127 guns, hundreds of wagons, tons of equipment, and a gift of 135,425 bags of flour from Canada to Britain.[68] The thirty-ship convoy moved into the Gulf of St. Lawrence on 3 October 1914. The day before, Minister of Militia and Defence Sam Hughes "had sailed around the fleet, distributing bundles of printed flyers entitled 'Where Duty Leads.'"[69]

After an uneventful ten-day voyage, the Canadians arrived at Plymouth, catching first sight of the rolling hills of the south of England. They encamped on Salisbury Plain, not far from Stonehenge. For 89 of the next 124 days, it rained.[70] Men slept with their clothes on and smuggled oil stoves into their tents to keep from freezing. "If it doesn't rain on our way out to the drilling area or during our exercises," Scanlan wrote, "it rains as we are coming in, and when the boys are dismissed they all begin quacking like ducks."[71] The tightly fitted tunics split at the seams, the cheaply made greatcoats "resisted neither rain nor cold,"[72] and the shoddily manufactured boots dissolved in the mud. The men took to calling Sir Sam Hughes "Sir Sham Shoes." Fortunately, the British War Office supplied durable clothing and hobnailed boots.

In mid-February 1915 the Canadians crossed over to France, docking at the Atlantic port of St. Nazaire. From there they travelled forty-eight hours in freight cars, taking over from the Seventh British Division south of Armentières.[73] Regina boy Art Chatwin informed his parents: "I had a few pot shots at the Germans today. It is just like shooting gophers at home.

Try to keep out of sight and take a shot as a nose shows up. I'll never shoot gophers again without thinking of this shooting today."[74] Jack Burton, also from Regina, described his first experience of heavy fire in March 1915:

> I did twenty-four hours in the firing line. The enemy's trenches were only about 75 yards away. We were under heavy bombardment for about twenty minutes, shells falling all around. One dropped about fifteen yards in rear of my trench, pieces of mud hitting me on the head and hands. It was an interesting time while it lasted, and we were thankful when the British guns put a stop to it.

To reach the front trench, Burton had to cross open ground in full view of the enemy, a risky venture attempted only at night. The Germans sent up rockets that lit up the whole country "as bright as day." "You would have laughed to see how quick we laid down flat till the light went out," he wrote. "I was expecting a maxim to open fire on us.... There are several dead bodies lying in front of the trenches, but it is impossible to get them on account of the enemy's fire."[75]

Reg Bawden, whose sister worked at the *Leader*, admired his comrades' composure. A machine gunner was knocked off his emplacement and fell to the bottom of the trench amid a pile of sandbags and earth. He was pulled out, unhurt, and, without pause, set up his gun to resume firing. The mechanism was jammed. Unperturbed, he methodically disassembled the weapon, cleaned it, and put it together again, "just as though he were in the drill hall instead of being in a trench with shells and bullets flying all round." "Yes," Bawden marvelled, "they are some bunch, all right, and I would back them against their number of any troops in the world."[76]

Soldiers' letters to family and friends published in the newspaper gave those at home insight into trench life. "We realize, although but dimly, no doubt," the *Leader* noted on 3 April 1915, "what it means to spend hours on duty in the trenches standing ankle or knee deep in mud, wet, cold and at times hungry, with the bullets whistling about and every now and then a comrade falling, killed or wounded."[77] The paper invited readers to contribute to a tobacco fund it had set up. For twenty-five cents, the *Leader* arranged to send to the front sixty cigarettes, one-quarter pound of compressed tobacco, and some matches, together with the name of the donor on a postcard.[78] In less than two weeks, $105.75 was raised, enough to supply over 25,000 cigarettes and more than 100 pounds of tobacco.[79]

In April 1915 the Canadian First Division occupied trenches in the Ypres salient (just within the Belgian border), which projected into German-held territory and was surrounded on three sides by high ground.[80] The British Twenty-Eighth Division was positioned to the right, and the Forty-Fifth Algerian and Eighty-Seventh French Territorial Division on the left. At about 5:00 p.m. on Thursday, 22 April 1915, the enemy released 150,000 kilograms of chlorine gas, a weapon the Hague Convention of 1907 had specifically banned. As the yellowish-green clouds rolled across the trenches, the Algerians and French Territorials panicked and fled. The Canadians did their best to fill the gap in the line, battling fiercely for every inch of ground. On Saturday, 24 April, at about 4:00 a.m., the Germans launched a second gas attack, this time aimed directly at the Canadians. Men soaked their handkerchiefs in urine and held them over their noses as makeshift gas masks. Others ripped open their tunics and shirts in a desperate effort to breathe. The dying writhed in agony, greenish foam on their lips.[81] The Ross rifle jammed after rapid firing and was rendered useless, except as a club. Soldiers were "crying in their trenches because they couldn't fire their damned rifles."[82]

The Canadians did not panic or run. Though forced to cede some ground, they accomplished the major objective of preventing a German breakthrough. Finally, on Sunday, 25 April 1915, relief came in the form of British reinforcements. The First and Third Canadian brigades were allowed to withdraw, followed by the Second Brigade on 27 April.[83] The official British communiqué stated: "The Canadians had many casualties but their gallantry and determination undoubtedly saved the situation."[84] The praise was deserved, but the cost incredibly high. The Battle of Second Ypres took 6036 Canadian casualties, fully half the infantry strength of the First Division.[85]

In the days leading up to the gas attack, G. Wall Row, an accountant who worked for the Department of Telephones in Regina, had been billeted behind the lines close to an artillery outpost. The Germans periodically lobbed shells into the area in an effort to take out the Canadian guns. Next to the battery was an open field, where Row and his fellow soldiers played baseball. Every time a shell came whistling through the air, they dropped to the ground, waiting for the hit. As soon as it exploded, they got up and resumed the game. The shells came to be regarded as nothing more than a minor nuisance interrupting otherwise enjoyable recreation. After five days in the billet, Row's unit moved up the line to relieve the French. "The Germans soon got after us," he wrote, "when they knew Canadians were in the trenches. Shells started to come over and landed twenty to fifty yards behind our trench, and, believe me, they were not small shells either. This went on every day for three days, and it got boring after a while."[86]

The next afternoon, 22 April, was quiet. Towards evening, the shelling started up again. Row, lying in his dugout, felt his eyes getting "sore as blazes," and he had trouble breathing: "At first I didn't know what was going to happen. I thought, 'Oh, my God! I am blinded,' and then I expected to drop dead from the suffocation, but found nevertheless I was still alive. My eyes were so bad I couldn't keep them open, and I was choking in the bargain."[87] All through the bombardment, he crouched as closely as possible to the trench parapet. Two boys standing beside him were killed, and another two wounded. The shelling continued all night long, and the next morning, when Row looked out over the horizon to the left, he noticed a yellow-green haze, the remnants of the chlorine gas still hovering over the landscape.

Row's battalion was ordered to fall back to a nearby wood and to a reserve trench. To get to the trench, they had to cross 400 yards of sloped, open ground, exposed to machine gun fire. Row thought, "Well, I suppose this is the end for us." But, unaccountably, the Germans did not shoot. However, as soon as the Canadians settled into the reserve trench, they heard the sound of bugles, as the enemy prepared to advance. "The sound of the bugle I'll never forget," Row recalled. "It sounded like a death note." "Well, enough of war," he concluded wistfully. "I wish to God it was over and I was again in civilian life."[88]

Don Grant, another Regina boy, found time in the midst of the Ypres battle to jot down a quick letter: "This is the fifth day of it and it has been terrible. Our artillery at the present time is something fierce. I can feel the ground trembling as I write.... I only had a couple hours sleep the first four days. I had my first baptism of fire the first day."[89] His job was to deliver ammunition to the guns at the front, which meant that he had to pass through the German line of fire. The road was strewn with dead horses and wreckage, and he encountered streams of wounded soldiers heading towards the dressing stations. Some were carried in stretchers; others walked or hobbled along. "I can't see how it can last much longer," Grant scribbled hastily. "Am expecting to be called out at any minute, and we never know if it is to be the last trip."[90]

Robert Ferguson of the Third Field Troop, Canadian Engineers, had just finished supper "when the fun started." "We got a little whiff of the gas," he informed friends in Regina, "but not enough to hurt us ... we sent out a patrol under Jimmy McNeil (You know him, he used to come up and play checkers). Mac was killed, but the other two reported.... There were so many wounded that the A.M.C. [Army Medical Corps] couldn't get them all in, so we were sent out to carry them in." At first, Ferguson and his companion fell flat on the ground every time a flare went up, but, finding that they were not accomplishing anything, they decided, "Well, if we get hit, we'll get hit." They improvised a stretcher out of an old sack and a stick about twelve feet long and, thus equipped, attended to the wounded. On Sunday morning (the battle had started the previous Thursday evening), they were ordered to dig a reserve trench. "If you ever want to see how fast you can dig," Ferguson grimaced, "get someone to point a machine gun at you and start it up. And then when the bullets and Jack Johnsons [powerful shells named after a famous boxer of the day], coal boxes [named for the loud, rumbling sound they made] and shrapnel are coming good and fast, just start digging. You will be surprised. We remained there the rest of the day. I bet they threw

10,000 shells into that place in that one day. When they burst you could feel the ground shake."[91]

Albert Hazell, star player on the *Leader* football (i.e., soccer) team, felt oddly detached during the Ypres battle: "When you are in the firing line, you never seem to think of getting killed, although you see men falling all around. All you think of is getting Germans. I was surprised the way my nerves stood the fire. I never felt them move at all, but I felt queer just the same."[92] Elmer Boomhower, an employee of the Northwestern Electric Company in Regina, observed off-handedly: "The next day towards evening we went into the firing line, we lost a large number of our boys, my chum had his head blown off while standing a few feet from me, some of the shell hit me but did not do any serious harm." He added, as though bemused at his own reaction: "It seems when we are in action that way we lose our heads as we think nothing of seeing our chum shot down beside us, or seeing the dead lying around. All we think of is to beat the Germans back, and we did."[93]

Twenty-year-old Joseph Hilsenteger worked for his father, who owned an excavation contracting business. The family attended St. Mary's Church, where most of the German Catholics in the city worshipped. In the fall of 1914, Joseph was one of the first Regina boys to volunteer.[94] In his last letter, dated 21 April 1915, he described the thoughts running through his mind:

> I felt as though I had seen it all before. When we were shelled I was one of the fellows not in the shrapnel-proof huts and I never went in but stayed out until it was all over, just in the open, in fact it never bothered me at all. We go into the trenches again tomorrow night and then we do four days again. After we come out we go to a town for a rest. Ypres is the name. They are shelling Ypres pretty hard and quite a number of people are killed.... Please write me some letters, as it is a month now since I have received any from home and it is very lonesome out here.[95]

Sergeant Wilfred A. Jeffs, in civilian life an employee of the Saskatchewan Public Works Department, was overcome by the horror of it all. He saw "shells literally bursting all around, and the road outside seemed alive with them. Huge holes were being torn in the ground almost at our feet, and shrapnel bursting overhead sent down a deadly hail of bullets and jagged splinters of metal.... God! It was awful."[96] When darkness fell, the scene was surreal. Fire cast a "sullen red glow" over the streets of Ypres. "Everything—the ruined houses, the dead lying so quietly by the roadside, the wrecked transports and smashed gun limbers—showed up mysteriously in the fitful gleam from the cathedral as the light rose and fell."[97] Wilson M. Graham, a Regina lawyer, was at a loss for words: "Honestly, it is quite impossible to give any idea of the horrors of real war.... To have the dead and wounded piled all around, not being able to spare a man to attend to the dying even, to hear cries and groans amidst a perfect inferno of rifle and shell fire—and a lot more—words simply fail to express it. Talk about civilization. Barbarians never thought of machinations of hell such as are used in modern warfare."[98]

Grief sharpened the desire for revenge. Jeffs deplored the German outrages, the shooting and bayoneting of helpless men as they lay in the trenches, overcome by gas fumes, or crawling and wounded, trying to get help, and the merciless shelling of ambulances and hospitals. "And yet," he said incredulously, "we are told to love our enemies!"[99] D. McLennan, who worked for Canadian National Railways' freight department in Regina, boasted that the Germans referred to the Canadians as "White Gurkhas," a tribute to their ferocity. But, like Jeffs, he felt bitter at the way the enemy had treated his wounded comrades. "Poor sports," he said of the Germans, "they can't play the game.... When it comes to a man-to-man fight with the bayonets, they either surrender or beat it in quick time. They take a special delight in shelling towns and villages occupied by civilians."[100]

The German use of chlorine gas was a particular sore point. "It came over to us like green, pink, yellow clouds of gas," recollected Oswald Monteith. "You see they wait on the wind then when the wind favors the devilish thing they pump it out in tons and the wind brings it right on to you, then the coughing, spitting—it turns you blind, useless for days. It was three days before I got over it. By heavens I don't mind dying but I would like a fighting chance."[101] Regina lawyer Frederick Bagshaw confessed that after Ypres he felt "like a tramp, dirty, lousy with the itch, pants in rags, eyes bloodshot and sore, and a cough through having been gassed, nerves all shot to pieces, tired and sleepy but unable to sleep. Yet still on the job doing business for the Canadian Department in the firm of John Bull and Co. We came out on the 6th [of May], after 21 days of the real thing." The men were ready "to go in again and do things to make up for our wounded who were bayoneted. We only want to come to grips with them and there will be the deuce for a while, no quarter asked or given; we all have a score to wipe out for our chaps who were gassed and didn't get a chance."[102]

Rumors circulated of the Germans having crucified Canadian soldiers in full view of their comrades. The *Leader* asked E.A. West of the Sixteenth Light Horse whether the story was true. West, who had "stopped the butt end of a German rifle with his nose in a hand-to-hand fight," was back in Saskatchewan on leave. He replied that he had not witnessed the deed firsthand, but three of his pals had told him that they had buried a Canadian who had been nailed to the door of a barn.[103] The story acquired mythical status. Everybody had heard it, but always from someone who had heard it from someone else. And yet the story refused to die. Whether literally true or not, it had psychological validity. It captured the essence of the ordeal of the Canadian soldier as he experienced it.[104]

Regina Reacts to the Battle of Second Yypres

Reginans took pride in the accomplishments of their men on the battlefield. "The soul of every Canadian will be thrilled today," exulted the *Leader* on 26 April 1915, "as he reads of the splendid daring and heroic conduct of the brave representatives of this Dominion in the great battle now raging around Ypres in Belgium."[105] Canada's achievement would be "kept green as long as the Dominion endures."[106] There was a surge of revulsion against German atrocities, especially "the diabolical use of poisonous gases in Flanders." Reginans, said the *Leader*, who up till now had been quite restrained in their opinions, now "expressed themselves in no uncertain language." A wave of patriotic emotion swept the city, coupled with "a desire to throw every interest and all considerations to the winds and seize a rifle and bayonet and do [one's] share towards utterly annihilating the German army."[107] Whereas at the beginning of the war, the fight was said to be have been against the kaiser and his minions, and not the German people as such, now the distinction was lost. The atrocities in Belgium, the use of poison gas at Ypres, and the sinking on 7 May 1915 of the *Lusitania* (with the loss of 1195 civilians, 100 of them Canadian) stiffened public opinion. According to the *Leader*, men in Regina of the mildest disposition were now frankly stating their "desire to kill."[108]

The paper reaffirmed that the main issue was "autocracy and militarism versus democracy and peace, the divine right of kings versus the sovereign will of the people." German victory would result in autocratic rule and "a reversion to the ethics of paganism and a relapse to the age of barbarism," while the triumph of British arms would secure the continuity of constitutional government and a peaceful world order. More than ever, the war was perceived as a holy crusade. Britain and Canada, the *Leader* asserted, were fighting for "the principles of the Prince of Peace."[109] They were engaged in a struggle "to save the world from a reversion to the state from which the teachings of the Great Master have lifted it."[110] Those who were physically able to fight had a paramount duty to do so. The *Leader* quoted the Gospel of Matthew to show there was no excuse for holding back: "For whosoever will save his life shall lose it, but whosoever shall lose his life for my sake and the Gospel's, the same shall save it."[111]

Thunderbolts of "holy war" resounded from the pulpits. Rev. Murdoch MacKinnon at Knox Presbyterian discerned a religious ideal "at the bottom of our enterprise in Europe, compassion for the weak, the integrity of plighted word, the deliverance of the oppressed."[112] Race and creed were united in "the praiseworthy endeavor to overthrow once and for all a power that implicitly denies the very foundation of morality and religion." The very "framework and constitution of the universe" stood opposed to Germany, "the evil-doer." Just as favourable winds had helped destroy the Spanish Armada, and a hailstorm had rescued the Israelites from the Amorites, so, too, the God of righteousness and truth would lend his assistance to the British Empire.

MacKinnon portrayed the Canadian soldier as the modern-day version of the chivalrous knight of the Middle Ages or the crusader to the Holy Land. Flanders was now sacred ground, and the man in khaki the new Sir Galahad, who had the strength of ten because his heart was pure. The Canadian soldier followed in the footsteps of Jesus Christ. "To behold the Man," MacKinnon said, quoting Pilate in reference to Jesus, "is to play the part of a man.... Stand fast in the faith. Quit Ye Like Men."[113] While the soldier's bones might rest in wretched Flanders mud, his soul had been lifted to heaven.

MacKinnon reflected, too, on the implications of the war for the building of the Canadian nation. "We thought we could glide into nationhood without an effort," he said. "Now we find that we must show our mettle before we can take our places in the councils of the Empire and in the affairs of the nations." After Ypres, Canada could no longer be dismissed as a bystander in the great affairs of the world. The country had won a place on the international stage; the price had been paid in blood. When the war was over, Canada would have a seat at the table, a voice in shaping the new world order.[114] For MacKinnon, nationalism was not a declaration of independence. Canada remained loyal to the Empire, but something had changed. Canada had gone through a rite of passage. She was no longer a colony.

In the aftermath of Second Ypres, recruiting assumed a new urgency. During the winter of 1914–15, 400 men were quartered in the Winter Fair building at the Regina exhibition grounds. Originally attached to the Ninety-Fifth Rifles and the Sixteenth Light Horse, they entered, respectively, the Forty-Sixth Infantry Battalion and the Tenth Canadian Mounted Rifles.[115] Most left the city in the spring. In late June 1915, Ottawa ordered the mobilization of two more infantry battalions for Saskatchewan, one based in the northern part of the province and the other in the south. The latter (the Sixty-Eighth) was under the command of Major T.E. Perrett, principal of the normal school in Regina and an officer with the Ninety-Fifth Rifles.[116]

The *Leader* made a special point of encouraging the Canadian-born to enlist. Both the first and second contingents had included a large percentage of British-born, but that supply was virtually exhausted. It was now up to Canadians to do their part. The war, the *Leader* insisted, was Canada's as much as it was Britain's. It was a fight to uphold the basic principles for which the country stood: freedom, democracy, the rule of law, and civilization itself. Canada's very survival was at stake, for, if Britain fell, Canada was next in line. It was infinitely better to fight the Germans overseas than to face them on home soil.[117]

"Why are YOU not in khaki?" the *Leader* demanded in July 1915.[118] The failure to raise Sixty-Eighth Battalion to full strength would be "a disgrace to our city and Province and to our young manhood."[119] Unmarried, physically fit young men lounged in billiard parlours, bowling alleys, and moving picture theatres.[120] "To say the least of it, I am disgusted," a recruiting officer complained bitterly. "To think that in the city of Regina during one whole week there were only about forty men to respond to the call to the colors is not very encouraging."[121]

Unlike Britain, where recruitment was conducted on a national plan, complete with centrally produced posters, billboards, advertisements, and rallies, Canada followed a decentralized approach. Once the Department of Militia and Defence had ordered the mobilization of a battalion, it left the actual raising of men to local officers. Ottawa did not even provide funds to hire recruiting agents or pay for advertising. All the money was raised locally, often coming out of officers' pockets.[122] In the absence of central coordination, recruiting was a free-for-all, in which battalions raided one another's territory in pursuit of volunteers. A more chaotic system could scarcely be imagined.

Women played a vital role in recruitment. Initially, a wife had veto power over her husband's enlistment. If she did not sign the form, he could not go. The rules were changed in August 1915, allowing a man to join without his wife's consent.[123] But even without formal authority, women exercised moral influence. She could provide a convenient excuse for a man not to enlist. Alternatively, she could make him feel guilty if he stayed at home. The *Leader* called on wives to let their husbands go, even if it meant "smiling through tears" as they bid them farewell.[124] Rev. Walter Western, in a sermon delivered at St. Paul's Anglican Church, spoke of how Cleopatra had made a coward of Mark Anthony: "A woman could make a man forget his duty, but love was not true love if it had not first consideration for the honor of the man loved... Many women could say the word, which would make a man face duty, see it and do it." Looking into the faces of the women of the congregation, he asked directly, "When are you going to say the word?"[125]

Men gave various reasons for failing to enlist. One said that he had not started the war, so why should he fight it? Others refused to talk to recruiting officers, or crossed the street to avoid an unpleasant encounter.[126] The Regina summer exhibition in 1915 brought rural men to the city for the annual festivities. Recruiters for the Sixty-Eighth Battalion with knots of coloured ribbons in their caps circulated through the crowd, buttonholing likely candidates.[127] The Travellers' Day parade featured a float decorated with Union Jacks and a banner that read: "Your King and Country Need You." Britannia sat enthroned, surrounded by young ladies representing the Allies, and, at each corner of the float stood a soldier at attention.[128] The film "England Expects" played at the Rose Theatre in March 1915. In the pivotal scene, a young man hesitating to enlist watches as his children, gathered around their grandfather's knee, listen to the story of how the old man had won the Victoria Cross. The little boy, face upturned, earnestly inquires, "Will papa save the colors, too?" "I will enlist tomorrow," the father instantly declares.[129]

According to a spokesman for the Regina Football League in July 1915, "the best of the players ... [had] quit the game for the more serious game of war. Some were now in the trenches; others, as one of the boys had recently put it in a post card had gone into the hospital for repairs; while still others had paid the supreme sacrifice for their King and country."[130] Lance-Corporal Morris of the Sixty-Eighth Battalion, formerly of the Moose football club, addressed a recruiting rally in September 1915. Three of

Regina's best-known "pigskin-kickers" stepped forward: Hoskins of the city hall team, Harvey of the Moose, and Butterfield of the Canadian National Railways.[131] Winnipeg's Seventy-Ninth Cameron Highlanders recruited Albert Gibson, star inside right of the Thistle football club,[132] and hockey players Charlie Otton and Roy Hamilton. The latter set up a recruiting office for the Seventy-Ninth in Charles A. Wood's sporting goods store on Eleventh Avenue.[133] Their teammate, Austin Creswell, captain of the Regina Victoria hockey club, which won the Allan Cup in 1914, and Fraser Stewart, a talented lacrosse player, stumped for the Sixty-Eighth.[134]

Fully one-third of Regina's fire department (twelve out of thirty-six) joined the colours by September 1915,[135] as did seven of eighteen members of the *Leader*'s printers' union.[136] Seven senior officials in the provincial Department of Agriculture enlisted, including livestock commissioner J.C. Smith; weeds and seed commissioner H.N. Thompson; assistant secretary of the Statistics Branch W. Waldron; and district representatives A.J. McPhail, E.H. Hawthorne, and W. Betts. Deputy Minister of Agriculture A. Frank Mantle was the highest-ranking civil servant to sign up.[137] His staff presented him with a pair of binoculars and a wristwatch. "I thank you from the bottom of my heart," he said. "I hope we will see each other again."[138]

* * *

On the first anniversary of the war, 4 August 1915, Regina held a parade. First in the line of march came the Sixty-Eighth Battlalion, followed by Red Cross nurses, the Mounted Police "resplendent in their striking uniforms," the Imperial Band, the Boy Scout band, the boys' brass band from the File Hills reserve east of Regina, fraternal orders, sports clubs, and members of the general public, who walked or rode in automobiles. Bringing up the rear was the fire department's ladder truck, covered from top to bottom with firemen cheering the seven comrades who had just joined the Princess Pats.[139] The parade halted at Broad Street Park, at the corner of Broad Street and Victoria Avenue, where citizens gathered around the platform to hear the speeches.

Provincial cabinet minister George Bell introduced the resolution that had been proposed by the Central Committee of the National Patriotic Organization of Great Britain for consideration in all parts of the Empire: "Resolved, that on the anniversary of the declaration of a righteous war this meeting of the citizens of Regina records its inflexible determination to continue to a victorious end the struggle in maintenance of those ideals of liberty and justice which are the common and sacred cause of the allies." The motion was seconded by Mayor James Balfour and unanimously approved. Member of Parliament for Regina William Martin said that, for him, defeat was unthinkable. It would lead to the "the Germanization of Canada, the obliteration of the British navy that rules the seas, the loss of British traditions and of all that is near and dear to every citizen of Canada. Canada is just such a country as Germany wants."[140]

Mayor Balfour was last to speak. He dared to hope that the anniversary they were commemorating would be the last of its kind in Regina. Surely, before another year had passed, the war would be over. He may have been thinking about his son and namesake, Jimmy Balfour, a student at the University of Saskatchewan in Saskatoon when the war broke out. Jimmie joined the Princess Pats and was wounded at Ypres.[141] Others in the crowd had similar thoughts. What were their loved ones, fathers, husbands, and sons overseas doing at that very moment? Would they come back home alive? "I pray," said the mayor, addressing his fellow citizens in the dying summer light, "that within the present year we will again gather on these grounds to celebrate peace, peace with honor that will ensure happiness to the world."[142]

Chapter 3

Brave New World

THE WAR, FAR FROM DETRACTING FROM SOCIAL REFORM MOVEMENTS, galvanized and strengthened them. Neither prohibition of alcohol nor women's suffrage had been successful before 1914. The war pushed both over the top. The key factor in both cases was the identification of the war overseas with the war at home against the "foreigner." The intertwined and mutually supportive prohibition and female suffrage movements enabled activist middle-class Anglo-Protestants to impose their values on the rest of the population. World War I gave British Canadians the moral authority to accomplish what had previously been out of reach.[1]

The War against Liquor
"Temperance" in the early nineteenth century referred to the temperate or moderate use of alcohol, but, by the middle of the century, it had come to mean total abstinence.[2] It was widely believed that "moderation" was

impossible, since one drink led to another and then another, and down the slide to drunken debauchery. The first temperance society in North America was established in Nova Scotia in 1827, and in the ensuing years lodges spread throughout eastern and central Canada.³ When the western frontier opened up, temperance organizations followed closely behind. In 1886 Mrs. Letitia Youmans, president of the Dominion Women's Christian Temperance Union, visited a number of Prairie towns, including Regina, appointing temperance workers and setting up WCTU locals.⁴

The anti-alcohol campaign received a boost with the formation in 1907 of the Saskatchewan Social and Moral Reform Council, a joint endeavour of the Anglican, Methodist, Presbyterian, and Baptist churches, together with the Royal Templars, the Trades and Labor Council, and WCTU.⁵ At the council's urging, the Scott government in 1908 introduced local option legislation, which allowed cities, towns, and rural municipalities to ban the sale of liquor in their respective jurisdictions.⁶ Seventy-three local option contests were held in Saskatchewan in December 1910, the "wets" winning thirty-six and the "drys" thirty-seven. Among the larger urban centres—Regina, Moose Jaw, Saskatoon, and Prince Albert—only Moose Jaw voted against liquor.⁷ The tally was close in Regina, where temperance forces lost by fewer than 100 votes. The holdout was Germantown (Ward 1), which voted 406 to 95 for the sale of liquor. The other five wards, taken together, voted 934 to 748 against for an overall victory of 1154 to 1049 for the "wets." It was truthfully said that Germantown ruled Regina in the matter of liquor sales.⁸

For the non-British population, stopping at the hotel bar for a convivial drink or raucous evening was part of community life. The bar was a place for socializing, the exchange of information, a clearinghouse for job opportunities, an "anti-home" where men took a break from domestic responsibilities, drank too much, and got into fights.⁹ Social reformers saw only a den of iniquity. When Regina Presbyterian minister E.H. Henry alleged that alcoholism in Germany led to a high crime rate, *Der Courier* set the record straight: "What does Pastor Henry know about Germany? Nothing! He's never been there. He took his information from that false, exaggerated, lying prohibition literature."[10] Every week leading up to the local option vote in 1910, *Der Courier* carried a full-page advertisement opposing the temperance campaign and defending the citizen's right to his glass of beer.

Prohibitionists adopted a new strategy in November 1913. Instead of aiming at a total ban on liquor, they set their sights on abolishing the bar. They hoped that once voters saw the benefits of putting an end to public drinking, they would be ready to embrace the total elimination of liquor consumption, even in the privacy of one's home. Thus was launched the Banish-the-Bar crusade,[11] headed by a group that called itself the Committee of One Hundred. The president was Rev. George Exton Lloyd, principal of Emmanuel College, the Anglican divinity school in Saskatoon, with Rev. W.J. Stewart (Presbyterian) and layperson C.B. Keenleyside (Methodist), respectively, office secretary and general secretary.

Regina Roman Catholic Bishop O.E. Mathieu lent his support, appearing on public platforms with Lloyd and promising that Catholic priests "would be at one in any fight against alcohol."[12] Nonetheless, Catholic involvement was muted. In Regina, for instance, Catholic parishes did not participate in Ban-the-Bar Sunday, 14 June 1914, when temperance orators occupied Protestant pulpits.[13] An editorial in *St. Peter's Bote*, published at the Benedictine St. Peter's College in Muenster, Saskatchewan, took a firm stand: "Prohibition violates a fundamental right of an individual. It shatters national unity, it fosters discord, foments enmities, gives rise to an endless series of quarrels and suspicions.... The leaders of the prohibition leagues are ... filled with a virulent hatred for the Roman Catholic church and all that belongs to it."[14]

Premier Scott introduced a bill late in 1913 to hold a plebiscite on the abolition of the bar. The Ban-the-Bar forces were delighted, but their joy was short-lived, for the premier suddenly and rather mysteriously withdrew the bill on 19 December. It was later revealed that liquor sellers had bribed Liberal MLAs to oppose the legislation.[15] A letter from C.E. Eymann, editor of *Der Courier*, to J.A. Calder, head of the Liberal Party organization, warned that if the bar were to be abolished, "our party [i.e., the Liberals] will have lost a number of very active supporters who at any time would be willing to materially assist financially." Eymann suggested that the liquor licence act be amended so that no licences could be issued without the approval of the Licensed Victuallers' Association. Under this scheme, no one but Liberal Party supporters would get licences, thereby shoring up the already powerful Liberal election machine. With the "solid support of the German-Canadian Alliance on the one hand and the liquor interests on the other," Eymann predicted that the Liberal Party could be "re-elected again and again."[16]

The coming of the war confounded these calculations. In the heightened emotional atmosphere, prohibition was indistinguishable from patriotism. "It is more than hinted," charged the *Ban-the-Bar Crusader*, the official temperance publication, "that some of the bars are meeting places for our Empire's enemies and breeding-places of sedition. This is intolerable. Surely the province cannot continue to license convenient centers for spies and plotters against the country's peace."[17] The Ban-the-Bar convention in December 1914 resolved to take direct political action. Candidates in the next provincial election would be asked to pledge their support for closing the bars. If they refused, a temperance candidate would be nominated to contest the seat.[18] The gauntlet was thrown down to the Liberal Party, which was now at risk of losing the "reform" vote.

Rev. Principal Lloyd, who had two sons at the front,[19] scathingly attacked the premier: "We have received a cold shoulder every time we have visited the Parliament Buildings." He said that Scott's statement that prohibition would damage the economy by putting hotels out of business and men out of work was an argument "worthy of a child, and not of a man." "The churches are here to stay," Lloyd thundered. "The barroom has to go."[20] Rev. Dr. Samuel Dwight Chown, general superintendent of the Methodist Church of Canada, addressing a temperance gathering in Regina on 23 February 1915, called for the complete suspension of liquor sales for the duration of the war. It made his blood boil, he said, to see the Union Jack draped in these drinking places: "The liquor traffic was killing off men by the thousands when the country demanded the best of its sons and when every living person was an asset.... Our slogan is to destroy this trade during the period of the war, and then let the people say whether it shall be brought to life again later."[21]

Premier Scott made his move on 18 March 1915. He announced that as of 1 July 1915, all bar and club licences in the province were to be abolished and all private liquor stores replaced with government-owned "dispensaries." After the war was over, a referendum would be held to determine whether the bars should be reopened. The ultimate fate of the "dispensaries" was also to be determined by referendum, tentatively scheduled for 1919.[22] This was more than the Ban-the-Bar crusaders had asked for. Not only were the bars abolished (and without a referendum!), but also private liquor stores had been put out of business. This meant that the liquor interests would not be a significant factor in the upcoming referendum contests.

The prohibitionists could scarcely contain their enthusiasm. "I can hardly realize that our wishes have been so sweepingly met," Lloyd swooned. "It is splendid and the Government will be returned to power when next it appeals to the country by an overwhelming majority."[23] Professor E.H. Oliver, principal of St. Andrew's Presbyterian College in Saskatoon, was equally complimentary: "It is the most important step in advance which Liberalism has ever made in this province and those of us who are not in politics, but who have been asking for such a policy will support Mr. Scott in the action he has taken."[24] Walter Murray, president of the University of Saskatchewan, normally reticent on matters touching on partisan politics, pronounced Scott's action "most advanced." Nothing more could have been expected or desired.[25]

Rev. Murdoch MacKinnon at Knox Presbyterian congratulated the government on "its sanity, its originality, and courage in bringing these [temperance] proposals forward." The liquor traffic, he said, was one of the "greatest scandals" of modern civilization:

> If this war is the outcome of any one of our many social sins it must be the sin of intemperance, for most of our other sins are near relatives of this one which has become the stumbling block of our civilization, the blight of the home, the bane of business, the foe of labour, the corrupter of governments

and the outstanding social pervert of modern times. When the truth becomes known, it will be found not only that the iconoclasts of the Louvain incident [the German soldiers who burned down the university library] were under the influence, but also that the man or men responsible for this war were drunk.

The closing of the bars was evidence that "evil may be converted into good and the world may yet see Providence in the European war."[26]

The war transformed prohibition from possibility to necessity. According to the *Leader*, it "created and crystallized public opinion in opposition to the traffic as nothing else could have done. Thousands of men are today prepared to stamp out the drink evil who would not have been willing to do so a few months ago."[27] Military metaphors abounded. Bishop Lloyd reminded prohibitionists that while they had succeeded in shutting down the bars, they still had work to do. Their next target was the government dispensary. The temperance army now knew that the enemy was not as well entrenched as had been thought. "The battle is in front of us and has to be won," Lloyd exhorted. "All that has to be done is state the case. If anyone who claims to be a man doesn't get up and do his share, he is no kind of a man anyhow."[28]

St. Peter's Bote and *Der Courier* deemed it an injustice to deprive hotel keepers of their livelihoods. Prohibition was an infringement on personal liberty and an insult to German customs and tradition.[29] Scott, however, had no choice but to abandon his erstwhile friends. The war made the alliance untenable. Besides, where were the "foreigners" to go? Eymann and company could hardly vote for the Conservatives, who were even more pro-British than the Liberals. In response to Scott's bold stroke, the Tories polished their temperance credentials. Opposition leader Wellington B. Willoughby proposed an immediate referendum on *total* prohibition, not to close down just the bars, but the dispensaries, too. He was against any government involvement in the liquor business. It could only lead to corruption.[30] The Liberals in turn whispered of a secret deal between the Conservatives and the liquor interests. It was "Scott and Sobriety" versus "Willoughby and Whiskey."[31]

As Joseph Gusfield argues, prohibition was a *symbolic crusade*. It is best understood in terms of how "a cultural group acts to preserve, defend, or enhance the dominance and prestige of its own style of living within the total society."[32] The "cultural group" under siege in wartime Saskatchewan were middle-class British Canadian Protestants, who were threatened by the flood of "foreign" immigrants into the province. Were the newcomers educable? Would they learn English? Could they be assimilated? It had been an open question before 1914, and the war brought matters to a head.

The goal of the dominant group was "the construction of an Anglo-Canadian identity that celebrated all things British and advanced Canada's destiny as part of the British Empire."[33] The non-British, who made up almost half the population of Saskatchewan, were not as keen on that. Meanwhile, the British Empire was engaged in a struggle for its very existence. If Germany won the war, the Empire would be finished. War is a time when "identities become polarized into good or bad, for or against, friend or foe, enemy or compatriot."[34] Prohibition in this context became a flashpoint. It symbolized the larger struggle to defend "Britishness" against its enemies, both at home and abroad.[35] This was why it came into effect during the war and not before.

The spirit of sacrifice aroused by the war undercut the argument that prohibition violated individual liberty. The survival of the nation trumped the freedom of the individual. As Rev. Harry T. Lewis preached at Metropolitan Methodist Church in April 1915, the "very fact of our soldiers going to the front to fight our battles demanded of those at home a new standard, and we were being tested out by the very conditions under which we lived."[36] Prohibitionists also made the case that the liquor industry undermined the efficiency of the war effort. The "drunken soldier was unfit to fight, an alcoholic worker was unable to produce, and grain distilled into whiskey could not be used to feed starving allies."[37] But these arguments were too rational to account for the emotion that enveloped the prohibition movement. British Canadians were fighting for who they were. They lashed out at "foreigners," who were perceived, not only as non-British, but potentially anti-British, plotting in their barrooms to overthrow the British Empire.

Prohibition Goes into Effect

On 1 July 1915, 406 bars, 38 wholesalers, and 11 clubs were put out of business and replaced by twenty-three government liquor dispensaries.[38] The change, said the euphoric *Leader*, signalled "a veritable revolution in the social, economic and moral life of the Province."[39] Regina police reported a sharp drop in arrests for drunkenness: 52 in the three-month period from July to September 1915 compared to 220 for the same period in 1914.[40] Mrs. Robert Sinton, president of the WCTU, was pleased to see fewer drunks on the streets, especially around the railway stations.[41] "The Province and its people are better off financially, commercially, morally and physically," crowed the *Leader*. "Many men are happier, healthier and more industrious and their families have gained in self-respect, comfort and happiness.... Few young men are contracting the habit, and the future is bright with promise that the day is not far distant when drunkenness, yes, even moderate drinking, will cease to exist."[42] Even the horses were happy. No longer did they stand in the bitter cold, "waiting, tired and hungry for the creature for whom they patiently toiled, helping to make the money he has been giving in exchange for that which makes him also a 'beast' with a mighty poor showing in comparison."[43]

The 250 delegates at the Ban-the-Bar convention in Regina in July 1915 were in a celebratory mood. J.F. Bole, former Liberal MLA for Regina, now in charge of the provincial liquor commission, stated his intention to sell as little liquor as possible.[44] During exhibition week in Regina, when demand for liquid refreshment was at a peak, he shut down all the local dispensaries, lest the visitors imbibe too freely.[45] According to the *Evening Province and Standard*, Bole went out of his way to stock the dispensaries with "rotgut stuff which even the hardened topers disdain to purchase." The editor hastened to add: "Our knowledge of the matter is secondhand, but the complaints are certainly widespread and bitter."[46]

In the local option votes held in December 1915, prohibitionists scored victories in Gull Lake, Watrous, and Biggar, all of which voted to shut down their dispensaries. Prussia, Churchbridge, Wadena, and Vonda, where dispensaries had not previously existed, all voted against their establishment.[47] Nationally, temperance campaigners had the wind in their sails. Manitoba and Alberta were on the brink of total prohibition, with British Columbia and Ontario not far behind. The Maritimes were almost dry, and even Catholic Quebec was beginning to come around. Saskatchewan, which had taken the early lead, now risked losing its trendsetter status. "Walter Scott captured the first line trenches of the liquor traffic," the *Leader* proudly observed. "He bore the brunt of the battle at the most dangerous period. The reserves are now coming into action in all the other Provinces."[48]

Originally to be held in 1919, the referendum on the dispensaries was moved forward to 11 December 1916.[49] The ballot question asked simply: "Shall the Liquor Stores System be Abolished?"[50] Residents of villages, rural districts, and towns under 1000 did not have to register to get on the voters' list. They merely showed up on referendum day and cast their ballot. Those who lived in cities and towns of more than 1000 were required to pre-register during a week in September set aside for the purpose. This gave an advantage to the prohibitionists, who were well organized at the grassroots level and did their utmost to get supporters on the voters' lists. Eligible voters included all persons, male and female, twenty-one years of age or more, who were British subjects, either by birth or naturalization, and had resided in Saskatchewan for at least twelve months and in their electoral division for at least three months.[51] Registrants were obliged to appear in person, or, in the case of illness or absence from the city, have their name placed on the list by a family member or friend, who swore an oath that the person so registered was a duly qualified voter. "Canadian soldiers are doing their duty at the front," the *Leader* admonished. "One of the first duties of Canadian men and women at home is to exercise their franchise, and in order to do so they must register. Keep the home fires burning by driving intoxicating liquor out of Saskatchewan. Do not make the mistake of thinking that the liquor interests are already beaten. Like the Germans, the minions of King Alcohol will fight to the last ditch."[52]

As referendum day approached, sensational accounts appeared in the press of drunken debauches in Germantown. John Bidniuk wanted to have a party—"there was some fete to celebrate, whether it was the defeat of the Austrian army or not was not ascertained." He dispatched John Wigtiuk and Bill Kokogauzuk to the liquor dispensary to purchase an eight-gallon keg of beer and "a gallon of whiskey in a little brown jug." On the way home, the two men took a detour and settled down to some heavy drinking. In no time at all, both keg and jug were drained. Bidniuk found them "rolling around in a glorious state of hilarity." They spent the night in jail, waiting until they sobered up enough to answer charges of theft.[53]

In a second incident, Miladin Petrov got into a fight with his brother, who accused him of stealing a bottle of whiskey. A scuffle ensued, and Miladin was stabbed with a knife and rushed to hospital, where he lay unconscious.[54] A few days later, a Rumanian Canadian soldier, dressed in uniform, was gravely injured at a dance in Germantown. "Here is a soldier, let's beat him," shouted a gang of Galicians. He might have been killed, had not a "British subject, Austrian born" come to the rescue. For his troubles, the Good Samaritan "got a thick ear" and "left some of his blood on the floor."[55]

Such scenes contrasted with that of respectable citizens devoutly wending their way to church on "Temperance Sunday," a special day set aside for prohibition sermons. In pulpits across the city, demon rum was excoriated. It was said that a vote for liquor was a vote for the kaiser.[56] Voting day was stormy and cold. Women swathed in scarves and bundled in heavy fur coats scurried to the polls.[57] The WCTU stationed a representative at each poll "to give any assistance in the way of the correct manner of voting and so on, but principally for the moral effect." This was the first time women in Saskatchewan had participated in a province-wide vote, and it was thought that "if they found other women at the polls, they might not feel so reticent at entering the booths."[58]

The results in Regina were conclusive: 4208 in favour of closing the dispensaries and 961 opposed. Four of five city polls voted dry by huge margins. Germantown, as usual, marched to a different drummer, supporting prohibition by the slim margin of 244 to 235.[59] Across the province, the victory for temperance was complete: 95,249 to 23,666.[60] However, it was still possible to import alcohol from outside Saskatchewan's borders, since the provincial government did not have jurisdiction over interprovincial trade. Not until April 1918 did the federal government close this loophole, too.[61] King Alcohol was completely overthrown. Now, if only Kaiser Bill could be so easily dealt with.

Women and the War

Women and children were perceived as principal victims of the liquor trade, since drunken men often wreaked havoc on family life.[62] According to Letitia Youmans, who founded the first local of the WCTU in Canada in 1873, women who campaigned against liquor were fulfilling their traditional maternal obligations. Prohibition, she said, was synonymous with "home protection." At first, the WCTU did not seek the vote. They lobbied governments and signed petitions in the hope that legislators would see the light of day of their own volition. It was soon evident, however, that the lack of voting power was a serious handicap. The WCTU came to the conclusion that male politicians would pay more attention to them if women had a say in who was elected.[63] The vote was not so much an end in itself as the means to an end. As the popularity of prohibition surged during the war, so, too, did the demand for the female franchise.

The vote was also seen as fitting recognition of women's war service. It was a way to acknowledge contributions to the Red Cross, IODE, Patriotic Fund, and other wartime charities, not to mention the sacrifice of husbands and sons to military service, the pain of separation, and the loss of loved ones.[64] Women were esteemed allies in the war effort and, as such, partners in democracy. The war, after all, was being fought in the name of democracy. It did not seem right to exclude half the adult population from the privileges and responsibilities of citizenship.[65] Moreover, why should German and Ukrainian men have the vote, and not British Canadian women? There was a strong racial component to the women's suffrage movement. As Carol Lee Bacchi astutely observes, "the suffragists were predominantly members of an Anglo-Saxon, Protestant social elite, dominated by professionals and the wives of professionals, who endorsed women suffrage as part of a larger reform programme designed to reinstate Puritan morality, Christianity, the family, and the rule of the professional."[66] Maude Stapleford, wife of the president of Regina College, bluntly stated that women's suffrage "was no longer a sex matter but a race matter."[67] But, despite what Stapleford said, it was inevitably a "sex matter," too, because it changed the balance of power between men and women. Whether intentionally or not, it opened opportunities for women that had not existed before.

The IODE was at the heart of women's war effort. Founded in Canada in 1900, it aimed to forge "an Anglo-Canadian identity in the image of Britain."[68] It took for its motto "one flag (the Union Jack), one throne (the British monarchy), one Empire (the British Empire)." Its badge displayed the crown and Union Jack, "surrounded by a seven-pointed outward-radiating star, one point for each of the major territories of the Empire."[69] World War I marked the apex of the organization. It enrolled 50,000 members across Canada, before falling to 20,000 in the post-war period.[70] In this way, it followed the trajectory of the rise and decline of British Canadian nationalism.

The Regina chapters of the IODE kept up a ceaseless round of activity. The Forget Chapter in January 1915 contributed funds to the Duchess of Connaught Hospital and to the national chapter of the IODE. In March they served refreshments at the Forty-Sixth Battalion concert and presented the battalion with a portrait of the king and queen and royal family. On 30 April 1915 they hosted a field comfort shower at the YMCA, which collected supplies that exceeded $500 in value and raised $51.35 in cash. In May they sponsored the Mile of Pennies scheme, placing collection boxes in all the public schools of the city. The boxes were opened on Empire Day (May 24), when it was found that the children had contributed $163.35 for field comforts. The ladies presented first and second prizes to grade seven and eight students for the best essays on the subject of "Canada's Duty in the Present War." The winners were awarded *The Princess Mary Gift Book* and *King Albert of Belgium*.

In June the chapter shipped a large collection of blankets and linen to the Canadian Red Cross at Toronto, which was forwarded to Cliveden Hospital in England. In September the ladies served tea at a Regina Golf Club tournament, realizing the sum of $106.50, which was donated to the Saskatchewan Hospital Unit. A tag day in October netted $1012, and, in response to an appeal from the provincial chapter, $200 was voted for the sailors of the Grand Fleet. The ladies assisted with a shower for the sailors on Trafalgar Day (October 21), and in November contributed $100 to the British Red Cross and $143.50 to the Saskatchewan Hospital Unit. They supplied Christmas presents for the soldiers, as well as apples and cakes that were sent to France.[71]

The municipal chapter, which comprised the Forget Chapter and the other chapters in Regina, boasted an equally ambitious program. It opened rooms in June 1915 on Eleventh Avenue, which were fitted up with sewing machines donated by the Singer Sewing Machine Company and cutting tables on loan from Knox Presbyterian Church. In November new quarters were found in the Masonic Temple building, where the owners provided space at no cost apart from the heating bill. The municipal chapter in 1915 purchased 2953 yards of flannel, 976 yards of cotton, and 1075 pounds of wool, which were used to make 740 day shirts, 1966 pairs of socks, 60 pairs of mitts, 172 scarves, 42 helmets, and 2444 handkerchiefs.[72] Volunteers came to the rooms to sew, or, if it suited them better, took the materials home and worked on them there. Groups of women all over the city organized sewing circles, meeting regularly in one another's homes "to do their bit." For example, twenty ladies gathered on 22 June 1915 at the home of Mrs. George Robinson, 2067 Rae Street, to form the West End Patriotic Club. They met every Tuesday afternoon to roll bandages, cut handkerchiefs, and make other articles for the soldiers. According to the informal rules of the club, the hostess was not allowed to serve anything other than tea, one kind of cake, and sandwiches. In one session alone, they folded forty-five yards of bandaging, and cut 150 handkerchiefs and face cloths, and 110 mouthwipes.[73] The municipal chapter's 1915 annual report acknowledged contributions from the West End Patriotic Club, the Cheerful Workers' Club, Arlington Beach Ladies' Aid, Motherwell Circle, Victoria Circle, Metropolitan Ladies' Aid, Knox Ladies' Aid, St. Paul's Ladies' Aid, Grace Church Ladies' Aid, among other groups.[74]

The first annual meeting of the provincial chapter of the IODE convened at the Regina YMCA in June 1915, with Mrs. William Melville Martin in the chair. She reported that since October of the previous year the number of chapters in the province had increased from twenty-three to thirty-eight.[75] Their principal work had been to supply field comforts for Canadian soldiers and raise funds for the Red Cross, Belgian Relief Fund, Patriotic Fund, and other war charities. In seven months, contributions totalled $20,039.04.[76] The IODE also undertook educational projects, with the aim of teaching "our children, particularly our young foreign-born population, the greatness, the glory and justice of the British Empire." To this end, it donated to the schools "good historical pictures, illustrated historical books and lantern slides illustrative of scenes in the British Empire and Canada." The IODE also sought to raise the profile of Trafalgar Day, the anniversary of Nelson's victory over the French and Spanish fleets in 1805, which laid the foundation of British sea power and on which the supremacy of the Empire depended. Nelson famously said on that day, "England expects every man to do his duty," words well suited to the First World War.[77]

At the second annual meeting of the provincial IODE in April 1916, there were fifty-two chapters (up from thirty-eight) representing 2409 members. Mrs. Martin, who was still president, proposed the erection of markers at historical sites in the province, starting with those commemorating the Northwest Rebellion of 1885. She thought it was important for the province to memorialize the patriots who fought at Cut Knife Creek, the RNWMP constable shot at Frog Lake, and the settlers who had defended Fort Carlton.

For the IODE, the British Empire was not something remote and distant; it was part of the social fabric of Saskatchewan. They affirmed a national identity that was British to its core.[78]

When the ladies of the Salisbury Chapter of the Regina IODE gathered to knit and sew, they took turns reading aloud letters from soldiers at the front. The soldiers thanked them for the care packages of "cigars, cigarettes, chocolate, gum, oxo, soap, stationery, candles, playing cards, shaving brushes, mouth organs, candies, condensed milk, cocoa, malted milk, and other articles."[79] Private Medley K. Parlee wrote: "I kissed all the girls I knew when I left Regina. I hope I kissed some of you. If I didn't, you're out of luck for I've married since. Besides, our battalion is getting too good a name, and I'm afraid we'll be wiped out soon. We've lived more than our share anyway.... Don't think I'm a morbid pessimist. I'm not. Who could be mirthful in such circumstances?" He told the story of a comrade, who stopped to chat with a sentry. The conversation went on for some time, so he set down his sack, and, when he left, forgot to take it with him. The sentry called out, "Hi, you've forgotten your rations." The retort came back, "Oh, that ain't the rations. Them's Jones and Snider. I picked 'em up out of the last trench mortar-hole. There's a blame good tooth in the bag. I'll rout it out if you want a souvenir. I saved one of Snider's to send home to his girl. Thought she'd like it. Dashed good fellow, Snider."[80] Arthur J. Dix related the news that his battalion was earning a fine reputation at the front, the officers "basking in immense popularity with the men." His thoughts turned to home: "We feel that Canada is doing her best for us boys and we are doing our best for her. The members of the IODE have showered gifts on us and we shall not forget. Please God, we shall return some day. Those who are lucky enough to do so will have lots to tell their friends."[81]

Like the IODE, the Regina Red Cross contributed immense quantities of field comforts and medical supplies. The annual report in November 1915 summarized the year's work: 1098 surgical shirts, 347 night shirts, 426 suits of pajamas, 696 grey flannel shirts, 48 dressing gowns, 1300 pairs of socks and wristlets, 176 scarves, and dozens of other items.[82] Nearly $9800 had been raised, $2886 of which was spent on sewing materials and $5742 forwarded to head office in Toronto for the purchase of food packages for Canadians in German prisoner-of-war camps.[83] Red Cross headquarters was in the Kerr block on Scarth Street north of Twelfth Avenue ("one floor up, take the elevator, first door to the right"). On one side were piled hanks of yarn and bales of flannel and linen. Other shelves contained cut-out garments, and still others returned parcels. Work schedules and the times of various meetings were posted on a large blackboard.[84] Regina Red Cross president Mrs. A.B. Perry (wife of the RNWMP commissioner) praised the dedicated work of the volunteers. One woman, with two small children to look after, found time in 1915 to make thirty suits of pajamas, seventy-four shirts, and twenty-one pairs of socks. Another, despite being ill and bedridden, managed to knit twenty-seven pairs of socks.[85]

The Red Cross put on a sports day in July 1915 at the RNWMP barracks. Reginans turned out in large numbers, some 3000 people passing through the turnstiles in the course of the afternoon and evening. The program began at two o'clock with a "tilting the ring" contest, followed by "a very brilliant exhibition of slicing the lemon." "It was a matter of great wonder to the majority of the onlookers," noted an observer, "to see the adroitness of the men with their swords." The highlight of the day was the musical ride—"Nothing finer has ever been seen in the Dominion in the way of a military display."[86] The day's activities ended with a vaudeville program in which "several of the best performers of the force" took to the boards. Over $1000 were raised.[87]

Tag days were ubiquitous in wartime Regina. A streetcar motorman boasted in October 1915 that the Red Cross was not going to get any money out of him. A lady ran in front of the car and refused to budge until he handed over his ten cents. "And if you start the car," she threatened, "I'll ride on the cow-catcher till you get ready to be decent about the Red Cross." The driver gave in.[88] A tag lady approached a soldier in uniform. He answered mildly that he did not think it was the duty of those in khaki to support the Red Cross. "Oh," rejoined the woman, "I have tagged many soldiers this morning." The soldier put a quarter in the box and moved on.[89] By 1916 tag-day exhaustion had set in. For every woman who volunteered to help, four or five made excuses: "One is house-cleaning; one is entertaining a guest; one doesn't feel fit as a fiddle; and the other one has not a maid." Only the indefatigable responded cheerfully, "Why yes, of course, I'll help. Where would you like me to be standing?"[90]

Women turned to raffles as a substitute for tagging. This annoyed the Ministerial Association, who deemed raffles a form of gambling and "not in keeping with the dignity of the cause." "Peter Pan," the pseudonym for the women's columnist at the *Leader*, shot back that women had "raked their brains hundreds of times to think out dignified methods of raising money which would receive a response from the public at all in proportion to the efforts spent upon them." They had "invented and offered every form of legitimate entertainment, and every variety of breakfast, dinner, or supper." Yet the need for war funds did not abate. Belgian, Serbian, and Russian refugees were still dying of hunger, and wounded soldiers went without the care they needed. If "their Reverences," the columnist acidly continued, had any influence in persuading their fellow citizens "to offer their dollars, and half and quarter-dollars and their ten-cent pieces direct to the Patriotic Fund, the Red Cross, Refugees' relief, and Field Comforts funds, without taking a chance on a doily, a nightie, or cushion-top, not a sanctimonious heart would be more glad to have raffling banished forever than the hearts of the women who have been selling tickets and tags ever since August 1914."[91]

In addition to fundraising, women organized auxiliaries to the various battalions raised in the city. They invited soldiers for meals—a welcome break from barracks food—and visited them in hospital.[92] They raised money for "extras," such as band instruments and special regalia.[93] At Wascana Park on 20 April 1916, the ladies' auxiliary of the Sixty-Eighth Battalion "presented the colours," a ceremony that involved the formal handing over of the King's colours (the Union Jack, with "68" in large gold letters at the centre) and the battalion colours (the crest of the Sixty-Eighth inscribed on a blue field). The men were drawn up in a rectangle on three sides, with drums piled in the centre. The senior lieutenant carried the king's colours to the senior major, who offered them to the lady representing the auxiliary. She presented the flag to the senior lieutenant, who knelt before her. The junior lieutenant carried the battalion's colours to the junior major, and the ritual was repeated. The colours were then placed on the piled drums and consecrated by a clergyman who recited the prescribed prayers.[94] The lieutenant-governor, the mayor, and the police magistrate all gave speeches, expressing the pride of the city in the battalion and extending wishes for success at the front and a safe return. The spectators, unsure about whether to applaud, maintained a perfect silence until the magistrate mentioned that not one soldier of the Sixty-Eighth had appeared in police court, at which point they broke out in loud clapping and cheering. The program ended with a march past, "first by companies, then by column of platoons, and then in column of route, and thus off the field and to the barracks."[95]

Although women did not serve in combat roles, many volunteered as nursing sisters. The first Red Cross nurse from Saskatchewan to go overseas was Miss E. Bolster, a graduate of Toronto General Hospital, who had worked as assistant nurse for the public schools in Regina. She left for the front in March 1915.[96] Prior to her departure, the teachers of the four schools in which she had worked held a reception in her honour and presented her with a "purse of English gold," sovereigns and half-sovereigns having a value of $65.[97] Nurse Dale sailed with the St. John Ambulance Association nursing contingent in May of that year,[98] and Mrs. A.D. Smith, who had been superintendent of a nursing home in Regina, departed at about the same time under the auspices of the Florence Nightingale Chapter of the IODE. Her husband had volunteered with the third Canadian contingent in training at the Winter Fair building.[99] Husband and wife headed for France at about the same time.

A reception was given in October 1916 at the nurses' residence for five women shortly to leave for England. In attendance were many of the city physicians and their wives, and members of the board of governors of the General Hospital. The mayor gave a speech, and R.H. Williams, chairman of the hospital board, presented gifts. Nurse Elsie Shannon received a gold wristwatch; Miss R.E. Wass, a steamer rug; Miss C. Elliott, a writing case; Miss Margaret C. Reid, a travelling case; and Mrs. Cochrane, a fountain pen.[100] The women were given a hearty send-off as they headed overseas.

Catherine Creswell, sister of hockey star Austin Creswell, made the journey in May 1917. As the transport rounded the coast of Ireland, a German submarine torpedoed it, and Miss Creswell, along with the other passengers, spent several hours in a lifeboat on the open water. They took up oars and rowed until they reached land. On arriving in England, Miss Creswell was sent to Bramshott, where she nursed Canadian soldiers, and, subsequently, to No. 2 British Expeditionary Hospital in France. Soon after, the hospital was bombed, and she was taken prisoner. Thankfully, after twenty-four hours, the Germans released the nurses, and she returned to London, where she was able to meet up with her brother, who was recovering from wounds sustained at the front.[101]

Miss Best, a Regina nurse on Red Cross duty in England, wrote about her experiences at the Duchess of Connaught hospital at Cliveden. Hundreds of wounded were coming in from France. One night when she was on duty, a Zeppelin was sighted almost directly over the hospital, and the lights were ordered out. "We all went shivering around in the dark, the goose flesh almost raising our collars. I slid down among my Canadian men where I somehow always feel safer." The next time she was in London, she went to see where the bomb had dropped. It had left a large crater and broken all the windows for blocks. At the time of her writing, the hospital was discharging all those who could possibly be released to prepare space for 5000 wounded waiting on hospital trains and ships. "Sometimes we get so homesick we think life is not worth living," she said, "but the wonderful spirit of these men shames us."[102]

Elsie Chatwin, another Regina woman with a brother in the Canadian Expeditionary Force, intended to join the nursing corps, but on arriving in London, discovered that there was a shortage of motor drivers. She registered for the driving course and passed all the examinations with flying colours. "The driving in the traffic didn't bother me at all," she said proudly, "and I was the only Canadian to get through."[103] Taken on as an ambulance driver in France, she found the job difficult and challenging, but also rewarding. "This morning we had an inspection of cars," she wrote. "The inspector said to me, 'Very nice,' and passed on. The blessed thing takes a good four hours of my time every day, so it should look 'very nice.'"[104]

As nurses, ambulance drivers, suppliers of field comforts, and patriotic fundraisers, Regina women made notable contributions to the war effort. They also paid a price in the emotional toll of separation from husbands, boyfriends, fathers, sons, and brothers. Many lived in constant fear and anxiety, dreading the casualty lists and yet obsessively scanning them for mention of loved ones. "It isn't very merry is it," conceded the *Leader*'s women's columnist at Christmas 1915, "this trying to make-believe celebrate, with half one's men friends somewhere in France or Belgium or the Dardanelles, and the knowledge that several of the others haven't spirit enough to be there. There's nothing for it, but to see that the children have a cloudless day, and for the rest of us to think of happier Christmas Days in the past, or better still, those in the future."[105]

Votes for Women
As with prohibition, the women's suffrage movement predated the war. Conservative MLA J.E. Bradshaw introduced a motion in the legislative assembly in December 1912: "That this House hereby signifies its approval of the extension of the franchise to women." Although many MLAs favoured the proposal, the resolution did not come to a vote. Premier Scott said that he did not want to proceed until the women of the province had demonstrated that they wanted the franchise.[106] Bradshaw introduced a second motion in 1913: "That, in the opinion of this House, the question of the Extension of the Franchise to Women should receive the earnest consideration of the Assembly at the present session." After less than an hour's debate, the resolution passed unanimously. Scott reported that in the past year he had received petitions signed by about 2500 women, but he did not consider this sufficient to justify moving ahead with legislation.[107]

The Conservative *Evening Province and Standard* reprimanded the premier: "There are some questions in which the right is so palpable that in reality there is but one side to them, and women's suffrage is one of them."[108] The paper saw no merit in the prove-that-you-want-the-vote approach. If even one woman wanted to vote, she had the right to do so.[109] Conservative MLAs J.E. Bradshaw, Joseph Glenn, and D.J. Wylie (whose sister, Barbara Wylie, was a militant suffragette in England)[110] led the fight in the House. On the suffrage issue, the Liberals were reluctant reformers.

The Saskatchewan Grain Growers' Association at its annual convention in February 1912 endorsed equal voting rights, as did its partner organization, the Women's Grain Growers' Association. Equal franchise leagues sprang up in Moosomin, Battleford, Prince Albert, Yorkton, and Moose Jaw.[111] They coalesced, along with the WCTU and WGGA, in February 1915 to form the Provincial Equal Franchise Board.[112] Between 10,000 and 15,000 signatures were presented to the legislature in May 1915, but Premier Scott still hesitated. He thought that petition gathering was useful for its educational value. As women went about the province, collecting signatures, they raised awareness of their citizenship responsibilities.[113] There was one small advance in 1915. Married women who owned property were given the right to vote in municipal elections (unmarried women and widows already did so).[114]

The Equal Franchise League met in Regina in November 1915. Among the speakers was Mrs. A.D. Miller, a member of the IODE, whose husband was in charge of the Regina Home Guard.[115] She contended that equal voting rights were necessary for "the main good of civilization."[116] The "women-slavery system," which, in her opinion, prevailed in Germany, was partially responsible for the war. If women in Germany had been able to vote, she argued, they might have halted the kaiser's "mad lust for conquest." Mrs. Miller believed that it wasn't just the knitting and other types of women's war work that was important, but also the spirit of sacrifice that lay behind it, which helped fortify the men. Ten New Zealand nurses had gone to their deaths when their hospital ship was torpedoed and sank. Instructed to take to the lifeboats, they stoutly answered, "Fighting men first." Such gallantry, said Mrs. Miller, exemplified the wartime spirit of Canadian women. They were doing everything in their power to help win the war.

Mrs. Maude Stapleford, a bachelor of arts graduate from Victoria University, Toronto,[117] also made reference to the martyred nurses. Women in New Zealand, she reminded the audience, had been voting since 1894. The franchise had not in any way diminished their capacity for self-sacrifice or womanly virtue. It was entirely unjust that German and Austro-Hungarian men should be allowed to vote, but not British women. Further, women were now attending universities in large numbers. Canada could ill afford to waste their intellectual talent and training, which must be utilized to build up the country. How ironic, Mrs. Stapleford commented with just a hint of acerbity, that in a war being fought for democracy, "we have but a partial democracy in which fewer than half of the adults have a share in the government."[118]

The discussion continued at the Women's Educational Club at Regina College. Miss Grace Morgan, professor of English, addressed the topic, "What Women have done for the War, and What the War has done for Women." Women, she pointed out, were taking men's jobs, releasing them to go to the front, "even acting as postmen, drivers, conductors, chauffeurs and farm laborers." This could not help but "strengthen the cause of women's rights."[119] Miss Bollert, dean of women at Regina College, maintained that it was scarcely to be believed that when the war was over and a new order of things established, governments would return to their "silly and time worn arguments against women in public affairs." The "mothers of all the nations of the earth" would remember their sons, who had been used "to feed the cannon's mouth" and daughters, who had suffered a "fate worse than death." They would expect to have a say in shaping the post-war world.[120]

Suffragists met at the home of Mrs. C.O. Davidson in Regina on 11 February 1916. They counted up the signatures that had been collected in the city, more than 1200. It was anticipated that in the next few days another 2000 would be turned in. At least 8000 were expected from rural areas, and to these would be added 11,000 names gathered the previous year. The smaller towns gave strong support, Wadena, alone, submitting seventy-one names.[121] The delegation proceeded to the legislature on Valentine's Day, 14 February 1916. Mrs. Alice Lawton of Yorkton, president of the Provincial Equal Franchise Board, opened the speeches: "Women have had a hard uphill climb to regain their place beside the men. I believe the women have at heart the interests of the race. We were called upon to give up our men. When they shouldered their arms and marched away, we had to take up their duties. Women by thousands today are working in ammunition factories and shops. They are proving as efficient workers as the men and as conscientious."[122] Men, in turn, "must be just." They must acknowledge that women had "a right to a voice in the industrial conditions which they must endure as the men do. If we want to keep Canada Canadian, it must be done through the home. The women have the keenest interest there, and should have a voice in making the conditions for it."[123]

Mrs. Zoa Haight, a representative of the Women's Grain Growers' Association, stated that women had given ample proof of their devotion to war work, and, in recompense, sought full citizenship rights. They wanted to build a society that embodied the ideals for which the war was being fought. This included a chance to vote on the temperance question and to help make the public school an effective instrument for the "Canadianization" of the "foreigner." Men and women, jointly, must ensure that Canada stayed British. Harry Perry, the sole male speaker in the delegation, brought the good wishes of the provincial Trades and Labor Council. Wartime women, he maintained, were proving themselves to be "very capable in directions hitherto not thought of." Organized labour supported equal voting rights so that women might "assist the men in the building up of the province along the right lines."[124]

Mrs. W.W. Andrews of the WCTU reminded the MLAs that her organization had been on record in favour of women's suffrage for forty years. Women knew the devastation caused by alcohol and the tragedies inflicted on home life. They were ready to work, alongside temperance men, to abolish the liquor scourge and the evils it brought in its train. Mrs. Charles Robson, Regina Local Council of Women, stressed that she did not come to the legislature "in a spirit of criticism or sex-antagonism." "We have given our husbands and sons," she declared, "and they are in Flanders upholding the ideals of democracy, meaning the government by all the people. The women at home were asking for a place in this democracy."[125]

Last to speak was Mrs. C.O. Davidson, president of the Regina Equal Franchise League. "We did not raise our boys to be soldiers," she said, "but we went down to death's door to bring them into the world and then in these recent months we have seen them put on the King's uniform and have smiled as bravely as we could to see them go. We have surely done what we could for our land.... It isn't as if we were strangers, who were asking this of you. We are your mothers, your sisters and your wives, and we ask you to honor us as we deserve."[126] The applause was deafening.

Premier Walter Scott rose to speak. He was reminded of the day war had been declared in August 1914. He had been in Saskatoon that night, observing the scene as bands played and a torchlight procession made its way through the streets. Happy throngs of people rejoiced, as though they had heard good tidings. "It astonished me," Scott said, "that news of that kind should make people light-hearted." Now in 1916 the citizens of Saskatchewan knew better. They had a more profound understanding of the burdens of citizenship and the price that had to be paid to preserve democracy and freedom. He promised to introduce legislation to give women the vote, but he emphasized that voting was a responsibility as well as a right. It involved sacrifice such as the women of the province had already shown they were capable of making.

The women caught the premier's mood. When he sat down, there was no loud cheering or burst of applause. Mrs. Lawton waved her handkerchief, and, by pre-arranged signal, the other women did the same. The legislative chamber was a sea of white, fluttering handkerchiefs. Mrs. Lawton began her reply with a little joke: "Mr. Premier, this is so sudden." "Our quiet manner of receiving this news," she continued, "does not mean we are less jubilant than we ought to be. But we know the responsibility it carries. We must now ask that women will study to do that which is right for our country and homes." E.H. Devline, Liberal MLA for Kinistino (soon to be jailed for highway-contract fraud),[127] started up a chorus of "For They Are Jolly Good Fellows," and all the men joined in. When they had finished, the ladies reciprocated with a verse; then, arm-in-arm, men and women, one step closer to equality, they exited the chamber.[128]

* * *

Aviator Katherine Stinson made a guest appearance at the Regina summer exhibition in 1916. "Somehow then it seemed that such a slip of a girl was out of place in the snorting monster that roared across the infield and shot in the air," mused the *Leader*. "But once the biplane settled into graceful flight, Miss Stinson seemed a natural part of the big bird that soared, dipped and spiraled for the entertainment of the crowd."[129] The "pièce de résistance" was a heart-stopping nosedive: "After rising to a height of about eight thousand feet, the little bird-girl suddenly swooped her plane like a wounded bird and then sloped the wings and executed some thrilling spirals, dips, banks and volplanes." Descending to about 3000 feet above the ground and pointing the nose of her plane straight at the earth, she fell to within 500 feet, before righting the machine and landing in a graceful glide in the exhibition enclosure. The telephones at the *Leader* rang off the hook as callers, who had spotted the descent of the plane, anxiously inquired if there had been an accident.[130] Miss Stinson was an unlikely candidate for such heroics. A "girlish person with curls hanging down in front of both shoulders," she was "slight and spirituelle." In the brave new world of wartime Canada, there was no limit to what a woman could do.[131]

A branch of the University Women's Club was organized at Regina College in November 1916, with an initial membership of sixteen. Eligible members had to have earned a university degree. The stated goals of the club were "to stimulate activity among university women, to work for the practical advancement of arts, science, literature and civic reform, and to promote the social welfare of the college-bred woman."[132] Coincidentally, at the Regina Public Library, a change was made in the seating arrangements of the reading room. In the past, women had been segregated in a space set aside for their exclusive use. It was well stocked with magazines full of "sandwich recipes, beauty hints, fashion notes and house decorations." Now, women started to take their place in the general reading room, where books and magazines covered a much wider range of topics, including politics, social issues, and current affairs.[133] Miss Sadie Bigelow, professor of modern languages at Regina College, gave a lecture in May 1916 on "The Opportunity of the Enfranchised Woman." She defined feminism as the effort of women "to meet life undaunted; to labor, to succeed or to fail, as human individuals; to seek their own success in self-chosen, appropriate paths, unhampered by laws or conditions from which men are exempt." These goals, she went on, constituted "the ultimate object of the revolt of the women."[134] No one had mentioned "feminism" or the "revolt of women" in the legislature on Valentine's Day. The delegation had said they wanted "to keep Canada Canadian." They had not come in a spirit of criticism or sex-antagonism.[135] Mrs. Stapleford said that women's suffrage was "a race matter not a sex matter." But now it seemed it was. What had happened?

In the crucible of war, women's rights were temporarily subordinated to the ideology of service and sacrifice. The politics of war overshadowed the politics of gender. Women were deemed worthy of the vote because they raised patriotic funds, knit socks, rolled bandages, cared for the wounded, took up jobs that released men to go to the front, and surrendered husbands, fathers, and sons to the battlefield. They were partners in the project of keeping Saskatchewan British. "We are your mothers, your sisters and your wives, and we ask you to honor us as we deserve," Mrs. Davidson had said. Who could resist such a plea, and who could appreciate its long-term ramifications for the equality of women?

Chapter 4

The Battle over Schools

THE BATTLE OVER SCHOOLS WENT TO THE HEART OF WHAT PEOPLE IN Regina and Saskatchewan thought the war was about. It was cast as a battle for British civilization waged on two fronts: overseas and at home, where the domestic equivalent of the firing trench was the public school. The fight was for British ideals, values, and institutions. In Europe, the enemy had to be killed; at home, the non-British had to be "Canadianized," which in this context meant assimilated to "Anglo-conformity."[1] As Philip Buckner rightly says of British Canadians in this period, "they were not cultural relativists. Most were committed to an aggressive evangelical Protestantism and a belief in the innate superiority of the British character ... [while] they preferred to see acculturation take place voluntarily rather than at the point of a bayonet, they never doubted that it was to the evident advantage of cultural minorities to abandon their own cultural traditions."[2] In Saskatchewan both Liberals and Conservatives were in agreement on this point. Both supported a carrot-and-stick approach to "Canadianizing" the "foreigner," or, as some liked to say, the "New Canadian." The only difference was that Liberals preferred the carrot to the stick, and for the Conservatives, it was the reverse. But both knew exactly where they wanted the cart to go.

The public school, also referred to as the "national school," was the primary site of Canadianization. It was where "foreigners" learned to speak English and absorbed British culture and ideals of citizenship. No other institution could be relied upon to do the job, neither family nor church. In many immigrant homes not a word of English was spoken, and church services were often conducted in the foreign tongue of the congregation. Hence the rallying cry: "one flag, one school, one language." As one Saskatchewan Education Department official put it in 1913: "Teach the children to speak, to read and to write English—this is our first and great educational commandment. Our second commandment is like unto the first—through the common medium of English, within our schools build up a national character."[3]

The public school had symbolic, as well as instrumental, significance. Just as prohibition had a patriotic subtext, the battle over schools masked a deeper struggle over cultural control of the province. From a purely rational perspective, it did not matter a great deal whether one hour of the school day was allotted to foreign-language instruction. Such a minor concession was not likely to vitiate the mission of the public school or wreck the assimilation project. But fine points of pedagogy were not the issue. The real question was: Who was in charge of the province? Who would prevail, the British Canadian or the enemy alien?

According to the terms of the 1875 North-West Territories Act, the religious minority in any school district, whether Catholic or Protestant, had the right to establish a separate school and support it through self-taxation. A territorial board of education was established with Protestant and Roman Catholic sections, each responsible for the supervision of its own schools. This system was replaced in 1892 by a unified government-controlled council of public instruction, which evolved into the Department of Education in 1901.[4] The religious minority in each district retained the right to establish a separate school, but such schools had to follow the regulations laid down by the Department of Education respecting curriculum, teachers' qualifications, examinations, and school operations in general.

In the first draft of the Saskatchewan Act, which created the province of Saskatchewan in 1905, the Laurier government attempted to reinstitute the school system that had existed in 1875. This provoked a fierce backlash among English-speaking Protestants and led to the resignation of the federal Minister of the Interior, Clifford Sifton. As a result of the furor, the prime minister backed down. The legislation was rewritten to bring it in line with the educational status quo of the Northwest Territories in 1905.5 Tax-supported separate schools for the religious minority were allowed, but they had to obey the rules and regulations of the Department of Education. A primary course (grades 1 to 3) could be offered in French, and other non-English instruction was permitted during the last hour of the school day (three to four o'clock). In the latter case, a special levy was imposed on the parents of the children registered in the non-English course to cover the cost of hiring a teacher with the required expertise.

At the spring 1915 sitting of the legislature, Premier Scott, who was also Minister of Education, introduced an amendment to the School Act, which stated that if the regular teacher was competent to give non-English-language instruction, he or she might do so, thereby saving the "foreign" parents the expense of hiring a supplementary instructor. Scott claimed that the amendment did not substantially alter the act; it merely clarified what was already not illegal. However, the Conservative opposition pointed out that in districts where one non-English group predominated, the school trustees had an incentive to hire a "foreign" teacher, for the sole reason that he or she had the ability to teach the non-English course at no extra cost. This would result, the Conservatives believed, in the hiring of teachers who lacked proper professional qualifications. The *Evening Province and Standard* suggested that the amendment was an attempt to legitimize bilingual schools by the back door: "It is a deliberate and dastardly attack upon the public school system, subtly and cunningly concealed, but as dangerous as open recognition of the German, Austrian, Galician or French language as of equal status with English in our public school system."⁶

Conservative Party leader Wellington B. Willoughby questioned whether foreign-born teachers had sufficient understanding of British culture and values. In making the point, he hastened to say that he "was not actuated by any other than kindly feelings for the foreign settlers, and it was in their own interest as well as that of the country, that English should be the language taught in the schools."⁷ David J. Wylie, Conservative MLA for Maple Creek, worried that English was "becoming merely a book study." "If these foreign-born people now in our country are not prepared to become Canadians, why are they in Canada?" he wondered.⁸ Fellow Conservative MLA John E. Bradshaw commented: "This war makes us think, and specially directs our thoughts to those districts with their German-speaking settlers.... It is our duty to make the children Canadians. They live in a British country, and under the British flag. They must forget their own country or else they are no use in Canada. The place where the teaching must commence is in the public school."⁹

Bradshaw alluded to an incident that had occurred at Blaine Lake, where the teacher, "an English gentleman of education," had taught his pupils a patriotic song, which included the line, "We'll show this German bully." The children were instructed to shake their fists as they sang these words, and they soon developed the habit of doing so in the faces of their German classmates. A local German ratepayer lodged a complaint which led to an investigation. George Langley, Minister of Municipal Affairs, reported to the legislature that the complainant, not the teacher, was the true "villain of the piece." It was obvious that the kaiser was a bully and needed to be put in his place. The minister admitted, however, that the teacher did not have a proper teaching certificate. Nor had he received any formal teacher training. This explained his controversial method of instruction, or so the minister surmised.¹⁰

The Conservatives proposed that none but Canadian- and British-born should teach in Saskatchewan schools. Scott replied that the suggestion was not in accord with the "British spirit of tolerance."[11] He said that, prior to the war, Germany had tried forcibly to Germanize its subject populations, and the policy had failed abysmally, causing nothing but resentment in the conquered territories. The British were more astute. By respecting the rights of minorities, they won them over, with the result that the entire empire was now fighting at Britain's side. The carrot worked better than the stick. The solution, Scott maintained, was to integrate "foreigners" into the life of the community, encouraging them "to identify themselves with Canada and Canadians, to follow the same pursuits, engage in the same businesses and professions and take part in the municipal and political affairs of the country, in a word, to become one with Canadians and assume their full share of responsibilities attendant upon Canadian citizenship and enjoy all the privileges which such citizenship confers upon them."[12] For this reason, he refused to expel foreign-born teachers from the schoolroom. But he did make one concession to the Tories. The government withdrew the amendment to the School Act that would have allowed the regular teacher to give foreign language instruction in the final hour of the school day. Scott said it was redundant, since nothing in existing law prohibited the practice, but that begged the question of why he had introduced it in the first place.

The Better Schools Movement
Toward the end of the spring 1915 legislative session, Scott announced that he intended to initiate a comprehensive inquiry into the school system.[13] The scope of the review went well beyond foreign language instruction and addressed a wide range of issues, including curriculum, teachers' qualifications, school attendance, length of the school year, consolidation of school districts into large units, and so on. It was a bid to take the school issue out of the arena of partisan politics and into the realm of "objective" scientific study, defusing what otherwise was a ticking time bomb for the Liberals. The *Evening Province and Standard* dismissed the proposal as an insincere, self-serving manoeuvre. Scott, the paper charged, had ignored blatant violations of Department of Education regulations in order to secure political

advantage. He had "made the educational laws a catspaw to secure the foreign vote, winking at the introduction of bilingualism, which invalidates the whole purpose of our public school system."[14] Certainly, reform of the school system was in order, but Scott was not the man to carry it out.

At the annual temperance convention in Regina in July 1915, delegates appointed a citizens' committee for school reform, structured along the lines of the Committee of One Hundred to abolish the bar. At first glance, the twinning of temperance and school reform seems strange and illogical. What had one to do with the other? However, the pairing made perfect sense as a joint effort to enforce Anglo-Protestant hegemony over the non-British population. To keep Saskatchewan British, it was necessary both to stamp out liquor, which was culturally identified with the non-British, and to implement Canadianization in the schools. The Ban-the-Bar crusaders, fresh from their victory over King Alcohol, were now fighting on another front, but it was the same war.

Delegates to the temperance convention attended a luncheon at the King's Hotel, where Dr. Norman F. Black was guest speaker. Vice-principal of Regina Collegiate Institute and author of *English for the Non-English*, Black was an expert on the latest "progressive" trends in education. He sketched in broad strokes the major challenges facing the school system: the difficulty of securing qualified inspectors and teachers; inaccessibility of schools in sparsely settled areas; gaps in the curriculum; insufficient attention to agriculture; the need for schools to serve as social and community centres in rural areas; and the "deplorable exodus" of population from the country to the city. Above all, Black emphasized the necessity of directing education towards "one great governing ideal." "Our schools were the training place for the youth of the country in Christian democracy," he said. "Their goal should be self-realization of the individual for and through free-hearted service to others."[15]

The discussion at the temperance convention led to the formation of the Saskatchewan Public Education League in Regina on 22 September 1915.[16] The *Leader* simultaneously inaugurated a full-page feature in the Saturday edition of the paper titled "The Crusade for Better Schools," which appeared weekly from September 1915 to March 1916. Edited by Norman Black, it included articles, editorials, speeches, reprints from other publications, and letters from teachers, trustees, and interested citizens. For Black, the school campaign was part of a "great wave of reform, not imposed from above, but rising from below out of the awakened intelligence of the general citizen body." It was a "mighty continental movement" that had already swept away the liquor trade and was beginning to penetrate other sectors of society. Democracy was "at last coming to its own"; the people "were on the march." All across the United States, school reform was a top priority, and now "the tide of genuine public opinion" had reached Saskatchewan. The citizen body of the province was "lining up as one of the regiments in the mighty democratic army whose cohorts are organizing, drilling and doing battle in every section of the American continent north of Mexico. Have you enlisted?"[17] There was a reciprocal relationship between the overseas war and the social reform movement at home. Each reinforced the other; both were being fought in the name of democracy.

Rev. Hugh Dobson shared Black's crusading zeal. He, too, believed that school reform was "not an isolated phenomenon but is a part of the rising tide of democratic feeling that is spreading over Canada and indeed over many nations in these perilous times when daily they are challenged even unto death." He linked it with the "overthrow of that tyrant king 'Alcohol,'" equal suffrage, direct legislation (legislation by popular referendum), and consumers' and producers' cooperatives. School reform was destined to "strengthen all who hope and work for a 'better day,' if we are fairly seized of the fact that 'the tide is rolling in,' a tide that may engulf those who try to stop it and is too strong that any man's hand should prevail against it." Dobson's optimism was nonetheless tempered by the realization that the forces of reaction would not give up without a fight. Success was not guaranteed. It had to be achieved through ardous struggle, or, as he put it, it was "a long way to Tipperary."[18]

F.X. Chauvin, a Saskatchewan school inspector, saw the war as "a turning point in the history of the world," one that was "revolutionizing the whole universe." Out of it would emerge a new civilization "based on the indefectible principles of true freedom, a civilization founded on the respect for the rights of individuals, races and small nations, a civilization based on the respect for God and the institutions of the Almighty."[19] A sign of the coming revolution was the steady advance of progressive reform. "Have you noticed," he asked, "how the tremendous wave of temperance has swept the illegitimate liquor traffic from the pedestal on which immorality placed it?" New ideals superseded "time-rotted habits," and fresh viewpoints upended "time-honored opinions." School reform was but one aspect of the total transformation that was underway. "The war," Chauvin wrote excitedly, "has precipitated its development in the same manner as it has helped swell the tide of public opinion against liquor and the liquor traffic."[20]

Intuitively, social reformers fastened on metaphors of vast upheaval in the natural world. Black celebrated the "great wave of reform," Dobson detected "the tide rolling in," and Chauvin heralded the "tremendous wave of temperance." All felt that the world was on the brink of momentous change. They sensed a titanic struggle underway between good and evil, reform and reaction, democracy and dictatorship. The world was on the threshold of utopia, a great leap forward in the development of the human race. The conflict with Germany was not just a run-of-the-mill war in a long succession of bloody wars. It was a righteous crusade of epochal significance.

There was no doubt that Saskatchewan schools were ripe for reform. Twenty-two percent of children and young people aged six to eighteen were not even registered as students. Only 5.48 percent of those aged fourteen to eighteen were in high school.[21] Even among those who were formally enrolled, attendance was spotty at best. In 1916 attendance in rural schools averaged only 53.47 percent. In other words, children, on the average, missed every second day of school.[22] A survey of 250 "Slavonic" schools revealed that, out of a total enrolment of 4806 pupils, 2577 (more than half) were in grade one, 692 were in grade two, and 635 in grade three. The decline in numbers continued dramatically through subsequent grades, ending up with only thirty-nine out of 4806 in grade eight.[23] "Foreign" children could not be "imbued with the story of the Canadian people, including its struggles against physical obstacles and the forces of nature, and the great men it has produced, with the lofty ideals for which they have striven," if they did not make it beyond grade three.[24]

The Rural Myth and Saskatchewan Schools

The war did nothing to debunk Saskatchewan's rural myth; quite the opposite. The promotion of agriculture emerged as a central theme of the better schools movement. Premier Scott made it the focus of the speech he gave on Better Schools Day, 30 June 1916, a public holiday set aside so that people could get together to discuss school reform.[25] Scott recalled his childhood in rural Ontario, where it had been drummed into him that the duty of every boy was to turn his back on the farm and find his true calling in the city. The farm was derided as "the place for the inferior boy."[26] The result, the premier contended, was the depopulation of the Ontario countryside. In Denmark, by contrast, the school curriculum highlighted the positive aspects of rural living. As a consequence (or so Scott believed), the farm population was growing. The aim of education, the premier said, was "to fit boys and girls for life work," and "the life work in Saskatchewan is agriculture." While the school should not disqualify the country boy for urban occupations, neither should it degrade the "dignity of agriculture." It would be a good idea, Scott thought, to teach the basic subjects of reading, writing, and arithmetic by using vocabulary and references familiar to those who lived on a farm.[27]

Rev. George Exton Lloyd, leader of the Ban-the-Bar crusade, was another advocate of adapting the school curriculum to the needs of agriculture. He based his opinion on the premise that "Saskatchewan is primarily and chiefly an agricultural province and probably will always remain so." It unsettled him to see high school graduates filling "the offices, business colleges, and professions with a non-producing race at the expense of the agricultural population." To his critical eye, young people on the streets of cities and towns presented a "spindly and weedy appearance." They did not look fit to reproduce "a sturdy race and population." Rural youth who moved to town to attend high school were "weaned away from the land and know very little of its real attraction." To reverse this unfortunate trend, he suggested shortening the high school year to a term extending from November to March, in place of the existing term that began in September and ended in June. This would allow young people to work the land from early spring to late fall. Under this regime, it would take longer to complete high school (eight years instead of four), but the prolongation, in Lloyd's view, was more a benefit than a hardship. By the time rural youth finished high school in their early twenties, they would be just at the right age to take up homesteads.[28]

Other school reformers took up the paean to agriculture. Rev. W.P. Reekie, a Baptist minister and chairman of the Saskatchewan Public Education League, suggested that school grounds be transformed into model farms and school buildings into "miniature sanatoriums" where health and hygiene could be taught: "Why not have a beauty spot in every community? The construction of a rose is of more value than a knowledge of the War of the Roses."[29] A.W. Cocks, supervisor for agricultural teaching in the elementary schools,[30] expressed the hope that nature study and agriculture would slowly subordinate "the other branches of study as formal and accessory, while it remains substantial." Surrounded "with the living things of Nature," the child in the rural school was given the opportunity "to properly develop his body and mind by natural methods before he is worried with the artificialities of our modern civilization." The school garden functioned as a laboratory of learning, transporting the child into "a state of continual wonder at the marvelous work of his Maker." It made possible "original research" in the intriguing world of plants and animals. The child who cultivated his own garden plot developed "those elements of character which are fundamental to civilization—such as willingness to work for one's daily bread; respect for the property rights of others; love of country and courage to fight and die for the home."[31] In Cocks's opinion, the "tricks" of reading, writing, and arithmetic were highly overrated. They could be learned in one-tenth the time, if only the child were "allowed to develop as nature intended he should, before an attempt is made to mould him into that particular shape which our civilization demands." Cocks exhorted, "Let us throw off the shackles of modern education and get back to the fundamentals so that there may be developed in Saskatchewan a race of men who prefer the natural life in the country to existence in the city."[32]

J.B. Musselman, secretary of the Saskatchewan Grain Growers' Association, echoed that the flawed educational system was responsible in large measure "for the drifting of so many of our people from the farms, where they ought to be happy and prosperous, to the towns and cities to enter the non-producing classes." "Now that the hotel bars—that ugly blot upon civilization—have become a thing of the past," he reflected, "the question of educational reform easily assumes a position in the front rank of the important questions of the day." What was the point of having a mind "crammed with facts or a knowledge of history and dead languages?" Of what use was it to be able to say "the yellow dog" in three languages? It was much better to have "three ideas regarding the dog which one can express clearly in one language."[33]

The government, at the urging of the Saskatchewan Public Education League, appointed Harold Foght, specialist in rural school practice at the Bureau of Education, Washington, DC, to conduct a survey of education in the province. In his 1917 report, Foght indicated that 90 percent of Saskatchewan's wealth was derived from agriculture.[34] It was entirely appropriate, therefore, for schools to "help the rural population to wholesome, joyous, remunerative living on the land."[35] While it could not be expected that city people would become farmers, they must have instilled in them a healthy respect for the agricultural life on which their prosperity depended. Foght recommended the introduction into city high schools of practical courses in agriculture, rural sociology, and farm economics in order to "forge a bond of sympathy and understanding between town and country people" and "place agriculture on the lofty plane which it should occupy in the esteem of all Saskatchewan people."[36]

The Language Issue

The other burning issue of school reform was language of instruction. H.S. Lovering, a staunch Liberal, speaking in Swift Current on Better Schools Day, got right to the point: "The ideal of every school should be to NATIONALIZE [emphasis in original]. Here is where we must make Canadians of our children. Let our schools be so conducted that Canadians, Americans, Jews, Greeks, Germans and all the rest are put through the melting pot and moulded into CANADIANS. To do this we must have ONE LANGUAGE taught and ONE ONLY. There is no place in our public schools for any language but English, and English doesn't include French." "This is OUR country," he continued, "and does not belong to the Foreigner. When he becomes Canadian he can say 'our' too, but not before. If these people insist on their language being taught in our public schools under any condition, let them know plainly it WILL NOT be taught. If they won't stand up for this treatment—well, the train that brought them into the country is still running and it runs out as well as in."

Lovering fretted that demographic trends did not favour the Anglo-Saxon. "In another ten or twenty years," he warned, "your Johnny and Mary will go to the polls and poll two votes. John Petrofsky's 13 children will walk up and outvote Johnny and Mary 13 to 2. We must make those 13 children into Canadians and must do it NOW.[37]

The German-Canadian Alliance held its annual convention in Regina in March 1914, with 500 delegates in attendance. Gerhard Ens, Liberal MLA for Rosthern, identified the object of the convention as "the cultivation of the German spirit," adding: "We are Germans and will remain Germans but we will be good Canadians, too." A resolution was passed requesting amendment of the School Act to allow two hours' instruction in German daily, instead of the one hour per day already provided for.[38] St. Mary's Catholic School in Regina obtained an exemption to the rule that confined German instruction to the final hour of the school day. The German teacher began at nine o'clock, taught for an hour in one room; moved to the next room, taught for an hour there, and so on throughout the day. The Deputy

Minister of Education approved the practice, saying that the original rule had been intended for rural schools and did not apply to city, multi-classroom schools.[39]

The German-Canadian Alliance lobbied before the war for more prominence to be given to the German language in the high schools, colleges, and normal schools of the province. It also requested the creation of a German section in the Saskatchewan Grain Growers' Association and the translation of Dominion legislation pertaining to farmers into German.[40] The Saskatchewan Deutsches Volksverein (German Catholic Association) attracted hundreds of delegates to its convention at Humboldt in June 1914. They passed a resolution declaring "religion the fundamental basis of all education, the purpose of the school to be the moral education of the child as well as its intellectual training." The association committed itself to defending "the right of minorities against unlawful oppression by majorities."[41]

The fight for German language rights did not cease with the coming of the war. A calendar issued by *Der Courier* announced in 1916: "We German Canadians should consider it our honour and advantage to care for the rich German culture. The growing Canadian nation can only succeed when the best things in the German elements take root in it and continue to develop." Among *Der Courier*'s demands were: "instruction in German in every public school where German-Canadians are strong enough, more attention to the German language and literature in the high schools, and training of German-English teachers."[42]

The first convention of the Catholic Association of Polish-Canadians met at Regina in July 1914 with 500 delegates present. Rev. Father Pander proclaimed that "the school is the backbone of the church; so, Polish fathers, use your votes, elect your trustees, and be masters of the education of your children!" Resolutions were passed expressing "a determination to speak Polish wherever possible" and "the need of Catholic education for children and encouragement of vocations for the priesthood."[43] Francophones were also active, organizing in 1912 L' Association Franco-Canadien of Saskatchewan "to promote unity amongst the French people" and "place the French language in the Schools upon an equality with English."[44] In the face of these multiple demands, A.H. Ball, Deputy Minister of Education (who later enlisted for military service), could only say: "Canada is an English-speaking country, and is English in the full meaning of the word. We cannot give you Ruthenian schools, to the Germans, German schools, to the Poles, Polish schools and so on." To do so would make Canada "a Balkan Peninsula."[45]

Edmund H. Oliver, University of Saskatchewan professor and principal of the Presbyterian College in Saskatoon, took up the question of the German Mennonites, whom he regarded as dangerously resistant to Canadianization. Mennonites in Saskatchewan fell into two groups: those who had come from the United States, directly from Russia or, in some cases, from Manitoba and had not settled in closed communities; and Reinlander Mennonites from Manitoba, usually referred to as Old Colony Mennonites, who had settled on reserves set aside exclusively for their use.[46] The former were generally willing to send their children to public schools. The latter refused to do so, setting up their own private schools, which were not under the jurisdiction of the provincial Department of Education. Oliver was mainly concerned about the Old Colony Mennonites, who numbered about 6000, and were clustered in two reserves. The first, comprising five townships, was located near Hague, not far from Saskatoon, and the second, a block of six townships, was south of Swift Current. Oliver visited a number the Old Colony schools in 1915 and was appalled by what he found. The German language was used almost exclusively in the schools, and the curriculum consisted of catechism, New Testament, and Old Testament, supplemented by prayer and hymns.[47] He urged the Department of Education to enforce the teaching of English and the proper training of the children in Canadian citizenship.[48]

Oliver also surveyed a rural municipality in northeast Saskatchewan populated mainly by Ukrainians. Only 3 out of 100 families in the district were able to read an English-language newspaper. The Ukrainian newspapers were suspiciously nationalist in tone; that is, they promoted, in Oliver's opinion, Ukrainian, not Canadian, nationalism. He also alleged that Ukrainian was the de facto language of instruction in some schools, a flagrant violation of Department of Education regulations. He was adamant that rules be strictly enforced: "The way out of our difficulties lies not in making concessions."[49] "Are we to be a homogeneous people on these plains," he anxiously asked, "or are we to repeat the tragic sufferings of polyglot Austria?"[50]

J.T.M. Anderson, inspector of schools for the Yorkton district, did not think the situation was as dire as Oliver made it out to be. The municipality Oliver had studied was not representative of the whole area. In the school district just to the south, English was the norm. The Ukrainian parents, according to Anderson, would not have it any other way.[51] The main problem was not the attitude of the parents, but rather the shortage of qualified teachers. It was not easy, especially in wartime, to find Anglo-Saxons willing to venture out into the "foreign" areas where living and working conditions were inferior to those of the cities.

Anderson appealed to the missionary spirit of idealistic young Canadians. Addressing the congregation at Metropolitan Methodist Church in Regina in November 1915, he called for "a committee of one hundred school teachers" (echoing the Committee of One Hundred of the Banish-the-Bar campaign) to devote five years of their lives "to the intellectual, social and moral uplift of the stranger without our gates," thereby laying "the foundation of a type of ideal citizenship, the like of which the world has seldom, if ever, known."[52] The mission, as Anderson conceived it, went well beyond the teaching of the "three R's" and instruction in English. It was nothing less than modelling Canadian life "to these people who are waiting anxiously for an interpretation."[53] Anderson's speech was not unlike those directed at Canadian Expeditionary Force recruits. In his mind, teachers and soldiers formed one vast army ready to make sacrifices on behalf of British civilization and democracy. The soldier fought the external enemy, while the teacher engaged the internal alien. Since the unassimilated population at home was kith and kin to the foe abroad, the symmetry was complete.

Anderson maintained that "missionary" teachers did not have to be ethnically British. They had only to be British in culture and outlook. Indeed, some of the best "British" teachers were not British-born. A case in point was Michael Rasorabowicz, who had been rejected by a city school because of his foreign-sounding name. He was doing a fine job in a rural Polish school district, accomplishing more than an ethnic Briton might have been able to do because he knew the maternal language of his students.[54] Anderson believed that "foreigners" wanted to become Canadians. He quoted a letter from a soldier at the front: "See that you men who are in charge of education at home do your duty. We'll do our part over here. Don't fail us at home." The soldier had taught in a German district in Saskatchewan before the war. On the day of his departure, the pupils had sung "God Be With You Till We Meet Again." Now at the front, he continued to receive letters from them.[55]

Canadianization did not mean necessarily the total obliteration of the immigrant's culture, just its substantial obliteration. The more "progressive" school reformers patronized the "foreigner" with what Mariana Valverde calls a "a parade of clichés."[56] Norman Black did not think there was any such thing as a "typical Canadian." "The Bruce County type we know," he wrote, "and the Blue Nose, and the Habitant, and so on; but none of these—however admirable—is representative of the manners and viewpoint of all Canada. We must evolve a Canadian type fusing the warm emotions of Celt and Slav with Saxon practical common sense, Latin appreciation of grace and beauty, and that quick and competent individual initiative which is among the best things characterizing our neighbors to the south." For this fusion to occur, "we must have a common tongue [and] it is equally evident that, for obvious practical reasons, this common tongue must be the English language."[57]

On the basis of his pedagogical research, as well as extensive correspondence with education "experts," Black was a believer in total immersion as the best method to teach a second language.[58] For this reason, he advocated English-only instruction in grades one, two, and three. He was willing to accept non-English languages in grades four through eight, but only as a subject of study, not as language of instruction. His plan, if implemented, would have cancelled existing language rights: the right in all elementary grades to non-English language instruction in the final hour of the school day. Also, it would have taken away the right to a course in French in the primary grades (one to three). Further, since the majority of "foreign" children did not stay in school beyond grade three, the effect of his proposal was to deny them any instruction in their native tongue.

The wording of the French language clause in the School Act was slightly ambiguous. It allowed any district "to cause a primary course to be taught in the French language." Did this mean that all courses could be taught in French or that French was allowed as one of the subjects of study?[59] Opinions differed, but in either case, Black's total immersion policy took away existing French rights.[60] He professed deep sympathy for the French-speaking population, whom he regarded as "in an important sense ... more truly Canadians than are the members of the English speaking majority." "WE MUST," he stressed, "SHOW OUR FRENCH SPEAKING FELLOW CITIZENS THAT IN FACT AS WELL AS IN WORD WE LOOK UPON THEM AS OUR BRETHREN AND THAT WE ENGLISH SPEAKING CITIZENS ARE AS INTENT UPON PROTECTING THE LEGITIMATE ASPIRATIONS OF THE FRENCH-CANADIANS AS ARE THEY THEMSELVES" [emphasis in original].[61] Francophones, understandably, could not reconcile Black's profession of sympathy with his policy recommendations.

He took his "compromise" proposal to the annual provincial convention of Saskatchewan school trustees in March 1916, but it was not accepted. In its place, the trustees resolved that no language other than English be taught during school hours in grades one through five. The non-English trustees were furious, accusing their English counterparts of having railroaded the resolution through "by steam roller methods." Black was afraid of a non-English backlash, which would only further antagonize the pro-British element, leading to "a superlatively dangerous crisis."[62] The battle over schools was far from over.

***

The public school was at the centre of the effort to preserve Saskatchewan's rural myth and Anglo-Canadian identity. Children were supposed to learn to appreciate the rural way of life and the dignity of the farmer's vocation. School reformers and curriculum experts waxed eloquent as to the benefits to mind and character of cultivating a garden plot and teaching the basics of reading, writing, and arithmetic in the agricultural vernacular. City schools were admonished to show respect for the farming life, even as they prepared students for urban professional occupations. The second core mission of the school was Canadianization, by which was meant the assimilation of the "foreigner" to British Canadian cultural norms and practices. This necessitated, above all, knowledge of English without which assimilation was impossible.

The war interacted powerfully with both educational projects. The expansion of agricultural production, occasioned by the need to supply unprecedented quantities of food to soldiers and allied civilians, codified Saskatchewan's self-proclaimed identity as "breadbasket of the world." The war against Germany, portrayed as a battle to uphold British ideals and civilization, resonated with the selfsame campaign waged in Saskatchewan schools. The war aroused passions centred on identity, belief, ideology, heritage, and culture, which reverberated from the trenches to the home front and back again to the trenches in a continuous cycle. Who would control the schools? Who would win the war? For many in Saskatchewan, it was the same question.

Chapter 5

The Preacher and the Premier

THE BATTLE OVER THE SCHOOLS HAD A CASUALTY IN WALTER SCOTT, who lost the premiership in a bitter public dispute with Rev. Murdoch MacKinnon. The quarrel was triggered by amendments to the School Act, but, in a larger sense, it centred on the government's overall approach to assimilating the "foreigner." MacKinnon believed strongly in the use of the public school as an aggressive instrument of Canadianization. Scott favoured a more subtle strategy, arguing that overtly coercive methods caused resentment that made immigrants resistant to assimilation. Moreover, the Liberal Party monopolized the "foreign" vote, an advantage they did not want to give up. This made them tread carefully, while the Conservatives, having less to lose electorally, did not show the same restraint. Each party tried to "out-British" the other, the Liberals claiming to exemplify "British fair play," the Conservatives forthrightly defending "one school, one language, one flag." MacKinnon sided with the Conservatives. He was offended that the government catered to "foreigners," betraying, as he saw it, the sacrifices of Canada's men on the battlefields of France and Flanders.

Born in 1867 in Middlesex County, Ontario, Walter Scott left school after grade eight and headed west. Arriving in Regina in 1886, he took up newspaper work, ascending the ladder from printer's devil to co-owner of the *Standard* in 1892. Less than two years later, he purchased the *Moose Jaw Times* and, in 1895, the Regina *Leader*.[1] Scott invested wisely, and his net worth in 1920 was estimated at $507,000, or about $5 million in today's dollars.[2] His political mentor was James Hamilton (Jim) Ross, a Moose Jaw rancher and Liberal Party kingpin, who became surrogate father to the ambitious young newspaperman.[3] With Ross's help, Scott won election to the House of Commons in 1900 and re-election in 1904. He was seen as a "comer" in Liberal ranks—perhaps even a future prime minister of Canada.

Scott left the federal arena in 1905 to become the first premier of the newly established province of Saskatchewan. He faced the electorate in December of that year, securing sixteen seats out of twenty-five in the provincial legislature.[4] He repeated the victory in the 1908 election (twenty-seven of forty-one seats)[5] and again in 1912 (forty-six of fifty-four seats).[6] As the years went by, his stock continued to rise. "Mr. Scott has industry, courage and originality, and a practical capacity for affairs which go far to explain his personal ascendancy in the constituencies," applauded the London *Times*' Canadian correspondent.[7] It seemed that Scott could not put a foot wrong.

From his earliest days in Regina, Scott attended Knox Presbyterian Church. His status was that of "adherent," not "communicant."[8] It is not clear why he held back from becoming a full member. Perhaps there were doctrinal scruples, or maybe there existed a more practical impediment: his inability to produce a baptismal certificate bearing the names of his parents. At the time he entered politics, he composed an autobiography, which he circulated among friends and acquaintances. In it he claimed that his parents were George Scott and Isabella Telfer. In fact, Isabella was not married at the time that Walter was born, and George Scott was probably not the father.[9]

Walter lived in fear his "shameful secret" would come to light, exposing him to public humiliation and making him an outsider in polite society.[10]

Murdoch MacKinnon, Scott's pastor at Knox Church, was born in Cape Breton in 1871. He was one of seven brothers, all of whom studied at Queen's University in Kingston.[11] Five obtained degrees in theology and two in medicine. Murdoch completed his MA in 1900 with the gold medal in moral philosophy. While at university, he met his future bride, Lilian Vaux, an honours and MA graduate.[12] They settled in Regina in 1910, when MacKinnon took up pastoral duties at Knox.

Lilian Vaux MacKinnon was a novelist of some repute. Her *Miriam of Queen's*, published in 1921, earned modestly favourable reviews. It was set at Queen's University in the late 1890s, when she and her husband had been students. The novel conjured the spiritual and intellectual atmosphere of the time, underlining the ethical idealism and call to service that pervaded the campus. Principal George Grant set the tone. An imperialist and nationalist, he urged his students to take up the task of building the new Dominion, especially in the West, which was the most dynamic and fastest growing part of the country.[13] For Grant, money-making and economic prosperity were secondary considerations. The most important thing was to establish the emerging frontier society on a solid moral foundation.[14] Lilian MacKinnon's novel captured the mood of inspired idealism: "Sermon followed the singing, and who could resist the appeal of the speaker to man's inherent nobility? A summons to latent worth, a call to action, a challenge to the slumbering soul of goodness. As the ringing, clear-cut words came hot from the speaker's heart, deep answered unto deep and many a soul was born anew to high endeavor."[15]

The hero of *Miriam of Queen's*, Hugh Stewart, a young farm boy from Cape Breton, excels at sports (just as Murdoch did) and impresses everyone with his manly character. Upon graduating, he sets out for Regina to take up a position in a law office. En route, he falls into conversation with a number of other Queen's graduates, who have decided to stake their future in the West. As the train nears Winnipeg, one of the them says:

"If any of you men want corner lots on Portage Avenue or Broadway, just call at my office."

"Going in for real estate?"

"Certainly. That will be the most important business out here for the next century or so."

"I question if it will," said the theologue, looking towards the colonist car with its swarthy occupants. "There's the business of the next century—making decent citizens out of a crew like that."[16]

Like the unnamed theologue in the novel, Rev. MacKinnon was imbued with a sense of national spiritual mission. As the years went by, he came to believe that Walter Scott had betrayed the vision of a society founded on British Protestant ideals, and, in the midst of the war, he threw down a challenge to the premier. In the battle that followed, one of the men, inevitably, was destroyed.

Rev. Murdoch MacKinnon's Attack on Premier Scott

The main elements of the dispute are readily summarized. In September 1911 Judge E.A.C. McLorg of Saskatoon handed down a ruling concerning the Vonda school district. He held that "the option of supporting the public or the separate school system rested with each individual ratepayer."[17] This meant that a Roman Catholic citizen had the right to direct his taxes to the public school, if he so chose. In response to McLorg's decision, the Scott government in November 1912 introduced an amendment to the School Act making it compulsory for religious minority ratepayers to support the minority school. In addition, the School Assessment Act was amended to give separate schools a larger share of business taxes.[18] Scott maintained that the amendments were "declaratory"; that is, they did not alter the School Act that had been in place since 1905, but rather reaffirmed the original intent of the statute, which, in Scott's opinion, Judge McLorg had misconstrued.

Rev. MacKinnon led a forty-member delegation to meet with the premier on 9 January 1913. The group included representatives of the Regina and Moose Jaw public school boards, the Orange Lodge, and clergymen of various Protestant denominations. Prominent among them was James F. Bryant, a Conservative lawyer and subsequently a cabinet minister in J.T.M. Anderson's government, an administration notorious for its lack of sympathy towards Catholic schools.[19] The delegation entreated the premier to refer the McLorg decision to the Saskatchewan Supreme Court for clarification. Scott refused, saying that he did not want to excite public discussion or friction over the issue.[20] The Synod of the Presbyterian Church in Saskatchewan, at MacKinnon's behest, condemned the amendments. The legislation, it said, was "calculated to encourage the Separate School at the expense of the Public School."[21] MacKinnon, along with Rev. Angus A. Graham, principal of Moose Jaw Presbyterian College, brought the matter before the general assembly of the Presbyterian Church in Canada. It, too, formally expressed "concern over the infringement on civil liberties in Saskatchewan where the minority was now precluded from supporting public schools."[22]

At the Sunday evening service on 26 December 1915, with Walter Scott and his wife in the pews, MacKinnon delivered a 100-minute sermon on the school amendments. He said that he wished to make it clear that he did not question the right of separate schools to exist. The 1905 autonomy act that created the province of Saskatchewan left no room for doubt on that score. His quarrel was with the amendments. While the number of separate school districts in the province was very small (only 19 out of about 4000 in 1918),[23] he believed the danger lay in the future. "All that is wanting," he said, "to divide every public school district in the province into two camps, as the city of Regina is today, is growth of population. By virtue of the amendments every public school district in the province may one day have a separate school formed within the very heart of its constituency."[24] This would lead inevitably to the weakening of Anglo-Protestant influence in the province.[25]

MacKinnon referred to the deliberations of a Polish convention, which had taken place in Regina in the past year. "The school," a Catholic priest was quoted as saying, "is the backbone of the church, and if your children do not get good principles in the schools it is useless for your priests to try and complete their education."²⁶ The convention pledged its devotion to the Catholic faith and the Polish tongue. Similarly, at a French congress held in Regina, "Frenchmen were urged everywhere to unite for the enthronement of French ideals and the Roman faith in the west." The president of the German association brought greetings to the congress and expressed his readiness to join with the French "in the noble enterprise of overthrowing the national school system and establishing separate schools throughout the length and breadth of the province." Although the Roman Catholic Church had endorsed both conventions, there had not been a word of protest from the government. Yet, when the Presbyterian Church dared to speak out on the school amendments, Scott had accused it of political meddling and denounced it as "a disturber of the peace and as a public enemy." Why the double standard? Why must the Protestant churches keep quiet? "Let the government of Saskatchewan do what no sane government in Canada ever did before in the matter of supplementing ecclesiastical discipline by provincial legislation," MacKinnon thundered, "but let the public be quiet about it. Keep silent. Do nothing. Lie down. 'St! Everybody in the attitude of the Brahman worshipper: Om! Om! Om!"²⁷

Referring specifically to the Vonda school district, MacKinnon noted that seven "Frenchmen" and ten "Ruthenians," who resisted the authority of the priest, had been "whipped into line" and forced to pay their taxes to the "dissentient school." This, MacKinnon said, was the modern-day equivalent of slavery, a derogation of the fundamental rights of citizens. The Saskatchewan government had taken away the very freedom that Canada was fighting for in the war against Germany, he argued: "Thousands of our men are fighting for freedom today. Shall freedom be defended upon the fields of Flanders and slain upon the plains of Saskatchewan? Men of Saskatchewan the issue is yours."²⁸

MacKinnon did not conceal his hostility towards the Roman Catholic Church and its educational work. He claimed that "the clerical school blasted out of Europe is being fastened on Saskatchewan and used to perpetuate non-Anglo-Saxon ideals and features which it should be the duty of statesmen and educationists to eliminate." In his view, the separate school stood for "pidgin English, much catechism, clerical skelping [sic], and general inefficiency."[29] He objected to the efforts of the Roman Catholic Church "to make its power felt with the political parties in order to gain influence and advantages" for itself.[30] MacKinnon said he knew personally English-speaking Roman Catholics in Regina, who, prior to Scott's amendments, had paid their taxes to the public school, an option now closed to them by force of law. According to MacKinnon, they resented having to support what they considered to be inferior schools dominated by their non-English-speaking co-religionists.[31]

For an hour and a half, Scott sat like a prisoner in the dock, while MacKinnon rang the changes on the iniquities of his government. As soon as he got home, he wrote a letter, which was published the next day in the *Leader* along with the full text of the sermon. "I begin to be doubtful," seethed Scott, "of a minister of the gospel who deliberately ignores important facts, and states half truths and hesitates to frankly admit errors to which all are liable." MacKinnon, he charged, had "prostitut[ed] his great gifts and adopted "the antics of the demagogue."[32] The *Leader* backed up Scott's position, accusing MacKinnon of having disgraced his pulpit: "People who had just commemorated the birth of Christ, and wended their way to church to worship, had their thoughts diverted into quite another channel, and left the sacred edifice in much the same spirit in which they would leave a political demonstration at the close of a red-hot campaign."[33] The *Evening Province and Standard* defended MacKinnon: "From the pulpit of Saskatchewan churches, the gospel must be preached, either the gospel of the Holy Writ or the gospel of the Grit campaign handbook. Following this rule, the pulpit is safe from all that is profane."[34]

On 30 December 1915 MacKinnon defended his right, as a man of the cloth, to speak out on the public questions of the day. John Knox had done the same and spent three years as a galley slave for his pains. MacKinnon beseeched Scott not to personalize the dispute, but rather to deal with the issues strictly on their merits.³⁵ The premier ignored the advice. His next letter, written just before midnight 31 December 1915 and published on New Year's Day, fiercely assailed the minister:

> You have not ceased to attack the amendments and my government and myself. In every church court you have done it.... You talked in your manse, you talked in other houses, you talked on railway trains, you talked on the street, persistently trying to poison any and all who would listen to you against this legislation and against me.... You always misrepresented, and with Jesuitical cleverness made white appear black.... For three years, month in and month out, you had attacked me, and the very moment I open my mouth in my own defence, you whimper like a baby. "Why not forget me, now that the matter is before the public?" you cry. Before I begin to deal with you, you appeal for mercy.... And from now on, depend upon it, I am going to talk in my own defence to you and about you in good, straight King's English, calling spades spades. Childish cries that "you are calling names" and "I am being abused" will not deter me.³⁶

MacKinnon, in reply, accused the premier of having turned the legislature into "an adjunct to the bishop's palace." The statute book, "so far as it deals with the question at issue," had been reduced to "a footnote to the book of common discipline of the Church of Rome."³⁷ He alleged that in most school districts where Catholics formed a majority,

> the public school bears no likeness to a public school, that it is conducted too frequently by nuns in religious garb, that the only educational qualification which some of these religious workers have is a colloquial knowledge of some language other than English, that sectarian doctrines are being taught in these public schools by these religious workers during regular school hours, that, on occasion, nothing is taught for three weeks at a stretch but obeisance, genuflections and catechism.

Presbyterians, said MacKinnon, were normally "an undemonstrative lot." They had been likened to "an iceberg with a volcano at the centre." But once their passions had been aroused, they fought to the bitter end: "You have allowed the Church of Rome to use the Legislature of this province for its own designs. You have betrayed your trust. Can you vindicate yourself? ...

The issue is between you, as the willing instrument of sectarian ambitions, and the people of this province. Therefore, to the amendments!"[38]

"Now, it is I, and not Tom, Dick or Harry," responded Scott angrily, "who takes the responsibility of declaring—it is I with that reputation behind me and at stake, who declare that you deliberately bear false witness against the school law amendments and against me." "You are a malicious mischief-maker," he fulminated, "and such persons are inevitably false witness bearers.... I have not had to run from charges yet, and I do not run from yours. No man has yet threatened me with war to the knife, and needed to chase me."[39] "War to the knife" was hardly the kind of language a premier normally used in reference to a clergyman. On purely legal grounds, Scott had a good case: it was meaningless to give separate schools the right to exist without also allowing them an adequate tax base. Why did Scott not stick to the facts? There was something in the Christmas sermon that triggered a fatal lapse of judgment.

MacKinnon now kept his silence, but this did not stop the premier from continuing the volley of letters, all of which were published in the *Leader*. Finally, hoping to end the dispute, MacKinnon invited members of the legislature, which was then in session, to a sermon at Knox Church on 23 January 1916. He promised to render a comprehensive judgment on the controversy. Long before the service was scheduled to begin, all the seats were taken, and hundreds stood outside. MacKinnon's address was high-toned and scholarly, complete with quotes from Kant ("God, Freedom, and Immortality are the three postulates of pure reason") and Hegel ("History is the gradual unfolding of the spirit of freedom in the lives and relationships of men"). "God Himself," MacKinnon declared, "did not use His omnipotence to force a man into the light." How, then, to justify a law that forced citizens of the religious minority to support the separate school against their will? The minister reiterated: "I solemnly and emphatically protest against THE LEGAL DISQUALIFICATION OF ANY MAN FOR THE SUPPORT OF THE UNDENOMINATIONAL PUBLIC SCHOOL OF THE PROVINCE" [emphasis in original].[40]

As the school debate raged, another serious crisis confronted Scott. The Opposition in the legislature had for some time been muttering vaguely about fraud and corruption in the government. Exasperated, Scott demanded an end to the smear campaign. Let the Opposition make a specific charge, he said. Otherwise, they should hold their peace.[41] Conservative MLA J.E. Bradshaw rose in the House on 10 February 1916 and alleged that Liberal MLAs had been bribed to oppose anti-liquor legislation; hotel owners had given money to Liberal MLAs to secure liquor licences; prosecutions had been stifled by the government as a reward for political support; and more than $50,000 had been paid out by the government on fake roadwork contracts.[42] The Conservatives clamoured for a Royal Commission. Scott refused, preferring to send the matter to select committees of the legislature, which were dominated by Liberals.[43] Not since taking power in 1905 had the Saskatchewan Liberals faced a crisis of this magnitude. Scott was fighting for his political life.

Scott Goes too Far

Hoping to clear the air with MacKinnon, Scott asked him to attend a sitting of the legislature on 24 February 1916. The request was published in the newspaper, making it a public event.[44] MacKinnon had invited the MLAs to Knox Church to hear his views on the school question; now Scott reciprocated. It would be MacKinnon's turn to sit in the pew and hear a sermon. On the appointed day, the chamber was packed. Seated in the front row of the visitors' gallery were Rev. MacKinnon, Rev. S.J. Farmer of First Baptist Church (who supported MacKinnon on the school amendments), James Balfour, former mayor of Regina and an elder at Knox Church, and "many other noted churchmen."[45] Scott began with an extensive review of the tortuous history of the school issue in all its legal complexity. Abruptly, he performed a stunning *volte-face*. The controversial school amendments were to be repealed. They were no longer necessary, Scott claimed. Judge McLorg had admitted to having made a mistake in the Vonda decision, and the amendments were now superfluous. This was pure fabrication. McLorg, as the next day's newspapers confirmed, had not made any such statement. The judge said that he "declined to act as the Premier's political scapegoat."[46] Even if he had made the comment Scott attributed to him, it would not have made a difference. A judge's remarks not uttered from the bench do not have the weight of a formal judgment.

The second part of Scott's speech was even more damaging to his reputation. Having changed his mind on the amendments, he proceeded to calumniate the character and conduct of Rev. MacKinnon. "What would be my duty," Scott wanted to know,

> if I knew we had in this assembly a leper, or if I knew we had in this city a leper? Could I allow the danger to circulate? What is the duty of every honest person who knows a moral leper is roaming through the household? ... To go farther, if an honest person shows in a position of sacred trust an intellectual and spiritual leper does he rest under any lighter duty than is the case when it comes to his knowledge that there is a physical leper in the community?[47]

He called upon the Presbyterian Church to remove MacKinnon from office. On them fell a solemn obligation "in relation to the character of their pulpit, which ought to be a shining light and a lamp to young and old alike. Is it? I ask them, is it? ... [they] must decide, and in deciding that the eternal fate of scores, if not hundreds, of little children may depend upon their failure or fulfillment of this duty."[48] As an adherent, not a communicant, Scott had no standing in church courts. Therefore, he could not lay a formal charge against the "moral leper" in the pulpit; it was up to others to do so. The scene of 26 December 1915 was exactly reversed. MacKinnon had tried to drive Scott from the premiership; now the premier was attempting to expel the preacher from the pulpit.

The elders of Knox Church held a special meeting on 25 February 1916 to discuss what had happened. Twenty-five were in attendance, and, of these, twenty signed a resolution supporting MacKinnon. A signature was also obtained by telephone from a twenty-first member, who was unable to be present. The resolution read, in part:

> We the undersigned ... desire to express our confidence in Mr. MacKinnon and in the splendid character of his work which has been carried on by him since he came to this city. We regret extremely that in the discharge of what he has deemed to be a public duty, he undeservedly called down upon himself the abuse of one whose position in the councils of the province gave us the right to expect that he would be able to deal with public matters without descending to the depths of abuse to which he gave expression.... Our sense of the nature of the outbreak is such that we can only characterize it as the most uncalled-for and indecent ever made in this free land upon a man discussing a public question of vital importance to the community.[49]

Among the signatories were two former Regina mayors, ex-aldermen, the chairman of the public school board, the vice-president of the Board of Trade, the city solicitor, the foreman of the city public works department, the secretary of the Banish-the-Bar committee, and the principal of Regina Collegiate Institute.[50] Scott felt personally betrayed, shunned by the elders of his own church, thirteen of whom he had counted as "personal and political friends."[51] He broke off attendance at Knox Church.[52]

The Regina presbytery also repudiated Scott's speech,[53] as did Rev. A.W. McIntosh, moderator of the Synod of the Presbyterian Church in Saskatchewan.[54] Manitoba College in April 1916 conferred on MacKinnon an honorary Doctor of Divinity degree.[55] The Regina Ministerial Association reaffirmed its confidence in his "high moral character and its appreciation of his great influence for good in the community."[56] The newspapers buzzed with comment. "A Presbyterian Liberal" put forward the view that MacKinnon had merely voiced "the principles of civil and religious liberty for which Presbyterianism and all Protestant religious bodies have stood and advocated since the Reformation and under which the civilization of the British empire has developed since that time."[57] Scott had "prostituted" the ideals of the Liberal Party and would pay the price on election day.[58] "Daylight's Dad" wrote that it made him blush to hear the premier's abusive language. Rev. MacKinnon was "one of the ablest men in the Presbyterian Church in Canada" and "without a peer among the Presbyterian ministers of Saskatchewan,"[59] "a gentleman, a scholar, and a man of outstanding integrity."⁶⁰ When the premier stooped to attack such a man, he "insult[ed] the Presbyterian Church of Canada" and "call[ed] every Presbyterian to arms against him and the government."⁶¹

According to rumours in the Conservative press, Scott had not wanted to repeal the school amendments, but had been pressured into doing so by senior Liberals, who feared going into an election "with a live issue of that nature dragging them down."⁶² Scott also had to back down on the question of appointing a Royal Commission to investigate the corruption charges. He had initially opposed a Royal Commission, but now gave in to the demands.⁶³ A split was opening up in the ranks of the Liberal Party; Scott was no longer in control.⁶⁴ Behind everything was the fear of losing the next election. Presbyterians, who comprised one-fifth of the population of Saskatchewan,⁶⁵ were not a voting bloc to the trifled with.

Scott's Fall from Power
Scott's health had always been fragile. He suffered a severe asthma attack in December 1905 just before the last rally of the election campaign. In the winter, when hotels, schoolhouses, and other buildings were sealed up against the cold, he was sometimes overcome by the panicky feeling that there was not enough oxygen in the room.⁶⁶ He gave up travelling in rural Saskatchewan during the winter months and took long trips to the southern United States, the Caribbean, and the Mediterranean. He treated himself to a round-the-world sea voyage in 1913 that lasted nine months.⁶⁷ To heal his shattered nerves, he periodically sought treatment at the Philadelphia clinic of Dr. Silas Weir Mitchell, reputedly "the most noted nervous specialist in America."⁶⁸

Now, in February 1916, the battle with MacKinnon and the uproar over the Bradshaw charges wore Scott down. He was getting only about three hours of sleep a night, and confided to Sir Wilfrid Laurier on 2 March: "Only those who have been in real nervous depression know what it is, and few in as far as I was in, ever come back to tell others what it is."⁶⁹ He left Regina at the end of March on a previously scheduled trip to the Bahamas.⁷⁰

His political enemies did not let up. "What would be said of a general," the Conservative *Province* growled, "who, in the midst of an important battle, deserted his post and left for the rear, leaving his subordinate officers to fight it out as best they could?"[71] Scott wanted to write more letters attacking MacKinnon, but by now their content was stale and repetitive, and the *Leader* declined to publish them.[72] The elders at Knox Church, anxious to restore peace to the congregation—for Scott still had some supporters—counselled MacKinnon not to say anything more on the school question.[73] Everybody wanted a break from the emotional harangue.

Rev. Angus Graham, principal of Moose Jaw College, wrote in the pages of the *Presbyterian*, the national journal of the Presbyterian Church, that Scott's scourging of MacKinnon "exceeded anything ever heard in the legislative halls of Canada."[74] He added cryptically: "There is an explanation for this unpleasant incident which human kindness and Christian charity will not even mention."[75] Scott asked W.R. Motherwell, Minister of Agriculture, what he thought the comment meant. Motherwell answered that the reference, "while not specific could only be justly made in respect of a person who was a whore-monger and an habitual associate of harlots."[76] Later, when Graham confronted Motherwell about this odd interpretation, the minister of agriculture said that since "so many men err in the respect referred to," he thought that people would assume that it was Scott's "besetting sin" also.[77] Graham assured Motherwell that he had meant nothing of the kind. He had merely wanted to allude, as delicately as possible, to the premier's nervous condition.[78] In any event, Scott took the incident badly. "I think that at the time," he wrote, "I was like an engine on dead centre, just then it was 'touch and go' whether I should swing into normal health or 'go under.'"[79]

Scott was back in Regina in July 1916, still depressed and feeling "all in." "I made a pretence of being 'on the job,'" he later recollected,

> until a day in September, when one memorable morning something snapped; I saw the Premier's office no more ... and by-and-by Senator [James Hamilton] Ross arrived from Montreal and yanked the 'sick slacker' out of bed and off to a hospital in Philadelphia where there were some weeks (or was it months?—

some weeks are months anyway) which it is just as well not to remember. Then California and the same bed during an interminable seventeen months, or seventeen interminable years more like.[80]

Ross arrived at the clinic and presented the premier with a letter of resignation. "After several days of reflection and advice from his physicians,"[81] Scott signed it, thereby ending his political career. He was forty-nine years old.

In the spring of 1918, Scott's depression began to lift. "I have considerable road yet to travel to reach the state of health I crave," he recorded in July of that year,

> but it is true I am vastly improved and finding genuine enjoyment in the improvement. For one who has never broken down it is, I am sure, wholly impossible to appreciate the delight that the mere ability to write an ordinary letter can yield, or the strength to do such a simple, easy thing as to see and have a chat with a friend without effort and strain amounting to torture.[82]

Scott received more good news at the end of the month. The Privy Council, the highest court of appeal, handed down its judgment on the Bartz case involving a Regina Roman Catholic who wished to pay his taxes to the public school. The court ruled against Bartz, deciding that once a separate school district had been established, minority ratepayers were legally bound to support it.[83] This vindicated Scott's belief that his school amendments, withdrawn in 1916 under pressure from MacKinnon and others, had been declaratory; that is, they had restated, rather than altered, the intent of existing law. Scott took further comfort from the fact that, two weeks after the ruling, MacKinnon resigned from Knox Church and accepted a post as military chaplain.[84] A letter to the editor of the *Leader* signed "Presbyterian" maintained that the minister owed the ex-premier an apology.[85] Another requested that the anti-Scott resolution still on the church's books be expunged.[86]

Writing to J.A. Allan, one of the elders who had signed the resolution, Scott confessed that it [the resolution] "disturbed me greatly and continues to disturb me." He felt that it was an obstacle to his worshipping with his old congregation. He did not want to enter a church that had unjustly condemned him.[87] Allan answered that, regardless of the legal aspects of the case, "the point of cleavage between yourself and the members of session so far as I understand the views of the latter had therefore to do only with the manner in which the controversy was carried on."[88] Scott had sullied MacKinnon's motivation and character in a manner the church elders found unacceptable. For them, the style of the attack, not the final disposition of the court case, was the crux of the matter.[89]

Ex-Mayor James Balfour rendered an even harsher judgment. "You had been playing for the Catholic and non-English support ever since getting to be Premier," he wrote. "You followed the policy that a Government's first duty is to stay in power. You amended the School law to gain Catholic support, and it was a good thing for this Province that Dr. MacKinnon had the courage to do what he did."[90] Not stopping there, Balfour indicted the entire Liberal approach to governing Saskatchewan: "You furthered the desire of the Catholics to get a bigger hold on this Province. You played for the foreign vote to keep you in power, and may I ask you what particular thing or things did you accomplish in all that time that any ordinary man could not have done? You have been a time-serving politician, not courageous enough to follow high ideals, but trimming your sails to every wind."[91]

There it was—a fundamental disagreement over how to deal with the "foreigner." Everybody supported the public school as the instrument of Canadianization. The question was how strictly to enforce the policy. There were very few separate school districts in the province. It was hardly an emergency. But MacKinnon and his supporters were looking ahead to the future. They were worried that the tax regime Scott had put in place would bear bitter fruit. As the province filled in, more separate schools would be set up because their financial support was enforceable by statute. From MacKinnon's point of view, Scott was a traitor to British Canadian ideals. The preacher had made it his life work to build the moral foundations of Anglo-Protestant nationality. He could not keep silent when it came under attack. "Shall freedom be defended upon the fields of Flanders and slain upon the plains of Saskatchewan?" he wrote.[92]

Scott might have survived had he handled the controversy more skilfully. The Bradshaw corruption charges, as serious as they were, did not bring about his downfall. The Liberal Party was able to weather the storm. In due course three Royal Commissions were appointed to investigate the various accusations. The government accepted the findings and implemented the recommendations. Two Liberal MLAs (J.A. Sheppard and S.R. Moore) were found guilty of receiving money from hotelmen to secure liquor licences; Liberal MLA H.C. Pierce was convicted of accepting a bribe to oppose the 1913 ban-the-bar bill and sentenced to eighteen months' imprisonment and a fine of $500; Liberal MLA C.H. Cawthorpe was found guilty of receiving money to stifle prosecution against a liquor licensee; and Liberal MLA E.H. Devline pleaded guilty to charges of forgery and fraud, and was sentenced to jail for three years.[93] All were expelled from the legislature and appropriately punished. The government cleansed its own stables to the satisfaction of the voters.[94]

The school issue, too, might have blown over, if Scott had maintained his composure. The tipping point was the Christmas sermon. Something happened to Scott that day. He felt publicly humiliated and persecuted, rejected and outcast. The sermon triggered a series of developments that led to his undoing. His personal fate became enmeshed in the wartime struggle over Anglo-Canadian identity. He was perceived as too sympathetic to "foreigners" and Catholics, and he had to go.

**

When Walter Scott came west as a young man, he had no money, no friends, and a grade eight education. By dint of talent and hard work, he made a small fortune and climbed to the top of the greasy pole. He had a breadth of perspective and depth of insight that set him apart from his contemporaries. For eleven years he was premier of the province he had helped to create. The legislation he introduced won accolades and gave Saskatchewan the reputation of "banner province." But beneath the façade of public success lurked private insecurity and fear. He made up a story about who his parents were, because he was ashamed to have been born out of wedlock. It must have been hard for him to receive plaudits and praise, winning election after election, hailed as Saskatchewan's man of vision and great province builder, all the while hiding who he really was. When he took his place in the accustomed pew in Knox Church on 26 December 1915, he had no inkling of the disaster about to befall him. He thought he was among friends, the people of his city and church, who liked and respected him. Then came the blow. For an excruciating hour and a half, the father figure in the pulpit lit into him. He was powerless to speak; he had to sit there and take it. Later, when he thought about what happened, the image that kept coming into his mind was that of the pastor attacking him with a knife.[95]

It was downhill from there. The letters to the *Leader* became increasingly shrill, betraying deep hurt. "I am no Tom, Dick or Harry," he wrote. "I am somebody." "You are a malicious mischief-maker." "I am not a moral leper, you are." The climax came in his speech to the legislature on 24 February 1916, when he retaliated against MacKinnon in a manner so abusive that he destroyed his own reputation. What he had imagined to be happening now actually came to pass. He was now the outcast of his own worst nightmares. He fled to the Bahamas, but there was no peace. He returned, defeated. Jim Ross, the mentor who had introduced him to the political game those many years ago, when Regina was but a cluster of shacks and tents on a vast, empty prairie, arrived with a letter. Wearily, Scott looked into the face of his old friend. He signed the letter.

Chapter 6

News from the Front

THE CHRISTMAS GIFTS SOLDIERS SENT TO REGINA GIRLS IN 1916 WERE a little unusual. Instead of jewellery, perfume, and boxes of chocolates, they gave their loved ones German helmets, gas masks, belts, pins, medals, battalion badges, and other war trophies. Some of the parcels contained pieces of French lace or little squares of silk embroidered with inscriptions: "To My Darling," "For My Love," or "Sweetheart." From Salonica an absent boyfriend sent a little drinking cup, embossed in fantastic colourings. Two young ladies, both wearing battalion badges, were overheard in conversation at the downtown post office. "Look what George gave me," boasted one, pulling out a silk kerchief with "To My Little Love" written on it. The other replied that her soldier boyfriend had sent her a precious item, too, but, to the disappointment of the crowd gathered at the stamp wicket, she did not reveal what it was.[1]

News from the Front

The flow of goods and information moved back and forth between home front and battlefront. Private A.G. Hazell, a football player on the *Leader* squad, left in September 1914 and was drafted into the Fifth Battalion. Wounded in early summer 1915, he returned home and talked to reporters. He said that Flanders was a "death-strewn, shell-torn waste of desert": "Corpses lie around everywhere, the stench of corrupting bodies fills the air and all round nothing but carrion, flies and rats are to be seen. I have never seen anything like the rats in Northern France. They are terrific. They prowl around the trenches and live on the dead bodies of fallen soldiers. Without exaggeration, I have seen rats there as big as bulldogs."[2]

James Allan, a student at the Anglican St. Chad's College in Regina, marvelled at the "queer mixture of excitement and philosophy" among French civilians. During one bombardment, he saw a man "running round in the middle of the village in a circle for all the world like a puppy trying to catch its tail," while another "was down on his knees in front of the Church door, praying aloud and crossing himself for all he was worth." Five minutes after the bombardment was over, an old woman was seen "sweeping the debris out of her house and getting things shipshape inside the house." Allan strolled over to the church to see what damage had been done. He found "a mass in full swing, the priest and server fully vested and a congregation about a hundred strong." Everyone seemed to think it was a shame that the Germans had chosen Sunday morning to bomb their church.[3]

Other soldiers revealed personal feelings. Private F. McIvor Williams, a Regina post office employee, served with the Tenth Battalion. On 23 April 1915, while charging a German trench, he took a rifle bullet in the foot. He managed to crawl back three-quarters of a mile to the field station, where an ambulance picked him up.[4] Before the battle he had been "full of ideas and theories" about how he would react. Every shell seemed to have his name on it, but, after a time, a mood of fatalism overtook him. He moved forward with the idea fixed in his mind that he would not get hurt. It was not the danger of impending death that rattled him, but rather the physical discomfort of the "sudden bursting of the shells, the screaming of the coal boxes, the 'whiz-bang' of the shrapnel and the concussion caused by the high explosive shells." When asked to describe his reaction to seeing a man drop at his side, he replied that "it was curious that instead of generating a feeling of fear, it only made the men who witnessed the incident the more savage and filled them with a desire to revenge their comrade."[5] Williams was not sorry his wound had placed him on the unfit list: "I cannot begin to describe all the horror of the war. Looking back it appears to me as if I had been living in some horrible nightmare." And yet there was "something grand in the way the men go out to fight, something thrilling and I am proud that I am a Canadian, and proud of our record."[6]

"What struck you most during the fighting in France?" Sergeant E.L. Hall was asked. "Well, to tell the truth, I am inclined to think that it was the shrapnel shell that put me out of action." He recalled that the first time he went into the firing line he felt shaky, but gradually the feeling wore off, and he settled into the routine. "Excitement grips you," Hall explained, "your breathing quickens, the heart beats faster, in fact muscular activities are increased tremendously. The nearer the trenches the greater is the excitement, and the more desperate and intense the fighting."[7] Men were totally absorbed in the moment: "Their attention is directed solely to their hostile vis-à-vis. They look neither to the right, to the left, nor behind. The gaze is fixed upon the parapet of the hostile trench."[8]

For some, the strain was too much. They suffered nervous breakdowns or became hysterical, but the vast majority made the adjustment and maintained "a state of indifference to the constant danger in which they are placed." The artillery barrage tried the nerves most—"the concussion of the shells, the shriek of the flying shrapnel, and that awful feeling of being shot at and not being able to see the enemy." Just before the battle, men were keyed up to the very limit, until they found relief in physical action, attaining "supreme forgetfulness" in hand-to-hand fighting. At such moments, the soldier did not feel his injuries. Often they had to be pointed out to him. "War was no easy game," Hall concluded. "I have done my bit, and I am glad of it, but it is up to every Canadian to do his share and they should start doing it right away."⁹

All through training, Private Stanley Kay had pictured to himself what the first taste of battle would be like. He was afraid that "when I got into a tight corner I should funk miserably," but when the time came

> I became possessed with a hate that is terrible to describe. I saw my pals fall all around me. Every time I stopped to put in a fresh clip of bullets in the magazine of my rifle I had to look down at the headless body of my best friend. This made me savage and I just pumped that gun as fast as the trigger would go. In front of me I could see a man pitch forward and throw up his arms. 'That's another of them,' I said to myself, and strange to say I did not feel in the least happy or elated at the fact. The idea that had by this time fixed itself in my brain was that the men in the grey coats coming up had to be stopped and that I was there to do the stopping.... The barrel of my rifle by this time was so hot that it had blistered my hand, but I never felt any pain from it at all. It was not until the fight was over and we had retired that I found that I was burned.¹⁰

Soldiers found solace in black humour. Private Hazell remembered that just before the attack, an American in the company dryly remarked, "Thank goodness, at last we will get something to eat."¹¹ (It was thought that the Germans feasted on sausages and cheese, while Canadians had to make do with hard biscuits and bully beef.) Sergeant W.J.A. Ensor, a time-sheet man at the Regina freight sheds of the Grand Trunk Pacific Railway, wrote cheerily:

> I have been in the trenches since October 6, 1914, and am not yet tired of the sport—in fact, I like it first class. Possibly from reading your American papers you will be led to believe these 'Deutschers' are 'hot stuff' at fighting. Such is not the case, however. Man for man, and given ammunition, we can lick them to a frazzle, and our men are tickled to death to get at them. They always show their dominant spirit, namely, tin gods when top dog, but like whining curs when in a difficulty.¹²

Other letters made no pretence at bravado. Private J.V. Preece, a Regina post office worker, confided gloomily:

I feel very lonely these days. Nearly all the boys are either wounded or sick.... They dropped forty of the black devils within two hours and all so near that we thought each one had our name on it. My nerves were very shaky after the ordeal and I don't wonder at it at all. We were just waiting—first we could hear the gun, then the awful gloating shriek, which those big shells let out, and then we went through the seemingly endless moment between the shriek and the burst. Our flimsy old dugout would just rock and tremble and each one of us would manage a sickly smile and say 'that was near,' or something like it. In any case it was more like a castanet dance helped out with a few gurgles. The weather is terrible now and our trenches in a corresponding condition. The communication trenches are in some places knee-deep with slush. The only thing that keeps us going is the small issue of rum we get each morning at daybreak. I firmly believe that if some of those teetotal cranks had their way we should get only drinks of pop or lemonade. Let them come out and do a week and then hear their song. When one is chilled to the marrow with an all-night stand to (as we get now and again), it is the only thing to make one's feet warm and help us to get a sleep.[13]

The Germans were at times amazingly well informed about the Canadians they faced in the trenches opposite. When Signaller Harold Martin of the Twenty-Eighth Battalion went into the line, a German soldier called over to him, "Say, Canuck, how's banish the bar in Saskatchewan?"[14] At another location, the Germans set up signboards in excellent English: "Hello Brandon," "Hello Winnipeg," "How's Manitoba?" or "What's on at the Walker [a Winnipeg theatre]?" The Canadians assumed that the German soldiers had lived in western Canada before the war and returned to Germany to fight for the fatherland. Responding to the taunts, the Canadians put up signs reading: "Winnipeg is all right and so is Brandon and you'll wish you were back washing dishes and slinging hash before we get through with you."[15]

The most wrenching reports brought news of the dead and wounded. Major A. Frank Mantle, Deputy Minister of Agriculture, signed on with the Sixty-Eighth Battalion in August 1915, before proceeding on draft to the Twenty-Eighth Battalion. He was killed on 26 September 1916, shortly after taking command of his company. On that fatal afternoon, he left his headquarters to inspect a platoon, which was holding a cemetery. He walked along the communication trench, visited a platoon doing duty towards the middle of the front line, and returned to the communications trench. To get to the cemetery, he had to cross a stretch of open ground, and as he did so, a German sniper shot him through the heart. He fell on almost the exact spot where J.W. Ward, a Regina lawyer, had been killed a few days earlier.[16]

Agriculture Minister W.R. Motherwell voiced Regina's overpowering grief: "In losing such a valued officer, not only the Department of Agriculture but the government of Saskatchewan feel that their loss at this formative period in our provincial life is beyond measure." George Langley, Minister of Municipal Affairs, added: "I feel we have lost one of the men from the province of Saskatchewan which the province needs very badly. To speak truthfully, I regard it almost as a misfortune that he enlisted, from the point of view just outlined."[17] At a memorial service held at Westminster Presbyterian Church, where Major Mantle had been superintendent of the Sunday school, the pastor eulogized his "unswerving devotion to duty, human duty, duty in the common service, duty to church and state or in whatever work he was engaged. After all, duty was the highest motive in the man. It was a tribute to the man that in service he found his highest reward."[18] Charles Dunning felt that if Mantle had lived "he might have risen to the highest office in the gift of the people." Motherwell glimpsed "the kingdom of God ... in the breast of the late Frank Mantle. He left here in the King's uniform, but he would be met hence robed in the uniform of the King of kings."[19] Dead at age thirty-four, he left behind a wife and three children, aged eleven, seven, and two.[20]

Captain John Arthur Cullum came west with his parents in 1884. Graduating with degrees from Toronto and Edinburgh, he took up the practice of medicine in Regina.[21] He went overseas with the Canadian Expeditionary Force in September 1915. In short order, he was awarded the Military Cross, the Bar to the Military Cross, and the *Croix de Guerre*. On one occasion, when the Germans exploded a mine under the trenches occupied by the Twenty-Eighth, Captain Cullum jumped over the parapet under heavy fire and helped dig out the buried men. He did this a number of times in various battles, bringing in the wounded men from No Man's Land at great peril to himself. Two battalion commanders recommended him for the Victoria Cross. "He doesn't know what fear is," one officer wrote.[22]

Lieutenant Colonel H.W. Laird paid a visit in May 1916 to the Twenty-Eighth Battalion, then occupying trenches in the Ypres salient. In a corner of the officers' hunt, Captain Cullum, his face lathered, stood shaving in front of an old broken piece of mirror. He turned around to see who had come into the hut and, as he did so, his razor slipped and he gashed his lip, the blood flowing profusely. Smiling, he joked, "I've wasted more blood over you than I have in the whole war." He asked question after question about Regina and all the people he knew there. He wanted to know every detail of what was going on in his home city.[23]

As the men of the Twenty-Eighth Battalion made their way to the mess hut for dinner on 9 November 1916, the Germans sent over four high-velocity shells. The second of these exploded on a metal shelter, killing two men outright and injuring Captain Cullum and Lieutenant A.H. White. White recovered, but Cullum died the next day. "Good Old Doc" or "Pills," as he was affectionately known, had just transferred from the medical corps to take a commission as combatant officer.[24] He was survived by his wife and three-year-old daughter. At the memorial service held at St. Paul's Anglican Church, Rev. Canon G.C. Hill took as the text Ecclesiastes 44:1: "Let us now praise famous men." "There was one name that stood out," the rector said, "a man whose fearless and undaunted devotion to duty, have endeared him to the hearts of every one of us especially, who had the honor of knowing him in life—Dr. J.A. Cullum."[25]

Joe Potts's barbershop was a busy place Christmas Eve 1916. Austin Creswell was back in town. Before the war he had captained the Regina Victorias hockey club, and now he looked the same as ever, except for the right arm encased in a sling. With his usual grin, he extended his left hand to friends and acquaintances. He was "mighty glad" to be in Regina, he acknowledged, but also anxious to return to the front.[26] He had taken the bullet that immobilized his arm at the battle of Courcelette in September.

His men had been held in reserve, while the company ahead of them charged the German line. The Canadians seemed to be wavering when Creswell jumped up and called out, "Come on there you boys from Regina, let's take that trench." The rush was so fierce and quick that they were carried right into the German trench and engaged in hand-to-hand combat. When the enemy retreated, Creswell, with bandaged arm, directed the cleanup operations. As soon as the work was finished, he asked for a cigarette, which he smoked calmly until he arrived at the hospital.[27]

Creswell's hockey teammate, Edward Lyman "Hick" (for "Hickory") Abbott, a twenty-four-year-old student-at-law and clerk in the attorney general's department,[28] went overseas with the Sixty-Eighth Battalion. He was assigned to instructional duties in England, but, finding the job too dull, volunteered to go to France. On his first day in the trenches, he was bowled over by a shell and sent back to England.[29] Shrapnel was removed from his left shoulder, and he recuperated in hospital for thirty-two days. By December 1916, he was back in the line,[30] where, on 4 September 1917, he took a gunshot wound to the face. A giant magnet was used to remove shell fragments from his right eye. In recognition of "conspicuous gallantry and devotion to duty," he was awarded the Military Cross and Bar.[31] He was killed in action on 14 August 1918.[32]

Charles Edward (Charley) Otton, another Vics player, twenty-four years old and an accountant, joined the Forty-Third Battalion in September 1915. At Ypres on 4 July 1916 a bullet passed through his left thigh, just missing the bone. He breezily reported that he was "OK," but had lost weight, now tipping the scales at only 184 pounds: "I am afraid I am through with taking an active interest in sport, as I will have slowed up considerably and will probably lose a limb before we get through with the Boch." He mentioned that he had seen "Old Hickory" Abbott "covered with mud from head to foot and you would believe he had been playing a game of football in no man's land. We had a great reunion I assure you."[33] Otton received a second wound at Lens on 20 July 1917. A machine gun bullet struck his left elbow, causing severe damage. Despite prolonged treatment and therapy, it remained so weak that he could not lift a thirty-pound weight from the floor to the table.[34] His hockey-playing days were over, but he made it through the war. When war broke out again in 1939, he signed up and served as the officer in charge of the training camp at Shilo, Manitoba.[35]

Bob Boucher was considered to be one of the best all-around athletes western Canada had ever produced. Though he excelled in rugby football and lacrosse, his passion was hockey. He "lived and talked hockey and nothing else." In a legendary game against the Saskatoon Pilgrims, "he went down the ice so fast that all the spectators could see was a streak. He shot the puck past Fowler so fast that he didn't even see it."[36] When he was killed at the front in March 1917, sports columnist James O'Phelan grieved:

> Here was a man, who died the noblest death that is given to the lot of anyone, that of shedding his blood, of giving his all, for his country.... He was first of all, God's noblest work, an honest man.... I tender on behalf of the people of Regina and, I might say, the Province of Saskatchewan, to his family and relatives, the sympathy that always goes out to an honorable life. I express further on behalf of his close friends the admiration we have always felt for his rigid sense of duty and finally I hope that all of us, who survive him, may when our time comes, die as noble and patriotic death as he did.[37]

The *Leader* said of Boucher and his teammates: "That Victoria hockey team was composed of real men, not only great hockey players and their work since that time has proved this assertion."[38]

Rugby player Clarence Russell (Clarrie) Dale was such a sports fanatic that he had *Sporting News* sent to the front so that he could keep track of major league baseball scores.[39] He enlisted at age twenty-six, just two days after the war started. Wounded at Festubert in the spring of 1915, he was honourably discharged. He might have sat out the rest of the war, but instead re-enlisted with the Sixty-Eighth Battalion. On the night of his death, he led his company from their billets to the forward trenches. It was pitch black and drizzling. Mud, shell holes, and broken ground made walking difficult. All through the march, he went up and down the line, asking the men how they were doing and whether they were going too fast. After they had covered about two-thirds of the distance, they halted at an old trench. The Germans were shelling to the right, but everything seemed quiet in their area. They had just resumed walking when a big shell landed close by. Above the din, the men could hear Dale, "cool as a cucumber,"[40] shout, "Keep going boys, and don't scatter." At that very moment, two more shells came down, and he was killed.[41]

Howie Longworthy was famous for his zigzag running style. He had helped Regina win the western Canadian rugby football championship in 1914. His father was foreman in the city Waterworks Department, and his mother president of the Metropolitan Methodist Church Ladies' Aid.[42] Howie's death at Vimy Ridge came as a terrible shock. The only consolation, the *Leader* said, was that he had "proved himself to be a hero in the greatest game of all, just as he was a hero on the gridrion."[43]

Airman Homer Waring Laird, the son of Conservative senator Henry Willoughby Laird, was killed in action on 8 October 1917.[44] His plane nose-dived from about 1200 feet and crashed into the ground. Laird flew with Jimmie Balfour, the son of James Balfour, mayor of Regina in 1915. The two boys grew up next door to each other on Victoria Avenue in downtown Regina. Soon after "Warrie" arrived in France, he and Jimmie took a plane out on a Sunday morning and flew about seventy-five miles to visit some of their Regina chums, including Billy Martin, nephew of the premier. The day before his death, Laird wrote prophetically: "I can plainly see now that there is no chance of beating this game and sooner or later I will get knocked out. What I have to do is try and beat time. If I can hang on for three months I will consider myself lucky and that I have done 'my job.'"[45]

Neil Joseph ("Piffles") Taylor (for whom Taylor Field, home of the Saskatchewan Roughriders, was named) quarterbacked the Regina rugby football squad in 1915. On 19 September 1917, seven German fighters dived out of the sun and attacked his plane. His observer, George Mumford, was put out of commission almost immediately, with eight bullets through his coat and one through the helmet. Taylor took a machine gun bullet in the shoulder and another through his cheek, which removed two teeth on one side and a tooth and a half on the other, exiting via his mouth. The third bullet did the most damage. It was an explosive bullet, which hit the strut above his head. Three splinters got into his eye, several bits around the eye, one on the side, and one in the back of the head. His goggles were shot away, and the other eye filled with blood so that he was blinded and forced to land. As soon as he touched ground, he was taken prisoner.[46] The eye that had been hit had to be removed and replaced with a glass substitute. "It's a bit rotten," Neil wrote his brother Sam, "but I am not complaining. I was lucky to get out as well as I did and it is a small sacrifice to make compared with what others have suffered, so I am wasting no time in self-pity."[47]

Life in a German prisoner-of-war camp was no picnic for the 3842 Canadians who endured the experience. The diet was a recipe for slow starvation, and beatings were all too common. A common punishment was *stillgestanden*, "two or more hours of standing rigidly at attention, preferably facing the rays of the sun." For able-bodied soldiers, it could be an ordeal. For those suffering from partially healed wounds or weakened by poor nutrition, it was agony.[48]

Taylor's main preoccupation, as prisoner of war, was getting enough food to eat. In the hospital at Mons, his diet consisted "chiefly of two sucks at a thermometer daily."[49] The food at the Mulheim convalescent hospital was better, but "never enough to satisfy"—a bowl of vegetable soup twice a day, at twelve o'clock and at six, and a ration of black bread and imitation coffee at nine and three. On Christmas Day, each prisoner received an egg, a bit of butter, and milk and sugar for their coffee.[50] At Saarbrücken camp, Taylor dined at a table with ten officers. They all laid out their plates, and one of the men served out the soup and spuds as equitably as possible. "Every eye," Taylor recorded in his diary, "is riveted on the grub and follows the spoon from bowl to plate and back again."[51]

Neil's brother Sam also joined the flying corps. Shortly before going to France, he confided to his mother: "I hope to come through alright, but of course, it is always dangerous, but death is not the worst thing that can happen to one if they have tried to do what is right."[52] Sam and two other Canadians crossed the lines on 7 July 1918 and attacked a German two-seater. A large formation dived on them in turn. Only one Canadian got back alive.[53] Sam was killed when his plane crashed just within Allied lines. His body was recovered by Australian infantry and buried about eleven miles east of Amiens.[54] When Neil was released from prison camp, he visited his brother's grave. He wrote their mother in Regina: "What everybody here says of Sam makes me more and more proud of him."[55]

For most of his thirty-one years, William Maunsell Scanlan led a charmed life. The city editor of the *Leader*, where he was known as "Scan,"[56] he was active in local theatrical productions, secretary of the tennis club, and a member of the boat club. He joined up in September 1914 and rose steadily through the ranks from lance corporal to corporal to sergeant and quartermaster-sergeant.[57] In the fall of 1916, he fought at Courcelette and was awarded the Military Medal.[58] At Vimy Ridge, he was struck by shell fragments and carried to the regimental aid post.[59] He seemed to realize that it was all over, but remained calm, even cheerful. He died at nine o'clock that evening.[60] Among his belongings was found a poem he had written titled "Notre Dame de Brebière." It was inspired by the half-destroyed Albert cathedral, where, after the shelling was over, the statue of the Virgin Mary in the bell-tower toppled over, but unaccountably remained suspended in mid-air rather than falling to the ground:

> I stand upon a hill in Picardy,
> And there, outlined against the fading light
> Of dying day, fast reddening into night
> I see a figure, grim with tragedy.
> An image of the Virgin and the Child
> Suspended as though held by a mystic power
> Hangs prone in mid-air from the ruined tower
> Of Albert's fair cathedral, Hun-defiled…
> Far from the stricken town the people flee
> But mid the ruin wrought by savage hands
> The Virgin with the Child still lonely stands
> And in her holy pity, breathes this plea:
> "Oh, Men of Earth to whom the Christ Child came,

The Gift of God, to teach the ways of peace
That war and strife for evermore should cease—
Have you so soon forgot His Holy Name?"
In answer to the plea a screaming shell
Burst through the air; a crash, a blinding flame—
The Virgin prostrate falls—with deadly aim
Has come the War Lord's messenger of Hell.
The simple peasant gazing up with awe
Of that grief-stricken figure, says that when
The Statue falls, "'Twil mean that Peace to men
Has come, and they once more obey God's law."
I stand upon a hill in Picardy,
And gazing on the tragic Statue there—
Above the ruined city, breathe a prayer—
That peace once more shall reign, and men be free.[61]

Recruitment Woes

It was hoped that stories of brave deeds would inspire volunteers to take the place of the fallen soldiers, but it became increasingly clear in 1916 that Canada faced a recruitment crisis. Prime Minister Borden, after a visit to the front in the summer of 1915, increased the authorized strength of the Canadian Expeditionary Force from 150,000 to 250,000. Then, in his New Year's message on 1 January 1916, he increased it again to 500,000.[62] Meanwhile, the demands of the war economy lured more men into well-paying jobs in industry and agriculture. The double pressure—more soldiers needed, not as many to be had—laid the groundwork for the imposition of compulsory military service in 1917.

In January 1916 recruiters for the Sixty-Eighth Battalion set out to visit every business establishment in Regina. The manager in one office invited about ten young male employees to hear the recruiting officer's presentation. Following the talk, the boss told the men that their services were no longer required, but if they enlisted, a job would be waiting for them when they returned.[63] In another incident, a teenager, not yet eighteen, who was employed as a deliveryman on the north side of the city, complained that two recruiting officers had approached his employer and demanded that he be fired. The young man had tried to join the army, but had failed the eye examination. He said that he did not want to lose his job because he was supporting his widowed mother and three young sisters, who were still in school.[64]

Officers of the Sixty-Eighth swarmed the streets and places of amusement.[65] Single, young men without dependents who were unemployed or who worked in non-essential occupations were easy targets. In one case, battalion headquarters received an unsigned postcard with information about two unemployed young men who were living in Regina's west end. The lead was followed up and in short order the men were in the army.[66] On another occasion, the recruiter was given the excuse: "My girl has said to me 'get into uniform and I am through with you.'"[67] He interviewed the woman, who denied having made the statement, and the young man signed up. A "six-foot giant, whose chest appeared to be about forty-four" was asked why he was not in khaki. It turned out that he was from a small town east of Regina. After a short conversation, he agreed to take the medical test, but, soon afterwards, he got cold feet and abruptly left the recruiting office. The sergeant delivered "such an unmerciful tongue-lashing that he started to walk out of the city rather than wait for his train, which was to pull out two hours later."[68]

According to regulations, recruits had to be at least eighteen years of age, but the rule was often ignored. A lad barely seventeen received four visits from recruiters, and there would have been a fifth, had not his parents intervened. A distraught mother begged the battalion to leave her son alone. In exchange, she supplied the names of "a dozen grown men, able-bodied and without dependents."[69] A Regina soldier, who was already in the trenches, wrote his younger brother back home:

> If they are recruiting young fellows in Regina, 16, 17 and 18 years of age, something ought to be done to stop it. I know they are doing the same thing in Toronto. This is no place for any fellow under 21 years old. I am glad you are willing to do your share, but I honestly think it would be a mistake for you to enlist yet. I can see why you wish to go with your school chums. But don't imagine for a minute that this is a sort of holiday outing.[70]

The Sixty-Eighth Battalion was due to leave Regina at the end of March 1916, but it was still 100 men shy of a full complement. The regimental band was sent downtown, where its lively performance of parade marches attracted a large crowd. Sergeant-Major Roach, formerly morality officer with the Regina police force, stood up on an automobile seat and, in booming voice, appealed for "men whose hearts were not in their shoes, men whose loyalty to the cause of right and justice was not a minus quantity, men whose spine was not weak, men, in final, whose feet were not cold."[71] Six men raised their hands and were immediately whisked to the recruiting hall. At the end of the day, fifteen fresh bodies were in the king's uniform, including two Russians, "who gave every evidence of being able to perform as their Cossack brothers are doing on the east front at the present time."[72]

The battalion departed the city on 23 April 1916. The *Leader*'s description of the send-off seemed a bit forced, as though the reporter felt an obligation to pump up patriotic emotions and tearful parting scenes, which at the beginning of the war had been more spontaneous: "Deep-throated cheers, handkerchief waving, and shrill whistling greeted the boys, while here and there mothers and wives and sweethearts smiled back the hot tears that tried to force their way out as they realized their sons and husbands would soon bid them good-bye." Friends gathered around for a final handshake. "God bless you my boy," cried one elderly woman, tears running down her cheeks. "This is my second boy to go," she confided, half-apologetically, "but I am very proud." "Don't forget to write," called out a father to his son. "Surest thing you know," came back the answer, "but the eyes of both were hard and stern and the handclasp was long and firm." A burly soldier stood with a broad smile on his face. "Did you kiss your girl good-bye?" he was asked. "No, I was just thinking what a peach of a time that bear of ours is having over there, and whether his girl kissed him good-bye." He pointed to the battalion mascot, pawing his cage and staring out the window of the baggage car. As the train pulled out, "smiles and tears mingled like sunshine and rain, but throughout there was the unmistakable evidence of a people content in the powers of their sons to take their part with valor and glory in the world-fight for freedom."[73]

Beginning in the fall of 1915, the department of militia and defence modified its recruiting policy. Militia regiments (such as the Ninety-Fifth Rifles in Regina) were bypassed in favour of community-based organizations.[74] It was hoped that this bottom-up approach would arouse local pride and stimulate enlistment. The new battalions were to be identified, not with a militia regiment, but rather with a locality or self-defined group whose members had something in common, for example, Scots, Scandinavians, sportsmen, university students, or temperance men, who formed a "dry" battalion. The policy shift led to the authorization of the City of Regina Battalion (195th) in February 1916. Appealing to civic pride, it incorporated the city coat of arms in its regimental badge and adopted the city's colours as its own.[75] Lieutenant-Colonel A.C. Garner, who had worked for many years as chief surveyor in the land titles office, was the commanding officer.[76]

Recruiting began on 10 February 1916 with the goal of raising 1100 men in three months.[77] Garner did not shrink from making an appeal to schoolboys. When two teachers at the Regina Collegiate Institute signed up, a wave of patriotism swept the school. Young men, often below the minimum age, tried to enlist. The collegiate board intervened, banning recruiting speeches on school property.[78] At Regina College, a private institution run by the Methodist Church, a recruiting officer, who happened also to be a member of the board of governors, challenged the boys: "Some of you fellows will have a pretty poor excuse to offer for not being in khaki when the war is over … There's a uniform to fit every man down at Earl Grey barracks, all the clothing you need, a rifle, and everything that goes with it—we give you an invitation to come down and see us."[79] The college presented a gold watch to each boy who enlisted, as well as automatic credit for the academic year.[80]

An editorial in the Conservative *Evening Province and Standard* expressed concern about the "militarization" of youth: "We are impressing upon their minds the ancient shibboleths of military honor and loyalty to a bit of bunting. We spend more time glorifying our own military strength and too little explaining that militarism is a thing accursed, the thing that the British Empire is unitedly [sic] striving to banish from the world's ken." One had only to observe boys of any age from six to sixteen to realize that they were military-minded through and through. They spoke continually of wanting to "lick those Germans" or to "shoot those Germans." They constantly aped army customs, marching instead of walking, saluting instead of speaking. "What we want is to impart to our children as their one great patriotic ideal," concluded the editorial, "the fact that freedom is all important, and that militarism destroys freedom. Teach them that Canada's sons, along with the Empire's best, are fighting, suffering and dying for freedom, and fighting that accursed creed of militarism, not the German people."[81]

Despite such qualms, the main priority was to fill the ranks of the 195th, and not to be too fussy about how it was done. Quite apart from the dishonour of having the "City of Regina" battalion fall short of its goal, the unit was a boost to the local economy. While the men were in training, $20,000 to $50,000 per month was spent on food and other provisions.[82] At a rally at city hall on 3 March 1916, Chief Justice Sir Frederick Haultain encouraged the city to get behind the recruitment drive.[83] A citizens' recruiting league was organized to distribute cards to employers, asking them to identify young men who could be spared for war service. In addition, the league conducted a house-to-house canvass to identify eligible men.[84] The survey revealed that there remained in Regina only about 3500 men of military age: 818 single, 484 married without children, 1571 married with children, and 781 who had already enlisted and were in training.[85]

Even after all these efforts, the 195th in the third week of March 1916 was still short 500 men.[86] A second canvass was conducted, this time zeroing in on homes where eligible men were known to reside. Men were divided into four categories: those who did not want to enlist, those who planned to enlist, those who were unfit, and "those who for some good reason or other [were] prevented from joining the colors at the present time."[87] In the opinion of the recruiters, 375 men did not have a valid reason for staying at home.[88] It was apparent that even if all 375 signed up, it would not be enough, since 500 were needed. By the first week of April 1916, the battalion had fifty agents scouring the surrounding countryside.[89] The cost of recruiting was estimated at $3 to $5 per recruit, but that did not include the cost of a band, which was another $1200 to $1800. Bands were considered a necessity, not a luxury, because they bucked up morale and instilled esprit de corps. Altogether, the 195th needed about $7000 to cover recruiting expenses. Fortunately, the IODE came through with a large donation, and the remainder came from fundraisers, such as concerts, raffles, dances, and officers' contributions.[90]

By the second week of April 1916, the 195th Battalion had 100 recruiters in the field, each instructed to bring back at least two men. Lieutenant Houston and Sergeant Cunning set a good example, signing up every eligible man in the town of Wawota.[91] In the city of Regina, recruiters were "on the warpath," visiting the same men again and again to wear down their resistance.[92] *The Battle Cry of Peace* was shown at a local theatre in late April 1916. It depicted the imagined invasion of the United States by "a first-class power who would spell culture with a 'K' and introduce it with machine guns turned ruthlessly on the non-combatants."[93] Although it had been the practice for censors to delete scenes that displayed the American flag (it was considered an insult to the British Empire, since the Americans were not yet in the war),[94] an exception was made in this case, because the film was effective as a recruiting device.[95]

Britain Prepared played at the Rex Theatre in May 1916. Produced with the cooperation of the British Admiralty, the British War Office, and Ministry of Munitions, it showed Kitchener's army in training, the bustle of munitions factories and dockyards, and the operations of the British fleet on the high seas.[96] The immense guns of the super-dreadnoughts threw up "black clouds like those of a tropical storm."[97] During the intermission of the two-and-a-half-hour-long film, Rev. George Hill of St. Paul's Anglican Church exhorted every man, whether "English, Irish, Scotch, Welsh, Scandinavian,

Russian, or Serbian," to join the colours. "If this country is good enough for you to live in and work in, it is good enough for you to fight for."[98]

Seven hundred school children attended a special screening. When images of bulldogs appeared, the youngsters cheered lustily, and "when the Union Jack was shown the cheers were even louder; the bumps which the motorcycle men got on a bad road were greeted with 'gee's' from the boys and 'oh's' from the girls."[99] At the end of the movie, the children stood for "God Save the King." When the orchestra struck up "Keep the Home Fires Burning," a boy in the audience spontaneously started to sing the chorus. Soon, every child in the theatre was humming the song. "They're a great bunch," nodded manager H.L. Gage, as he closed the doors. "They sure understand things, and they are one of the best audiences I have ever seen."[100]

Nine-year-old Milton Brown, whose father was in France with the Tenth Canadian Mounted Rifles, showed up at the offices of the 195th Battalion at 1776 Scarth Street. He told the recruiting officers that he wanted to see his father, and he thought that by joining the 195th he would be able to get transferred to his father's company after arriving in England. The officers did not have the heart to tell him that he was too young, so they sent him home to get his mother's permission. The next day he reappeared with the letter they had asked for. When he was definitely turned down, he applied to the 217th Battalion, where he got the same answer.[101]

Enlistment in the 195th climbed to 804 by the middle of April.[102] Finally, at the beginning of June, the target of 1000 was reached.[103] All through the long, intense campaign, the battalion had forged a bond with the community. Its fundraising dances and entertainments were always well attended, the regimental band was a fixture at public events, and the men entered teams in the football and cricket leagues. The recruits were initially quartered at Earl Grey School, with the overflow being sent to Benson School. When the Sixty-Eighth Battalion left for the front, the 195th took over the vacated space in the Winter Fair building at the exhibition grounds, where they trained until departure in the fall.[104]

Earl Grey School became home to the Sixtieth Battery Canadian Field Artillery, which was also recruiting in the city. The battery hosted an "at home" on 14 May 1916, with the assistance of the IODE, who served tea and cakes. Visitors toured the barracks and learned the difference between "a kit inspection and a common one."[105] The school was decked out with flags and bunting, palms, cut flowers, and houseplants in bloom. Decorating the tea table was "a small field gun, and a modern 18-pounder shrapnel shell with fuse." The design of a Sixtieth Battery field gun appeared in the icing of a large cake, set off with streamers in red, white, and blue.[106] The battery was at full strength in a little over two weeks' time[107] and left the city on 28 May 1916.[108] The Seventy-Seventh Battery began recruiting almost immediately,[109] departing for the front on 9 August.[110]

Reginans caught a glimpse what the battlefield looked like, or at least an idealized version of it, in late 1916, when Camp Exhibition (as the exhibition grounds barracks were now called) conducted a grenade and bombing training school for officers.[111] "The noise of the exploding bombs was terrific," reported the *Daily Post*, "and the destruction which they dealt even to frozen Regina gumbo gave some indication of the death-dealing properties of the hand-thrown bomb."[112] A network of trenches was constructed, including main fire trenches, communicating trenches, dugouts, sanitary trenches, parapets, and "every other device known to soldiers for their protection in modern warfare."[113] The men practised "going over the top," a dress rehearsal for what they would soon face at the front.

By mid-1916 enlistment was plummeting. In western Canada, 21,897 men were raised in the last three months of 1915 and 22,593 in the first six months of 1916. From July to October 1916, only 896 men were found.[114] Each of Canada's four infantry divisions required from 12,000 to 20,000 new men a year to replace casualties.[115] Without reinforcements, they would waste away, losing their effectiveness as fighting units. Undeterred by the grim recruiting numbers, Lieutenant-Colonel C.B. Keenleyside, a Regina alderman and leader of the Ban-the-Bar crusade, set out in the fall of 1916 to raise yet another Regina battalion.[116] He tackled the task of filling the ranks of the 249th Battalion with the same enthusiasm that he had previously given to the campaign to rid Saskatchewan of alcohol.

Beginning in January 1917, the 249th ran a series of newspaper advertisements. The first was titled "You Are Wanted!" and read: "Stand by your fellow countrymen in their hour of need. Help to win the war.... Provide yourself with an answer to the questions of the future, which will be showered upon you from all sides, 'What part did you take in the war?'"[117] The second ad announced: "The Hun Declares for Unrestricted Murder on the High Seas." It flayed "the German maniac," who sank hospital ships and slaughtered women and children.[118] The third was more graphic still, depicting the German soldier as a "Fiend Whose Orgy of Murder Must Be Ended." He "swaggered through Europe like a bully with threats and insults forever on his tongue," wantonly killing innocent civilians, firing upon Red Cross wagons and stretcher bearers, beating, starving, and assassinating prisoners, bombarding defenceless and unfortified towns, "encourag[ing] the Turks to murder one million Armenians, sinking the *Lusitania* and shooting Nurse Edith Cavell, outraging and torturing women, mutilating and slaying 'wee kiddies,' crucifying wounded Canadian soldiers, and gouging out the eyes of others." "Does this plain recital of facts not stir your blood?" the ad asked. "Come on, lend a hand. Do Your Bit ... The 249th Overseas Battalion has a place for you. It has a good suit of clothes that will fit you. It will train you, feed you, arm you and give you a chance to shoot Germans. What more could any healthy man want? Come Along, You Are Needed."[119]

The 249th hoped to raise about 525 men, half its strength, in Regina, but enlistment proceeded very slowly. By the first week of March 1917, only thirty city men had come forward.[120] The Citizens' Recruiting Committee, chaired by lawyer D.J. Thom, launched Win the War Week on 18 March. Lieutenant Augustus H. Ball, who had resigned his position as Deputy Minister of Education to join the military, addressed the congregation at First Baptist Church. "The appeal of men in uniform now largely fails," he conceded. "The eligible men who are left are almost army-proof, and are so used to the approaches and arguments of the soldiers that no headway can be made with them. Many are not above giving a wholly false excuse for non-enlistment. I recall a case where a man had stated that he could not enlist because he was supporting a wife and six children. He was not even married and was not making much of success in supporting himself."[121]

As the supply of soldiers dried up, non-Anglo-Saxons were increasingly sought after. According to the *Leader*, Rudolf Bocz, whose mother was German and his father Austrian, had been accepted into the Seventy-Ninth Highlanders. Despite their foreign heritage, Rudolf's parents were described as "Canadians in the full sense of the word since 1896, when Mr. Bocz became a naturalized Canadian."[122] Bishop Nykyta Budka, who had issued the much-condemned pastoral letter just before the war broke out, estimated that as of December 1916, there were 2000 Ukrainians in the Canadian army, many of them having enlisted as Poles or Russians in order to escape the stigma of their Austria-Hungarian origins. Alternatively, they assumed British names such as Smith, Jones, and O'Connor.[123]

Mayor W.D. Cowan addressed a recruiting meeting at the Rumanian hall in Regina in February 1917. Orthodox clergymen were on hand to lend their support. They said it was important for Rumanian-Canadians to enlist, not only for Canada's sake, but also for Rumania, which was fighting on the side of the Allies. The meeting concluded with the singing of both "God Save the King" and the Rumanian national anthem.[124] Norman S. Edgar, officer commanding Military District No. 12 in Regina, warned against enemy aliens who were trying to pass themselves off as Rumanians or Serbs. He ordered a thorough investigation of all "foreigners" who tried to sign up.[125] In addition, he forbade enlisted men in Regina from entering "hotels, dance halls, pool rooms and other public places east of Broad Street." This was to prevent fights and disturbances between soldiers and the "foreign element" in Germantown.[126]

Win the War Week proved a dud, and a note of desperation began to creep into the recruiting effort. According to new regulations, officers were allowed to go out in mufti (civilian clothes) on Sundays. Strolling down the street, Major Thornton happened to fall in behind two strapping young fellows, "who gave every indication of being physically fit and capable of getting into the trenches." As he passed by them, one said to the other, referring to Thornton: "There's the kind of gink that ought to be in uniform."[127] The major said that the comment was all too revealing of the state of opinion among a certain class of people who were avoiding military service.[128]

The Local Council of Women opened a registry office, where women could volunteer for jobs currently held by men, thereby releasing them for the front. Although seventy-one women registered, most of them were unskilled, and a large number were already working and merely wanted to upgrade their jobs.[129] This did not help to get men out of the labour force and into the army. A woman from the small town of Estlin scoffed at Regina men: "I am a soldier's wife with one little daughter two years old and am now a housekeeper on the farm here. I would be willing to do anything, even sweep the streets, to release one man for the army. I think it is time we women should make the physically fit men join the army or else put them in skirts and don the khaki ourselves."[130]

A city-wide canvass was conducted, with two recruiters assigned to each of the fifty-one polling subdivisions in the city.[131] The goal was to find 200 men within the week, but results were meagre—only three new recruits after the first day. One young man, single, English-born, and physically fit, who was employed as a cashier, brazenly declared that he had no intention of enlisting. When asked why he was not in khaki, he told the recruiter that it was none of his business. He refused even to give his name. "Quite a patriotic citizen," the canvasser sneered.

A recruiter confronted two "strapping fellows," aged about twenty-two to twenty-four, who had arrived in the city the week before. They were looking for work, and when they were told that King George had a job for them, they answered curtly, "We don't want that job, … we have been in five or six places in the province so far and everywhere we went we met with the same invitation; we don't intend to enlist, so you needn't waste any time."

A woman, walking down the street, spied a young man not in uniform. She went up to him and inquired:

"Why don't you enlist?"

"Why don't you?"

"My dear young man, are you waiting until the women enlist before you do your duty?"

"Why don't you go to work in a munitions factory?"

"Why don't you?"[132]

And there the conversation ended.

The Citizens' Recruiting Committee's "great patriotic demonstration" at the auditorium rink flopped badly.[133] Only 225 people showed up, "a goodly number of them women." Mayor Cowan regretted "that during the last three months a great apathy had taken hold on the people of the city." There had been a time when Regina had been enthusiastic about the war, but now support seemed to have dwindled. War-weariness had set in. Rev. Canon George Hill said that he had lived in Regina for seventeen years and had always been proud of the city, but now he felt a little ashamed, "not of those who were present at the meeting, but of those absent, of the thousands who were not there and who should be there." Back in school days, when a lad had done something dishonourable, he was "put in Coventry." Hill advised similar treatment for slackers. They should be shunned, neither spoken to nor acknowledged, until they came to their senses and remembered their duty to their country.[134]

Win the War Week drew to a close on 25 March 1917, with fewer than a score of new recruits, well short of the goal of 200. "What is the matter?" anguished the *Leader*. The physically fit young men, who appeared nonchalantly on the streets and in the theatres, were "deficient in red blood and the qualities which go to make a man."[135] They might consider themselves men, but they were rather "a sort of contemptible nonentity for which there is no word sufficiently descriptive in the English language." These "things" leaned over pool tables, shouted themselves hoarse at hockey matches, and wore vapid grins on their faces, while "real men" donned the king's uniform and carried rifles in their hands. When the real men came home from the war, they would "scorn to call by the name of comrade those who left them and their country in the lurch when the bullets and shells were flying."[136]

The 249th failed to recruit up to full strength, enlisting only 550 men, about half the required number.[137] The shortfall was not unique to Regina. Voluntary enlistment was collapsing all across Canada. Part of the problem was inefficiency in the recruiting system. Ottawa gave no funds to assist local battalions, and the recruiting drive lacked overall coordination. In Regina the local battalions faced competition from units based elsewhere. At various times the Ninety-Sixth Battalion (Saskatoon), 217th Battalion (Moosomin), 128th Battalion (Moose Jaw), 210th Battalion (Moose Jaw), 239th Battalion (railroad construction), 200th Battalion (Winnipeg), 253rd Battalion (Queen's University), 152nd Battalion (Weyburn), Strathcona Horse, 238th Battalion (lumbermen), Naval Recruiting League, 197th Battalion (men of Danish, Icelandic, Norwegian or Swedish descent), 203rd Battalion (temperance men), 212th Battalion (American-born, whose motto was "We'll fight for God and justice as we would for the Stars and Stripes"), Western Universities' Battalion (196th), and the 224th Forestry Battalion (bushwhackers, teamsters, and carpenters) were active in the city.[138]

By late 1916 those who wished to volunteer had done so, and those who did not had abundant job opportunities at home. In January 1917 the new Militia and Defence Minister, Sir Edward Kemp (Sir Sam Hughes had been fired for incompetence in November 1916), announced that no new overseas battalions were to be raised. The 249th was the last of its kind in Regina. Henceforth, recruits were sent over in drafts to replenish existing units.[139] In Regina men signed up with First Depot Battalion, stationed at the exhibition grounds.[140]

* * *

"Offer such excuses as we will, and seek to disguise it as we may, recruiting for overseas service has come practically to a standstill."[141] So concluded the

Leader on 28 April 1917. Moreover, the "industrial fabric of the Dominion" was at risk. Men who were of more service to their country working in industry or agriculture had left for the trenches, while those whose labour was non-essential stayed at home. The haphazard, mindless arrangement made no sense. The voluntary system had outlived its usefulness. The war for "democracy" now required compulsion and rational planning at the top.[142] There was also the matter of simple justice. The *Leader* knew of four Regina families. Each had four boys of military age, all of them physically fit. In three of the families, not one boy had enlisted. All were at home making good wages. In the fourth, one son had been killed in action, two were in the trenches in France, and the fourth had recently enlisted.[143] Was that fair?

Chapter 7

The Twenty-Eighth Battalion

MOST OF THE BATTALIONS RAISED IN REGINA WERE EVENTUALLY BROKEN up to reinforce other units. The Sixty-Eighth Battalion arrived in England in May 1916 and was absorbed into the Thirty-Second Reserve Battalion in July.[1] The 195th Battalion sailed in November 1916, and drafts were taken into the Fifth Battalion and the 102nd Battalion. On 11 November 1916, what remained of the 195th went into the Thirty-Second Reserve, which in turn was folded into the Fifteenth Canadian Reserve Battalion.[2] The 249th reached England in March 1918 and was immediately taken into the Fifteenth Canadian Reserve Battalion.[3]

The exception to this pattern of absorption and loss of identity was the Twenty-Eighth Battalion, which was ordered to mobilize on 19 October 1914. The "originals" were men from Regina (12 officers and 246 men), Moose Jaw (6 officers and 246 men), Saskatoon (6 officers and 228 men), Fort William (4 officers and 114 men), Port Arthur (3 officers and 114 men), and Prince Albert (3 officers and 97 men).[4] J.F.L. Embury, officer commanding, was a Regina lawyer, thirty-nine years old when the war broke out.[5] Alexander Ross, thirty-four, also a Regina lawyer, was second in command. On 4 August 1914, a beautiful day in Regina, Ross played a round of golf at the Wascana Country Club, southeast of the city. As he approached the twelfth fairway, Embury drove up in his automobile. The conversation was brief and to the point:

> Embury: "I guess there is going to be a war. Are you going?"
> Ross: "Sure! Alright."
> Embury: "I'll send a wire offering our services."
> Ross: "Goodbye."[6]

The battalion mobilized in Winnipeg on 31 October for preliminary training. There was no problem finding recruits. Indeed, many had to be turned away, and Embury had his pick of whom to take. The battalion was quartered in the Horse Show building in Winnipeg, an entirely unsuitable accommodation. It lacked proper flooring, and the ground was "impregnated with horse manure." The building was poorly ventilated, drafty, and cold. As a consequence, many of the men took ill—200 were on the sick list at one point—and several died, mainly from pneumonia. Eventually, some improvements were effected, a wooden floor installed, windows caulked, and leaky roofs repaired, but by then most of the damage to the health of the men had already been done.[7]

Embury maintained strict, but fair, discipline. Any man found drunk was discharged, though abstention was not insisted upon.[8] The men were almost entirely raw and inexperienced (only 5 percent had previous military training),[9] but by dint of hard drill and physical training over the winter, they were "transformed from slouching civilians into upright soldiers."[10] The battalion passed inspection on 7 and 8 April 1915. Col. H.B.B. Ketchen, officer commanding, Sixth Infantry Brigade, reported, "I consider it made the best appearance of the whole Brigade at my Inspection.... There is also a very strong Esprit de Corps in the Battalion—reflecting the greatest credit on all ranks."[11] Performance in the field was commendable, and the battalion had been worked into fine physical condition, notwithstanding bouts of influenza and pneumonia. The musketry standard in range shooting was high—about 85 percent all round. All in all, Ketchen considered the battalion to be "under excellent discipline and having done generally very creditably for the time it has been mobilized and the opportunities afforded it."[12]

The Twenty-Eighth was brigaded with the Twenty-Seventh (City of Winnipeg) Battalion, the Twenty-Ninth (Vancouver), and the Thirty-First (Alberta). The four units together constituted the Sixth Canadian Infantry Brigade, Second Canadian Division, nicknamed the "Iron Sixth."[13] The Twenty-Seventh Battalion was the first to leave Winnipeg, followed on 26 May 1915 by the Twenty-Eighth. It was a glorious morning, "early summer when Western Canada is always at its best."[14] The men marched to the Canadian Pacific Railway station, where a vast crowd had assembled, and they boarded the trains amid loud cheering and fond farewells. On the journey out, a sergeant was discharged for pulling the communication cord, causing the train to make a sudden stop. When reprimanded, he was insolent to the officer of the day. As punishment, he was dropped off at Fort William and returned to military headquarters in Winnipeg.[15]

The trains arrived in Montreal on 28 May 1915, where the Governor General, Duke of Connaught, inspected the battalion. They boarded the *S.S. Northland* and sailed from Montreal at three o'clock in the morning on 29 May. The ship reached Plymouth on 8 June 1915, and from there the battalion with a strength of 36 officers and 1084 other ranks proceeded to Dibgate Camp.[16] Training continued through the summer in musketry, bayonet fighting, bombing, entrenching, methods of trench warfare, and route marching. Finally, on the morning of 17 September 1915, the battalion left for France.[17] The mood was generally cheerful, the men eagerly anticipating the adventures that lay ahead. The glamour of war had not yet worn off.[18]

Into the Trenches

The battalion moved "up the line" on 25 September 1915 into the trenches at Kemmel, south of Ypres. As Alexander Ross observed, "that mysterious 'front,' an unbroken line of winding, zig-zagging, interlocking trenches, miles in length with barbed wire, out in front ... was to be for so many months our principal care, our glory, our life and for many of us, our death."[19] "The tyranny of the trenches," he continued,

> had us in its grasp and for many months it was a tiresome programme of 'in' and 'out'. There was something about trench warfare that sapped the vitality of those who were compelled to take part in it. The deadly routine varied only by different degrees of unpleasantness, lowered the morale and weakened the fighting qualities of even the finest troops, more so, perhaps than any other form of warfare in vogue in the First World War.[20]

Early in the evening of 8 October 1915, just as darkness fell, the Germans exploded two mines under the trenches held by a Regina platoon. Although several men were buried, the survivors managed to hold back the enemy, who attempted to seize the craters created by the explosion. It was a severe test, but the untried troops showed their mettle.[21] The battalion was taken out of the trenches in early February 1916 and billeted in farmhouses behind the line. It rained steadily, and the fields were drenched. The men "endeavored to get rid of trench crouch and crawl by physical training and parade ground exercises," only to sink ankle deep in mud.[22] After this "interlude of so-called rest," the battalion returned on 8 March 1916 to the Kemmel sector. But their stay was short-lived. Orders were received at the end of the month to move to a new section of the line.

Ross described the march down the poplar-lined road from Locre:

> Although the winter still lingered, there was a feeling of spring in the air and the country now looked fresh and green.... Evening came on and darkness fell and way to the North over Mont Rouge could be seen the 'Varey' lights from the Salient and ever and again the fitful flash of a gun. Now and then such a flash would become one great series of flashes and single detonations would become a sustained roar, telling of fresh alarms in the Salient. To us, to whom the Ypres Salient was still unknown, for we had been in the Kemmel Sector, came strange thoughts and forebodings of the morrow. For many months we had been able to observe from a safe distance the ceaseless activity going on in that particular piece of hell.... It was not a very cheerful prospect, yet no one was considered to be a real soldier until he had held fast the Salient.[23]

On the night of 3 April 1916, the Sixth Brigade relieved the British regiments at St. Eloi. The Twenty-Seventh and Thirty-First battalions held the front line, with the Twenty-Ninth in support and the Twenty-Eighth in reserve at Dickebusch. The enemy attacked in the early morning of 6 April, delivering a stunning artillery barrage on a narrow front of less than 1000 yards. Even before the assault, the area had been torn apart by a series of explosions, forming craters, large and small. The Twenty-Eighth Battalion was called into action on the evening of 6 April, and bombing parties were sent out. Gerald D. Murphy, a bank clerk from Moosomin, and his unit of bombers eventually reached the craters and gained possession of three of them. Captain A.G. Styles (of Regina rugby football fame) "continually exposed himself, with a total disregard for his own skin, in an attempt to consolidate scattered units of the 28th and 31st."[24] The efforts were in vain. The Germans could not be pushed back. The toll on the brigade was 617 killed and wounded.[25] Respite for the Twenty-Eighth came on 8 April, when the Nineteenth Battalion relieved it.

After nine days of rest and recuperation, Embury received orders to occupy the trenches lying south of the Ypres-Comines Canal. "By this time of the year," Ross related, "the trees in the neighborhood had acquired their foliage and nature was trying her best to disguise the ravages of War. Birds sang sweetly from the poplars on the canal, and an officer on night duty going out to view the sunrise and get a few mouthfuls of fresh air before turning in on a beautiful May morning, would be entertained by a cuckoo which invariably greeted the dawn."[26] One morning a shell hit the cookhouse, "completely upset[ting] the culinary arrangements and caus[ing] a number of casualties."[27] Other shells landed in the huts where men were sleeping, and one detonated on a steel rail supporting the structure that housed the D Company officers. It blew the roof off their shelter, but left them unscathed.

On the night of 6 June 1916, the Germans launched an attack at Hooge, a small village on the Menin Road, the gateway to Ypres and the English Channel. The enemy brought up heavy railway howitzers to add to their arsenal. Ross, who was in charge of the battalion during this action (Embury had temporary command of the Sixth Brigade), described the barrage as "a current of fire of absolute density and impenetrability."[28] Fortunately, most of the shells overshot their target and landed behind the lines. At two o'clock in the afternoon large mines were exploded under the Canadian trenches, practically burying the whole of A Company. Wurtemburger regiments charged in masses, "fully equipped with packs as if they, this time, intended to stay."[29] Flame-throwers sprayed liquid fire on the beleaguered battalion. The enemy captured the front line with ease, but that was the extent of their progress. The Twenty-Eighth Battalion machine guns, posted on either side of the Ypres-Menin Road, put up fierce resistance. The Canadians waited until the Germans were about 200 yards away and then opened fire. This saved the day and barred the route to Ypres.[30] The defensive victory came at heavy cost. Of the 650 men who had gone into the line, over 300 were killed, wounded, or taken prisoner. Divisional Commander Major General Sir R.E.W. Turner commended the Twenty-Eighth and Twenty-First battalions on their "splendid fight." "Everything was done," he said, "that could have been done."[31] The depleted ranks were filled, in part, with a draft of 170 men from the Sixty-Eighth Battalion, who largely had been recruited from Regina and surrounding area.[32]

From Flanders to Courcelette

The battalion departed the depressing mud of Flanders on 20 August 1916. They marched through the back country, which was "unblemished by War, with the harvest everywhere ripening in the August sunshine."[33] The men were billeted in the village of Volkerinchove. Here they abandoned their Canadian-manufactured Ross rifles, trading them for "trim little Lee-Enfields." Only the snipers regretted the exchange. This "gang of cheerful murderers," as Alexander Ross called them, preferred the old Ross rifle "souped up" to the "individual tastes of users." They were of the opinion that the Canadian-made rifle allowed for a more precise shot. The snipers, Ross acknowledged, "were most useful members of our fraternity, deserving to be greatly encouraged in their untiring efforts to make good Germans—dead ones."[34]

The Twenty-Eighth moved on 27 August 1916 into billets west of St. Omer, where they took possession of a lovely chateau set in a magnificent park. The only drawback was that the owner had removed every stick of furniture and everything else that was transportable, including the doorknobs. The battalion was able to squeeze into the chateau and the adjoining barn, and, for a time, enjoyed the amenities of the stately mansion and grounds. Sergeant W.T.H. Cripps composed a review, for which bandmaster W.H. Foote supplied the music. Lieutenant F.C. "Bubbles" Whigham performed in the role of the leading lady "and rather fancied himself in paint and powder, much to the delight of all concerned."[35]

The luxurious chateau interlude ended on 4 September 1916, when the battalion left St. Omer by train for the Somme. Arriving in Picardy, they were impressed by the "wide open fields without hedges or trees, slightly rolling and no high hills,"[36] which reminded them of the landscape back home in western Canada. At the town of Albert, they caught sight of the great tower of the cathedral with the figure of the Virgin suspended horizontally over the street. The Germans had bombed the cathedral, but, strangely, the statue had not fallen, although it hung precariously and seemed ready to crash at any moment.[37] The Twenty-Eighth settled down in an area known as the Brick Fields, northwest of Albert.

The main objective of the Canadian infantry was the village of Courcelette, a key factor in the German defence line. The Sixth Brigade was assigned the job of taking heavily fortified approaches to the village, while the Fourth Brigade was ordered to capture the Sugar Factory to the south, believed to harbour clusters of machine gunners. Once these two tasks had been accomplished, the way would be clear for the Fifth Brigade to storm Courcelette. The attack was set for 15 September 1916. In the ranks of the battle-seasoned Twenty-Eighth, there was "no excitement, no hurry, no confusion." They marched from their billets to the assembly trenches, while the band played the "Iron Sixth," a tune the bandmaster had composed to commemorate the brigade's past achievements. Their step was light, their heads held high. Arriving at the assembly point, they waited calmly until 6:20 a.m., when the attack was scheduled to begin. Sleep was impossible. German shells fell incessantly, wounding and killing indiscriminately.

This was the hardest time of all. "You crouched down in your hole in the ground," Major Ross wrote,

> while the cold raw chill of the early dawn ate into your overtired body and seemed to penetrate the very marrow of your bones, waiting for the signal, shortly due to sound. It was here that you were given time to think—of the machine-guns out in front, of the barbed wire, of shells and shell-splinters, of the enemy battened down, alerted and waiting for your approach a few hundred yards away. Short as it was, you also had time to think of the home you had left, of those you had left behind and, then and only then, to realize that War was hell. A hell of a peculiar devilish character.[38]

At zero hour the artillery provided a "curtain of fire" for the advancing troops. The battalion moved forward slowly and deliberately. "Instead of walking into the face of death," an observer recorded, "one would have thought they were on a peace maneuver somewhere back home."[39] Men fell here and there, but the wave inexorably pressed forward, "disappear[ing] in the depths of the enemy's trench." Runners and stretcher-bearers clambered across No Man's Land, seemingly with no thought given to personal safety. In the midst of battle, there were even flashes of humour. The line was halfway across to the enemy trench when a sergeant turned around to pick up something he had dropped. It was the rum jar, which he had been carrying behind his back to protect it from German fire.[40]

British airplanes buzzed overhead, maintaining steady contact with those on the ground. Airmen helped pinpoint the location of German guns. The "Crème de Menthe" and the "Cordon Rouge," primitive tanks, lumbered over the battlefield, alarming the enemy and boosting Canadian morale. German prisoners of war called them "terrifying monsters," and accused the Allies of unfair methods of warfare.[41] By 7:40 a.m. on 15 September the Twenty-Eighth Battalion had established itself in the enemy trenches. However, there was still fire from outlaw machine-gun posts. A party of bombers rushed to the rear of the German emplacement, fired a hail of bullets, and put the gunners out of action.[42]

The day was a triumph for the battalion, at the cost of nearly 300 casualties,[43] including officer commanding J.F.L. Embury. Just as his unit was moving into position, a shell landed at headquarters hitting him in the arm and foot. Ignoring the injuries, he directed the attack, refusing to leave his post until the operation had been declared a success. He did not report to the dressing station until twenty-four hours after receiving the wound.[44] Subsequently, he was made Companion of the most Excellent Order of St. Michael and St. George and Companion of the Order of the Bath,[45] and placed in command of the Tenth Training Brigade and, later, the Second Infantry Brigade, with the rank of Brigadier-General. With Embury gone, Alexander Ross assumed command of the Twenty-Eighth Battalion.[46]

Vimy Ridge

The battalion departed from the Somme battlefield in early October 1916 and settled in billets in "the pleasant little village of Halloy-les Pernois." "It was heaven on earth," Ross recalled. "We soon forgot the horrors of war which we had left behind and reveled in the joys of just being alive. Here all ranks had access to very much needed and welcomed bathing facilities.... With the grime of battle once more washed away and again living like white men in a civilized community we soon regained our old snap and were ready to face anything."[47] The last weeks of October 1916 found the battalion near Vimy Ridge, on the Souchez front. The good weather came to an end, and cold rain fell steadily. Life became "distinctly amphibious."[48] To ward off trench feet, inspections were carried out twice daily, and orders were given for "frequent brisk rubbing with whale oil and changes of socks, as often as necessary."[49] A special sock-drying apparatus was put into operation. The efforts were largely successful, and incidents of the disease were kept to a minimum.

The officers celebrated New Year's Eve 1916 in a rude YMCA hut with an earthen floor and oiled linen windowpanes. The long dining table was covered with "cheese cloth, newspapers, oilcloth or whatever material was available in place of table linen," and the cutlery consisted of odds and ends, "perhaps a spoon from the Fort Garry in Winnipeg, a knife from the *S.S. Northland* or a fork from the London Southeastern and Chatham Railway." The battalion band accompanied the singing of barracks room songs and music hall favourites: "If You Were the Only Girl in the World," "Keep the Home Fires Burning," and "The Long, Long Trail," embellished with the usual parodies. The Scots burst into loud renditions of the "auld songs," and the Irish responded with their own version of musical bedlam. Evenings such as this, Ross wrote, "gave us both esprit de corps and morale.... It helped to make life in these trying days, such as it was, well worth living."[50] On New Year's Day, in accordance with regimental custom, the officers served the men of other ranks a turkey dinner with all the trimmings.[51]

Preparations were underway for the great assault on Vimy Ridge. A narrow stretch of land extending some 8000 yards, it had the appearance of an impregnable fortress,[52] dominating the countryside and offering unrivalled observation of a wide expanse of land east and west. For the Allies, it was a symbol of despair, which had cost thousands of lives in futile attempts to take it. Now the Canadians were going to have their chance. For the first time, all four divisions of the Canadian Corps fought together in one coordinated assault. Preparatory to the battle, a miniature plan of the battlefield was laid out in the fields behind the lines. Trenches, roads, machine-gun nests, and other natural features were marked out in detail so that each man had fixed in his mind "where it was intended he should go, how he was to arrive there, and his tasks when once he had arrived."[53]

Easter Sunday, the day before the battle, the men attended a church parade. "There, among the bare splintered trees of the Bois des Alleux," Ross remembered, "with guns thundering along the whole front, with the sound of the enemy shells breaking over Berthonval Farm, with incessant aeroplane activity overhead, the bark of the 'Archies,' the pop of anti-aircraft shells and an occasional burst of machine-gun fire, we worshipped and thought of the morrow."[54] Brigadier General H.D.B. Ketchen, officer commanding the

Sixth Brigade, offered words of encouragement, and in the afternoon the Twenty-Eighth regimental band put on a concert. The men wrote letters, played sports, and did routine chores. As Ross put it, "the angel of death did not seem to beat his wings on this sunny day."[55]

As evening fell, the battalion moved into position. The roads were jammed with vehicles, and the whole backcountry was filled with music, as "brass bands, bugle bands, pipe bands, fife and drum bands [played] their respective units out to victory."[56] In the distance, the men could see "the constant steady rise of white flares, the occasional reds or greens or combinations of both." The Germans seemed on edge, occasionally firing volleys of heavy shrapnel or gas shells. "It all seemed weird and unreal," thought Ross, "but unspeakably thrilling, a night which would be long remembered by those who would be fortunate enough to survive."[57]

Zero hour was 5:30 a.m. on Easter Monday, 9 April 1917. As the first rays of dawn lit the sky, the artillery opened up a tremendous barrage. Edwin Sneath from Regina felt that the world was coming to an end. The earth, he said, shook and rocked like a wagon on a stony road. Mines went up all over the place, and whole hills simply disappeared in the enormous explosion.[58] Steadily, the well-trained Canadian troops advanced across the shell-pocked terrain. The whole operation was carried out with clock-like precision, just as it had been practised on the simulated battlefield behind the lines. The Twenty-Eighth Battalion, forming part of the second wave, moved forward at 9:35 a.m. The weather had turned cold, sleet and snow blowing in from the northwest. The battalion soon seized the machine-gun-infested village of Thelus on the western slope. The troops swept on according to plan and attained the summit. "Units on the right and left were also up and Vimy Ridge was ours,"[59] Ross declared with satisfaction. The trophies of the Sixth Brigade included 1000 prisoners, 14 guns and howitzers, a large trench mortar on wheels, and 25,000 rounds of ammunition.[60] After the battle, Rev. E.C. Earp, an Anglican chaplain from Regina, encountered a boy at the base hospital who had lost his hand. "I see you have lost your hand," the padre said. "Is there anything I can do?" The boy held up the stump of his arm and said: "I have not lost it, padre. I gave it."[61]

Vimy Ridge was one of those rare events, the long-term significance of which was immediately appreciated. Prime Minister Borden, then in London, wrote in his diary: "All newspapers ringing with praise of Canadians." The *New York Tribune* extended congratulations: "Well done, Canada. No praise of the Canadian achievement can be excessive." The *New York Times* predicted that the battle "would be in Canada's history ... a day of glory to furnish inspiration to her sons for generations."[62] Back home, the *Leader* exulted: "The Battle of Vimy Ridge will live through the centuries that are to come, and will ever stand an imperishable monument to the valor, the courage, the unconquerable spirit of the men of Canada. Vimy will ever remain one of the great sign-posts along the road to World Liberty."[63]

The battle marked a transformation in Canada's understanding of itself. The country was still British, but not as British as it had been before the war. The soldiers sensed this. They had come from all parts of Canada and had enlisted for various and diverse reasons. Some fought to defend the empire against German aggression, others to uphold liberty and justice. Still others had joined the army out of a sense of adventure or merely to escape unemployment and poverty. But, when they journeyed overseas and fought together as the Canadian Corps, something unusual and unexpected happened. They discovered who they were, and in so doing helped other Canadians discover who they were, too. Ross wrote that at Vimy Ridge he saw "Canada from the Atlantic to the Pacific on parade. I thought then, and I think today, that in those few minutes I witnessed the birth of a nation."[64] In the tunnels under Vimy, where the men crouched as they waited to go into battle, can be found today, carved into the chalk walls and shielded by Plexiglas like a precious icon, a single, small Canadian maple leaf.[65]

Across Canada, newspapers rejoiced in the victory and honoured the 3598 Canadians who had given their lives. The battle acquired additional resonance from the fact that it took place on Easter Monday, the birth of a nation coinciding with the commemoration of the resurrection of Jesus

Christ.[66] Vimy entered deeply into the national psyche, and in a literal sense became part of Canada, since the site was turned over to Canada in perpetuity by the government of France.

To Passchendaele

After Vimy, the Twenty-Eighth Battalion moved towards the mining town of Lens. The fighting commenced on 15 August, the First Division advancing on the left, the Second Division in the centre, the Fourth Division on the right, and the Third Division in reserve. The dawn light "turned to a lurid glow" and the earth was churned to a "likeness of a scene from Dante's Inferno."[67] The Canadians penetrated the German lines and captured Hill 70, a well-defended elevation to the north of Lens, as well as the suburbs of the city. The Sixth Brigade, including the Twenty-Eighth, was held in reserve. However, in the continuation of the battle on 21 August, the battalion played a prominent part. The attack was directed against two strong German positions known as Nun's Alley and Cinnabar Trench. After intense fighting, the Canadians won the day.[68] A platoon of the Twenty-Eighth, nicknamed the Piccaninnies on account of their small size and relative youth, won the praise of the entire brigade. The plan was to keep them in reserve, but their services were needed and they splendidly rose to the occasion.[69]

The Twenty-Eighth Battalion on 18 October 1917 headed once more into the Ypres salient. "The shadow of that loathsome salient settled down on all ranks," reflected Ross. "It seemed to be our nemesis, and there was none of the gaiety usually noticeable when awaiting a move to new adventures."[70] The battalion arrived at Bavinchove, the very spot where they had detrained two years earlier on their first journey to France. For Ross, it was an eerie experience: "Memories of old friends now gone seemed to crowd in around us. We were a little war-weary but ever so much wiser and filled with the same determination to see the War through, no matter how long or how hard might be the contest."[71] Orders came down to proceed to Passchendaele, "a luckless piece of territory" that had already taken thousands of casualties. Once again, the Canadians were called upon to succeed where both

British and French troops had failed. The officers of the Twenty-Eighth held a dinner on 31 October 1917 to celebrate the third anniversary of the unit's mobilization in Winnipeg. The party was not an altogether happy affair. "Already," Ross said, "it seemed to all that the Battalion was again under the grim shadow of the salient. Already it seemed as though the beatings of the Wings of Death could be heard." Within a few days, many "would have paid the supreme price."[72]

A blot on the landscape more dismal than Passchendaele could scarcely be imagined. As Ross eloquently put it, "we lived, moved and had our being in a sea of filth and mud."[73] Craters were filled to the brim with water, forming miniature lakes. Stepping off the duckboards, men sank knee-deep in mud and slime. Enemy aircraft patrolled overhead and bombed the Canadian shelters. Tents had to be taken down at dawn because it was too dangerous to have them visible in daylight hours.[74] The attack began at 6:00 a.m. on 6 November 1917. Because of the mud, the advance was slow, a mere 100 yards in eight minutes, less than half the usual pace. In short order, three company commanders fell, but, fortunately, junior officers and non-commissioned officers were well prepared to take their places. H.L.N. Salmon from Regina took command of D Company, leading with such verve that he was awarded a Bar to his Military Cross.[75]

The advancing infantry met heavy shell and machine-gun fire. Hostile aircraft swooped down and poured out deadly fusillades. One by one, the German pillboxes were put out of commission. By 7:40 a.m. the Twenty-Eighth Battalion had attained its objectives, but the German artillery did not relent. Shells continued to fall on the main roads, making communication and transportation extremely hazardous. One runner had his heel shot off, but still managed to deliver his message. Private A.L. Doner of D Company traversed the distance from the front lines to battalion headquarters three times on 6 November, making it safely each time. The next day he volunteered to guide a party delivering rations and was killed by a stray shell. Posthumously, he received the Military Medal.[76]

The muddy conditions made evacuation of casualties next to impossible. The wounded men cursed the medics for failing to take them out. Finally, as the battle eased, rescue work began. The mud was so thick that it took as many as eight men to carry a single stretcher. When they reached the dressing station, there were no ambulances because they could not get through the mire. The stretcher bearers had to carry their burden another two miles.[77] The Twenty-Eighth had casualties of 11 officers and 257 other ranks.[78] They dubbed Passchendaele "Passion Dale" or "Easter Valley." As battalion historian D.G. Scott Calder summarized: "It is not too much to compare the Canadian troops struggling forward, the pangs of hell racking their bodies, up the Ridge, their dying eyes set upon the summit, with a Man who once crept up another hill, with agony in soul and body to redeem the World and give Passchendaele its glorious name."[79]

After the battle, the battalion was transferred back to the Vimy sector, where conditions were much quieter. As a bonus, they received news that for the first time since 1915, they would not have to spend Christmas Day in the trenches. They moved to St. Hilaire, "a very pleasant little village tucked behind the lines."[80] Large quantities of turkeys were delivered, although the wagon carrying them was very nearly bombed by enemy aircraft. Each man feasted on "soup, at least a pound of turkey with trimmings, all the vegetables he could eat and plenty of plum pudding, followed by a ration of rum and a bottle of beer."[81]

Training resumed on 27 December 1917, with emphasis on the integration of new recruits with the survivors of Passchendaele. The battalion took over the trench line near the ruined village of Avion. The talk was of the anticipated German offensive,[82] which began on 21 March 1918 on a wide front from the Scarpe to the Oise Rivers. All leaves were cancelled and training suspended.[83] The battalion marched twenty-two miles to Pommier southwest of Arras, where it was thought it might have to be called in to support the wavering line, but, fortunately, the positions were held, and their services were not required.[84] The Second Canadian Division (including the Sixth Brigade with the Twenty-Eighth Battalion) was posted to the Sixth

Corps of the Third Imperial Army and given the task of holding a portion of the front line, where the British had fallen back during the German spring offensive.[85] Here the Second Division stayed for ninety-two days.[86] Finally, on 29 June 1918, it was pulled out of the front line and rejoined the Canadian Corps.

***

The Twenty-Eighth Battalion celebrated Dominion Day, 1 July 1918, at Tingues. It was a great day because almost the entire Canadian Corps was out of the line at the same time and had a chance to celebrate together. There were sports, track and field events, and ample food and drink. Old friends met and shared stories, revelling in what they had achieved and speculating on what lay ahead. "There had never been anything quite like this before," Ross remarked, "and it spoke volumes for the quality of our young nation, that after all of these trying and critical months, we could all meet and enjoy ourselves to the fullest extent, while still within sound of the guns and while the force of the enemy's spring offensive had not yet entirely spent itself."[87]

The Twenty-Eighth Battalion proceeded to Saisseval in the Somme area west of Amiens at the end of July. Complete secrecy surrounded the march. Even Ross was in the dark as to what was about to happen. The battalion trained with tank formations on 3 August 1918, a sure sign that a major offensive was in the offing, since tanks were not generally used with infantry for defensive purposes. That evening the unit marched to Ferrières, where they joined the Second Canadian Machine Gun Battalion. The men were ordered not to move about during the day. They were confined to barracks on 5 August 1918. Church parade and baseball and football games were cancelled. Ross was let in on the secret of the impending offensive, but he was not allowed to say anything about it to subordinates until 6 August. The high command feared that the information would leak out to the civilian population, who might inadvertently give it to enemy agents.[88] The Last 100 Days were about to begin.

Regina (circa 1914), looking west down Eleventh Avenue, city hall on the right (GG).

Regina troops leaving for war in 1914. Civilians march alongside the soldiers, including a woman pulling a baby carriage (SAB).

Top: Views of downtown Regina, circa 1914. In the centre of the panorama, a bit to the left, the city hall is visible. Its tower projects slightly above the horizon and the windows are outlined in white stone. The building with a tall spire near the centre of the right photo is St. Mary's Catholic Church. The large church on the right is Knox Presbyterian (GG).

Above: Flag-bedecked Belgian Relief Fund wagon in front of Regina city hall (SAB).

Above: Arrival of a Western contingent at Valcartier camp near Quebec City, where the First Division underwent preliminary training before proceeding overseas in October 1914 (GG).

Left: A photographer takes advantage of the war to drum up business, *Leader*, 28 September 1914.

Recruits for the Canadian Expeditionary Force at the Regina exhibition grounds. Many do not yet have uniforms (SAB).

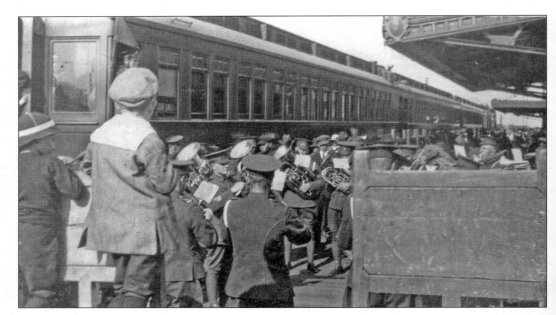

Top: The 152nd Battalion band playing for departing troops at the Regina train station (SAB).

Below: Miss Katherine Stinson next to her biplane. She gave a thrilling aerobatic display at the Regina exhibition in the summer of 1916 (SAB).

Clockwise from top left: Knox Presbyterian Church, facing Victoria Park, where Rev. Murdoch MacKinnon delivered his 1915 Christmas sermon, leading to the political downfall of Premier Walter Scott (GG).

Rev. Murdoch MacKinnon, pastor of Knox Presbyterian Church, in his military chaplain's uniform, 1918 (SAB).

Brigadier-General John Fletcher Leopold Embury, Officer Commanding 28th Battalion, 29 May 1915 to 17 September 1916 (GG).

William Maunsell Scanlan (left), city editor of the Regina *Leader*, killed at the Battle of Vimy Ridge, 9 April 1917 (SAB).

Clockwise from top left: Officers displaying the colors of the City of Regina Battalion (the 195th) in Victoria Park (SAB).

Walter Scott (right) and William Martin standing outside the Empress Hotel in Swift Current after a day of campaigning in the 1912 provincial election. Martin succeeded Scott as premier of Saskatchewan in October 1916 (GG).

Brigadier-General Alexander Ross, Officer Commanding 28th Battalion, 18 September 1916 to 1 October 1918. The 28th Battalion is perpetuated as the Royal Regina Rifles (GG).

Clockwise from top: Recruits practicing trench warfare at the Regina exhibition grounds (GG).

The Liberals painted Conservative party leader W.B. Willoughby as a pawn of the liquor interests, Regina *Leader*, 23 June 1917.

Mrs. C.O. Davidson, president of the Regina Equal Franchise League, and a member of the delegation to the legislature on Valentine's Day, 1916 (SAB).

Top: The "Big Interests" were accused of making excess profits on munitions and other war contracts, Regina *Leader*, 4 August 1917

Above: Food conservationists took up the slogan, "Lick your plate or be licked," Regina *Leader*, 22 January 1918.

Top: Regina Boy Scouts selling Victory Bonds in 1918 (SAB).

Above: The vacant lot garden movement encouraged householders to grow vegetables not only in their own backyards but in empty lots all over the city, Regina *Leader*, 30 April 1918.

Clockwise from top left: Soldiers returning to Regina in 1919. The sign reads, "From the Rhine to Regina, Saskatchewan. The Pride of the Prairies." (SAB)

Walter Davy Cowan, victorious Regina pro-conscription candidate, federal election, 17 December 1917 (SAB).

Canadian Patriotic Fund whirlwind campaign, Regina *Leader*, 22 September 1914

Eclipsed---Lost His Place in the Sun

Top: The defeat of Germany was taken to signify the triumph of liberty over despotism, Regina Leader, 8 June 1918.

Above: Returned soldiers in front of St. Chad's Military Hospital, Regina, May 1917 (SAB).

Top: Official opening of Regina's Soldier's Cemetery, the Cross of Sacrifice in the centre, 25 June 1922 (SAB).

Above: Memorial Gate to the Soldier's Cemetery, flanked by two captured German field guns (SAB).

Chapter 8

The End of Voluntarism

CANADA'S BATTLEFIELD VICTORIES CAME AT GREAT COST AND RECRUITMENT failed to keep pace with casualties. In April 1917 overseas casualties were 23,939, while volunteers for the Canadian Expeditionary Force numbered only 4761.[1] At this rate, the Canadian forces would collapse for lack of replacements to fill the depleted ranks. "Piffles" Taylor, serving with the Royal Flying Corps, wrote home to his father in Regina in June 1917: "I haven't any patience whatsoever for the boys who are left in Canada. I used to try to excuse some of them, but not any longer. No sacrifice is too great for the work that is to be accomplished. The people in Canada have not yet realized that there is a war going on.... I hope that Borden succeeds in establishing a coalition government and brings conscription into force."[2] This was the majority sentiment of the men overseas. When they had a chance to express an opinion on the matter in the federal election of December 1917, they voted 92 percent in favour of conscription.[3]

Compulsory service had its counterpart in the erosion of voluntarism on the home front. The voluntary principle seemed increasingly anomalous for the conduct of a modern war. Patriotic and relief organizations, though well intentioned, were too poorly funded and disorganized to get the job done. Government had to take charge, put efficient organization in place, and tell citizens what to do. For those who liked the old style of spontaneous philanthropy and voluntary giving, the increased level of state involvement was disconcerting. Some thought it was "Prussian." It seemed to go against the democratic ideal for which the war was being fought. To win the war Canada had to transform itself, to some degree at least, into the likeness of the enemy.

Compulsory Military Service

Prime Minister Robert Borden at the beginning of the war had promised not to introduce conscription, in large part in deference to francophone Quebec, which strongly opposed it. But for Borden the soldiers came first and politics second. The government authorized in August 1916 the appointment of a National Service Board. Led by Director-General Richard B. Bennett, the board distributed registration cards to be filled out by workers throughout the country "in order to gather basic information as to manpower location and distribution."[4] The scheme did not sit well with many trade union leaders, who regarded it as a prelude to conscription.

Borden and Bennett visited Regina on 19 December 1916, addressing a crowd of 4000 at the Winter Fair building. The prime minister announced that the cards would be mailed out to all men between the ages of sixteen and sixty. They were asked to provide information about age, health, marital status, dependents, job skills, and overall capacity to serve the country, whether in the civilian or military sphere.[5] Filling out the cards was voluntary, but the government strongly encouraged it.[6] A trade union meeting in Regina on 3 January 1917 condemned the plan, and launched a broadside against various aspects of wartime administration. It charged that war industries were "reaping profits for their owners out of all proportion to the effort put forth by the owners, and many of them operating under conditions which are doubtful or unfair to the people working in the industries."[7] Further, the trade unionists called upon Borden to resign in order to make way for a government "in which all classes of the nation will be represented and particularly in which the working people will have such trusted representation as their numbers and importance in the country would justify."[8] The resolution was forwarded to Bennett, who responded irritably: "I note that those who are stated to have been present have passed a resolution to defy the law of the country in which they live, and under whose institutions they enjoy liberty, which at times I fear is mistaken for license."[9]

On returning from a visit to the front in May 1917, Borden declared his intention to introduce conscription. Organized labour was up in arms. The Canadian Trades and Labor Congress, in convention in the first week of June, pronounced itself "emphatically opposed" to the conscription measure and called upon workers to resist it "with every means in their power."[10] There was even talk of a national general strike to prevent implementation of the legislation.[11] James Watters, national Trades and Labor Congress president, demanded "the nationalization of the mines, railways, munitions works, and other establishments necessary for the prosecution of the war including the banking system and warned the organized workers not to permit themselves to be shackled with the chains of conscription."[12]

Regina workers scheduled a meeting at the Labor Temple on 31 May 1917 to discuss the situation. The agenda was taken over by 150 members of the Great War Veterans' Association, who marched en masse from their clubrooms to the hall. When an elderly gentleman hazarded the opinion that many men in the first contingent had joined the army because they were hungry and starving, he was hooted down with cries of "That's a slur," "Sit down," "Get off the floor," and "You insult us."[13] Ernest C. Kirk, a returned soldier, insisted that the most important thing in the present crisis was to secure men for the trenches. He did not think that conscription would harm the trade unions. Its main impact would fall on those "who loitered on street corners or lounged in the poolrooms."[14] The meeting passed a resolution stating: "The workingmen here assembled put themselves on record as pledging their loyalty to the king and empire to the just cause of the allied peoples in their defence of the rights and liberties of the workingmen, and our pledge to support the government of Canada in their endeavor to place men in the firing line in France to defend our homes and the lives of our women and children."[15] After the meeting, the veterans marched to Germantown, where they sang patriotic songs in front of the offices of *Der Courier*.[16]

Unionist Government

Borden on 29 May 1917 proposed to Opposition Leader Sir Wilfrid Laurier that a coalition government be formed to enforce the conscription policy. Laurier declined, mainly out of fear of losing his political base in Quebec.[17] In mid-September, the prime minister introduced two new electoral laws, the Military Voters' Act and the Wartime Elections Act.18 The former disenfranchised persons from enemy countries who had come to Canada after 1902 and gave the vote to women who were next-of-kin to soldiers. That latter provided for the "pooling" of the military vote and its allocation to constituencies where it would do the government the most good. Taken together, the measures greatly increased the chances of a pro-conscription Tory victory in the upcoming election.

In Regina on 13 September 1917 a group of prominent Liberals gathered at city hall to support "national"—that is, coalition—government.[19] It was a hard pill for them to swallow. For years they had never tired of denouncing the unholy cabal of manufacturers, railways, and banks, supposedly in league with the Tories to rob farmers and oppress the West. Now, suddenly, they were about to form an alliance with Borden. The *Leader* argued, somewhat lamely, that Liberals could fight the Big Interests more effectively if they were inside, rather than outside, the coalition government:

> There can be no quitting the war of Democracy at home any more than we can afford to quit the war for Democracy in Europe. Just as for the first years of the war Prussian autocracy seemed to be able to work its will in Europe, and go

forward from one conquest to another, so Big Interests autocracy in Canada succeeded during the first three years of the war in achieving victory after victory over the masses of the people.... Naturally, the Big Interests scored success after success, until today they are entrenched in a Hindenburg line of their own choosing. It will be a long and stubborn fight to oust them.[20]

With the formation of a Unionist government on 12 October 1917, the Big Interests, said the *Leader*, no longer held "supreme and undisputed possession and control of the main citadel": "We have friends in the front line trenches now. But they require supports. They alone cannot achieve the victory we must have if Canada is not to lose at home all our brave lads are fighting for overseas."[21] The best way to defeat the Big Interests was to join them.

Saskatchewan's man in the Unionist cabinet was J.A. Calder, described by the *Leader* as "one of the biggest men in Western politics."[22] A former teacher and school inspector, he had served as Deputy Minister of Education until 1905, when Walter Scott appointed him as one of the four original members of the Saskatchewan cabinet.[23] Because of Scott's frequent and prolonged absences from the province, Calder was de facto premier for months at a time. He was also in charge of the provincial Liberal Party organization, a well-oiled patronage machine, which he now abandoned.

Calder justified this "treachery" before a large Regina audience on 23 October 1917. More than 1200 people squeezed into Metropolitan Methodist Church, with an additional 800 seated in First Baptist Church across the street. He spoke at both venues so that everyone could hear what he had to say. "Some people scarcely realize that we are at war," he began, "and very few people will admit that insofar as Canada is concerned this is a war of defence, that we are actually defending our home and our families." Canada must rise to the challenge and do her part "in a manly way." This, he said, was his main reason for joining the Unionist government. He continued: "Let me say this in all sincerity and earnestness: if the call to duty comes to any man and it is a clear call, there is only one thing to do. That call to duty came to me and regardless of my own personal feelings or of anything I thought as to what I would be or would like to be there was only one thing for me to do and that was to respond to the call."[24] He had in effect "enlisted" in the Borden cabinet. He hoped, too, that he would be able to play some part in improving the efficiency and competence of wartime government. A more methodical approach and a general housecleaning were badly needed.[25] Above all, it was necessary to keep the armed forces at full strength. If Canada did not win the war, nothing else would matter.[26] He was still a Liberal at heart, determined as ever to oppose the protective tariff and the Big Interests. It was just that winning the war came first.[27]

Since Calder was nominated in Moose Jaw, the Unionists decided, as a trade-off, to run a Conservative in Regina. This was almost more than the Liberals could bear. The *Leader* hastened to allay their anxiety. Having to put up with a Tory M.P. was but a small sacrifice compared with that "made by our heroic men overseas who have given up business, home, loved ones, comfort, their bodies and life itself, in the same great cause of humanity and civilization."[28] The nominating convention selected Walter D. Cowan, mayor of Regina, who had lost in a landslide to Liberal William Martin in the 1911 federal election.[29] To mollify erstwhile opponents, Cowan promised to follow "the wishes of the majority in the constituency" in the matter of the protective tariff. In other words, he could be counted upon to vilify the Big Interests.[30]

Not every Regina Liberal was willing to support the Unionist candidate. The diehards joined with organized labour to run Andrew MacBeth, a Liberal/Labour alternative to Cowan. MacBeth pledged "to defeat the big interests combination who are using the war to distract the attention of the public from the most outrageous profiteering that has ever disgraced a country."[31] The campaign was unusually bitter, even by Saskatchewan standards. Unionist ads asked, "How would the Kaiser vote?"[32] The Laurier Liberal/Labourites retaliated with: "How would the Big Interests and the war profiteers vote?"[33] Most Protestant clergy were emphatically pro-conscription.[34] Rev. George Daly at Holy Rosary Cathedral was more circumspect, saying that the Roman Catholic Church "left her children free to vote as they wished." However, he cautioned moderation in the expression of opinion: "Let us remember that when the smoke of battle will have lifted, when the din of the cannon will have been silenced, when our soldiers will have beaten their swords into plow shares, we will have to live together, work together, for the up building and future prosperity of our country."[35] *Der Courier* openly opposed conscription. It claimed that Unionist government was a Tory plot to cover up the corruption of the Borden administration.[36]

The Great War Veterans' Association and soldiers in training at Camp Exhibition held a rally four days before the election. Carrying torches, they marched from their clubrooms in the McCallum-Hill building (Scarth and Twelfth), arriving at city hall at about eight o'clock. They were greeted with rousing cheers, and the audience sang "trench choruses," which were printed on programs distributed at the door. Miss Gertrude Drummond recited "The Thin Red Line" and "Canadian Girls" to great applause. Rev. Murdoch MacKinnon spoke of the "necessity of union among the peoples, political parties, churches, every phase of Canadian life, for the preponderance of British ideals, the victory desired by every one so ardently." "Canada was today fighting for her very soul," he cried, "and the issue remains with us to say whether she shall be saved or shall be lost." The defeat of conscription "would send a chill to the marrow and the bones of the brave soldiers fighting at the front." Arrayed against the Unionist government were "every German sympathizer in the whole country, every Austrian who loved his native country before the country of his adoption, every Hungarian and every Turk."[37] Quebec must not be allowed to impose its will on the rest of the country. Too much was at stake to allow the betrayal of Canada's fighting men.[38]

An election-eve rally capped the Unionist campaign. Rev. Ernest W. Stapleford, president of Regina College, confessed that he had never voted Tory in his life and did not intend to this time. He was voting for Canada. The speeches continued for more than three hours, exhausting the audience, who finally sang the national anthem well past eleven o'clock.[39] The next day, 17 December 1917, Regina gave Unionist W.D. Cowan 76 percent of the vote (7674 to 2478 for MacBeth).⁴⁰ Across the province, the result was virtually identical. Unionists took 74 percent of the vote and all sixteen seats.⁴¹

Even so, about a quarter of the electorate in Regina and the province had not supported the Unionist government. It is likely that they had qualms about conscription and could not vote for a party identified with the Big Interests. They demanded "conscription of wealth," by which they meant "heavy taxation of the abnormally high wartime profits of Central Canadian manufacturers."⁴² They could not forgive and forget the past sins of the Tories and Big Interests. For them, the war did not blot out the old grievances, but rather intensified them. "Conscription of wealth" was code for class conflict and regional protest, which for them trumped the win-the-war argument. Their friends might hold their noses and vote for the Borden government, but they could not.

Implementing Conscription

Under the terms of the Military Service Act, which became law on 29 August 1917, men were placed into six categories, according to age and marital status, beginning with single men aged twenty to thirty-four (Class 1) and ending with married men aged forty-one to forty-four (Class 6). The physically unfit, men in essential jobs or having special skills, the clergy, and conscientious objectors were allowed to apply for exemption. Their cases were adjudicated, in the first instance, by one of 1253 tribunals set up across the country. Each tribunal had two members, one appointed by the government and the other by the opposition. Appeals from the tribunal's decision were to one of 195 special courts. The final appeal lay with Mr. Justice Lyman Duff, a member of the Supreme Court of Canada.⁴³

Class 1 men were ordered to report for duty by 10 November 1917. Failure to do so could result in imprisonment for five years with hard labour.⁴⁴ Across Canada, 405,395 Class 1 men reported, and 380,510 filed for exemption. In 334,989 cases, exemption was granted.⁴⁵ The tribunals varied widely in their interpretation of the Military Service Act. Some were lenient, others very strict.⁴⁶ There were five tribunals in Regina, composed respectively of

J.H. Heffernan and J.W. Smith; Martin J. Bruton and H.E. Sampson; James Habkirk and James Balfour; H.G. Smith and W.G. Styles; and George Bradshaw and J.A. Wetmore.[47] Heffernan, former senior RNWMP inspector, was police magistrate for Regina. J.W. Smith, ex-mayor, had two sons at the front. H.E. Sampson, KC, was Crown prosecutor, and M.J. Bruton, chief of police. Both James Balfour and W.G. Styles had sons overseas. The sole trade unionist was James Habkirk, a city alderman, who was in charge of the mechanical department at the Leader Publishing Company.[48] As a whole, this was not a group likely to go easy on exemption applicants.

Conscripts occupied the Winter Fair building at the exhibition grounds.[49] In the early morning hours of 18 December 1917, the day after the federal election, A.B. LaDrue of the Seventy-Seventh Battery awoke with a choking sensation and the smell of smoke. He picked up his bugle and sounded the alarm. Within a few minutes, 700 men piled out of the building into the bitter cold. Some ran to the nearby Grey Nuns' Hospital, where nurses looked after them, while others took refuge in neighbourhood homes. A large contingent headed downtown to find shelter at city hall and Knox Church. Wearing flimsy canvas shoes and clad in light clothing, blankets pulled over their heads, they pluckily sang "Pack Up Your Troubles in Your Old Kit Bag."[50]

The fire raged out of control, shells by the thousand exploding and whizzing through the air, ricocheting from the big steel beams. Horses released from the stables ran wildly over the grounds and into adjacent residential areas. Rumours abounded that the fire had been deliberately set, perhaps by German spies. However, formal investigation identified the cause as a kitchen blaze set by a drunken cook, who had consumed "a bottle of whisky, a bottle of lemon extract, and some two per cent beer."[51]

Moose Jaw and Saskatoon were quick to take advantage of Regina's misfortune. Both applied to have the First Depot Battalion relocated to their respective cities. Regina vigorously opposed the transfer. If the battalion were to leave, so, too, in all likelihood, would Military District Headquarters.[52] The latter had come to Regina in June 1916, when Military District 10, which was based in Winnipeg and included both Manitoba and Saskatchewan, had been divided into two parts. Regina became headquarters for Military District 12, covering Saskatchewan only. It was quite a boon for the city, since it involved the acquisition of general staff officers, quartermaster general and deputy assistant adjutant, assistant director of medical services, district paymaster, records department, and numerous other personnel, an establishment worth about $4.5 million a year.[53] City council scrambled to find alternative accommodation for the troops. It leased the recently vacated Sherwood department store building at Albert Street and Victoria Avenue for $847 per month and handed it over to the military at no cost.[54] The economic benefits to the city more than compensated for the monthly rent the city had to pay.[55]

A steady flow of conscripts entered Sherwood barracks. Major Graham, general staff officer for Regina, said he was generally pleased with their quality and demeanour. "I believe they are made of stern stuff," he said with satisfaction, "and will follow creditably in the footsteps of their comrades who preceded them."[56] In one incident an "Irishman" strode in the front door and challenged everybody in the building to a fistfight. He claimed that he could "lick any man in the Depot battalion—aye, any man in Regina." When he regained consciousness, he had the presence of mind to quip, "I must have made the mistake the Kaiser did—I tried to cover too much territory."[57]

By 24 November 1917, some 10,000 applications for exemption had been processed in Saskatchewan. Of these, 8000 were allowed and 2000 refused.[58] Farmers complained that they were being treated too harshly. A man near Humboldt with seventy-five head of horses was given only three weeks to dispose of them. A farmer, who in the previous year had broken 600 acres with a steam plough, was denied exemption. Farmers who were too proud to claim an exemption were automatically put into the army, even though their farm production was arguably of greater value to winning the war than their military service. There was no mechanism to grant an exemption to someone who did not apply for one.[59]

The issue came up at the annual convention of the Saskatchewan Grain Growers' Association in February 1918. The delegates called for the release from the army of all bona fide farmers and farm workers. They further demanded the closing of all non-essential businesses and the conscription for farmwork of men employed in such businesses.[60] Thomas Molloy, director of the provincial Labour Bureau, explained that under federal government regulations, any man who owned land and intended to crop it in 1918 would be given an exemption, and men who did not own land, but could show that for the preceding three years they had been continuously employed in farmwork, and had a farm job to go to in the current season, were likewise exempted.[61]

The rulings of the appeal court in Regina reflected Molloy's understanding of the regulations. Judge Hannon on 9 January 1918 confirmed exemptions for seven farmers and farm labourers, while non-farmers received differential treatment depending on individual circumstances. William Clink, plumber, was granted exemption until 1 April by reason of the shortage of plumbers and the great demand during cold weather, and Claude Burrows, a law student, had his military service postponed to June to allow him to write final examinations. W.J. Ledster, Canadian Pacific Railway yardmaster, received an exemption on the representation of the company that he was a necessary employee. Similarly, F.M. Quance, a professor at the normal school, was allowed to continue teaching on the basis of statements from the acting principal and the Department of Education that he could not easily be replaced. J.J. McIsaac, student, was denied an exemption, and B.D. Hogarth, barrister, withdrew his appeal for one.[62] The same pattern was evident in Judge Hannon's rulings on 21 January 1918. Seven farmers and three farm hands were exempted, but W. Stanley Holmes, science teacher, Arthur Davidson, hardware merchant, Frank Fillmore, retail salesman, and Archibald Todd, teacher, were all conscripted.[63]

During the major German offensive launched 21 March 1918, exemptions were cancelled for all men, including farmers, farmers' sons, and farm labourers, aged nineteen to twenty-two inclusive.[64] This affected about one in twenty farmers.⁶⁵ Farmers felt betrayed because during the December 1917 election campaign they were promised a blanket exemption, and they had been told repeatedly that increased agricultural production was a top priority. In the government's defence, the German offensive created an emergency that had not existed at the time of the election. However, in Saskatchewan this excuse had little purchase. Farmers, already suspicious of the Borden government because of its ties to the Big Interests, had their mistrust confirmed.

Under the 1917 Wartime Elections Act, naturalized British subjects of enemy alien nationality who had come to Canada after 1902 were not allowed to vote and were not subject to conscription. The *Leader* and most Saskatchewan Liberals disagreed with this policy: "What do our Canadian and British fathers and mothers think of the situation, and the future before their daughters, if all their sons of British breed and blood are sent away to war, while the sons of the alien nationalities in our midst remain in comfort and security in Canada, growing richer because of the dearth of labor and the high price obtained for the products of their labor?"⁶⁶ The Tories took away the "foreigners'" votes and the Liberals blasted them for not being eligible for conscription. The "foreigners" were made out to be villains on both counts.

All told, 99,651 Canadians were conscripted into the Canadian Expeditionary Force, and, of these, 47,509 proceeded overseas. A total of 24,132 were in France when the war ended.⁶⁷ By the time they entered the trenches, the worst of it was over. But on 18 May 1917, when Prime Minister Borden made the decision to conscript, he could not foresee how long the war would last. For him, the most important thing was to make sure that the men in the field had the support they needed. He would not let them down, and judging from the outcome of the December 1917 election and the subsequent implementation of conscription, most people in Regina and Saskatchewan agreed with him.⁶⁸

Voluntarism Falters on the Home Front

Conscription was but one instance, though by far the most drastic, of the wartime trend towards coercive government intruding upon individual freedom. Another was the transformation of the Patriotic Fund from a strictly voluntary organization to a public-private hybrid. By May 1915, 103 soldiers' families in Regina (including 177 children) were receiving help from the fund, which had been set up at the beginning of the war. To get on the list, a family first had to be investigated to determine the level of need. The investigator's report was sent to a local committee, who reviewed it and made a recommendation. This in turn was forwarded to the general executive of the local branch of the Patriotic Fund. If everything was in order, the forms were filled out and submitted to the secretary of the provincial Patriotic Fund and reviewed by the provincial advisory board. Only then were the cheques mailed out.[69]

Because the Patriotic Fund depended on voluntary donations, it strove to keep administrative costs to a minimum, thereby avoiding criticism that the money was not reaching the intended beneficiaries. The investigators were unpaid volunteers, as were the members of the various committees. The office of the Regina branch of the Patriotic Fund was provided rent-free in the McCallum-Hill building,[70] and the provincial government covered the salary of the assistant secretary, who, initially, was the only paid employee.[71] As the number of cases increased, it became necessary to hire a female investigator, who received a modest remuneration.[72]

The Regina Patriotic Fund in October 1915 assisted 235 women and 350 children at a cost of over $5000 per month. Contributions for the month of September amounted to only $3400.[73] The branch appealed to city council, which provided a small grant of forty dollars per month, enough to cover some of the increased costs of administration.[74] But the bigger problem lay in the discrepancy between income and expenditure, a gap that was likely to grow as more men joined the Canadian Expeditionary Force. The success of the recruitment campaign hinged, in part, on adequate provision for soldiers' dependents. A married man was not likely to enlist if he believed that his family would suffer economic hardship as a result.

At the annual meeting of the Regina branch in 1915, vice-president J.A. Allan defended voluntarism. The army, he said, was voluntary; the Patriotic Fund should follow the same principle. This argument later backfired when conscription was introduced, but in 1915 it was still valid. Allan maintained that the most important element of morale was the spirit of sacrifice, which lay at the heart of the war effort. For those not able to enlist, the next best thing was to give generously for the support of soldiers' families. If the government were to cover the cost through taxation, the gesture would not have the same moral value.[75] The Patriotic Fund gave everybody a chance "to do their bit." It was "an outlet for their patriotism, a stimulus to self-sacrifice, a means of satisfying a conscience restive under the imperative character of the call of duty." To make the Patriotic Fund a government responsibility would be to choke "the fountains of private giving," for "why should an individual pay his own share of the tax and also make a free contribution to redeem the share of the tax to be borne by his fellows?"[76] It was further assumed that if the government took over the fund, partisan politics would tarnish its reputation, a legitimate concern in an era of patronage and cronyism in the Saskatchewan government.[77]

These arguments, as cogent as they were, could not withstand the logic of the balance sheet. The amount raised through voluntary contributions in 1915 covered only half the expenditures for 1916.[78] To help make up the shortfall, the Department of Education issued an appeal to the schoolchildren of the province. Deputy Minister Augustus H. Ball encouraged schools to hold fundraising concerts, "songs and choruses, musical drills, dialogues, recitations and essays by the pupils and their friends, addresses on patriotic subjects and topics connected with the war, instrumental music, tableaux and plays." Receipts from such entertainments totalled $24,192. A similar collection for Belgian Children's Relief raised $46,037.[79]

H.H. Christie, MD, president of the Esterhazy Patriotic Fund, found fault with the voluntary system. He thought it placed too great a burden on patriotic citizens, while allowing "slackers in charitable giving" to get off easy. It was a known fact, he wrote, that "washwomen with their scanty hard-made earnings have conscientiously remitted their monthly donations, while many others whose financial returns are materially greater as a direct result of the war have as yet to learn the joy of giving."[80] He noted that Britain was in the process of adopting compulsory military service. Should not the same principle apply to patriotic fundraising?[81] T. Watson decried the injustice to the soldier and his family: "Charity for him and his is an insult. It is JUSTICE and not charity that is due to them" [emphasis original].[82] The Regina Trades and Labor Council amplified the complaint, endorsing a tax-based Patriotic Fund, to which all citizens would contribute according to their means.[83]

The Regina *Daily Post* countered that it would be a mistake to place the fund under government control. If that occurred, all soldiers' families would have to be given the same amount of assistance in accordance with a set formula, as was the case with the separation allowance. It would be difficult to calibrate relief to need, with the result that some would get too much and others too little. Secondly, the *Post* contended that the cost of administering the fund would be much greater than it was under the voluntary system. As things stood, "in every town there are willing workers who gladly contribute their time, labor and thought to the philanthropic fund." If the government assumed control, all the workers would have to be paid, and the work would not be as well done. Government departments tended to perform their duties in an "automatic matter." The "friendly, personal, helpful relationship" that existed between voluntary administrators and the families of the men overseas would be lost, to the detriment of both parties. The "flow of human kindness would cease if the fund were to come within the cogs of the machinery of government administration."[84]

Despite these objections, the provincial government moved partway to bring the Patriotic Fund within the ambit of the public sector. In 1916 it passed the Patriotic Revenues Act, which levied a tax of one mill on all ratable property for the purpose of raising funds for a variety of patriotic and relief projects, including the Patriotic Fund, Belgian, Serbian, and Polish Relief, the Red Cross, and the Military Hospitals Commission. The Patriotic Fund received the lion's share.[85] Beginning in July 1916, the provincial government contributed an average $55,527 monthly to the approximately 400 branches of the fund in Saskatchewan. Voluntary contributions, by comparison, were about $24,000 a month.[86] The fund was now primarily a government-supported operation, though administration and disbursement still remained in private hands.

Premier William Martin in November 1916 launched the Regina Patriotic Fund campaign. "Above the din of arms in Europe," he urged, "let our soldiers hear reverberating the answer of the people at home, in one loud, swelling chorus, that ready and noble response will be made to the appeal for funds in behalf of the near and dear ones left behind."[87] Lawyer Norman MacKenzie added: "We have every incentive to help this Fund. When we read the casualty lists day after day and see the names of those we know, see the names of those who only a few years ago were walking around our city in short pants, and are now fighting our battles for us, I say we have every incentive to help this great fund." E.W. Stapleford pledged $600 on behalf of Regina College faculty and students.[88] Notwithstanding the enthusiasm, the campaign fell short. Only $40,940 was collected in 1916 compared with $75,000 the previous year.[89] Now that the fund was tax-supported, people seemed less willing to give.

The Patriotic Fund offered more than material support to soldiers' families. The Regina branch, assisted by the IODE, put on a Christmas party in 1915 for 460 children. As the *Leader* reported, the fun began "when the house lights were turned off, sleigh-bells jingled, and a spot-light was turned on the chimney down which a pair of legs was soon seen to dangle. From then till Saint Nick and his pack of toys were safely landed you could have heard the same old pin drop had anyone been thinking about dropping pins." Grocers donated pails of candy, cases of oranges and raisins, and sacks of nuts. Each child received a bag of treats, along with "a book or a woolly lamb, a little perambulator" or other toy.[90]

The Patriotic Fund executive, mostly business and professional men, were available every Wednesday from three to six o'clock to give advice about taxes, insurance benefits, pensions, and other legal or financial matters. On a typical afternoon, thirty to forty soldiers' wives dropped by.[91] When the provincial government in 1917 exempted soldiers' homes from the property tax,[92] a number of wives who applied for the exemption discovered that they did not have title to the property they thought they owned. The Patriotic Fund executive helped them obtain the necessary documentation. In addition, Regina's medical doctors attended soldiers' dependents free of charge, and the General Hospital gave free treatment.[93]

Patriotic Fund investigators Miss Galbraith and Miss Allan (the latter a Presbyterian deaconess) saw themselves as friendly visitors, not mean-spirited inquisitors. Their job was not just to assess financial need, but also to give comfort and advice. In 1917 Miss Allan made 1874 calls and visited 544 different homes in the city and the various annexes.[94] However, her interventions were not always welcome. A correspondent to the *Leader*, who signed himself "Engineer," claimed to have spoken to a number of soldiers' wives who felt they were being treated in a "patronizing and meddlesome manner." "I personally," Engineer wrote indignantly, "have too much respect for my wife and family to submit them to the interference of any person who is capable of suggesting that they ought to be fed on oatmeal porridge, as I am told the visiting agent of the fund suggested to my neighbor."[95]

Patriotic Fund caseworkers took it upon themselves to supervise family budgets, assess sanitary and building conditions, monitor nutrition and child care, and, in some instances, remove children from women who cheated on their husbands.[96] It did not follow, however, that their ministrations were uniformly resented. Miss Allan organized a popular Soldiers' Wives Club, which met Wednesday afternoons at St. Paul's parish hall.[97] It alleviated "the loneliness, not to mention the anxiety, that gnaws at the heart of many a woman left alone, or with a little family, hourly waiting in unrelieved suspense news of some kind from the front."[98] At the annual meeting of the club in December 1917, condolences were offered to Mrs. McDonald, whose husband had recently been killed, and to Mrs. Thackeray, whose son had died in the trenches. Club members, who numbered between 100 and 125, in 1917 knitted 129 pairs of socks, 15 sweaters, and 2 scarves. Initially, the programs were structured and formal, but, as women started to bring their babies and young children, the meetings became more relaxed. Lectures were abandoned in favour of knitting circles and "chatting over current events, the latest news from the trenches, etc. and enjoying a short musical program and a cup of tea." "Our greatest work," reported Miss Allan, "no doubt has been to link together the women who are most concerned in this great war so that the burdens have been shared and lightened, and in the hour of deepest need the tender sympathy and love of the members have been freely given."[99]

The Patriotic Fund had to compete for public attention with other worthy causes, such as Victory Loan campaigns. The province was expected to raise $12 million in the fall of 1917, of which $1,500,000 was to come from Regina.[100] The campaign was a highly orchestrated affair, complete with telegraph forms stamped with the Victory Loan logo and eight-minute short films shown before the main feature at movie theatres.[101] Premier Martin sent a letter to schoolchildren, soliciting their donations. War bonds, he said, were "silver bullets" and "explosive shells": "It is more important to buy a bond than to buy an automobile. It is more important to buy a bond than pay the mortgage on the farm. Buying a bond is clothing and feeding and arming a soldier boy and giving him new courage to fight."[102]

A Victory Bond parade was held in Regina on 15 November 1917. Led by a procession of returned soldiers, it included veterans of previous wars, troops of the 1st Saskatchewan Depot Battalion, the RNWMP, and 2000 schoolchildren. The latter were in a boisterous mood, singing patriotic songs and shouting out school yells as they marched. Others joined in, including a young mother who sported a Victory Bond button and pushed a baby carriage. At the saluting stand, the premier, mayor, and other dignitaries stood at attention. "Miss Canada" waved at the crowd, and Kaiser Bill was burned in effigy.[103] The Victory Loan drive far exceeded its target. Saskatchewan raised $21,752,250, Regina contributing $2,061,950.[104] Schoolchildren alone bought $30,000 of bonds, more than the children of any other province.[105]

The rival claims of multitudinous charities led to overlapping, confusion, and donor fatigue. A meeting was held at city hall on 24 April 1916 to sort out the problem. In attendance were representatives of the Alexandra Club, IODE, Local Council of Women, 195th Battalion, Red Cross, Homemakers' Club, YMCA, Returned Soldiers' Welcome and Aid League, Board of Trade, Patriotic Fund, Boy Scouts Auxiliary, and St. John's Ambulance Association. The discussion centred on the lack of coordination. Several campaigns competed for donations at the same time, with the result that individual appeals were drowned out in the general melee. The majority favoured some form of civic regulation and oversight. The limits of voluntarism had been reached; government supervision was considered necessary to bring order to the chaos of private philanthropy.

Following the meeting, a civic approvals committee was set up, with a mandate to establish a schedule for concerts, public subscriptions, tag days, raffles, teas in public places, and "all fund-raising functions whatsoever." The committee consisted of the mayor, police magistrate, clerk of the police court, and representatives from the Local Council of Women and Board of Trade. Any organization wishing to appeal to the public for charitable donations had to submit an application to the committee, together with a statement of how the funds were to be used. The committee refused applications that did not conform to their pre-existing approval plan, or which diverted funds to other than patriotic, charitable, or military purposes.[106]

A group came before the approvals committee in late April 1916 with a proposal to raise $3000 for a brass band by canvassing the city for five-cents-a-week subscriptions. In return, the band promised to perform twenty open-air concerts and offer its services at civic and patriotic functions. The committee turned down the application on the grounds that other calls on the public purse were more pressing and because the mode of collection was thought to be inefficient and a waste of time.[107] The committee also rejected an application from the Regina Society for the Prevention of Cruelty to Animals to hold a tag day in June. All the Saturdays in the summer had already been spoken for. It offered the society 1 November as a substitute and recommended that the funds be used to care for wounded horses at the front.[108]

The Red Cross applied for tag day on 14 July 1917 but was refused because it had already been granted one for 8 September. It went ahead with the July tag day in defiance of the committee, who then appealed to city council to back up its authority.[109] The council passed a bylaw in August 1917, which required all persons, societies, or organizations soliciting contributions from the public "on or in the streets, lanes, squares or public places on behalf of any person, cause or organization" to obtain a permit from the "Board to Regulate the taking of Public Contributions." This put legal muscle behind what had previously been a voluntary arrangement. Persons soliciting donations had to wear a badge indicating that they had a permit. Those soliciting without due authorization were liable to a fine of not less than five dollars and not more than fifty dollars for each offence, together with the costs of prosecution. In the event of non-payment, the guilty party could be jailed for a period not exceeding thirty days with or without hard labour.[110]

The Board to Regulate Public Contributions encountered an unexpected snag. The federal government passed a War Charities Act purporting to coordinate and regulate private philanthropy. Uncertain as to the impact of the federal legislation, the local board suspended operations. The city solicitor asked Ottawa for clarification, but received no response.[111] Meanwhile, the backlog of charity applications piled up. Exasperated, Regina city council reactivated the local board in March 1918 "until such time as they were officially notified by the Dominion government that they had no power to deal with such matters."[112] To ease pressure on donors, the board tried to limit tag days in the summer to one every two weeks,[113] but this did not prove practicable. There were just too many charities wanting to make an appeal to the generosity of the public, and the weekly tag days had to be resumed.[114]

The Regina Rotary Club in August 1918 floated the idea of a "war chest" or "community chest," such as had been tried in some American cities.[115]

Under the scheme, the various charities got together and agreed on a common budget, allocating a share of the money to each participating organization according to need. They then held a joint annual fundraising campaign to secure the agreed-upon amount. The public had to respond to only one appeal per year, eliminating incessant tag days and charity drives. The agencies stood to benefit, too. Instead of spending an inordinate amount of their time fundraising, they were able to focus on delivery of services. In short, charity was "modernized" and made efficient. The *Leader* backed the reform, calling it "pure patriotism ... to suggest a change in our methods of collecting and distributing funds for the benefit of our worthy heroes of war and their dependents."[116]

But the idea was not accepted in Regina because it clashed with the spirit of independence and individuality. Charitable organizations did not want to have to report to a superior body. Nor did they want to be told how much money they could raise or how to spend it. Bureaucracy and regulation killed the generosity of spontaneous giving. It made charity seem like a job, rather than a matter of the heart. Regina did not adopt the community chest idea until 1935, when the Great Depression brought a more profound crisis to private philanthropy.[117]

* * *

Nonetheless, the war suggested the trend of future developments. Voluntarism gave way to a measure of government involvement and control. The civic approval board brought order to patriotic charity, and the Patriotic Fund depended on government subsidy to maintain its operations. The *Leader* in October 1917 wanted the government to take the next step and assume full responsibility for the care of soldiers' dependents. It was "a war measure," the paper argued, "and all matters pertaining to war come solely within the scope and jurisdiction of the Ottawa authorities."[118] No country could ask more of its men than to conscript them for battle. If the state demanded so much of its citizens, surely it owed them something in return. Support of soldiers' families was a matter of public entitlement, not private charity. Thus were sown in World War I the seeds of Canada's modern welfare state.[119]

Chapter 9

The Economy and the Rural Myth

THE WAR WAS A BOON TO THE SASKATCHEWAN ECONOMY, AT LEAST IN THE short run. The total value of field crops and livestock rose from $264,398,237 in 1914 to $609,588,065 in 1917, before dropping slightly (because of drought) to $585,733,357 in 1918.[1] Acreage seeded in wheat doubled between 1914 and 1919, and the price was fixed at $2.21 a bushel in 1917, triple its pre-war level.[2] Saskatchewan farmers were told to grow as much wheat as they could, and that is exactly what they did, reinforcing their dependency on a single staple crop. More than ever, Saskatchewan self-identified as the "wheat province." Although the number of dairy cattle, beef cattle, sheep, and hogs increased between 1914 and 1919, the rate of increase lagged behind that of field-crop acreage.[3] The easy money was in wheat. Whereas it took three years to raise cattle to market weight, the turnaround for a wheat crop was only three months.[4] The war played a "cruel trick" on the Saskatchewan farmer, keeping him on the treadmill of cereal monoculture.[5]

Agrarianism helped account for the relative lack of labour radicalism in Regina during the war. Although 1918 saw a rise in militancy, it was muted in comparison with other parts of Canada. Saskatchewan was basically an agricultural province, not fertile ground for industrial unionism. The city imbibed the agricultural ethos, both figuratively and literally. The Soldiers of the Soil campaign recruited high school students and office workers to help with seeding and harvest. Food production moved into the city under the auspices of the vacant-lot gardening movement. It was the city dweller's patriotic duty, not just to conserve food, but also to grow it. Everyone was expected to till the soil.

The Economy Goes into High Gear

Munitions production in Regina during the war was nil. Almost all the increase in industrial capacity occurred in central Canada, reinforcing the basic structure of the National Policy. The Big Interests, shielded by the tariff wall, were masters of the situation. According to the census, the population of Regina fell from 30,123 in 1911 to 26,105 in 1916, the decline a testament to the severity of the pre-war recession. The 1916 number was hotly disputed, as usually happens in such circumstances. The *Leader* maintained that the census had been carried out "in the most slipshod, incomplete and careless manner."[6] L.T. McDonald, secretary of the Board of Trade, calculated that in 1911 the total number of schoolchildren had been about 3000, or 10 percent of the population. In 1916 it had risen to 4000 children. From this he deduced that Regina's population was close to 40,000, far higher than the census indicated.[7]

Whatever the true figure, the city's prospects were definitely looking up. The Imperial Oil Company in 1916 announced plans to build a refinery to serve western Manitoba, Saskatchewan, and eastern Alberta. The plant employed 200 men in the construction phase and 50 in permanent, full-time jobs.[8] Rental housing was in short supply in the fall of 1916,[9] and home construction, which had stalled since the collapse of the pre-war boom, now started up again. A tour of the "best districts" in the southern part of the city in June 1917 revealed a dozen substantial new homes under construction, not to mention more modest dwellings on the north side and on the outskirts. One builder had received ten offers to rent and two to purchase for a structure that was not yet framed.[10] Non-residential construction also picked up. In the spring of 1917, the Royal Bank opened a new branch at the corner of Hamilton Street and Eleventh Avenue. Plans were also underway for a Union Bank on Scarth Street and an automobile garage at the corner of Hamilton Street and Twelfth.[11]

"People have money and they are spending it," gloated a Regina merchant in December 1916. "If we would just get a little let up in this severe weather business would pick up perceptibly." Another noted a heavy demand for better quality and luxury goods: "We're finding difficulty in securing stock of the better class."[12] Farmers poured into the city Christmas week and spent lavishly, every store reporting increased sales over the previous year.[13] According to a salesman who travelled the entire province, farmers were leading the way in the purchase of automobiles. "The farmer today," he said, "wants the large car. He does not seem to want the small car at all. He wants a big car and is ready to pay cash for it."[14]

The 1917 crop was down in volume from the previous year, but the quality was good and prices were high.[15] In dollar terms, it was by far the largest in the history of the province.[16] "The financial condition of the people," provincial Treasurer Charles Dunning beamed in December 1917, "generally is such that it has never been before." Conditions in 1914 had been dismal, prices for farm products "dangerously near—and in some cases below—the cost of production." The war, he said confidently, had been the "economic salvation of western Canada and particularly Saskatchewan."[17]

R.B. Bennett, Director of National Service in the Borden government, declared in March 1917 that it was the duty of Saskatchewan farmers "to crop every acre and crop it properly." The highest quality of seed must be sown on "the most efficiently prepared land." The outcome of the war depended on it.[18] Food production, he emphasized, was every bit as important as munitions production. Armies could not fight on empty stomachs, and if shortages were to develop among the civilian populations in allied European countries, there would be a decline in the health and vigour of munitions workers and a corresponding diminution of output.[19]

Charles Dunning was "loaned" to the Dominion government in 1918 to supervise the greater production of foodstuffs and conservation of food supplies. At the SGGA convention that year, he called on farmers to seed at least ten acres of wheat in 1918 for every seven sown in 1917. Canada needed to increase wheat exports by at least 180 million bushels.[20] The provincial government had already introduced the Saskatchewan Greater Production Loan program. Organized along the lines of the Victory Loan, it offered the public ten-year bonds in denominations of $20, $100, $500, and $1000, bearing an interest of 5 percent per annum payable half yearly. The money was used to extend credit to farmers to cultivate more acres.[21]

Labour Shortages

As agricultural production increased, so, too, did the demand for farm labour. The Department of Education amended its regulations in May 1917 to permit high school students whose services were needed on the farm to proceed to the next higher grade without examination, provided that they had been in regular attendance for at least six months prior to leaving school to do farmwork and their school work was deemed satisfactory by their principal or teacher.[22] In a two-day period, seventy students at Regina Collegiate volunteered for farm work,[23] among them Blanche Watson, who drove a Ford car "with an attachment which transformed the machine into a tractor." It just went to show, the *Leader* complacently observed, that farmwork, assisted by modern machinery, was "not too strenuous for the average Canadian girl."[24]

The provincial Bureau of Labour in the years 1912 to 1914 placed 1591 female domestic servants on Saskatchewan farms. In 1915 and 1916, by comparison, only sixty-five girls could be found, even though every effort was made to recruit in the United States and Britain, as well as eastern and western Canada. Typically, domestics stayed in service for about a year and then married or found some other kind of job. A steady intake of new domestics was required to fill the places of those who moved on. When the war cut off the flow of immigrants, a shortage quickly developed.[25] One farm woman, who came into Regina in June 1917 to hire help, was told there was not the slightest chance of her finding a girl. The woman thought she could hold out until harvest time. "Then," she sighed, "I must have help of some kind for the work is more than I want to tackle alone, and if I can't get a girl I think I shall have to try and get a Chinese assistant."[26]

A Regina matron lamented that she had placed a help-wanted ad in the newspaper for ten days running and had received only one applicant. She knew of five families "within a stone's throw of my house" who were badly in need of a maid, but unable to hire one. Servants were demanding eighteen to twenty-five dollars a month, which employers were more than willing to pay, if only they could find someone to do the work.[27] Another correspondent, who signed herself "One Who Would Go If She Could," saved her sympathy for the overworked farm housewife with a gang of harvesters to feed. She suggested that city women release their maids to do farmwork for a couple of months. "I can think of no act that would be more patriotic," she wrote. "You would be forty or fifty dollars in pocket, which would be more than you could possibly make by teas and tagging in that time for the Red Cross."[28]

The Canadian Pacific Railway hired women to clear the right-of-way, mow grass, cut down thistles, and shovel sand. They were mostly Austrians and Germans. Wearing plain calico dresses, with good bonnets, they toiled in the hot sun. Asked if they found the work tiring, they replied that "it was not any worse than the garden work, except that it was a little warmer on the tracks."[29] The annual report of the Regina Board of Trade in February 1917 noted that women now occupied positions vacated by men in banks, wholesale houses, and other places of business.[30] On the whole, however, because Regina lacked major secondary industry, apart from the oil refinery, women did not have the range of job opportunities that were available elsewhere. Until the 1920s, over half the women in the paid workforce in Saskatchewan were employed as domestic servants. The rest worked mainly in agriculture, sales, and clerical positions, or as seamstresses, telephone operators, and waitresses. Only about 5 percent were professionals, mostly teachers and nurses.[31]

By 1917 large numbers of alien enemies were being released from the internment camps to work on the farms. A group from Brandon arrived in Moose Jaw in early May, when RNWMP officers registered and photographed them. They were placed on farms near Vantage and ordered to report to the nearest police station once a month.[32] Five "Austrians" (Joseph Dishorn, Joseph Lukon, Karl Mokah, John Dyonski, and Joseph Gravetch)[33] were arrested in Regina in August 1917 on charges of vagrancy. They had been loitering on South Railway Street, demanding $4.50 a day for farm labour plus "cakes and lodging."[34] Magistrate Heffernan set them straight:

> You men are alien enemies and as such you will not be permitted to hold up British farmers of this province for absurdly high wages, especially when these farmers' brothers and sons are fighting in the armies opposed to the country from which you came.... You had better go to work as soon as you leave this court. In the event that you do not you will be arrested and I instruct the police now that if they find you loafing around the city they are to arrest you and bring you before me, when you will be given work for several months, and for this work you will not get wages.[35]

The Regina Trades and Labor Council objected to Heffernan's ruling, which they characterized as a "a threat to every working man."[36] It was unfair, they said, to arrest the men for bargaining for a better wage. The going rate for farm labour at the beginning of the 1918 season was $4.50 a day for a full-season contract. Even if the farmer did not need help for the entire summer, he had to keep his man on the payroll or risk not having anyone to assist in the harvest. By the fall of 1918, men were getting five dollars, $5.50 and, in some cases, even six dollars a day. Some wanted as much as seven dollars and threatened to quit if they did not get it. Farmers complained to local justices of the peace that employees were breaking their contracts, and in almost every case they secured a conviction.[37]

Soldiers of the Soil

Thomas Molloy, director of the provincial Labour Bureau, estimated that 10,000 men were needed for spring seeding in 1918. He called on business and professional men to give a month of their time to put in the crop. Labour committees were organized in cities, towns, and villages to drum up volunteer farm workers. "Do not be timid," Molloy implored, "in asking your women, your boys and girls to take charge of your shops, lumber yards, restaurants, hotels, pool rooms and even livery stables for a few months in order that the men may be released to assist in farm work."[38] The *Leader* lectured: "The clerk must be taken from the office, store and shop; vacations hitherto spent by city men at the seashore, lake or in the mountains must be spent in health-giving, war-winning work on the farm; the labourer in non-essential work must be transferred into essential productive work on the farm."[39]

By 20 March 1918, 235 farm labour committees had been set up in the province.[40] The Regina committee distributed 5000 cards to employers in the city, requesting them to release men for spring seeding. One businessman pledged that he would be happy to "go out for couple of weeks to milk the cows, drive a tractor, or a team of mules."[41] Women, too, volunteered, but Molloy thought they were of more use in the kitchen, helping the farmer's wife.[42] Even so, it was reported in September 1918 that many Regina women were out stooking sheaves on the surrounding farms.[43]

Boys joined the "Soldiers of the Soil" campaign, under the direction of L.E. McCormick of Regina, chairman of the provincial boys' work committee.[44] The Soldiers of the Soil recruited youngsters, aged fifteen to nineteen, from school or office jobs to work on farms at regular wages. Boys as young as thirteen to fourteen were enrolled, but they were sent only to the farms of friends or relatives.[45] The Soldiers of the Soil held a rally at Regina city hall on Sunday, 17 March 1918, for the "holy war against the Huns."[46] Jack Storey, an instructor at Regina College, "pictured to the lads" the sufferings of the people of France and Belgium, who did not have enough to eat. "Many a boy in this audience will find it hard going for a few days," he warned. "But stay with it. You'll get a kink in the back and your muscles will be tired but remember that what you are doing is for those overseas."[47] Within a few days, close to 100 boys from Regina Collegiate and 100 boys from the elementary schools signed up.[48] Over 2000 Saskatchewan boys were enrolled under the banner of the Soldiers of the Soil by mid-July.[49]

Labour shortages were evident in the city as well. "Boy! Oh boy! Where is that boy?" was the exasperated cry heard in telegraph companies, stores, and business offices. If the typist had her back turned, there would follow "a more or less mild expletive that you would never hear at a Sunday school picnic." "We could use quite a few right now," acknowledged Mr. Shamrock, superintendent of the Canadian Pacific Telegraph Company. "Boys could make as much as forty and fifty dollars a month with us just now, but there are none offering." "Boys," exclaimed Mr. K. Cornwell, local manager of the Robert Simpson Company, "why we have put advertisements in all the papers, and we could use a hundred more if we could get them." When school started in the fall, the shortage was even more acute. "The office boy will have a hard time to get away to football and hockey games this year," the *Daily Post* reported, "and has to have at least a couple of grandmothers die before his excuse will be accepted by the boss."[50]

Labour Unrest

The labour shortage and rising cost of living stimulated the growth of labour unions. By 1917 the Trades and Labor Council had almost twenty-five affiliated unions and a membership of over 1000.[51] About 250 marched in the Labour Day parade, led by Grand Marshal McRoberts, president of the teamsters' union, dressed in a cowboy outfit and sitting astride a chestnut steed. The ladies of the bookbinders' union put on an especially fine show, with their white dresses and purple sashes emblazoned with the number of their local. In the afternoon, there was a sports day at the exhibition grounds. The lieutenant-governor and premier were on hand to award the prizes, their presence a clear indication of the prestige enjoyed by the skilled trades in the community.[52]

In Saskatchewan there were only two strikes in each of 1914 and 1915. In 1916 the number jumped to six, fell to five in 1917, and rose again to nine in 1918 (seven of which were in Regina).[53] The city carpenters in March 1917 demanded a wage of fifty-five cents per hour for a nine-hour day, ten cents an hour higher than the 1916 scale.[54] They said the increase was justified because of the increased cost of living (consumer prices rose nearly 40 percent between 1916 and 1918).[55] The Regina Builders' Exchange offered fifty cents, which was rejected out of hand, and the carpenters threatened to go out on strike. The employers responded with an offer of fifty-five cents an hour for a ten-hour day, with Saturday afternoons off in the months of May through August. The carpenters accepted it. Although they had wanted a nine-hour day, the Saturday half-holiday during the summer translated to almost the same reduction in number of hours worked.[56]

The forty-six workers at the municipally owned powerhouse asked in February 1917 for a 10 percent increase in the salaries of all employees earning less than $125 a month. After a brief strike, lasting no more than a few hours, the city capitulated.[57] Another strike erupted at the city stables, where teamsters wanted the same salary in winter as they earned in summer ($70.20 per month). Management argued that this was unwarranted because in winter business was lighter and hours were shorter. The day after the strike began, Martin Besta arrived at the stables to take his team out. Jack Dusanko and Pete Zarona confronted him and said some "nasty things." Besta told the manager that Dusanko and Zarona had threatened to kill him if he did not support the strike. The man in charge of the stables went to the police, and Dusanko and Zarona were arrested for uttering threats.[58] Over the course of the day, fourteen more strikers went back to work, and by the next morning another seven were on the job. In short order, the strike was broken.

Regina postmen walked out on the morning of 23 July 1918, followed by postal clerks in the afternoon. They demanded payment of a promised war bonus, a minimum wage, and the appointment of a conciliation board.[59] The strikers presented their grievances before a joint meeting of city council, the Board of Trade, and the Wholesale and Retail Merchants' Association. All agreed with the request for a conciliation board, with the exception of Regina Member of Parliament W.D. Cowan, who condemned the strike and insisted that the postmen get back to work.⁶⁰ The Trades and Labor Council polled its affiliates to see whether they supported a sympathetic general walkout. The bricklayers and masons voted in favour, but before there was time for the other returns to come in, the federal government settled the strike, largely in the union's favour.⁶¹

Female telephone operators went on strike on 18 October 1918. The work stoppage was ill-timed, since the flu epidemic was raging and telephone communication was important to coordinate health services.⁶² The female telephone operators volunteered as nurses, but the gesture was not enough to counter the negative publicity caused by the walkout. Provincial Treasurer Charles Dunning blamed the strike on a "Bolshevik agitator" from the United States (a representative of the International Brotherhood of Electrical Workers). He said that the main issue was whether the people of Saskatchewan were to be allowed to manage their own telephone system without dictation from outsiders.⁶³ After two weeks, the union went back to work and submitted to a compromise settlement.⁶⁴

A federal order-in-council in April 1918 made it illegal, punishable by fine or imprisonment, "for any male resident of Canada between the ages of 16 and 60 to be living in idleness."⁶⁵ The so-called "anti-loafing law" was partly a response to the Great War Veterans' Association, who demanded that enemy aliens be put to work. International law forbade alien forced labour and, as the *Leader* reminded its readers, "to defy and repudiate international obligations is not the British way."⁶⁶ Further, if Canada bent the rules in this regard, the Germans might retaliate against Canadians held in prisoner-of-war camps. The anti-loafing law applied to all male residents, British and non-British alike, and therefore could not be seen as discriminatory. The Regina police clamped down on "loafers," "butterflies," and "IWWs" (Industrial Workers of the World). In May 1918, they arrested Joseph Kit, John Resoski, Mike Kosowski, John Lysck, Steve Lajoe, and John Hayish on charges of "playing cards for a period of two weeks in a public rooming house in the city."[67]

The absence of substantial secondary industry in Regina dampened labour militancy. In addition, the demand for high-priced farm labour acted as a safety valve. Discontented city labourers had only to hire themselves out to farmers, who were begging for assistance with seeding and harvesting. The Great War Veterans' Association functioned as a policing force, taking control, for example, of a protest meeting that was called in May 1918 to protest conscription. After the meeting, the association's members marched into Germantown, sending a clear message to the non-British population that patriotism trumped working-class solidarity. When in October 1918 the Borden government banned strikes and lockouts for the duration of the war, the Regina Trades and Labor Council talked vaguely about a strike to protest the measure, but nothing came of it.[68] The *Leader*, a self-proclaimed friend of organized labour, insisted that working-class grievances took a backseat to the war effort. It totally supported the federal government's decision to outlaw strikes: "In these trying times Canadian workmen, in common with all classes of Canadians, should confine themselves to just one kind of strike—that is, strike at the Hun with every ounce of strength and weight they possess. That is the way their comrades on the field of battle are striking; it is the way we should all be striking at home."[69]

Vacant Lot Gardens

The province's campaign to increase agricultural production had a spillover effect on Regina residents, who took up with enthusiasm backyard and vacant lot gardening. Gardens added to the supply of foodstuffs and brought down the cost of living.[70] The man who neglected horticulture was deemed "as much a slacker as the unmarried young man of military fitness who refuses to don the khaki."[71] Residents who did not have a backyard of their own, or who wished to grow more produce than their property would allow, applied to a central committee and were assigned a vacant lot. The committee arranged, at nominal cost, to have the lot ploughed and organized the bulk purchase of seed. Both the gardener and the city benefitted, the former from his harvest of vegetables and the latter from the elimination of "the unsightly vacant lot, breeding places for flies, mosquitoes and vermin of all kinds."[72]

The vacant lot gardening movement began in Regina in 1913, when seventy-two lots were cultivated.[73] The number increased to 650 in 1917, when gardening was transformed from congenial hobby to patriotic service. The vacant lot committee adopted the slogans "every potato a bullet" and "help win the war by producing."[74] Mayor Cowan's gardens were said to be "among the finest in the city."[75] Although he was too busy to wield the spade himself, he conscientiously supervised the work of others. Aldermen, professional men, merchants, professors, and men from every walk of life took up gardening,[76] as did women, including soldiers' wives.[77]

The value of the 1917 vacant lot crop (not including backyards) was estimated at between $20,000 and $25,000.[78] Masses of green foliage were seen everywhere. On the side facing the street gardeners planted profusions of "marigolds, sweet peas, California poppy, lobelia, geraniums, Joseph's coat, mignonet, hollyhocks, golden glow, zinnia, begonia, tulips, bicornis, stocks, phlox, dahlias, shasta daisy, bleeding hearts, sweet william, and poppies."[79] Some grouched that flowers were an unnecessary indulgence, but the *Leader* begged to differ.[80] While there was no excuse in wartime for "flaunting display, extravagant entertaining, and the spending of large sums of money upon non-essentials," modest pleasures were quite justified. People needed a bit of beauty in their lives. "We would like to see every war vegetable garden brightened with a border of flowers," counselled the *Leader*, "or at all events, with some little space devoted to flower culture."[81]

The vacant lot garden committee renamed itself the Regina Food Production Association in 1918 and set as its goal the cultivation of "every available foot of vacant property in and about the city of Regina."[82] Vegetable patches were now dubbed "war gardens,"[83] and gardeners enlisted as Soldiers of the Soil under the slogan, "Watch Reginans Grow."[84] "They may wear no uniform, display no badge, but blistered and calloused hands and aching backs will be honorable 'wounds,'" proclaimed the *Leader*. "Let everybody 'carry on' in the backyards and vacant lots."⁸⁵

"With flags and banners and pennants flying, with bells, auto horns, and whistles," the Regina Rotary Club donned stetsons and caps, gathered up hoes and rakes, and piled into their automobiles. Their destination was a ten-acre potato plot located three miles south of the city. Each motorcar displayed a sign on the windshield that read "Food Will Win the War: If You Cannot Fight Produce Food." After a tour of the business and residential districts, with much tooting of horns, the cavalcade headed out into the open country. Two Fordson tractors, on loan from the Saskatchewan Motor Company, churned the earth. The Rotarians took turns at the wheel, each trying to outdo the other in the straightness of his furrow. Cigars were distributed, and there was much "good-natured joshing." "Men who never expected to see a farm in their lives cavorted in the 'dirt' with evident enjoyment."⁸⁶ Premier William Martin demonstrated high aptitude at the wheel of a tractor, his furrow being rated as highly commendable.

Agriculture Minister W.R. Motherwell initiated a "Raise a Pig," campaign to alleviate the shortage of animal fats.⁸⁷ He asked urban municipalities to amend their bylaws to allow the raising of pigs within city limits. A Regina bylaw dating from 1907 stated that "no hog, pig, goat or cattle of any kind (except cows) shall be kept in any shed, stable, pen, byre, yard or other enclosure in the City situated at a less distance than seventy-five feet from the nearest dwelling-house and twenty-five feet from any public highway not being a lane." Further, "no person shall keep more than one hog, pig, goat within any shed, stable, pen, byre or other enclosure within the City." If a cow were kept, the stable had to be a minimum twenty feet from the nearest house. For two cows, the distance increased to eighty feet.⁸⁸ Motherwell thought it would be all right to have pigpens closer to dwelling places, but Regina medical health officer Dr. Malcolm Bow objected.⁸⁹ After looking into the matter carefully, he deemed the proposal "very prejudicial to the public health."⁹⁰ City council followed the advice, putting a damper on the Raise a Pig campaign.

Food Conservation

The rising cost of living led a group of "concerned citizens" to wait upon Mayor Cowan and ask for a public meeting. Accordingly, on 30 August 1917, a large crowd occupied the main floor and gallery of the city hall auditorium. Rev. Hugh Dobson, to the best of his ability, exposed the machinations of the fruit combine, in which fruit sellers, using different company names to fool the public, colluded to keep prices high.[91] He also quoted figures to show that the price of bacon was higher in Regina than in any other city in Canada, and bread more expensive than in any other locality in Saskatchewan, save for one.[92] The meeting resolved to investigate the reasons for the high cost of food and to consider the possibility of setting up a consumers' cooperative to purchase goods in bulk. It recommended that grocery and department stores institute a "cash and carry" system, offering discounts to customers who did not use the delivery service.[93] This would have the added benefit of releasing liverymen and horses for work on the farms.[94]

The investigating committee met with representatives of the Retail Merchants' Association on 18 September 1917. The grocers claimed that the high cost of living was due "to the extravagant method of living in vogue on the part of the public." Notwithstanding the high prices, the public was "buying as freely, if not more freely, than ever in the history of Regina's business." One merchant cited a special brand of bacon priced at fifty cents a pound. It sold so quickly that he could not keep it on the shelves, while another brand priced at thirty-five cents a pound remained unsold. The merchants asserted that they were not getting any more profits than before the war. J.K.R. Williams of R.H. Williams and Sons (Glasgow House) even offered to open his books to the inspection of the committee to prove that his prices were fair and just. As for the cash and carry system, the merchants explained that they could not offer a discount because, even if some people carried their groceries home, the delivery wagons would still have to cover the whole city and costs would remain about the same.[95]

The federal government in June 1917 appointed W.J. Hanna as food controller. Beef and pork were restricted in restaurants on certain days, and eating places were allowed only a fixed amount of sugar per number of meals served.[96] However, the main emphasis was on voluntary compliance, not coercive regulation. To publicize food conservation, food committees were established in each province. Saskatchewan in June 1918 had local committees in seven cities, twenty-five towns, forty-six villages, and ten rural communities.[97] They handed out "food service pledge cards"[98] and distributed pamphlets produced by the federal government with titles such as "Can, Dry and Store for Victory," "Eat More Fish," "One Week's Budget," and "War Meals."[99]

The main burden of food conservation fell on women, who had primary responsibility for food purchase and preparation. Miss Fannie Twiss, Director of Household Science in the provincial Department of Education, decreed that it was "unpardonable" to take a larger helping than one needed or to leave "fragments" on the plate.[100] The Regina Local Council of Women in January 1918 vetoed the serving of refreshments at the meetings of its forty affiliated societies and the holding of teas to raise funds for charitable causes.[101] "What do you think about afternoon teas when one is careful not to use white bread or sugar?" inquired Mrs. Stapleford of W.G. Rook, special representative of the National Committee on Food Conservation. "All serving of refreshments at other than meal times must be considered a waste," he replied, "except in the case of invalids or children or travelers."[102] His slogan was "Lick your plate or be licked."[103]

A window display at the Glasgow House department store featured a female figure representing the province of Saskatchewan, clad in gold crown and tricoloured drape, carrying a shield decorated with wheat sheaves. She supervised the loading of rail cars of No. 1 hard wheat bound for England, France, Belgium, and Italy. At one end of the window, a Canadian child sat at the table, partaking of a substantial breakfast and shamelessly discarding large quantities of food. At the other end, a European waif gazed longingly at the scraps in the garbage can.[104] The propaganda apparently had some effect. It was estimated in 1917 that the amount of kitchen refuse in Regina had declined 50 percent since the beginning of the war. This was calculated on the basis of the number of dump cars that were needed to haul trash to the city incinerator. The daily load in 1912 and 1913 had been thirteen or fourteen cars. In late 1917 it was down to between five and nine cars.[105]

The Local Council of Women took aim at hotels and restaurants, which were accused of serving oversized portions. The ladies also protested against cutting off crusts of bread for sandwiches, demanded the prohibition of the slaughter of calves or hogs weighing less than 200 pounds, and sought restrictions on the manufacture of candy and ice cream. Restaurants, they said, should not serve food at times other than recognized meal hours except to travellers. The same rule ought to apply to private homes (except in cases of sickness), although this, they acknowledged, would be hard to enforce.[106] "The government found it necessary to legislate in the matter of making those who can serve their country at the front," Mrs. Stapleford declared, "and those who have to remain behind should be legislated in the saving of food for those who have gone."[107] Mrs. Oman concurred: "Our men are proving themselves heroes on the field of battle, and the women of Canada are waiting for the moment to be called on."[108]

* * *

Food was at the heart of Saskatchewan's war effort. The province was built on wheat, never more so than during the war. The rural myth governed both the provincial psyche and the war economy. Regina did not get any munitions contracts that might have helped to diversify the economy from its dependence on agriculture. On the contrary, provincial and federal government leaders exhorted farmers to put every available acre into wheat. Feed the hungry Allies, they were instructed, and so they did. As a result, the rural myth—"In Wheat We Trust"—was consolidated and entrenched.

City dwellers became honorary farmers. Young men were pulled out of high school to seed the crop. Businessmen emptied their offices to bring in the sheaves. The vacant lot gardener was lauded as a war hero, the blisters on his hands the home-front equivalent of injuries sustained in combat. Wasting food was almost sinful. "I stopped all food waste in my kitchen and adopted war menus a year ago," boasted Mrs. D in June 1917, "not for the nation's sake exactly, but because I was forced to do so if I wanted to have anything left over for sending to my sons at the front." But "while we are pinching and scraping, whether in order to have food for ourselves or for the army, or for the Belgian and French refugees," a few men "are juggling with food prices." The solution in her mind was simple: "When three of the men responsible for prices upon the commonest foodstuffs going up while supplies are cornered are backed up and shot, perhaps we can economize to some purpose."[109]

Chapter 10

Religion and Social Reform

THE SOCIAL REFORM MOVEMENT IN WESTERN CANADA PREDATED THE war. The rapid expansion of the wheat economy after 1900, the flood of "foreign" immigrants, and the problems of rapid urban growth gave rise to demands for tariff reform, direct legislation, better schools, public health improvement, prohibition, women's suffrage, and other progressive measures. Although the movement crossed party lines, it was mostly identified in Saskatchewan with the Liberal Party, who liked to think of themselves as at the forefront of reform. The movement's "common philosophical denominator" was the social gospel, which emerged in the late 1800s and peaked during World War I.[1] Far from being sidetracked by the war, it reached new heights of intensity and influence.

The social gospel rested on the premise that Christianity is a "social religion," concerned primarily with "the quality of human relations on this earth." Expressed in more vivid terms, "it was a call for men to find the meaning of their lives in seeking to realize the Kingdom of God in the very fabric of society."² It took hold most notably in the Anglican, Methodist, and Presbyterian churches.³ Catholics were less interested. George Thomas Daly, priest at Holy Rosary Cathedral, said dismissively of social gospel adherents: "With them Christianity is nothing more than social welfare inspired by a vague philanthropy."⁴ The goal of "building the Kingdom of God on earth" sounded good, but what did it mean exactly? "What serves justice in particular situations?" "How do we create peace?" "On closer inspection," writes Pope Benedict XVI, "this whole project proves to be utopian dreaming without any real content, except insofar as its exponents tacitly presuppose some partisan doctrine as the content that all are required to accept."⁵

The social gospel was at heart a critique of individualism. Christians were called upon to set aside the pursuit of selfish goals for the sake of the common good. In the words of Walter Rauschenbusch, a major theologian of the social gospel in the United States, "The next great principle ... is *association*. Now men are free, but it is often the freedom of grains of sand that are whirled up in a cloud and then dropped in a heap, but neither cloud nor sand-heap have any coherence. New forms of association must be created. Our disorganized competitive life must pass into an organic cooperative life."⁶ Or, as progressive economist Richard T. Ely expressed it, "Social solidarity means that our true welfare is not an individual matter purely, but likewise a social affair, our weal is common weal; we thrive only in a commonwealth, our exaltation is the exaltation of our fellows, their elevation is our enlargement."⁷ The message was ideally suited to wartime, when individuals were called upon to make sacrifices for the sake of the nation, just as the men in uniform were doing.

Churches in Canada almost uniformly supported the war effort. Clergy and theological students enlisted along with citizens at large. Congregations "played an active role in recruiting, organized sewing and knitting circles, used their facilities to provide recreation for soldiers away from home, and promoted victory loans."⁸ Sermons were at times bloodcurdling. Challenged by the pacifist argument that it was impossible to imagine Jesus Christ plunging a bayonet into the heart of a human being, Samuel Dwight Chown, general superintendent of the Methodist Church, answered belligerently:

> For myself it is enough to know that Christ, as I perceive Him, would not stand with limp hands if a ruthless soldier should attempt to outrage His holy mother as the women of Belgium were violated. To Him all motherhood is sacred; nor would He retreat and give place to the armed burglar, breaking with murderous intent into His home; nor would He witness, without any effort to prevent it, the destruction of the civil and religious liberty which His teaching has enthroned in our British Empire. His manhood is without seam throughout, and I believe Canada is right in this war.[9]

For Chown and other patriotic churchmen, the war was not merely a grim necessity, but rather a righteous crusade, one that Christ Himself would have sanctified. As J.M. Bliss perceptively observes, "No Methodist could fight a war that Jesus would not have supported. Therefore Methodists could fight only a holy war."[10] The social gospel rejected the doctrine of original sin.[11] Bad behaviour was attributed mainly to environmental causes, such as lack of education, poor upbringing, inadequate social programs, and so on. But if this were true, if men are not inherently predisposed to evil, what had caused the war? Only one explanation was possible. It must have been the result of a flaw in the international system, such as the unequal distribution of wealth. The answer was to build the Kingdom of God on earth, not in Canada alone, but across the entire globe. The war became, in United States President Woodrow Wilson's words, "the war to end all wars" and the "war to make the world safe for democracy." Utopianism overwhelmed *realpolitik*. The war was not just being fought to protect national interests. It was a righteous crusade.

The Social Gospel and the Spirit of Sacrifice

Rev. Salem Bland, a faculty member at Wesley College in Winnipeg (a hotbed of the social gospel),[12] gave an address in Regina in 1917 on the occasion of the thirty-first anniversary of Metropolitan Methodist Church. He preached that for too long the church had focused on personal, rather than social, salvation. It was time to "bring forward its other foot" and bring about "social regeneration."[13] The Christian who was "wrapped up in devotional saintliness" and deaf to social needs was "a sort of voluptuary."[14] Theology was all right in its way, Bland grudgingly conceded, but "it would take a lot of it to save a man."[15] The interest of the church must lie "no longer in doctrine, but in the appealing, intelligent Jesus." It must take His message into "the realms of business, industry, and politics."[16] The soldier at the front cared little for theology or inter-denominational doctrinal squabbles. It mattered not to him whether the man standing next to him in the trench was a Presbyterian or a Baptist. He was a brother all the same, and each was prepared to lay down his life for the other. The war, for all its horror and devastation, was a kind of blessing. Better than any church could do, it was teaching the gospel of sacrifice and brotherhood.

Rev. S.D. Chown also spoke in Regina in the fall of 1917. Freshly returned from France, he gave an account of what he had seen. The men in the trenches were "incurably religious,"[17] but not in a traditional, formalistic way. They were drawn to "the religion of sacrifice."[18] Christ was the centre of their spiritual lives, especially Christ on the cross. Theological doctrine was of little consequence and denominational distinctions scarcely thought of. He recounted an incident where a Catholic boy, wounded in battle, was dying. His superior officer, a Protestant, fashioned a small cross of twigs and held it for the boy to kiss, "and he died happy."[19] Chown noticed that soldiers, on the whole, were "poor haters." When prisoners were brought in, they just laughed at them. They had no desire to do them harm.[20] Chown believed that he had witnessed true Christianity, the essence stripped of all ornamentation, institutional trappings, and superfluous theology.

In keeping with the theme of sacrifice, Rev. C.W. Brown preached a sermon at Regina's Wesley Methodist Church entitled "We're Only Worth Sacrifice if We Straighten Up."[21] He told the story of David, who, pursued by his enemies and with a price on his head, asked for a drink of water from the wells he had known in his boyhood. Three of his men took his words literally and made their way through enemy lines to obtain water from the wells he had named. Despite the great danger, they returned safely. When David learned what they had done, he took the water and poured it on the ground as an offering to God. Brown applied the story to the war. Canada's soldiers were risking their lives daily for their fellow citizens. How were Canadians going to use the gift of liberty that was being won for them? Should they not follow David's example and "pour out their strength and service before the Lord?"[22] "Ease as Usual, or Drink as Usual, or Self-Indulgence as Usual" was no longer acceptable.[23] The only valid response to the soldier's sacrifice was a consecrated life.[24]

The "altar of sacrifice" was a familiar image in wartime oratory. At the annual meeting of the Regina Canadian Club in 1918, it came up repeatedly, as though embedded in the mindset of the time. J.F. Frame described home-front patriotic service as "tokens of the fine spirit of our people and their determination to defend democracy. We have brought these offerings to the altar of sacrifice, and placed them there with a willing hand, but what are these contributions of ours as compared to the contribution of human life which the sons of Saskatchewan have made and are making for their ideals of freedom?"[25] S.J. Latta echoed, "your sons and mine are over yonder amid the shell puddle muck of Europe. Their lives are on the altar of their country." J.A. Allan followed with, "but France rose and if it is overcome it will be because none of her sons are left to be laid on the altar of sacrifice."[26]

The psychology of sacrifice lent fervour to the condemnation of the Big Interests, who placed private gain ahead of the common good. Manufacturers, who before the war had unjustly benefitted from high tariffs, now raked in exorbitant profits on munitions contracts. Workers and farmers—"the productive classes"—struggled to keep pace with the rising cost of living while bloated capitalists piled up fortunes. A keen sense of injustice drove the progressive movement. It led to the cry for "conscription of wealth" along with conscription of men. The war was interpreted as the struggle of the "people" against the "interests," democracy versus the privileged elite. Opposition to the enemy at home (the Big Interests) intensified hatred of the enemy abroad (Germany and Austria-Hungary) and vice versa.

Social Reformers Gather

On Sunday afternoons in Regina during the winter months, little was available in the way of public entertainment. The picture shows were closed, and church services were normally held in the morning or evening. It is not surprising, therefore, that the "People's Forum" was well attended. Initially held in the labour temple and later moved to city hall, it featured a different speaker each week holding forth on a subject of current interest, often having to do with politics or social reform. After the lecture, there were questions from the floor, and the discussions were often quite lively.[27] Rev. W.W. Andrews, a Methodist minister and former president of Regina College, gave a talk in March 1916 about the need for "re-organization in our religion."[28] Old ideas of sin and salvation, he contended, were outmoded. The new theology was "a moral trend," which, to his mind, meant "international peace, fair wages, Wednesday half-holidays, children's welfare, and the right to be well born."[29] "Evil might triumph for millions of years, but it was doomed at last."[30]

Rev. Hugh Dobson, a stalwart of the People's Forum, was the heart and soul of the social gospel in Regina. He had a finger in every progressive pie. His letters to the editor bombarded the newspaper; his missives to the premier kept the government on the path of reform. Born in rural Ontario in 1879, he graduated from Wesley College in Winnipeg. After serving some years as a Methodist minister in Grenfell, Saskatchewan, he was hired at Regina College, where he taught biology and "human relations." In 1913 he was appointed field secretary of the Evangelism and Social Service department of the Methodist Church.[31] Said one who knew him well: "Rev. Hugh Dobson, B.A., of Regina, is one of those personalities who instinctively challenge and arrest the attention of men. You may agree with Mr. Dobson or you may not, but you will have to listen to him."[32]

The social gospel inspired the Moral and Social Reform Council of Canada (later renamed the Social Service Council of Canada), an alliance of church groups, labour unions, and other reform-minded organizations.[33] The Saskatchewan branch, in which Dobson figured prominently, sponsored a Social Service Congress in Regina in November 1916. Delegates from all parts of the province came together at Metropolitan Methodist Church for three days of speeches and discussion. They were the vanguard of social reform, in the words of one delegate, "keen, alert, sober-minded reflective men, with strong impressive faces, most of them in the prime of physical vigor, and women who are realizing the part they are to play in the social and political life of the future. Clergymen, lawyers, doctors, businessmen, politicians, grain growers ... Saskatchewan's best, come together to study how to make their country a better place to live in."[34]

Dr. F.A. Corbett, the first speaker on 27 November 1916, took for his subject "The Right of the Child to be Well Reared." The child, he said, had "no right to be born in a slum, where it could get no fresh air and this child of such great possibilities should not be placed under conditions which would make for ill health and immorality."[35] Rev. H.T. Lewis, Zion Church, Moose Jaw, continued with "The Children and Their Right to Play." Children must learn to play wisely, he argued: "The boy who had learned to play well had added much to his moral education."[36] Rev. A.M. McIntosh of Saskatoon contributed "Children Were the Nation's Greatest Asset." He regretted that "the nation seemed to take more interest in preserving the prairie chicken and big game than it did in preserving its children. It often happened that a community paid more to get some one to look after its livestock than it paid for a teacher for its children."[37]

The featured lecturer of the evening was Raymond Robbins of Chicago, who began by remarking how pleased he was to have the "opportunity of speaking to the people of this great Anglo-Saxon province." His focus was Germany, especially the many failings and deficiencies of that benighted country. Its ruling class was too materialistic. It trusted too much in "science and the general staff." "Economic and material greatness was no guarantee of your civilization and the protection of your institutions, but the guarantee of these things lay in the principle of Christianity."³⁸

The next morning the congress looked into the immigration problem. Rev. J.A. Doyle pointed out that half of Saskatchewan's 300,000 non-English-speaking people were German or Austrian. Among the non-English were 40,000 Scandinavians "of whom nothing was to be feared as they were a progressive and loyal people."³⁹ Rev. Principal Graham of Moose Jaw discussed "Citizenship Standards," saying the question of the hour was not what Canadians should do for "foreigners," but rather "what we should do for ourselves in order to be good examples for the foreign-born." He anticipated a flood of immigration after the war, which, if not managed properly, would be disastrous. "The people must brush the dust from off their own ideals,"⁴⁰ he said. School inspector J.T.M. Anderson pleaded for a better understanding of the foreign-born population. The best singing of "O Canada" he had ever heard was in a German schoolhouse.⁴¹ Foreigners wanted to become good Canadian citizens, he believed. They needed only to be shown the way. Rev. Dobson thought that Canada soon would be "all white," by which he meant entirely free of alcohol. But reformers must stay on their guard. The liquor interests had plenty of fight left in them yet.⁴²

The afternoon session continued the temperance theme. Rev. H.G. Cairns dismissed the argument that prohibition interfered unduly with individual liberty. No man had the right to harm his brother or sister, he said: "The aim of the people should be community interest, not self-interest."⁴³ Likewise, individuals should not be permitted to marry whomever they chose, regardless of the social consequences. In particular, in his opinion, the feeble-minded and unfit must not be allowed to reproduce. Rev. John H. Nicol recommended that the "age of consent" be raised from fourteen years to eighteen, and the seduction laws made applicable to women up to the age of twenty-one. "A man who dishonored a girl was punished only one-seventh as severely as the man who stole his neighbor's calf and was penalized no more heavily than one who stole a railway ticket." ⁴⁴ Rev. R.L. McTavish condemned the attitude of society towards "fallen girls." The young man in such cases was thought to have committed a minor indiscretion, while the girl was ostracized. To all sinners, men and women alike, "Jesus left open the door of hope ... there was no respect of persons with God."[45]

Rev. Walter Western took issue with those who said the church was losing its hold on society. The congress itself was proof to the contrary. He was a firm believer in the efficacy of religious instruction at home. For the first five years of the child's life, the parents had a monopoly over instruction. The simple act of saying grace before meals could make a big difference in character formation. He was also of the view that "it was necessary to train our boys in chivalry and our girls in modesty." "Immoral dress" aroused in the minds of young men "thoughts and impulses which did not make for clean living."[46] Rev. Hugh Dobson, addressing the congress a second time, dealt with "Present Provision in the Province for the Care of Dependents, Defectives and Delinquents." There was a desperate need for a juvenile court and a detention home for girls under eighteen years of age. Mentally defective children must be "detained all their lives" and "not allowed to marry."[47]

At Tuesday's evening session, Dr. John MacKay, principal of Westminster Hall, Vancouver, tackled the issue of "Patronage." He said the topic could not be considered without reference to the democratic ideals "for which our bravest and best are dying." "Vast corporations," such as the railway companies, had seized control of the nation, suborning political parties and the newspapers. It was essential that all political donations be made open and transparent. "Absolute publicity as to where money came from and where it went would remove danger from many a politician's path. Men who abused their trust must be punished and severely," said MacKay.[48]

W.R. Motherwell, Saskatchewan's Minister of Agriculture, blamed the protective tariff for the political corruption in the land. In his words, it was "the most subtle and insidious species of graft that can be thought of." For every dollar taken out of the taxpayer's pocket to pay for legitimate government services, he added, "two dollars or more is being legally grafted from the other pocket by means of the artificially inflated prices charged by home manufacturers and for which the tariff is designed and so eagerly retained and perpetuated." Peter (the honest producer) was robbed to pay Paul (the Big Interests), blighting politics and discrediting public life.[49]

The final speaker of the evening, Rev. George C. Pidgeon, president of the Social Service Council of Canada, reflected on the core meaning of the social gospel. Moral reformers, he said, had often been dismissed as mere dreamers, but their success in overthrowing the liquor trade showed that they were a force to be reckoned with. Canada was engaged in a struggle for her very soul, striving to build a righteous nation worthy of the victory her soldiers were fighting for on the battlefields of Europe. The call of service vanquished the spirit of selfish individualism: "We were coming more and more to see that the welfare of the whole community depended on the welfare of each." [50]

The next morning, T.M. Molloy, secretary of the Saskatchewan Labour Bureau, took up the question of "The Worker and His Wage." Labour was not just a commodity to be bought and sold. The "material things of the earth" were intended for all human beings, he said, not just the favoured few. It followed that the worker was "entitled to at least a living wage and as much more as he can command or the industry will bear." Molloy noted sardonically that he had never heard of an employer having been expelled from a church for having paid his workers less than a living wage, and yet this was a sin as grievous as any other. Nor was the so-called "right of free contract" an excuse for low wages. Said Molloy, "One might as well argue that the man held up at the point of a revolver is free to refuse to hand over his money and his valuables."[51]

Rev. S.L.W. Harton approached the topic from another direction. He said that "no man who is able to work has a right to live on the toil of others; every man, therefore, is under obligation to seek to the limit of his ability to find employment." The right to work implied a duty to support oneself, and the fulfillment of this obligation required "keeping oneself fit for work, the performance of one's work efficiently, the maintaining of a deep sense of responsibility, the looking to service and not accumulation as the idea, and other things."[52] Mrs. C.O. Davidson, who had been a member of the women's suffrage delegation to the legislature in February 1916, gave an overview of "Women in Industrial Life." She expected that women's role in the paid workforce would continue to expand, as had already happened during the war. Mrs. John McNaughton, president of the women's section of the Saskatchewan Grain Growers' Association, said she was encouraged by the fact that women were "attempting to change the color of political life today in federal, provincial, municipal and school government," while Rev. Mr. Reekie, superintendent of Baptist missions in Saskatchewan, praised women's involvement in social and religious activities: "Instead of the bridge fiend and money squanderer had come the woman who studied the problems of the country and gave her assistance in their solving."[53]

Wednesday afternoon, Rev. T. Albert Moore, DD, lectured on "The Ideal Social Service Organization—National, Provincial and Municipal," emphasizing the importance of coordination, efficiency, and economy to achieve concrete results. Rev. George Dorie dealt with "The Rural Church," praising the ability of small communities to work together for common purposes. Municipal hail insurance, he said, constituted "a victory for the spirit of Jesus Christ." H.E. Sampson spoke on "Modes of Gambling, Legislation and Enforcement." He condemned gambling as a double evil, one that "cursed him who won and him who lost."[54]

The rest of the afternoon was given over to Rev. Principal MacKay's speech on "The Social Obligations of Christianity." He believed that the war showed daily and ever more clearly that all men were neighbours, and added that "the supreme obligation of the Christian was the principle of love to God and love to man.... All religion," he affirmed, "was essentially a social passion." Many evils had to be addressed, and while it was impossible to do everything at once, a start had to be made. Critics and detractors claimed that social reformers had forgotten theology and were not preaching the true gospel. MacKay could not agree. To work for social reform *was* to preach the gospel. He added: "The first business of the State was to prevent wrongdoing, and if the State neither prevented nor punished wrongdoing, the nation had to stand responsible for wrongdoing."[55]

In the final session, the congress approved a number of resolutions: support for the better schools campaign, elimination of political patronage, supervised playgrounds for children, prohibition of racetrack gambling, raising the age of consent from fourteen to eighteen years, compulsory registration of tuberculosis and venereal diseases, direct legislation, improved care of mental defectives, and minimum wage laws. The state, the congress proclaimed, must "not forget the human values which may be served by the more equitable distribution of wealth and other forms of social justice." Its duty was to "limit the prizes open to speculation" and "conserve for industrial enterprises the legitimate rewards." "Conservation of the general happiness and morality of our people" was "the paramount end of government."[56]

By vote of the congress, the Social and Moral Reform Council was renamed the Saskatchewan Social Service Council. It reached out to a number of supporting organizations, including Christian churches, the WCTU, Local Council of Women, Equal Franchise League, Grain Growers, Women Grain Growers, Homemakers' Clubs, and Royal Templars.[57] Although Regina Roman Catholic Archbishop Mathieu was made one of the honorary presidents (along with Lieutenant-Governor Lake and Anglican Bishop Newnham),[58] the congress was mostly an Anglo-Protestant confabulation, British Canadians talking to other British Canadians about how to transform Saskatchewan in line with Anglo-Saxon Protestant beliefs. The agenda ran the entire gamut of social reform from gambling to age of consent, supervised playgrounds to the protective tariff, cleaning up politics to the minimum wage. The Protestant wartime mindset conflated domestic reform with the war against Germany. A new world was dawning, and social gospelers were its harbingers and foot soldiers.

Social Reconstruction

In 1917 the Saskatchewan Social Service Council articulated a "win-the-war platform for a united Canadian people."[59] It called for the conservation of resources, beginning with the termination of the "quite unnecessary" manufacture of automobiles. Rev. Hugh Dobson complained that people had "gone wild on motoring." Gasoline was being wasted on frivolous "joy riding."[60] Food, too, was being squandered. It cost twenty-five cents to get a baked potato on the Canadian Pacific Railway diner "and not a large one either."[61] Even so, people were leaving too much on their plates. Portions were obscenely large, with enough meat, Dobson said, to feed an entire family. The platform called for "national control of production, distribution and conservation; fixed prices on staple necessities of food and fuel, immediate and drastic control of coal and gasoline; [and] mobilization and control of all transportation facilities in the interests of the nation."[62] The needs of war demanded a massive increase of government involvement in the economy.

The Saskatchewan Social Service Council further proposed a national insurance program to deal with unemployment, accident, and old-age dependency. "If we are going to maintain unity and freedom from dissension," Dobson contended, "we must deal not only with the soldier who has given himself for his country, but also for the labouring man who finds himself, through no fault of his own, at the mercy of charitable people in our seasonal and cyclical periods of unemployment."[63] To pay for this, he advocated a progressive income tax, "amounting to expropriation of personal incomes above $10,000 and a surtax on unused and unoccupied land for speculation purposes."[64]

Infringement on personal freedom and confiscation of wealth were considered to be necessary sacrifices for the common good. According to the win-the-war platform, "All wealth is a social product. No hermit can amass a fortune.... The public, therefore, have a measure of right in all wealth won by private enterprise." The nation had "the same right to call into the direct service of the state the total wealth of its citizens as it has to demand the surrender of their lives. Justice demands that we should not ask the latter without a greater call upon the former."[65] Also required were the nationalization of transportation systems, natural resources, and "industries concerned in the manufacture and storage of food, and liquid and solid fuels," the fixing of "a minimum living wage as the first item in the cost of every manufactured article," and regulation of "the hours of labor and the working

225

conditions of our workers such as shall make the highest efficiency in the service of the common weal."[66]

The council also favoured a Dominion Board of Education to coordinate educational programs in all the provinces (disregarding the British North America Act, which placed education within provincial jurisdiction). The board was to aid in the training of teachers, the setting of educational standards across the country, and the creation of vocational and industrial training programs. In addition, the government was urged to establish a Dominion Board of Health with a mandate to safeguard public health and a Bureau of Child Welfare to tackle infant mortality, child labour, and poor school attendance. The formation of sound public policy depended upon the "scientific study of social economic conditions and the conservation of our human resources." Accordingly, the council supported the creation of a Dominion Bureau of Surveys to collect social data on which to base legislation.[67]

The council worried that the Big Interests had too much influence in shaping public attitudes. Consequently, it asked that "every newspaper, magazine, trade journal or other periodical that seeks to influence public opinion or give information to the public ... publish a sworn statement of the names of the owners and directors."[68] The Saskatchewan Social Service Council supplied articles, news items, and editorials to friendly newspapers and magazines, and distributed leaflets through Sunday schools, churches, the WCTU, Grain Growers' locals, fraternal societies, Great War Veterans' Association, Army and Navy Veterans, and other groups. It set up a speakers' bureau and cooperated with the provincial departments of Education and Health to distribute pamphlets through the schools. It experimented with non-print media, including slides for movie theatres "containing striking sentences of social service import to be thrown on the screen between films."[69]

To finance its activities, the council received an annual grant of $1500 from the provincial government.[70] Dobson corresponded on a regular basis with Premier Martin, nurturing a relationship that was beneficial to both parties. Martin secured his hold over the "progressive" voting bloc, while Dobson lobbied for pet projects, such as the Babies' Welfare Exhibit and Conference. In 1916, 2283 children under the age of five died in Saskatchewan, a mortality rate of 103.3 per 1000 live births. (In 1950, by contrast, the rate was 31.8 per 1000 live births.[71]) The Social Service Council aimed to cut the infant mortality rate in half through the introduction of baby clinics, safe water supplies, sanitary sewage disposal, and pasteurized milk.[72]

Better Babies' Week at the Regina exhibition in July 1916 featured lectures on baby- and childcare, which were printed up in the daily newspapers. Cash prizes of ten, seven, and four dollars were awarded for healthy babies in various categories, depending on the age and sex of the infant. Each entrant was scored on a 1000-point chart prepared by the American Medical Association, which covered every aspect of the child's mental and physical development. Seventy-two percent (147 out of 204) of the contestants were found to be "abnormal" in some way,[73] mainly because of adenoids, enlarged tonsils, or decayed teeth.[74]

The Social Service Council also campaigned for better control of venereal disease. It was a serious health problem among Canada's soldiers, by far the largest single cause of hospitalization during the war.[75] More than 10 percent of enlisted men were diagnosed with the disease.[76] After the armistice, "venereals" were kept in England until they were cured, but there was still a risk that the infection would spread.[77] In Saskatchewan in 1919, 205 cases were reported among civilians and seventy-one among military personnel. Eight percent of prisoners had syphilis and 65 percent of female inmates were diagnosed with gonorrhoea.[78]

Rev. Dobson addressed the topic at the Peoples' Forum in January 1918, boldly defying the taboo against discussing sexual matters in public.[79] A controversy arose over the showing in Regina of the film *Damaged Goods*. Although approved by both the Canadian Medical Society and the Saskatchewan Censor Board, it was considered too risqué for the public. Dobson arranged a private screening for a select group of prominent citizens, who were asked to vote on it. Forty-seven voted in favour of allowing it to play in the theatres, and only three were against.[80] Among the opponents was chief librarian J.R.C. Honeyman, who thought it was a good film, but people would go to see it for the wrong reasons.[81]

The opposition did not deter Dobson, and eventually his efforts were rewarded. In January 1918 the provincial government made it compulsory for anyone suffering from venereal disease immediately to secure treatment from a qualified doctor and to remain under treatment until the disease had been cured. Further, the physician was required to report the case to the provincial health authorities within three days of the first visit of the patient. The report had to include detailed information about the patient, including age, marital relations, occupation, and probable source of contagion. The patient's name was omitted, except when he or she failed to keep up the treatment. In such cases, the name was given to the provincial Commissioner of Health, "who was empowered to take such means as may be required to arrange for the treatment of the patient."[82] Dobson expressed his gratitude to the premier: "The action you have taken will give a good lead to the other provinces and will be a challenge to our Dominion Government."[83]

The Social Service Council was equally pleased in August 1917 when the Province established juvenile courts and appointed as the first judge Miss Ethel MacLachlan, formerly superintendent of the Neglected and Dependent Children's Branch.[84] The act separated young offenders (sixteen and under) from the adult criminal population, both as to legal procedure and type of punishment meted out. Emphasis was placed on moral guidance, education, and encouragement rather than retribution.[85] This reform legislation was followed in November 1917 by the passage of the Mothers' Pensions Act, which gave an allowance to "any mother, who is a widow and who on account of poverty is unable to take proper care of her child and children and who is otherwise a proper person to have the custody of such child or children."[86] The allowance was not to exceed three dollars a week for each child. However modest and hedged with qualifications, it marked a shift in social policy from laissez-faire individualism to the collectivism of the welfare state.

Moral Policing

Dobson said the aim of the social gospel was to build a "Christian democracy,"[87] the same phrase Norman Black used in describing the goal of the better schools movement.[88] The term comprehended both social welfare and moral policing, as in the prohibition movement. While the moral agenda was generally well received during the war, the proposals occasionally went too far for the broad mass of people to accept. When the WCTU chastised Canadian soldiers for smoking cigarettes and drinking rum, the *Leader* retorted that those who were fighting for their country must not be made the "targets of every oddity allowed under the name of reform."[89] Soldiers were not "wayward children," and war was not a "Sunday School picnic." The men were passing through "a fiery furnace, which may have purified them more than ourselves at home amid ease, comfort and idle temptations."[90]

As they were wrapping Christmas parcels for the boys overseas in 1917, the ladies at Wesley Church in Regina made a startling discovery. Tucked among the socks, neckties, and boxes of chocolates were decks of playing cards, also known as "the devil's prayer book." An emergency meeting of the church board was called to discuss the situation. Complicating matters was the fact that each package contained a message saying that the parcel was being sent courtesy of the pastor, seeming, therefore, to give the church's blessing to card playing and possibly even gambling. It was decided to open all the packages and remove all the cards before the parcels were mailed out.[91]

Towards the end of the war, the panicky sense of a decline in moral standards began to unsettle social reformers. The Social Service Council detected a "growing looseness in regard to moral conditions throughout the country,"[92] and a deplorable "prevalence of prostitution and adultery, Sabbath desecration, and other forms of violation."[93] Irresponsible parents were "sowing to the wind in the excessive liberties granted children." Young girls roamed the streets without supervision "from early evening until midnight or after."[94] Rev. Dobson said he had heard the "most revolting remarks being made by men on the street as young women and girls passed."[95]

For All We Have and Are

Moral conditions in Regina were such "as to put the large American cities to shame."[96]

The Local Council of Women decried the "endless dancing"[97] to which girls were addicted, risking their reputations, "if not their moral safety."[98] Dances, if they must continue, should be by invitation only. The IODE went so far as to cancel the dances it had been sponsoring to raise money for war charities. They decided that the funds obtained, even for so worthy a purpose, could not compensate for the loss of sexual decorum and female modesty.[99] The Local Council of Women joined with the Social Service Council in July 1918 to ask city council to provide better lighting in public parks and more frequent police patrols. The aldermen demurred, citing the prohibitive $900 cost, which they said the city could not afford.[100] More probably, the self-righteous zeal of the moral reformers was beginning to wear a little thin.

* * *

"Shall we be found on the side of democracy and the common people?" Regina Methodist minister Dr. Robert Milliken asked in a sermon in September 1917.[101] If Canada lost the battle for "social righteousness," all the sacrifices of the war would have been in vain. "We feel as if we were in the hands of the capitalists and the big interests on every hand," he lamented, "and when we find so much grafting in the necessities of life we feel our helplessness."[102] Ultimately, he felt, "Democracy and God" would prevail: "The finger of God was to be seen pointing the way down through history and it was through the experiences of nations in the past that we were to find the way of right and justice."[103]

"Democracy and God," the pastor assumed, went together, which justified both the war against Germany and the war against oppression and injustice at home. The social gospel built on the Saskatchewan tradition of state action to advance socio-economic equality, whether through cooperative elevators, government-owned telephones, municipal hospitals, or laws to protect workers. It fuelled the battle against the Big Interests and their wartime profiteering. The war did not divert Regina and Saskatchewan from social progressivism, but rather lent new passion to the cause, leading to practical reforms such as babies' welfare clinics, improved venereal disease control, juvenile courts, and mothers' pensions. It also inspired moral policing and the denial of individual liberty for the sake of what was alleged to be for the good of all, notably the ban on liquor consumption. Sacrifice was the highest ideal, especially when other people had to do the sacrificing. "Nothing so needs reforming," Mark Twain quipped, "as other people's habits."[104]

Chapter 11

Returned Soldiers

WOUNDED AND MEDICALLY DISCHARGED SOLDIERS BEGAN RETURNING TO Canada as early as January 1915. In June of that year the Borden government created the Military Hospitals Commission (MHC) to look after their needs.[1] The main priority was to find work for veterans at suitable wages, thereby enabling them to reintegrate into civilian life. It was agreed that the care of the disabled was "an obligation which should fall primarily on the state."[2] The commission acquired scores of buildings across Canada for use as hospitals, tuberculosis sanatoria, and mental asylums. It also built a factory in Toronto for the manufacture of "artificial legs, boots, glass eyes, and face masks for the hideously scarred."[3]

The federal government appointed the Canadian Board of Pension Commissioners in June 1916 to administer pensions for the permanently disabled. The amount of the pension varied with the severity of the disability and its "attributability" to war service. If it could be demonstrated that the soldier had a pre-existing medical condition bearing on the case, the pension was correspondingly reduced. The medical advisers were very strict. Only 5 percent of claimants received the top rate. The vast majority got 25 percent or less.[4] The system invited endless complaint and petitions for better treatment. Veterans' organizations took up the cause and eventually brought about some modest improvements.[5]

The Saskatchewan Military Hospitals Commission, the provincial branch of the federal body, was appointed in November 1915, with Mr. Justice E.L. Elwood, of the Supreme Court of Saskatchewan, as chair.[6] "The duty before us now," he told a Regina meeting on 19 November, "is to enable returning soldiers to be able to get their living."[7] He suggested that each city, town, and municipality establish a committee to scout possible job opportunities. The lists would be sent to a central clearinghouse in Regina. W.B. Willoughby, leader of the provincial Conservative Party, raised the case of two soldiers recently returned to Moose Jaw. He said they had been without means of support for "more than a few days," until, finally, work had been found for them at the post office. "What was the Government doing?" shouted a man at the back of the hall. Willoughby said he did not wish to blame anyone. He wanted merely "to see what practical men can do in the solution of the question that lies before us."[8] A resolution was passed to encourage the establishment of a Returned Soldiers' Welcome and Aid League in each community in the province, with a mandate to give each returning soldier a "hearty welcome" and to assist him in finding a job.[9]

The Regina Returned Soldiers' Welcome and Aid League was to have been founded on 30 November 1915, but very few people showed up. It was decided to call a second meeting and, this time, extend a special invitation to women, whose participation was deemed essential for the organization to succeed.[10] The meeting on 15 December attracted a large crowd, including representatives from a wide variety of churches and community organizations. Mrs. A.D. Miller of the IODE assured the men that women "were only waiting for the opportunity to do their share."[11]

The League's first project was to help furnish the convalescent home at St. Chad's College. Since almost all the students at the Anglican boys' school had enlisted, the building was practically empty and the diocesan authorities willingly handed it over to the Military Hospitals Commission. Although the federal government covered the basic costs, the league was called upon to supply the "extras."[12] The official opening took place on 9 April 1916. The Sixty-Eighth Battalion string orchestra provided the music, and the rooms were fragrant with daffodils and hyacinths. Guests brought gifts of preserves, jams, tinned and fresh fruits, cigarettes, tobacco, books, magazines, sandwiches, and cakes. A small boy lugged a large picture, which had been hanging on the wall of his bedroom. It depicted a fierce-looking British bulldog guarding the Union Jack. He said he wanted to give it to the soldiers for their hospital.[13]

Twenty desks were installed in the home and vocational classes offered in general subjects, bookkeeping, mechanical drawing, and telegraphy.[14] A poultry department was established with seventy-five pens of White Leghorns, White Wyandottes, Plymouth Rock, and other registered stock.[15] W.P. Hewitt, the agricultural instructor, arranged for the ploughing of two acres of land surrounding the college to set up a miniature experimental farm.[16] However, the main centre for vocational training was the University of Saskatchewan in Saskatoon.[17] Instruction in agriculture was emphasized, even though most of the soldiers showed a marked preference for motor mechanics and engineering.[18] The veterans were told that while life on the farm "for the first four or five years may be rough and hazardous yet there is a splendid future, a certain return and an independence which cannot be found anywhere else with such little effort."[19]

For the severely injured and bedridden, time dragged and boredom set in. The men were encouraged to take up knitting, an activity that settled the nerves. "And the work is not the rough style that might be expected," a discerning visitor noted. "Some splendid pieces of Hardanger, cross stitch, fancy matting, etc. were shown this week, and the work would easily stand alongside some of the best exhibits in the fancy work department at the recent exhibitions in Regina."[20] A large convalescent home was opened in Moose Jaw in 1917, supplementing the beds at St. Chad's. In addition, a sanatorium for soldiers with tuberculosis (which affected 8571 of the close to 600,000 members of the Canadian Expeditionary Force[21]) took up quarters in Regina's refurbished Earl Grey school. Large glass-enclosed balconies were built at the east and south sides of the building so that patients could get plenty of fresh air and sunshine. St. Chad's continued as the main clearing hospital, where returning soldiers temporarily resided until it was determined where they should receive treatment.[22]

In March 1917 the provincial government created the Saskatchewan Returned Soldiers' Employment Commission. It carried out a "careful and comprehensive industrial and commercial survey of the available sources of employment for returned soldiers within the province" and arranged for their placement in suitable positions.[23] As of February 1918, 2345 men had returned to Saskatchewan, of whom 1347 had been placed in jobs. Sixty-one were still waiting for employment, while the remainder were either undergoing rehabilitation and retraining or were too disabled to work.[24]

Harris Turner, a blind veteran who had been elected to the provincial legislature in 1917 as one of the soldiers' representatives, introduced a motion to dismiss all the men in government service who were capable of combatant military service and replace them with discharged veterans. Premier Martin opposed the motion. While he agreed with the preferential hiring of returned men,[25] he said that he "would regret if the impression was to be permitted to get abroad in Saskatchewan that the civil servants had not done their duty in the matter of enlisting … if the members of this assembly will go through the different offices in the buildings they will find few—hardly any—individuals liable to call."[26] George Bell, Minister of Telephones, mentioned that there were only five men in the province with the technical skills necessary to maintain and repair the automated equipment. If they were to enlist, telephone service would break down. The premier neutralized Turner's motion with an amendment that approved the actions the government had already taken for the raising of men for military service. The amendment carried, with only Turner voting against it.[27]

The Regina Returned Soldiers' Welcome and Aid League tried to ensure that all returning soldiers were greeted at the train station, but there were occasional glitches. Four wounded soldiers, who arrived Sunday morning, 27 August 1916, were not met by anyone. They wandered for hours in the hot sun, until a fellow returned soldier directed them to St. Chad's Convalescent Home.[28] "If they [the Returned Soldiers' Welcome and Aid League] can't do the work, they should leave it alone," blustered the Trades and Labor Council.[29] James Balfour, president of the Aid League, said that the military authorities in Winnipeg had failed to alert the committee in Regina of the soldiers' impending arrival. The information had not reached the secretary until an hour after the men had disembarked at the station.[30] To ensure that such incidents would not happen again, the League appointed seven reception committees, each consisting of six people. Two committee members, working in rotation, were assigned to meet every Winnipeg train.[31]

Over 600 citizens gathered at the train station on 25 March 1917 to welcome a large group of returning soldiers. As the "limping heroes" stepped from the rail car, a "mighty cheer" went up. The soldiers were escorted first to the clearing depot at the McCallum-Hill building and then to luncheon at the Assiniboia Club.[32] The ritual repeated itself on 1 April 1917, when a party of twenty-five men arrived. The Ninety-Fifth Rifles band, the Boy Scouts, Salvation Army band, and Army and Navy Veterans formed the welcoming entourage. At the Assiniboia Club, Chief Justice Sir Frederick Haultain and Rev. Murdoch MacKinnon paid tribute to the men for the sacrifices they had made in the service of their country.[33]

A Red Cross train pulled in on Sunday, 8 July 1917, with four cars full of soldiers, a hospital car, a diner, and two baggage cars. The hospital car had thirteen patients under the care of twenty-four-hour duty nurses. The train was covered with posters bearing the names of battles in France where Canadians had fought.[34] Over 3000 people came out to greet the men. Women circulated among the soldiers, "giving dainties here, cigarettes there, lighting a 'fag' for the men who had one arm only or could not use the two they still carried, for among the fighters who came back yesterday, several carried their arms in a sling, others had arms straightened out unable to bend, and others were hobbling along on crutches."[35] At Christmas 1916, the Returned Soldiers' Welcome and Aid League hosted a party at the Legislative Building. The guests dined at long tables "brilliant with crimson-shaded candles and baskets of fruit," and each soldier was presented with the gift of a briar pipe.[36]

Veterans organized their own entertainments. The Twenty-Eighth Battalion held a reunion in Regina on 31 October 1917, the third anniversary of the unit's mobilization. They gathered from all over the province and parts of Manitoba, some on crutches, others missing an arm or an eye.[37] The soup was "French Drizzle Somme"; the entrées, "Aerial Torpedo Sausage," "Bully Beef," "Turkey, Hun Dressed," "Duck Whizz Bangs and Coal Boxes"; the vegetables "Bayoneted Murphies," "French Peas à la Commode"; and the dessert "Sandbag Pudding, Shrapnel Sauce."[38] Sergeant J.R. Renton toasted the "dear dead, the comrades who were left under the sod of France."[39] Friends gathered in small groups, reliving old times. In one corner, the battle at St. Eloi was refought; in another, bomb-throwing techniques were debated. Corporal Tallet thumped out favourite tunes on the piano. Spontaneously, it was decided to send a telegram to the men still at the front. "Stay with the game," the telegram read, until victory is won and "the ideals of the battalion perpetuated."[40]

Veterans' Organizations

It did not take long for returning soldiers to form associations to represent their common interests. By 1917 most cities in Canada had a veterans' organization of some sort, and in Winnipeg on 10 to 13 April, delegates from a number of provinces gathered to form the Great War Veterans' Association (GWVA). A year later, also at Winnipeg, a pre-war club of mostly British veterans reconstituted the national Army and Navy Veterans (ANV). Both veterans' organizations "veered to the political right." They were generally not attracted to socialism or Bolshevism. Nevertheless, as Desmond Morton notes, "veterans' conservatism had an egalitarian, radical edge."[41] Members of the GWVA addressed one another as "comrade," and they did not accept passively the veterans' benefits Ottawa handed down. Instead, they argued their case before parliamentary committees and lobbied ministers on pensions, medical care, retraining, government hiring policies, assistance for widows and children, and the whole gamut of issues relating to veterans' welfare. Their claims were based on a sense of moral entitlement, not an appeal for sympathy. They had served their country, and they expected their country to do something for them.

The first inkling of the formation of a veterans' organization in Regina came in September 1916, when Col. G.F. Carruthers of the Army and Navy Veterans of Winnipeg paid a visit. The result was an ANV local with thirty members, which was open to veterans of all previous wars, not just World War I. Carruthers, himself a veteran of the Fenian Raids of the 1860s, promised that the organization would work in cooperation with the Returned Soldiers' Welcome and Aid League.[42] Both shared the same goal of facilitating the readjustment of the returned soldier to civilian society.

In May 1917, just before the provincial election, an anonymous notice appeared on the bulletin board of the ANV clubroom:

> Comrades: there is about to be a split in the ranks of the Army and Navy Veterans owing to the older veterans putting aside interests of the returned soldiers to back party politics.... Veterans who have served in military units and the Strathcona Horse of ancient days, are looking to their own welfare. While we are pleased to have their advice we trust that more consideration will be given the returned soldier in future, before the split takes place. Signed A RETURNED SOLDIER.[43]

The dissenter was likely a supporter of the Great War Veterans' Association, which had recently held its founding convention in Winnipeg. Unlike the ANV, its membership was restricted to veterans of the current war who had served overseas. Those in the military who stayed at home were given status as non-voting associate members.[44] The Regina GWVA seceded from the ANV on 7 June 1917. They resolved to stay out of partisan politics and to focus their efforts exclusively on the welfare of returned soldiers.[45]

Controversy erupted over the arrangements for the soldier's vote in the June 1917 provincial election. Rather than allowing Saskatchewan's 27,000 overseas soldiers to vote for candidates in their home ridings, the Martin government created three special "soldiers' constituencies." One MLA represented soldiers quartered in England; the second, those in France; and the third, men serving in Belgium. Premier Martin argued that the MLAS chosen in this manner would ably represent the soldiers' point of view in the legislature. The Conservatives saw the matter differently. The soldier vote was thought to be pro-Tory because of Borden's recent decision to implement conscription. If their votes were distributed in the existing constituencies, they might help defeat the Liberals in close contests.

When the government introduced the soldiers' voting act, Conservative MLA D.J. Wylie protested that "he would rather cut off his right hand than be a party to bringing such a damnable thing as the present bill before the house.... Talk about Prussianism and Kaiserism," he spluttered, "well, this takes the cake." It was "the most flagrant false political move ever made by the government and the men in Flanders and France today are just waiting to get the vote to put the government out of power."[46] Wylie wondered why provincial Treasurer Charles Dunning, only thirty-one years old and apparently in robust health, had not signed up. "It's dirty tactics," Dunning retorted. "I don't have to make a personal explanation to any man in this house. The honorable gentleman can secure the information he wants from his friends at Ottawa, from R.B. Bennett, from Sir George Foster, from any of the ministers. Play the man."[47]

The Regina ANV condemned the government's soldiers' representation bill, characterizing it as "class legislation."[48] Both the 179th and 217th battalions, who were in training in the province, signed petitions against it, as did the Moose Jaw Returned Soldiers' Association.[49] The Great War Veterans' Association refrained from comment. On election day, 26 June 1917, the Liberals captured fifty-one seats, the Conservatives seven, and the

Nonpartisan League (a farm protest group) one. The Liberals polled 57 percent of the popular vote to the Conservatives' 36 percent, the remainder divided among Nonpartisan, Independent, and Labour candidates.[50] "In many churches on Sunday," wrote Conservative leader Willoughby in an election post-mortem, "the priests openly said a Conservative vote was a vote for conscription. The vast majority of priests in Saskatchewan are French or German speaking.... It is true we obtained some votes on conscription but not one for 20 we lost."[51] The Liberal machine performed with customary efficiency. A Conservative worker noted: "At all the polls where the foreign born voted were Interpreters who were rather overzealous in the masters' cause. As we could not understand the language we were at a great disadvantage. At my own Poll I caught him several times placing his thumb where they should make their mark."[52] Premier Martin handily defeated Brigadier-General J.F.L. Embury, the Conservative candidate in Regina. In Germantown (eight polls), Martin polled 529 to Embury's 178, for a majority of 351. In the city as a whole (51 polls and 5984 votes cast), the premier's margin of victory was 856.[53] He would have won even without the "foreign" vote, but the race would have been closer.

In the wake of the election, the GWVA moved to consolidate its position as the leading veterans' organization. It established itself on a province-wide basis at a convention in Saskatoon in November 1917.[54] Premier Martin addressed the delegates, assuring them of his sympathy and support.[55] Shortly afterwards, he received a letter requesting a government grant to pay the salary of the GWVA secretary, office rental, the travel expenses, and other items.[56] "We will endeavor to make this association self-sustaining after its first year," assured GWVA president James McAra.[57] As it turned out, the $10,000 annual grants continued to flow in subsequent years.[58]

By the second annual convention in July 1918, the GWVA had expanded to twenty-four local branches in Saskatchewan (up from the original five) and 2700 members. It performed a variety of functions: helping with adjustments to separation allowances, assigned pay, pensions, post-discharge pay, administration of deceased soldiers' estates, and other matters. It lobbied to have the Patriotic Fund made fully a government responsibility and not dependent on charitable contributions. The request was rebuffed, but a GWVA representative was added to the fund's provincial executive.[59] In January 1919 the national GWVA started a campaign for a $2000 bonus to be paid each veteran as compensation for income lost during war service. The Borden government portrayed the bonus as a cash-grab that would cost the federal treasury $2 billion.[60] Premier Martin sided with Borden, and the bonus was not awarded.[61]

Putting the "Foreigner" in His Place

In July 1918 the Saskatchewan GWVA passed a resolution demanding that no person of "alien enemy birth or the progeny of unnaturalized enemy aliens" be allowed to work for the government.[62] This would have excluded from the civil service naturalized British subjects and Canadian-born persons of German or Austro-Hungarian parentage. Martin rejected the idea, saying only that "every person employed by the Government in this Province is required to take the Oath of Allegiance before he can draw his salary."[63]

The Regina ANV in September 1917 sent a delegation to the town of Prussia, located west of Regina about twenty-fives miles from the Alberta border. The veterans wanted the name of the town changed, as well as the street names, one of which was "Lusitania."[64] The residents put on a splendid banquet for the visitors, regaling them with patriotic songs, rendered in full voice and many verses. The mayor presented a handsome cheque, which the veterans gratefully accepted. The name was changed to "Leader" and the offending street names were likewise rechristened.[65] The veterans assured their hosts that "nothing more could have been done to entertain them, to make things generally pleasant and to convince them that citizens of Prussia were British and not hyphens."[66]

The school issue was not so easily resolved. The GWVA demanded that "the English language be the only language taught in the Public and Separate Schools of the Province of Saskatchewan up to and including the eighth grade, and that the English language be the only medium of instruction in all the schools of the Province of Saskatchewan."⁶⁷ Martin responded cagily: "This is a question which has been receiving the attention of the Government of the Province for some time past and I hope that when the proper time comes a satisfactory solution of the question will be reached."⁶⁸

In April 1917 Martin found himself seated on the platform at the Saskatchewan schoolteachers' convention next to James F. Bryant, chairman of the Regina Public School Board. Bryant, whose brother was seriously wounded at Passchendaele,⁶⁹ charged that schools in the province were using Austrian textbooks and children were being made to recite: "Our Emperor is the Good Francis Joseph, and Elizabeth is his good wife. We must speak reverently when we speak of them."⁷⁰ Martin, though not scheduled to speak, immediately got to his feet. "The man," he said, "who, in this critical stage of the British Empire raises religious and racial discord is not a true friend of Saskatchewan or of Canada or of the Empire."⁷¹ The teachers applauded heartily, making it clear whose side they were on. They also voted unanimously not to include Bryant's speech in the published version of the convention proceedings because his remarks were judged to be "political, rather than 'educative' in character."⁷² There was a good deal of irony in this, since school inspectors regularly reported on the political affiliation of teachers. Non-Liberals risked losing their teaching certificates, and school boards who hired Conservatives were in peril of losing their government grants.⁷³

During the June 1917 provincial election campaign, Conservative supporter Mrs. F. Newcombe said she knew of a school where the teacher had torn down the Union Jack, ripped it into pieces, and given the rags to the children to wipe their slates with. She had heard that the German-Canadian Alliance was blatantly advising its members to vote for candidates who promised to defend German language rights. "Fancy that," Mrs. Newcombe remarked incredulously. "Representatives of the Germans in our parliament. I do not agree with Premier Martin's expression of tolerance and go slow. Let me tell you this. When a child is born of German or Austrian parentage in this country, he is a Canadian. As he grows old under our present system does he become a Canadian, or a German or an Austrian? No. He becomes a mongrel."⁷⁴

The National British Citizenship League was founded in Moose Jaw in March 1917,⁷⁵ and a Regina branch soon followed. Men in uniform were honorary members. Adopting the slogan "One School—One Flag—One Tongue," the league advocated English only in the schools and the disenfranchisement of all those born in enemy countries, including those who had been naturalized, "until those who fight for the empire recover their franchise." It desired a tightening up of naturalization procedures, weeding out those who could not demonstrate the ability to speak English in open court before a judge.⁷⁶

Soon after the election, Premier Martin, who was also Minister of Education, toured some of the schools in the foreign districts. The "progressive" Mennonite schools he deemed "as good as any which existed in the Regina plains."⁷⁷ The Union Jack flew in front of all but one, and in that instance the teacher apologized profusely for the lapse. The Old Colony Mennonite schools were another story. Only German was spoken, and nothing taught but the Bible and catechism. Travelling from Vonda to Humboldt, the premier passed a number of Ukrainian schools and was delighted to see the Union Jack hoisted in front of each of them. He examined children's notebooks, which were written entirely in English, and observed "cloaks neatly hung in a cloak room and on each nail was also hung individual towels and individual drinking cups."⁷⁸

Critics were not appeased. Rev. Murdoch MacKinnon excoriated the school laws before the Great War Veterans' Association in February 1918.⁷⁹ The Grain Growers' Association approved a resolution to delete the provision in the School Act that allowed foreign-language instruction from three to four o'clock, such teaching to be permitted only after regular school hours.⁸⁰ Bitter allegations were hurled across the convention floor, prompting the chairman to caution against "wild and exaggerated statements." "A year ago last December," J.H. Hilton of Melville testified, "there was a school district seven miles south and west of Melville, Pearl Park, where they had a teacher who did not come up to the requirements of the inspector and who taught school in German for about two months."[81] The teacher had been let go, but was subsequently hired in the Wymer school district, where he taught nothing but German. A delegate rose to his feet and demanded that children of alien citizens be required to swear an oath of loyalty on the flag: "They should learn to respect our flag at the youngest period, and we should not allow the flag to be torn into slate rags as is being done."[82] This raised cries of "Rot" and other such expressions from various parts of the hall.

The 1918 convention of the Saskatchewan School Trustees' Association attracted more than 2000 delegates, about double the usual number. Saskatoon's Third Avenue Methodist Church was filled to the rafters, and an "overflow convention" spilled into Knox Presbyterian Church. "Foreign" trustees had stolen a march on the British delegates at the preceding convention. By packing the meeting, they had succeeded in tabling a motion that would have forced the province to adopt uniform school readers printed in English. The vote had been close—330 to 321—and the British trustees were determined not to be out-manoeuvered a second time.[83]

The resolution before the 1918 convention was that "no language except English be taught during school hours in any school which comes under the provisions of the School Act."[84] It was basically the same motion the Grain Growers and the GWVA had already approved. Rev. Father Pander of Melville told the delegates that he had been born and raised in Prussia, where German was the only language permitted in schools. The experience had not turned him into a Prussian. Children, he believed, would be at a disadvantage if they could not understand the language in which a church service was conducted. "Send them to an English church," someone bellowed. J.F. Bryant declared that he did not want Saskatchewan to become a polyglot monstrosity like Austria-Hungary, where multilingualism had led to a profusion of ethnic nationalisms and, ultimately, the breakdown of civil order.[85] Trustee J.L. Atcheson made the point that the resolution before the convention did not prohibit "foreigners" from holding on to their religion and language. All that was being asked was that during school hours the teacher "use only the English language and to impart the ideals and the fundamentals of the heritage which was theirs by right and had been purchased at the price of blood."[86] The motion passed by a standing vote with much enthusiastic cheering and applause.[87]

An attempt was made to protect French language rights. A trustee from Lanigan said that French-speaking Belgians were more patriotic than Australians, who had just given a "magnificent example of disloyalty" by voting down conscription. The comment raised such an uproar that the speaker had to sit down. A resolution was hurriedly drafted deploring the "disgraceful and untruthful" slur. Needless to say, there was no exemption for French. Indeed, a motion was approved that "no person shall be eligible to be elected as trustee unless he is a British subject" and "able to read and write the English language."[88]

Letters and petitions from municipal councils, school boards, and private citizens descended on the premier's office.[89] The School Trustees, Grain Growers, GWVA, Saskatchewan Association of Rural Municipalities, Orange Lodge, Baptist Conference, and Anglican Synod of Saskatchewan all called for English-only schools.[90] The Department of Education in March 1918 required all teachers to swear the oath of allegiance.[91] It was made compulsory for schools to fly the Union Jack, weather permitting, on the days the school was in operation, and for children to sing "God Save the King."[92] Parents in the Old Colony Mennonite settlements were forced to send their children to the public school. Those who refused were subject to fines. When eight ratepayers in Flora School District did not pay up, "three horses, a hog, and five cured hams were seized by police and sold at public auction." The local GWVA declaimed, "We are convinced that the only method by which these groups and sects can be Canadianized is by inculcation in their schools through the English language the elementary principles of freedom and democracy we enjoy."[93]

In April 1918, a mob of sixty men invaded the home of Henry Willners of Davidson, a small town about halfway between Regina and Saskatoon.

Willners, a German, had a son who had recently enlisted in the Canadian army. When he told his father of his decision, the son was ordered out of the house. Hearing this, the men invaded Willner's home and forced him to apologize to the boy, kiss the Union Jack, and donate $100 to a war charity.[94] The non-British population bent over backward to demonstrate their loyalty.[95] Gathering at Leschinsky's Hall in June 1918, the residents of Germantown organized a Red Cross fundraising campaign, with J.J. Bergl as chairman, H. Zimmer as secretary, and F.X. Kusch, treasurer. They divided the area into districts and assigned canvassers corresponding to the ethnicity of each neighbourhood.[96] A group from Germantown marched in the Red Cross parade, prompting the laudatory *Leader* headline, "East End is Enthusiastic for Red Cross."[97]

Der Courier suspended publication in September 1918. The editor feared a vigilante raid on the plant.[98] Publicly, he said only, "The one thing we certainly wish to avoid is the aggravating in any way of public sentiment, always prone to excitement in time of war."[99] A few days later, a federal government order-in-council banned publications in enemy languages (German, Austrian, Hungarian, Bulgarian, Turkish, Rumanian, Russian, Ruthenian, Ukrainian, Finnish, Estonian, Syrian, Croatian, and Livonian).[100] *Der Courier* later resumed publication as an English-language newspaper.[101]

The Martin government on 17 December 1918 introduced legislation abolishing languages other than English from the school.[102] A minor exception was made for French, which was allowed as the language of instruction in grade one and as a subject of study for one hour a day after grade one. Previously, it had been permitted as the language of instruction in the first three grades. The *Leader* justified the special treatment: "French is not a foreign language in this Dominion, it being an official language in Canada and having the same status in our Federal Parliament and courts as English."[103] It was also "the language of diplomacy and of the greatest of our Allies in the recent war." It would be unwise for Saskatchewan to prohibit French just as the peace conference was assembling in Paris, thereby providing "an instrument of propaganda for German agents to use in an endeavor to arouse feelings of ill-will between the British and French nations."[104] The Conservative leader responded dryly that he did not think the diplomats at Versailles were paying much attention to what was going on in Saskatchewan.[105]

* * *

In 1918 Anglo-Canadian patriotism, bolstered by returning soldiers, reached its apex. The veterans had given all they had to the cause. While they were overseas, "foreigners" had prospered, buying farms, cultivating more acres, and reaping record crops at record prices. Even the lowly farm labourer had never had it so good. The stories about "foreign" children tearing up the Union Jack for rags to wipe their slates, even if not literally true, had metaphorical verisimilitude. They expressed the fear that "foreigners" were wiping the Saskatchewan slate clean of British civilization. Something was owed the 4958 Saskatchewan men who had given their lives for their country.[106] Their sacrifice had to mean something. Saskatchewan must be Canadianized, and that meant English only in the schools.

Chapter 12

Victory

EASTER SUNDAY, 31 MARCH 1918, WAS A BLUSTERY, COLD DAY IN REGINA. Heavy, dark clouds rolled in from the west, bringing snow flurries; rain and sleet fell intermittently through the afternoon and evening. The Salvation Army band was out on the streets at an early hour, celebrating the day with Easter anthems. Despite the inclement weather, the churches were full. Ministers were gratified to see their congregations seeking the consolation of prayer in a time of trial and tribution.[1] Walter Murray, president of the University of Saskatchewan, found inspiration in the Easter message:

> The darkness of this war is as nothing compared to the time when the Prince of Peace was not received by the Jews, but was turned over to the unbelievers to be cruelly tortured and crucified until even Nature felt the shock and there was darkness in the land. The darkness was followed by the dawn of resurrection of the Prince in power, might and majesty. The darkness of this period will be followed by a period when the spirit of peace will be enthroned

with an irresistible power in the hearts of men.... In His own good way and time He will bring out of this turmoil peace.[2]

The Spanish Flu

But before peace arrived, one more ordeal had to be endured. Robert Callander died at the Regina General Hospital on 6 October 1918 of a mysterious illness.[3] It bore some resemblance to an ordinary flu, but the symptoms were much worse. Typically, the disease that had taken Callander's life began with a dull headache. The eyes burned, and the patient began to shiver. Then came a kind of delirium and feverish discomfort. The muscles ached and the head throbbed. The face turned brownish-purple, the feet black. The patient coughed up blood, and, at the end, usually a few days after the first onset of symptoms, gasped for breath. Reddish saliva foamed at the mouth, and the patient drowned in his own fluids. The autopsy revealed the lungs "lying heavy and sodden in [the] chest, engorged with a thin bloody liquid, useless, like slabs of liver."[4]

There was no cure or vaccine, and doctors did not even know what caused the malady. Nor was there a definitive test to determine whether a person was infected.[5] Scientists knew of the existence of viruses, but no one had ever seen one, since they were too small to be observed through an ordinary microscope, and the electron microscope had yet to be invented.[6] It was not known where the 1918 influenza came from or how it mutated into such a killer strain.[7] The first wave, relatively mild, appeared in the spring of 1918, when it infected eight million people in Spain;[8] hence, the name "Spanish flu." Other countries were hit as well, including much of Europe, the United States, and parts of Asia. Canada was mostly unaffected.[9]

The second wave, more virulent than the first, touched nearly every part of the globe. The average fatality rate was 2.5 percent of those infected, much higher than the one-tenth of 1 percent, which is normal for influenza.[10] Deaths worldwide were estimated at between 20 million and 100 million, considerably more than the 9 million combatant and 6 million civilian deaths caused by World War I.[11] In many cases the patient fell victim to secondary infections, when bacteria invaded the injured lungs, and it was often difficult to know whether death resulted from the flu or pneumonia.[12] Young adults aged twenty to forty were among the most vulnerable, while the very young and the aged were more often spared.[13]

In the second week of October 1918, medical doctors in Regina held a meeting to discuss the situation. There was no reason to panic, they said. The disease was "no different from the old influenza except that it was more epidemic." It was influenza "with complications." The doctors did not think it was necessary to "impede the commercial and social life of the city" by closing down the schools, theatres, places of amusement, or the street railway. They advised those who developed symptoms to stay in bed and avoid contact with others. Regina medical health officer Dr. Malcolm Bow suggested that caregivers wear a mask "of several thicknesses of gauze and spray their throat with eucalyptus as a preventive measure."[14] Within a day or two, all the drugstores in town were sold out of eucalyptus medicine.[15]

On 13 October, the flu claimed the life of Rev. Father A. Suffa, priest at St. Mary's Catholic Church. He felt unwell on Wednesday and after lunch took to his bed, but rose shortly after and carried on his usual round of activities for the rest of the day. The next morning, he was sick and stayed in bed. His assistant phoned the doctor, and Father Suffa was taken to Grey Nuns' Hospital, where he died early Sunday morning.[16] That same day, Jonathan Andrews, a farm labourer from out of town, was found delirious and fainting in Victoria Park. He was taken by ambulance to the General Hospital. Earlier that morning he had tried to gain admission to the hospital, but had been turned away. The assistant matron had said that she was under instructions not to take in any more patients because of the lack of space.[17]

There were no beds left at the General, Grey Nuns', or isolation hospital.[18] At a meeting of city council, Alderman MacKinnon expressed alarm, but others were more sanguine. Alderman John A. Rose, a medical doctor, characterized the flu as not so much "epidemic as endemic." It resulted in death only among "weakened or careless people."[19] Even so, on 15 October 1918, Dr. Bow ordered the closing of the city hall auditorium to all dances, since it was thought that they were a dangerous source of contagion.[20] He recommended the closing of places of amusement, including theatres, moving picture theatres, poolrooms, billiard rooms, bowling alleys, and dance halls, and the suspension of all public assemblies and public meetings, including church services. The Ministerial Association took umbrage, saying they wanted to keep the churches open so as not to "create panic," but in the end they complied with the medical health officer's advisory.[21]

Bow stopped short of closing the public schools, which had a staff of nurses who checked on the students daily. As soon as symptoms were detected, the child was sent home. "Eat plain, nourishing food," Bow instructed, "spend as much time as possible in the open air, keep the house well ventilated, and avoid crowded conditions anywhere, cover up all coughs and sneezes. If feeling ill go to bed at once and call your physician promptly." Norman Black, principal of Regina Collegiate Institute, reported an absentee rate of 16 percent, double the usual, but did not close the school.[22] Chief librarian J.R.C. Honeyman kept the library open as an antidote to the flu "in the form of healthy and entertaining literature to the state of mind produced by reports of the spread of the disease."[23] The books were thoroughly disinfected before being placed back on the shelves.[24]

City streets were now deserted at an early hour. Streetcars, which normally carried between forty and fifty passengers in the evening, had less than ten. Some twenty motormen and conductors were at home sick, and service had to be curtailed. A car was taken off the Red and White lines and two off the Blue and Green-Red lines.[25] About twenty-five employees were absent from the post office, and one department store reported that it was short twenty-six workers. The Board of Trade set up a labour bureau to recruit temporary replacements. "I am of the opinion," board secretary L.T. McDonald stated importantly, "that there are in the city a number of young women who are quite capable of rendering service in a clerical way and who have some experience as stenographers and others as clerks. Such as these would be rendering a most valuable service if they would undertake to fill, temporarily, the positions rendered vacant by the epidemic in many of our business offices."[26]

The separate board shut down its schools on 17 October (the public schools remained open) and offered St. Joseph's School as a temporary hospital to receive the overflow from the General. Classrooms were stripped of their desks and seats, and cots and beds installed. The General Hospital assumed responsibility for administration, assisted by volunteer nurses.[27] A military hospital for 100 patients was opened at St. Paul's parish hall to care for soldiers who could not be accommodated at the camp at the exhibition grounds or at St. Chad's convalescent home.[28]

Dr. Bow, meanwhile, supplemented his previous directives, advising the use of three or four thicknesses of gauze saturated with Lysol over the mouthpieces of telephones in public places. He requested that funerals be held in private to prevent the gathering of crowds[29] and asked employees in large business establishments to wear masks, provided they took care to change the masks frequently and burn them when they were discarded. He did not think it was a good idea to wear masks on the street, because they blocked inhalation of fresh air, which was "generally recognized as the best germ-fighter in existence."[30] People bought large quantities of alcohol, which, despite prohibition, was still available for "medicinal" purposes. Some doctors in Regina were writing 250 or more prescriptions a day for the much-sought-after remedy.[31]

Regina College instituted a strict quarantine of the 150 students living in residence. No cases had been discovered, but it was thought wise to take extra precautions. A nurse was kept on twenty-four-hour duty.[32] The collegiate institute closed its doors on 18 October. About one-third of the students had stopped attending classes, and one young man, Leslie Gardiner, had died of the flu. Principal Black admonished the students to keep up with their studies while they were at home so that they would not be at a disadvantage when it came time to write the final examinations.[33]

More than two weeks after the first flu fatality, the public schools were finally closed.[34] Nurse Cooper of the Public School Health Department, released from her school duties, took charge of home visitations. She divided the city into eight districts and assigned nurses and volunteers to each of them. Teachers, mostly female, volunteered as nurses, while citizens who owned automobiles chauffeured them from house to house. Nurse Cooper's organization was, literally, a lifesaver for the city, since the Health Department had proved entirely inadequate to the task, many of its staff members having succumbed to the epidemic.[35]

Each day, the casualty list grew longer. James Murray Ross, brother of Alexander Ross, officer commanding the Twenty-Eighth Battalion, died on 20 October.[36] W.F. Ridgeway, thirty-one, cashier in the office of the Saskatchewan Grain Growers' Association and Sunday school secretary-treasurer at one of the Baptist churches, succumbed, leaving two children, the elder three years old. Returned soldier James Wesley Hayward, who had managed to survive the war, met a deadlier enemy at home. Flight Lieutenant F.H. Parker had also served in France. One day, on a routine patrol, he encountered engine trouble at 7000 feet. His plane nose-dived and crashed down across a trench. He was picked up unconscious and carried to a field hospital. Although his skull was fractured and he was given little hope of recovering, he regained consciousness after seventy-two hours. The first thing he saw was the face of the Red Cross nurse watching over him. He was released from hospital on his nineteenth birthday and returned safely to Regina, only to die of the flu on 27 October 1918.[37]

Nurse Cooper's organization was handicapped by a shortage of volunteers. On Saturday, 26 October, for example, there were forty calls from homes with sick persons, and only twelve nurses to look after them. Rev. Hugh Dobson issued an appeal for twenty-five men and twenty-five women to help in the hospitals and private homes overnight, but only eighteen persons showed up. "There is quite the same need of taking up 'our cross' and 'going over the top' in this way," he pleaded, "as there has been for other men and women to face danger for us. If we turn back because of danger, we will hardly want to look others in the face who have risked their lives."[38]

According to one nurse, married women without children were letting the city down. She called them "slackers of the worst order." They thought they were "real honest-to-goodness Joans of Arc, when they timidly [ran] across the street with a bowl of gruel of something."[39] Single women, on the other hand, performed magnificently. Out of 125 teachers in the city, 76 volunteered as nurses, even at great risk to their health.[40] "Miss K" worked from fifteen to twenty hours a day for nine days in the home of a total stranger, preparing meals and looking after the sick. There was no remuneration of any kind.[41]

A *Leader* editorial on 29 October found fault with the city's overall response to the crisis. "Why was the city fighting the flu on the cheap?" it asked. Why were nurses not being paid? More than three weeks into the epidemic, there was still no clear assessment of the extent of the problem. A census was needed to secure the necessary information. Cards should be distributed to all households, explaining what to do in the event of illness, the language simple enough for children to understand, since they were often the ones healthy enough to care for the other members of the family.[42]

The city council Relief Committee had the cards printed up, and J.J. McLeod, boys' work secretary at the YMCA, enlisted scores of boys to distribute them.[43] A census of the city was planned for 30 October, but only forty volunteers came forward to conduct it, well short of the 350 hoped for. E.N. Weed of Minneapolis, a salesman for the Kill 'Em Quick Gopher Poison Company, offered his services. He had brought his car up from Minnesota, but with the flu raging throughout the province, business was slow to non-existent and he had been biding his time in one of the local hotels. He thought he might as well help out with the survey.[44]

John McCarthy, another volunteer, canvassed six blocks in Germantown. He noticed that most of the residents could not understand what was printed on the health cards, since the instructions were in English only. Nor could they read the labels on medicine bottles. Sick rooms were poorly ventilated. "In many cases," he reported, "fresh paint sealed the inside sashes and there was no evidence of windows having been opened to admit fresh air, even though the doctor had been present."⁴⁵ The canvass revealed 945 flu victims in an area encompassing half the city. Assuming the other half contained the same proportion of sick persons, there were roughly 1900 to 2000 flu cases in Regina, including the outlying districts of North Regina and North Annex.⁴⁶

The death toll reached 144 on 1 November. There were 64 patients at the General, 93 at St. Joseph's, 64 at the Grey Nuns', and 104 in the military hospitals.⁴⁷ The task of burying the dead now fell entirely on Speers Funeral Home, the Regina Burial Company having been put out of business by the death of its manager Percy Chapman.⁴⁸ Gravediggers could not keep pace with the number of dead, forcing the city to reassign street cleaners to the cemetery. It was impossible to schedule funerals more than two or three days in advance because of the backlog of corpses and the shortage of plots to receive the bodies.⁴⁹

To complicate matters, Dr. Bow fell ill, as did the acting medical health officer and the chairman of the Relief Committee appointed by city council.⁵⁰ Fortunately, Dr. Bow recovered and returned to work on 4 November, optimistically announcing that the worst of the epidemic was over.⁵¹ Nurse Cooper shut down her organization on Sunday evening, 10 November 1918, and transferred the remaining cases to the city Health Department.⁵² Under her supervision, 3070 cases of flu had been cared for (some visited more than once) and 3865 house calls made. Her work started on 23 October (the day the public schools were closed), when forty-two cases were dealt with. The peak was reached on 31 October when 258 patients were visited in their homes and 429 calls made. The first day of November the decline began, and, while slow at first, it accelerated after 4 November. On 10 November, the date of the transfer to the city Health Department, there were only eighty-eight patients.⁵³ Dr. Bow expressed the gratitude of the city for the efforts of the female schoolteachers, who had formed the backbone of the voluntary nursing corps. He hoped they would receive a week's vacation before school resumed, a request that was granted.⁵⁴

The number of patients at St. Joseph's Hospital was also declining. The total on 12 November was fifty-four, and new cases were no longer accepted, since the General and Grey Nuns' now had room for them.[55] The last patient was discharged from St. Joseph's on 27 November, and the school fumigated and prepared for the resumption of classes.[56] In the course of its forty-one-day life, the hospital had cared for 282 patients (172 male and 110 female). There were thirty-one male deaths (18 percent) and eleven female deaths (10 percent). Of the male deaths, more than two-thirds were between the ages of twenty-six and forty. Of the female fatalities, almost half were between twenty-six and thirty. Two children died between the ages of one and five, and there were no deaths between the ages of six and fifteen. Only one fatality over forty-five years of age was recorded, and he was forty-eight.[57] In the city as a whole, the flu took 330 lives.[58]

Church services resumed on Sunday, 24 November,[59] and theatres reopened four days later, to the general relief of owners and employees who had been without work for five weeks. The bill at the Roseland Theatre featured the musical comedy *Murphy in Society*, while the Regina Theatre presented *Balree, Son of Kazan*, with the added attraction of the song-and-dance team of McDonald and Curtis. *The Blindness of Divorce* played at the Rose, and *Out of the Clear Sky* was showing at the Rex. The latter was described as a "a tender little story with a beginning in desecrated Belgium and an ending in the Canyon of Colorado."[60]

The Last One Hundred Days

Thousands of miles away, the Canadian Corps entered the last phase of the war. On the morning of 8 August 1918 the battle of Amiens began. Regina's Twenty-Eighth Battalion, acting in support, moved forward at 5:50 a.m., and by 4:30 in the afternoon, the outer perimeter of the city had been reached.[61] That night the battalion slept well, officer commanding Lieutenant Colonel Ross snug in a dugout that had been occupied the previous evening by a German officer. The next morning the attack resumed. The line of advance was "over a plain as level as a billiard table and absolutely devoid of cover."[62]

To make matters worse, the troops to the left and to the right had been delayed, and there was little artillery support. On the right the troops fanned out on their exposed flank, opening up a space in the middle. Ross ordered B Company led by Captain A.F. Simpson and A Company led by Captain J.F. McKay to move in and close the gap, which they were able to do. By the end of the day, the Sixth Brigade had advanced over four miles into enemy territory. On every side wounded Germans could be heard, in Ross's words, "bleating like sheep."[63]

The battalion moved back of the line on 11 August. They travelled by train to Frevent and were assigned to support positions at the Telegraph Hill switch system northwest of Wancourt. Telegraph Hill had been captured with Vimy Ridge in April 1917. Orders came down for the taking of Wancourt, but, before that, Neuville-Vitassse was to be seized. Ross thought this was a bad idea. All the possible approaches to Neuville-Vitasse were exposed to German observation. The element of surprise would be entirely absent, but orders were orders, and Ross had to obey. "Fortunately," he sardonically recounted,

> time was on his side for in such limited operations plans had to be carefully made, orders issued, company commanders instructed and in turn their subordinates advised.... It was truly surprising how on this occasion, so much time was required to do all of this without any apparent wastage of that vital commodity. From the time the orders were definitely confirmed by 6th Brigade our Unit headquarters was a hive of activity, yet by the time all was ready and the troops prepared to move it was quite late.[64]

Higher Command ruled that, after all, Neuville-Vitasse could be bypassed, and the orders were rescinded. Wancourt, a key point in the Hindenburg line, fell to the Allied forces on 26 August 1918.[65]

After a short rest, the Twenty-Eighth relieved the Twenty-Ninth Battalion at the Canal du Nord. The area had been heavily bombarded with mustard gas shells, and "when the men got into confined quarters the gas fumes did their devilish work and some severe casualties resulted."[66] An attempt was made on 1 October to cross the canal and capture Cambrai. The Germans had massed artillery in nearby woods, and the falling shells caused a great deal of damage. Within a few minutes, three company commanders were hit.[67] As night fell, it was learned that Brigadier General A.H. Bell, commanding the Sixth Brigade, had been seriously wounded, and Ross was ordered to succeed him. Major G.F.D. Bond was brought up from battle reserve to take command of the Twenty-Eighth Battalion.[68] The final assault on Cambrai took place on 8 October. "Over to the right to the southeast," Ross wrote, "the glow of the fires from burning Cambrai [the fires deliberately set by the Germans] could be seen casting a weird light over the landscape, punctuated at intervals by the spitting flash of an 18-pounder gun, or the belching flame of a howitzer firing from a position out in the open."[69] The operation was a complete success, and Cambrai now belonged to the Allies.

On 11 October 1918 the Twenty-Eighth Battalion attacked Iwuy, "a compact village with the customary garden and orchard in the rear of each house, brick walls and thick hedges."[70] Braving the heavy barrage and fierce machine-gun fire, the men forced their way in. The enemy had to be hunted down and engaged in hand-to-hand combat. The village had been captured and cleared by 11:44 a.m., but the Germans launched a strong counterattack with tank support. For a while it looked as though the battalion might be surrounded and cut off. The men held on until relief came that night from the Fifty-First Scottish Division. Over the course of the day, the Twenty-Eighth had eighteen men killed, with fifteen missing, nine gassed, and ninety-six wounded. Ross considered it the battalion's finest hour. While the actions at the Somme, Vimy, Passchendaele, Amiens, and Arras had all been impressive, they were "set-piece operations with full reconnaissance, careful planning and carefully rehearsed, so that every man knew exactly what he had to do and which had been supported by overwhelming fire and carried out with the Unit at full-battle strength."[71] Iwuy was different. It was "a leap into the unknown, hurriedly planned, unrehearsed, and supported by an improvised barrage," and "it had been carried out by an undermanned unit, short of officers, and by men already tired, yet in spite of all, they had done everything that had been required of them."[72]

Word came that the Germans were retiring and that the area between Cambrai and Valenciennes had been evacuated. The nights were quieter now, the enemy bombers showing up only on rare occasions.[73] The Third and Fourth Canadian divisions took Valenciennes and, as soon as they had completed the job, the Second Division came in behind. The Twenty-Eighth Battalion rested at the Ancien Citadel in Valenciennes until 8 November 1918, when they moved to Frameries, arriving on 10 November. All along the march, villagers brought out their black, yellow, and red Belgian flags and waved them proudly. Grateful to be liberated, they welcomed and cheered the Canadians.[74]

On the morning of 11 November 1918, the Twenty-Eighth Battalion marched towards Mons, the site of the ignominious British retreat in August 1914. The battalion was ordered to take possession of the village of Havre and secure the line of the Canal du Centre to the north and east. Private George Lawrence Price, a twenty-six-year-old from Moose Jaw, Saskatchewan, and a few other members of A Company crossed the canal and entered the small village of Ville-sur-Haine to search a house from which a German machine gun had been firing moments before. The Canadians entered the house and found only the owner and his family, the Germans having hurriedly exited through the back door. Just as Price stepped back into the street at 10:50 a.m., a single shot rang out, and he slumped to the ground. He was dragged back into the house and attended to, but it was too late. He died at 10:58 a.m., just two minutes before the ceasefire. George Price was the last Allied soldier to die in the Great War.[75]

Regina Celebrates

The news of the end of the war reached Regina at about two o'clock in the morning on 11 November. Notwithstanding the late hour, people took to the streets with noisemakers of all kinds—horns, whistles, sirens, pots and pans, garbage cans, and a coalscuttle beat with a walking stick. At the offices of the *Leader*, a man with a megaphone bawled out the terms of the peace to the throng below. Baritone J.H. Arnett came to the window and in full voice sang:

> Kaiser Bill is of the past;
> Hindenburg is licked at last;
> Willie now is running, too;
> What a day for me and you.[76]

Happy carousers set ablaze an effigy of "Kaiser Bill" in front of city hall. A strong wind picked up the flames, and the fire brigade had to be called in to make sure that the kaiser was "extinguished in more ways than one."[77]

At seven o'clock in the evening on 11 November, 8000 citizens, led by the Salvation Army band, marched out to Wascana Park. Lieutenant-Governor R.S. Lake declared that the German dream of world domination had been shattered: "Tyranny and autocracy were things of the past."[78] Exuberant cheers greeted Colonel J.A. Cross, district officer commanding, Military District 12. It was a full minute before he could speak. "This is Der Tag," he said, "this is the day, this is the day of the British Empire and her Allies." The allusion was to the pre-war German military toast, "To the Day," "referring to the moment when German armies would be unleashed on the world."[79] Cross paid tribute to the Canadian Corps: "Throughout the years of the war, it had never been known that an objective had been assigned to the corps and that it had failed to plant the flag of Canada on top of this objective."[80]

Lieutenant Colonel Hodson, officer commanding, First Depot Battalion, set off a fireworks display, including a number of flares that had been taken from the Germans during the Somme offensive. The downtown streets were crowded with hundreds of autos, loaded to the breaking point. One carried a piper, a Highland fling dancer and "a bevy of young girls." Every time it stopped, the piper tuned up and the dancer executed a Highland fling in the middle of the street. A white goat drew a cart, with a placard reading, "We've got the Kaiser's goat." A red-cheeked John Bull strode proudly down the street, accompanied by a jubilant Uncle Sam. The students at Regina College lit a huge bonfire, and the farms around the city were ablaze with burning haystacks.[81]

* * *

Thanksgiving and memorial church services were delayed until 1 December on account of the flu epidemic. The Great War Veterans' Association and the Army and Navy Veterans marched en masse to Metropolitan Methodist Church. The First Depot Battalion band played Handel's "Dead March" from *Saul*, the congregation standing with heads bowed. J.H. Arnett sang "The Silent Hour of Our Immortal Dead." Rev. Dr. Milliken expressed "profound gratitude that sorrow and suffering (on this side) and horror, cruelty, and barbarity (on the other side) had passed." He praised the "courage and devotion of the men who had borne arms" and "had made possible this service of national thanksgiving." "Methinks," he said, citing Pericles, "death as theirs is the true measure of a man's worth."[82]

At Holy Rosary Cathedral, a high mass was celebrated for Catholic soldiers killed in the war. Archbishop Mathieu spoke feelingly of "the wonderful part Canada had played in the great war and how nobly she had done her part for victory." He exhorted the congregation to thank God for the success of Allied arms and ask for his aid in overcoming the problems of reconstruction so that "all peoples would be united for the greater good of Canada, which is favored above all lands of the earth by natural advantages."[83] Rev. A.S. Lewis at First Baptist Church struck a sterner note:

> Not until Germany brings forth fruits worthy of repentance should she have a place in the coming league of nations.... We must deal justly with Germany, and simple justice demands that her leaders should be punished and amends made for her hideous crimes, but all this must be done not in a spirit of revenge, but for the one supreme purpose of bringing about a change of heart in our enemies.[84]

At St. Paul's Anglican Church, Rev. G.F. Davidson read out a list of members of the congregation who had given their lives "in the empire's cause" and made reference to a tablet, on which the names would be inscribed as soon as the list was complete. Special prayers were recited, and the congregation sang "For All the Saints Who from Their Labors Rest." Rev. Davidson spoke of the necessity of keeping faith with the men who had borne arms "by establishing in the nation and throughout the world those principles for which they had suffered." The service ended with "a rendering of the War March of the Priests."[85]

Epilogue

Crown of Thorns

IT TOOK A WHILE FOR THE NEWS TO SINK IN THAT THE WAR WAS OVER. "Are you dreadfully happy?" a Regina woman, who had three sons go off to war, was asked. "I am," she replied,

> in the lucid intervals when I grasp the fact that the war is over. But for the most part I am utterly stunned. I go around with my face long and solemn, saying to myself, 'O, this awful war,' and wishing the boys were safe. You may not understand it, but my thoughts keep recurring along that strain. They act like a man freshly out from the penitentiary after serving a long term—he always has an impulse to run back to the spot he has grown accustomed to haunt. For four years, I have thought of nothing but the war, and the muddy trenches and the frightful guns. The nearest thing to heaven is not to have the guns going. In imagination I've been listening to them for four years, and I cannot keep it in my mind they are quiet. Perhaps in a little while I'll get my thoughts out of their old groove.[1]

Regina Commemorates

Regina did not want to forget. It wanted to remember. On 18 April 1919 Archie McNabb, Minister of Public Works, announced the government's intention to build a combined war memorial museum and natural history museum. It was to be located on Albert Street immediately to the south and west of the Legislative Building. An architectural competition was held, all entries to be handed in by 7 July 1919. The winner was the firm of Nobbs and Hyde of Montreal, who proposed a two-storey building with massive features. Entering the building through the main door on Albert Street, the visitor would pass into the Hall of Honour. To the left and right were the north and south courts of the war museum, where trophies and artefacts were to be displayed. A.G. Doughty, comptroller (later director general) of war trophies, shipped to the city one German airplane, five boxes of airplane parts, two aerial bombs, seven German machine guns, three Austrian machine guns, seven other machine guns, one hundred Mauser rifles, one naval torpedo and warhead, one German naval gun, one German 210 mm howitzer, one rangefinder, one trench periscope, as well as "various helmets, machine-gun belts, gas masks, bomb throwers, Zeppelin pieces, ammunition boxes and trench-fighting implements and weapons."[2]

The architect's plans were completed and two models constructed, but construction was delayed. The fall in wheat prices crippled the economy, making it difficult for the government to raise the half million dollars that was required. The project was not cancelled, but neither was it proceeded with. Finally, in 1926 it was officially abandoned. The collection of war trophies was kept in storage until, in the midst of World War II, they were melted down for scrap, realizing the grand total of $278.21, which was divided between the Regina Citizens' War Economy Board and the IODE.[3]

Although the museum failed, other commemorative projects went forward. Largely through the initiative of GWVA president Colonel James McAra, city council set aside a portion of the Regina cemetery for the burial of veterans. Uniform headstones marked the graves, the soldiers lying in death as comrades and brothers, with no distinction of "rank, race or creed."[4]

The Forget, Cecil Rhodes, and the Brigadier General Embury Chapters of the IODE raised funds for the memorial gate. The guns at the entrance were German field pieces captured during the war. In the centre of the cemetery stood the Cross of Sacrifice, designed by Sir Reginald Bloomfield for the Imperial War Graves Commission. Symbolizing the Christian ideals for which the war had been fought, it was officially unveiled on Sunday, 25 June 1922, by the Governor General, Lord Byng of Vimy. Fittingly, many of the men buried there had served under his command at the Battle of Vimy Ridge.[5]

On the first anniversary of the armistice, 11 November 1919, King George suggested that British subjects in all parts of the empire observe two minutes of silence in remembrance of the war dead. In Regina at eleven o'clock, a steam whistle blew and all business came to a halt; the city was momentarily stilled.[6] In the evening, the GWVA held an "open house" at their clubrooms, which became an annual event. In 1920 Lieutenant-Governor Richard Lake told the veterans: "We were in danger of having our institutions taken from us, but it is to you and those you represent we owe our thanks for being able to be here this evening as free men and citizens."[7] The 1921 program included vocal solos by GWVA members and twenty-one rounds of boxing, Premier Martin squeezing in a speech between the third and fourth bouts.[8]

The United Services Institute, an officers' organization, held an annual ball on the eve of Armistice Day (renamed Remembrance Day in 1931).[9] It was considered to be one of the highlights of the social season. It took place in 1921 at the Trading Company banquet hall, suitably decorated with flags for the occasion. Two hundred and forty couples attended, their names published the next day in the *Leader's* social column. The men wore full-dress military uniform and the women elaborate gowns. "The scene was a brilliant one," said the *Leader*. "The creations of brightest hue and of iridescent beads equaled in beauty only by the gowns of softest pastel shades and those statelier ones of black trimmed with jet."[10]

In the run-up to the third anniversary of the end of the war, 200,000 poppies, which had been manufactured by women and children in devastated areas of France, were distributed throughout the province. Harry W. Cook, GWVA provincial secretary, reported that demand outstripped supply: "In many cases the original order has been doubled and trebled, but letters and telegrams are still being received urging us to send more poppies for remembrance."[11] The following year, the poppies were made in a factory in eastern Canada, which employed disabled Canadian Expeditionary Force veterans. Fifty percent of the proceeds of sales went to them, the balance divided between the Last Post fund, which looked after the Soldiers' Cemetery in Regina, and the local branch of the GWVA. Boy Scouts and Girl Guides helped to sell the poppies, and another 3000 were distributed through the schools.[12]

In 1923 the GWVA sponsored an essay-writing contest on the topic "The Poppy as the Emblem of Armistice Day." Many of the schoolchildren wrote about John McCrae's poem "In Flanders Fields," which already had a place in the Armistice Day ritual. Some made the connection between poppies, opium, and sleep, while others wrote that the colour red symbolized the blood of sacrifice. There was also reference to the resilience of the flower that sprang up "round the ragged edges of the shell holes ... as if trying to hide the destructiveness of man." Elsie Japp of Spears pointed out pragmatically: "The poppy is not a large flower and can be easily duplicated in cloth or paper.... The corn flowers grow in great abundance in these fields, and they would have been much harder to imitate than the poppy."[13]

Running through many of the essays was a reiteration of the high ideals for which the war had been fought. "German autocracy was determined to conquer the world and to place it under a military system which would crush all individual effort," wrote Louise Sveinbjoinson, a junior high school student from Elfros, Saskatchewan. "We must hold the torch of democracy high, that other struggling, suffering nations may rise and become happy and contented," contributed Alice Fisher of Qu'Appelle. Grade eight student Eleanor MacKinnon from Weyburn (future secretary to Premier Tommy

Douglas) paid tribute to those "brave enough to fight and die so that we might have our homes and freedom." Eric McAughey from Saskatoon said that soldiers had given their lives "in the cause of liberty, justice and truth." The poppy "seems a little wreath of glory given by the Creator in honor of His brave dead." The "pretty red speck of nature" had cheered the soldier and "turned his mind back home—to his boyhood days, to mother and sweetheart, where all was calm and serene and full of hope.... It steeled his heart to fight all the harder for King and Country and to protect the homes of his beloved ones from the awful tyranny and savage cruelty of the Hun."[14] The patriotic rhetoric of 1923 was exactly what it had been in 1914.

Since Armistice Day fell on a Sunday in 1923, a memorial service was held at the Capitol Theatre in Regina at four o'clock. Special seats were reserved for returned men in uniform, who were asked to wear their medals and decorations. The crowd was huge, estimated at about 2000. Every seat was taken, right up to the highest balcony, "where a raising of the arm is enough to touch the lofty ceiling." Those who were unable to get in "stood around the spacious vestibules and retiring rooms of the theatre content to catch any echo of the music, the addresses or the prayers that might drift back from the platform."[15] The program was given under the joint auspices of the Regina Choral and Orchestral Society, the Regina Musicians' Union, the GWVA, the Regina Canadian Club, and the Women's Canadian Club of Regina. It consisted of hymns ("O God Our Help in Ages Past"), scripture reading, prayers, an address by Captain H.R. Nobles, and appropriate selections of music. The chorus performed "Te Deum" and "How They Shall Softly Rest," and Captain Dan Cameron sang "Land of Hope and Glory."[16] Among those seated in the reserved box was Major A.G. Styles, who had played in the western Canadian rugby championship on 31 October 1914, the day he joined the Twenty-Eighth Battalion, with whom he served for the entire duration of the war.[17]

The *Leader* portrayed the service as "a unique combination of the patriotic and religious sentiments ... a service of thanksgiving for victory and peace; a requiem for the fallen; a token of gratitude to those who had lived to return; an appeal for sympathy and help to those of them whose minds were still unsettled by war or who had failed of re-establishment."[18] As the years passed, and war faded from direct experience, the desire to remember only grew stronger. In 1923, for the first time, the last post was sounded at precisely eleven o'clock in three parts of the city. One trumpeter stood at the corner of Dewdney Avenue and Garnet Street, another at the corner of Fourteenth Avenue and Toronto Street, and a third in Victoria Park. Also, for the first time, the street lamps were lit for the two minutes of silence.[19]

The city memorial project, which had first been discussed in 1919, was now reactivated. One proposal was a memorial driveway on the north shore of Wascana Lake between Albert and Broad streets, which "would afford many opportunities for expression by the City and by various Civic organizations in a commemorative way of the great war." They included "formal gateways at the entrance to the drive, the construction of rest arbors, the erection of monuments, [and] the planting of trees." The plan was both utilitarian and aesthetic.[20] It had the further advantage of being carried out over several years, so that the cost in any one year would not be prohibitive.[21]

The alternative was a monument in Victoria Park in the centre of the city. The location would give the memorial the prominence it deserved, but at the sacrifice of the fountain that was already there. Old-timers felt that its demolition "would take away one of the links with Regina's early days, when the pioneers of the city took pride in erecting the fountain on a spot where, it was believed by outsiders, fresh water would never be available in any quantity."[22] Both the GWVA and the United Services Institute lobbied for a monument in Victoria Park. The ANV had yet another idea. They wanted a Soldiers' Home for disabled veterans. City council in March 1925 opted for the monument, the cost estimated at $30,000 (later reduced to $25,000) to be raised by way of a debenture bylaw submitted to the burgesses.[23]

The wording of the bylaw was somewhat vague. It did not specify the type of monument or where it would be placed, merely what it would cost.[24] It was defeated by 239 to 157 in the vote held on 7 May 1925, to the consternation of veterans, who were described as "shocked" at the result. Col.

A.C. Garner, a past president of the GWVA, said that he could not believe the vote was "a true expression of public opinion, because I cannot conceive of a city like Regina declining to honor the memory of the fallen when small cities, towns and villages throughout the length and breadth of Canada have erected memorials to their dead."[25] Some thought the adverse result was "due to the fact that the question had become beclouded because so many projects had been discussed," but none firmly decided upon.[26] The matter was mulled over in various pulpits, the consensus being that the vote did not represent the true feelings of the people of the city. Rev. I.B. Naylor at Fourteenth Avenue Methodist Church declared he had every faith that citizens "were really desirous of having some form of worthy memorial for the boys who fell in the war," while Father Kearney at Holy Rosary Cathedral insisted that "ex-service men deserved some form of recognition in a public monument for the services rendered to the Empire in the hour of need."[27]

The GWVA asked for the resubmission of the bylaw at the earliest possible date, while the Rotary Club and Anglican Church representatives thought it should be delayed until the next municipal elections in the fall. City council sided with the GWVA,[28] and a second vote was held on 17 July 1925. This time it passed by a substantial margin of 572 to 181.[29] Again, it was left to city council to choose the site, which they did on 15 October 1925, opting for Wascana Park near the Smith Street entrance. J.J. MacLean, GWVA local president, argued the case for Victoria Park: "There it would be seen by everybody as it would be practically in the center of the city. In all the large centers of population in the world, war memorials are located in central positions. Take the cenotaph in Whitehall, London, as an example.... How many people go to Wascana Park in the long winter months?"[30] Alderman McInnis asked if the GWVA had considered the fact that in order to give the cenotaph prominence, most of the shrubbery in Victoria Park would have to be cleared away. McLean replied that the people he represented did not desire undue prominence for the memorial: "As for the shrubbery, it was desirable to have it around the memorial so that the women for whom the memorial had a deep personal significance might go and sit near it.... It may be sentimental," he said, "but it's done the world over."[31]

A cenotaph, from the Greek, meaning "empty tomb," is a war memorial to a person whose body lies elsewhere. Edwin Lutyens had designed the one in London to which MacLean referred, a model that was widely copied in cities throughout the British Empire. Those attending the first ceremony in London had spontaneously covered the base with wreaths, establishing a custom that became a regular feature of Remembrance Day services.[32] The monument eventually built in Victoria Park, though distinctive, has a family resemblance to the Lutyens design. It is likely that the veterans had it in mind when they made their proposals to the city.

City council on 20 October 1925 reversed its earlier decision and settled on the Victoria Park site. A competition was held for the design[33] and forty-nine entries received. The judges, Cecil S. Burgess, nominated by the Royal Architects Institute of Canada, and L.A. Thornton, Regina City Commissioner, chose the design submitted by R.G. Heughan of Montreal. It was "of dimensions suitable to be a dominating feature in the park and to form a point of interest in the vista of Cornwall Street," and it commemorated "the citizens who fell in the war in a finely restrained and dignified manner." However, Heughan's soldier figure with reversed arms was very similar to the "brooding soldier" of the St. Julien Memorial near Ypres, which was the work of Regina sculptor Frederick Clemesha.[34] The judges were concerned about plagiarism so they made acceptance of the Heughan design conditional upon permission having been granted by both Clemesha and the Canadian Battlefields Memorials Commission.[35]

As it turned out, neither party raised an objection.[36] However, W.G. Van Egmond and eight other Regina architects were not so easily modified. They petitioned for the disqualification of the Heughan entry on the grounds that it was not original. The City sought the opinion of the president of the Dominion Institute of Architects, who replied by telegram: "FIGURE NOT SAME DETAIL AS CLEMESHAS. HEUGHAN AGE THIRTY SEVEN BORN IN SCOTLAND. IN CANADA SEVENTEEN YEARS. HAS GOOD DESIGNING EXPERIENCE.

IN FIFTH MOUNTED RIFLES. NOT OVERSEAS. DISCHARGED OWING TO ACCIDENT IN CAMP." C.S. Burgess telegraphed: "THE ORIGINALITY OF THE DESIGN CANNOT BE REASONABLY CONTESTED. ALL GOOD DESIGNS CONSIST OF WELL KNOWN ELEMENTS VARIOUSLY COMBINED. IN THIS CASE THE COMBINATION IS DEFINITELY ORIGINAL." Thus reassured, city council proceeded with the Heughan design.[37]

The grey granite monument was officially unveiled on Thursday, 11 November 1926, the mayor declaring a civic holiday from ten to twelve o'clock so that all could attend who wished to do so. Ten thousand citizens stood quietly and reverentially "in the cold November mist,"[38] including militia, naval men and airmen, ex-servicemen and their wives and children, and schoolchildren. Ex-soldiers who had lost limbs or were otherwise disabled were escorted to benches near the speakers' platform. Widows, mothers, and soldiers' wives were seated in places of honour. At a quarter to eleven, the Regina Male Voice Choir sang the first low notes of the processional hymn:

> Fight the good fight, with all thy might,
> Christ is thy strength and Christ thy right,
> Lay hold on life and it shall be
> Thy joy and crown eternally.[39]

Mayor Mason said two thousand men from the city's contingents had been wounded and 587 killed. "The memory of the war dead must be kept green, for the sake of the children and for the sake of the citizens themselves." [40]

The choir sang a second hymn:

> O valiant hearts who to your glory came,
> Through dust of conflict and through battle flame
> Tranquil you lie, your knightly virtue proved,
> Your memory hallowed in the land you loved.
> Proudly you gathered, rank on rank, to war,
> As who had heard God's message from afar;
> All you had hoped for, all you had, you gave,
> To save mankind; yourselves you scorned to save.
> Long years ago, as earth lay dark and still,

> Rose a loud cry upon a lonely hill;
> While in the frailty of our human clay,
> Christ, our Redeemer, passed the self-same way.
> Still stands his cross from that dread hour to this,
> Like some bright star above the dark abyss;
> Still, through the veil, the Victor's pitying eyes
> Look down to bless our lesser Calvaries.
> These were his servants, in his steps they trod,
> Following through death the martyred Son of God;
> Victor, he rose, victorious too shall rise,
> They who have drunk his cup of sacrifice.
> O risen Lord, O Shepherd of our dead,
> Whose cross has brought them, and whose staff has led,
> In glorious hope their proud and sorrowing land
> Commits her children to thy gracious hand.[41]

The trumpets sounded a long "G" followed by two minutes of silence, as the crowd stood with bared heads bowed. The construction workers who were building the new Hotel Saskatchewan across the street "paused astride lofty girders." A single factory siren wailed, and the bell of a clock tower boomed the hour of eleven. Mayor Mason gripped the cord that held the bunting in place and "two great Union Jacks trembled for a moment and fluttered to the ground."[42] The honour guard presented arms with Brigadier-General J.F.L. Embury saluting. Buglers of the Regina Rifle Regiment sounded the last post and the trumpets of the RCMP the reveille. Rev. Will Surman, an ex-serviceman and Baptist pastor, uttered a brief dedicatory prayer. The inscription on the monument read simply: "To the Glory of God and the Immortal Memory of the Men of Regina who gave their lives and service in the Great War, 1914–1919"; on the other side: "Dedicated by the people of Regina in grateful memory of their fellow citizens who fell in the Great War."[43]

Premier James G. Gardiner spoke, describing the monument as "a mark of respect to the dead and challenge to the living." Canada's soldiers had sacrificed themselves for justice and freedom, liberty, and equality of opportunity. It was incumbent on those who followed to "realize the spirit which our men embodied in themselves when they went to the other side." The Regina Pipe Band played a melancholy Lowland air, "Flowers o' the Forest," followed by the Salvation Army band's rendition of "Promoted to Glory." Mrs. A. Hilsenteger, whose son Joseph had been the first Regina man to fall in the war, placed a wreath at the base of the monument, followed by a long line of men and women representing scores of Regina organizations. Anglican Minister Edward Frampton pronounced the benediction, and the program concluded with the singing of "God Save the King."[44]

The crowd lingered long after the formal service had ended. All through the afternoon and evening, hundreds of visitors came to inspect the memorial. Quiet crowds gathered around shop windows where war pictures and relics, theatrical posters of wartime motion pictures, and other memorabilia were on display. Flags flew from every office building, a mark of homage "beautiful, simple and sincere."[45] The next year on 11 November, the weather was unseasonably cold. Snow covered Victoria Park, the mercury hovered at the freezing mark, and a chill gale swept the city. Even so, hundreds of people gathered at the cenotaph to pay their respects,[46] establishing an annual ritual that continues to this day.

The *Leader* described the 1926 unveiling ceremony as both "sacred and triumphant." It was "a time for tribute to these gallant dead and for re-consecration to the ideals for which they died." There was no hint of apology or second thoughts, no suggestion that the war had been a wasteful tragedy or that the men had died in vain. Quite the opposite, the hymns identified the fallen soldiers with the crucified Christ. Because they had sacrificed themselves for others, they lived on in glorious immortality, just as Christ rose from the grave to redeem the world. The inscription on the monument significantly began with words, "To the Glory of God."

Only in the second part of the editorial did the *Leader* strike a dissonant note:

> There is a recognition today, on a scale never known before that war does not provide its own antidote, and the talk of war ending war has long ago, perforce of actual experience, given place to the conviction that warfare sows

> the international fields with dragon's teeth and induces new hatreds and rivalries, pushing forward possibly towards another dreadful clash of nations ... the one fact made clear as daylight is that battling is no real remedy for national or international disputes, and the instrument of war is a two-edged sword which punishes the so-called victors in common with the supposed-to-be vanquished.[47]

This subversive thought hinted that war itself was the enemy, not the "Hun" or any other nation. If battling was "no real remedy for national or international disputes," and if it induced "new hatreds and rivalries, pushing forward possibly towards another dreadful clash of nations," it followed that World War I had not solved anything, but only created more problems. Having raised the issue, the *Leader* backed away from its full implications. The editorial concluded conventionally: "Regina's observance of the signing of the Armistice Day will not be one that includes any note of regret for sacrifice rendered. Hers was a tribute willingly paid—a stern, even cruel tribute but one offered willingly on the altar of liberty and chivalry. And it is in this spirit that the war memorial will be unveiled today. It will be a tribute to the chivalry, the honor, the glory of Regina youth. It will be a ceremony of remembrance, of gratitude, of devotion, of love."[48] And so it was. The thousands of people gathered at Victoria Park did not consider themselves "so-called victors." They believed that the war had been fought for a noble cause. For them, words like "gallant," "chivalry," "honour," "glory," and "liberty" did not ring hollow. They expressed the ideals of Canada's fighting men.

Crown of Thorns

By 1926, when the Cenotaph was unveiled, August 1914 was a failing memory. Although Reginans now had a better understanding of the costs of war, they were not disillusioned. The challenge had been met, the foe defeated. And yet there were cross-currents. Saskatchewan, with its large "foreign" population, had been a hotbed of contested national identity. The public school was the battleground where the issue was to be decided, the place where Canadianization would either succeed or fail. Emotions reached fever pitch, helping to bring down Premier Walter Scott in 1916 and obliging his successor, William Martin, to abolish non-English language instruction in 1918. Anglo-Saxon supremacy asserted itself, firmly and decisively.

Ironically, however, the war did much to erode the British-oriented Canadian nationalism for which it had, in large part, been fought. In May 1917 the Regina Sunday school association put on a patriotic concert attended by over 2000 people. Hung across the back of the stage was a huge painting, *The Beaver*. A chorus of 500 children sang the "Canadian song," which was "all about this remarkable little animal and the fact that he stands as Canada's emblem."[49] It was the composition of Professor F. Laubach, the choir leader at St. Paul's Anglican Church, who had charge of the program. The boys sang "On, Canadians On," as well as songs representing England, Scotland, Ireland, Wales, India, and the United States. At the end of the concert, the Sunday school association presented Laubach with a baton on which was engraved "The Beaver." It had a silver beaver at one end and a small plate inscribed with the details of the concert.[50] The empire was still important, but the focus had shifted to Canada.

Methodist minister Salem Bland, speaking in Regina in 1918, declared that 1 July had new significance: "no longer was St. George's Day, nor St. Patrick's Day, nor St. David's ... the day of days for any Canadian. Canada had been made sacred by her sons who have gone over the top. They were all Canadians. They have consecrated the Maple Leaf, and henceforth Canada must be the greatest name for all of us, short of the Kingdom of God."[51] The Canadian Club in Regina gained in popularity and membership, overshadowing old-world organizations like the Sons of England and the St. Andrew's Society.[52] It made a concerted effort to promote the study of Canada's past, awarding in 1917 gold medals to the high school student who wrote the best essay on Canadian history and the elementary school pupil who obtained the highest mark on the Canadian history examination.[53]

On Dominion Day 1917, the *Leader* posed the question, "Why are Canadians so reluctant to fly the flag [presumably the Union Jack] on the national holiday?" An anonymous letter writer replied that "Canada did not stand for anything but one of a number of dependencies of England, and, although it styled itself a nation, the word was a misnomer, that it was not a nation and never would be until it declared its independence." The *Leader* disagreed. Canada was just as independent as any nation in the world. It was not a colony of England, but rather a partner. The British Empire was the sum total of all the self-governing dominions—Australia, South Africa, and all the rest. Canada, if she so desired, could withdraw from the empire at any time without a drop of blood being shed. And, as for the war, Canadians were fighting for Canada, "for civilization, for world liberty, for humanity." They were fighting for those ideals just as truly as the United States was fighting for them.

Canadians too often made the mistake, the *Leader* continued, of making patriotic appeals "not to the Canadian sentiment, but to the 'Motherland,' meaning Great Britain." The appeal must be made, instead, to love of Canada. This was not to deny that Canada's institutions, her laws, and methods of government, had come down from Britain. This was an historical fact in which Canadians rightfully took pride. But the important thing was that Canadians should be "Canadians first, last and all the time. Not English-Canadians or Scotch-Canadians, or Irish-Canadians or German-Canadians, or French-Canadians, or American-Canadians, but Canadians pure and simple."[54] Regina's Alexander Ross said it best. Leading the Twenty-Eighth Battalion into battle at Vimy Ridge, he saw arrayed before him "Canada from the Atlantic to the Pacific on parade... I thought then, and I think today, that in those few minutes I witnessed the birth of a nation."[55]

Another legacy of the war for Regina and Saskatchewan was the reinforcement of the rural myth. More than ever, the province embraced the slogan, "In Wheat We Trust." The war brought great prosperity and a doubling of wheat acreage, but very little industrial development. The farmer, who had always been placed on a pedestal, rose even higher in public esteem. Food production was considered to be meritorious patriotic service, nearly on a par with fighting in the trenches. High school students, office boys, businessmen, and professional men went out to the farms en masse, helping put in crops in the spring and bringing in the harvest in the fall. City dwellers were expected to grow food in their backyards and on vacant lots. Only slackers and shirkers failed to arm themselves with rake and hoe.

More than ever, agriculture was destiny. No one doubted the growth mantra: more immigrants, more farms, more wheat, and more railways. J.A. Calder, Liberal cabinet minister and one of the best strategic brains in the province, said in 1916 that the biggest question Canada had to face, after winning the war, was "the settlement of vacant lands."[56] This may have been good policy in the short run, but over the long haul it was disastrous. The rural myth haunted Saskatchewan, inhibiting efforts to diversify the economy. Even today, when agriculture accounts for only 8 percent of gross domestic product, the province cherishes an image based on farming. When in 2007 the government tried to get rid of the wheat sheaf logo, which is used as a provincial identifier on everything from letterhead to road signs, there was a strong backlash. It was considered heresy "to drop a symbol so suggestive of the province's agricultural heritage."[57]

The rural myth was linked to Saskatchewan's obsession with the Big Interests, the combination of central Canadian manufacturers, railways, and banks who extracted wealth from the hard-working farmer. The war did nothing to mitigate the siege mentality. The Big Interests, who had always benefitted from the protective tariff, now reaped huge profits from munitions contracts, not a single one of which came to Regina. Hence the cry for "conscription of wealth" along with conscription of men.

Regina identified with the farmer. When he did well, the merchant and businessman made money. When he faltered, so did they. When farmers assailed the Big Interests, Regina chimed in. This lent a "progressive" tinge to the politics of the city and province. Even before the war, the Liberal government had intervened in the free-market economy to subsidize cooperative elevators and provide telephone service to rural areas. The Liberals also forged an alliance with trade unions by passing workers' compensation, a fair-wage clause in government contracts, and other pro-labour laws. By measures such as these, Saskatchewan appointed itself the "banner province," leading the country in progressive legislation.

Progressivism was infused with the social gospel, the Protestant movement away from traditional theology towards social reform, or, as its supporters liked to say, "building the Kingdom of God on earth." The war carried the social gospel to unprecedented heights. The soldier's sacrifice was identified with that of Christ on Calvary, an irresistible call to surrender selfish individualism for the betterment of society. The war became a holy crusade. King Alcohol was slain as a preliminary to the kaiser's overthrow. Women were given the vote so that they could participate as full partners in the great struggle for democracy. A 1917 *Leader* editorial, tellingly titled "Canada's Two Wars," compared the war against Germany with the war against the Big Interests. It was a spiritual struggle of right versus might, good versus evil, the kingdom of God versus its satanic opposite. The war was not just an external event occurring on distant European battlefields. It was being fought right here in Canada.

The politics of national identity, the rural myth, and social gospel progressivism lent a distinctive flavour to Regina's Great War. In other respects, the city was just one more little town of Stephen Leacock's imagining, doing its part in the greatest ordeal Canada has endured. French historian Annette Becker said the war was "an immense Good Friday,"[58] a time of immense suffering and purposeful sacrifice: young Joseph Hilsenteger going into battle at Ypres with the strange feeling that he had "seen it all before"; Catherine Creswell rowing for hours on the open water after her boat had been torpedoed; Dr. John Cullum digging with his bare hands to rescue comrades buried in No Man's Land; Alexander Ross deliberately delaying the execution of an order that he knew to be pointless to spare the lives of his men; government employees weeping at the news of Frank Mantle's death; J.F.L Embury directing his men in battle, heedless of the wounds he had suffered; Nurse Cooper supervising the female teachers of Regina heroically nursing the victims of the Spanish flu epidemic; the joy of Reginans who poured into the streets at two o'clock in the morning to celebrate the end of the war; the dignified grief and deep pride of Armistice Day services.

Was it worth it? Was the death and destruction justified? Neil "Piffles" Taylor, the young Regina quarterback, who joined the Royal Flying Corps, thought so. Released from a German prisoner-of-war camp at the end of the war, he wrote to his mother: "I can't regret the sacrifices that have been made. I am not going back elated, as I at one time dreamt I would, but I am going back contented. Sam, Lyman, Chester, Frank, Lavell, Howie and many others will not be there to greet me, but I shall feel that I am returning to a country which is free only because they were prepared to die that it might be so, and therefore I am content."[59]

Notes

Introduction

1. C.P. Stacy, "Nationality," *Historical Papers* (1968): 11.
2. For Canada's experience of World War I, see Desmond Morton and J.L. Granatstein, *Marching to Armageddon: Canadians and the Great War 1914–1919* (Toronto: Lester and Orpen Dennys, 1989); J.L. Granatstein, *Hell's Corner: An Illustrated History of Canada's Great War 1914–1918* (Vancouver: Douglas and McIntyre, 2004); Desmond Morton, *When Your Number's Up: The Canadian Soldier in the First World War* (Toronto: Random House, 1993). For local studies see Robert Rutherdale, *Hometown Horizons: Local Responses to Canada's Great War* (Vancouver: University of British Columbia Press, 2004); Ian Miller, *Our Glory and Our Grief: Torontonians and the Great War* (Toronto: University of Toronto Press, 2002). For an account of how Canadians interpreted the meaning of the war, see Jonathan Vance, *Death So Noble: Memory, Meaning and the First World War* (Vancouver: University of British Columbia Press, 1997).
3. City of Regina Archives (CORA), COR-R-F44, George Beach, *Municipal Manual, City of Regina* (Regina: City of Regina, 1919).
4. "Mothers of Soldiers," *Leader* (Regina), 13 May 1918.
5. "Major Mantle, Regina Officer, Dies at Front," *Leader* (Regina), 4 October 1916.
6. "In Wheat We Trust," *Evening Province and Standard* (Regina), 22 July 1915.
7. Canada, *1911 Census*, "Birthplace of the Population in Cities and Towns 7,000 and Over."
8. The phrase "imperial-nationalism" is used in Rutherdale, *Hometown Horizons*, 42.
9. Phillip Buckner, "Whatever Happened to the British Empire?" *Journal of the Canadian Historical Association* 4 (1993): 18.
10. Jay Winter, Geoffrey Parker, and Mary R. Habeck, eds., *The Great War and the Twentieth Century* (New Haven: Yale University Press, 2000), 3.
11. Ibid., 38.
12. Cited in Miller, *Our Glory and Our Grief*, 36.
13. Angus McLaren, *Our Own Master Race: Eugenics in Canada, 1885–1945* (Toronto: McClelland and Stewart, 1990), 48.

14 Peter Melnycky, "The Internment of Ukrainians in Canada," in *Loyalties in Conflict: Ukrainians in Canada During the Great War*, ed. Frances Swyripa and John Herd Thompson (Edmonton: Canadian Institute of Ukrainian Studies, 1983), 1.
15 David E. Smith, *Prairie Liberalism: The Liberal Party in Saskatchewan 1905–71* (Toronto: University of Toronto Press, 1976), 33.
16 *Der Courier*, 16 July 1913, cited in Katherine Luttmer, "The German Experience in Regina to the End of World War I," BA Honours paper, University of Regina, 1986, p. 29.
17 Smith, *Prairie Liberalism*, 33.
18 Buckner, "Whatever Happened to the British Empire?" 28.
19 Anderson, *Education of the New Canadian*, 88, cited in William J. Brennan, "A Political History of Saskatchewan, 1905–1929," PhD thesis, University of Alberta, 1976, p. 395.
20 There was a minor exception for the French language. See Chapter 11.
21 Tim Cook, *Clio's Warriors: Canadian Historians and the Writing of the World Wars* (Vancouver: University of British Columbia Press, 2006), 209.
22 Stacy, "Nationality," 11.
23 "Why Do Not All Choirs Learn How to Sing 'O Canada'?" *Leader* (Regina), 25 August 1917.
24 "Have New Version National Anthem," *Leader* (Regina), 15 June 1918.
25 "'O Canada' Not to Replace 'God Save the King,'" *Leader* (Regina), 6 August 1918.
26 Richard Hofstadter, *The Age of Reform: From Bryan to F.D.R.* (New York: Alfred A. Knopf, 1956), 24.
27 See Vernon Fowke, *The National Policy and the Wheat Economy* (Toronto: University of Toronto Press, 1957).
28 Paul Voisey, "The Urbanization of the Canadian Prairies, 1871–1916," *Histoire Sociale/Social History* 8, 15 (1975): 83.
29 Dale Eisler, *False Expectations: Politics and the Pursuit of the Saskatchewan Myth* (Regina: Great Plains Research Center, 2006), 47.
30 Elizabeth Mitchell, *Western Canada Before the War* (Saskatoon: Western Producer Prairie Books, 1981), xviii. First published 1915 by John Murray, London.
31 Gordon Barnhart, "Walter Scott," in *Saskatchewan Premiers of the Twentieth Century*, ed. Gordon Barnhart (Regina: Canadian Plains Research Center, 2004), 11.
32 Voisey, "Urbanization of the Canadian Prairies," 78.
33 Ibid., 87.
34 Department of Temperance and Moral Reform of the Methodist Church and the Board of Social Service and Evangelism of the Presbyterian Church, *Report of a Preliminary and General Social Survey of Regina*, 7.

35 William Brennan, *Regina: An Illustrated History* (Toronto: James Lorimer and Co., and Ottawa: Canadian Museum of Civilization, 1989), 57.
36 Mitchell, *Western Canada Before the War*, 114.
37 Voisey, "Urbanization of the Canadian Prairies," 78.
38 Alan Artibise, "Boosterism and the Development of Prairie Cities, 1871–1913," in *The Prairie West: Historical Readings*, ed. R. Douglas Francis and Howard Palmer (Edmonton: Pica Pica Press, 1992), 524.
39 *Report of a Preliminary and General Social Survey of Regina*, 28.
40 Gordon Barnhart, *Building for the Future: A Photo Journal of Saskatchewan's Legislative Building* (Regina: Great Plains Research Center, 2002), 22 and 51.
41 Gordon Barnhart, *"Peace, Progress and Prosperity": A Biography of Saskatchewan's First Premier, T. Walter Scott* (Regina: Canadian Plains Research Center, 2000), 59.
42 "Saskatchewan's Greater Production Loan," *Leader* (Regina), 19 Sept. 1917.
43 Government of Saskatchewan, *Budget Speeches*, Budget Speech delivered by the Hon. C.A. Dunning, 27 January 1920, 5–6.
44 "Grain Growers and the Church," *Leader* (Regina), 19 May 1917.
45 William Brennan, "The Public Career of Charles Avery Dunning," MA thesis, University of Saskatchewan, 1968, p. 30.
46 "Grain Growers and the Church," *Leader* (Regina), 19 May 1917.
47 J. Castell Hopkins, ed., *Canadian Annual Review of Public Affairs*. (Toronto: Canadian Annual Review Ltd., 1912), 553.
48 "Grain Growers and the Church," *Leader* (Regina), 19 May 1917.
49 Russel Nye, *Midwestern Progressive Politics: A Historical Study of its Origins and Development 1870–1958* (East Lansing: Michigan State University Press, 1959), 12–13.
50 Hopkins, ed., *Canadian Annual Review of Public Affairs, 1912*, 542.
51 Eisler, *False Expectations*, 29.
52 Hopkins, ed., *Canadian Annual Review of Public Affairs, 1912*, 561.
53 Barnhart, *"Peace, Progress and Prosperity,"* 116–117.
54 John Herd Thompson, *The Harvests of War: The Prairie West 1914–18* (Toronto: McClelland and Stewart, 1978), 55.
55 "Canada's Two Wars," *Leader* (Regina), 13 October 1917.
56 David Danbom, *The World of Hope: Progressives and the Struggle for an Ethical Public Life* (Philadelphia: Temple University Press, 1987), 209.
57 Ibid., 52.
58 "The Kingdom of Heaven in Regina," *Leader* (Regina), 5 May 1913.
59 *Christian Guardian*, 16 September 1914, cited in J.M. Bliss, "The Methodist Church and World War I," *Canadian Historical Review* 49, 3 (1968): 215.
60 "The War Is Another Step in Age-Long War Between Christ and Anti-Christ, Says Pastor," *Daily Post* (Regina), 18 December 1916.
61 Jim Warren and Kathleen Carlisle, *On the Side of the People: A History of Labour in Saskatchewan* (Regina: Coteau Books, 2006), 50.

62 Election ad, "Constructive vs Destructive Policies," *Leader* (Regina), 19 June 1917.
63 Bill Waiser, *Saskatchewan: A New History* (Calgary: Fifth House, 2005), 133.
64 Hopkins, ed., *Canadian Annual Review of Public Affairs, 1912*, 553.
65 Waiser, *Saskatchewan*, 88.
66 J.M Bliss, "The Methodist Church and World War I," *Canadian Historical Review* 49, 3 (1968): 229–30.
67 Marilyn Barber, "Nationalism, Nativism and the Social Gospel," in *The Social Gospel in Canada: Papers of the Interdisciplinary Conference on the Social Gospel in Canada*, ed. Richard Allen (Ottawa: National Museums of Canada, 1973), 213.
68 George Thomas Daly, *Catholic Problems in Western Canada* (Toronto: Macmillan, 1921), 82–83.
69 *Report of a Preliminary and General Social Survey of Regina*, 20–21.
70 Ibid., 29.
71 Ibid., 25.
72 Ibid., 26.
73 Ibid., 28.
74 Ibid., 26.
75 Ibid., 47.
76 Ibid., 38.
77 Ibid.
78 Ibid., 37.
79 Ibid., 36.
80 Ibid., 28.
81 Ibid., 46.
82 "Sworn Detailed Statement of the Circulation of the Regina *Leader*," *Leader* (Regina), 8 January 1918.
83 Notice, *Leader* (Regina), 5 December 1914.
84 Hopkins, *Canadian Annual Review of Public Affairs, 1912*, 549. Conversion to current dollars is based on the Bank of Canada inflation calculator, <http://www.bank-banque-canada.ca/en/rates/inflation>.
85 Hopkins, *Canadian Annual Review of Public Affairs, 1917*, 767.
86 Jeffrey Keshen, *Propaganda and Censorship During Canada's Great War* (Edmonton: University of Alberta Press, 1996), xii.
87 *Report of a Preliminary and General Social Survey of Regina*, 28.

Chapter 1

1 Hew Strachan, *The First World War* (New York: Viking, 2004), 3–64.
2 "Huge Crowds Assemble in Front of *Leader* Building Awaiting Britain's Momentous Decision," *Leader* (Regina), 4 August 1914.
3 "Patriotic Demonstrations of Unparalleled Fervor Called Forth by Germany's Challenge," *Leader* (Regina), 5 August 1914.

4 Barely 13,000 of Canada's half million volunteers in World War I were French speaking. Desmond Morton, *A Military History of Canada* (Toronto: McClelland and Stewart, 2007), 152.
5 Rutherdale, *Hometown Horizons*, 36.
6 Ibid., 37.
7 "YMCA Men Parade the Streets," *Leader* (Regina), 5 August 1914.
8 "Adopted Sons of Empire Speak in Praise of Britain," *Leader* (Regina), 5 August 1914.
9 "Practical Joke Is Boomerang," *Leader* (Regina), 5 August 1914.
10 "Found It Necessary to Appeal to Police," *Leader* (Regina), 7 August 1914.
11 Government of Canada, *1911 Census of Canada*.
12 "Foreign-Born Citizens Are Indifferent," *Leader* (Regina), 3 August 1914.
13 Brennan, "Political History," 285.
14 "Where Chivalry Is Needed," *Leader* (Regina), 7 August 1914.
15 "United Province the Ambition of President Murray," *Phoenix* (Saskatoon), 10 October 1914. The motto of Saskatchewan today is "From Many Peoples Strengths."
16 "Regina Farewells Overseas Contingent at Patriotic Concert in Auditorium Rink," *Leader* (Regina), 21 August 1914. An exception was the riot at Rhein, Saskatchewan, on 4 June 1915, involving about ten to twenty men. The combatants were "a number of elevator construction men just newly arrived and a number of German residents of Rhein and vicinity." According to the police report, the trouble started at the Rex Hotel "by one named Henry Swartz (German) striking A.C. Hepburn when the latter refused to include Swartz in the drinks and informed Swartz he had been bumming drinks from the elevator men all day." Saskatchewan Archives Board, Walter Scott Papers, M I IV.160, World War I: German Canadians, 1914–1915, Crime Report re: Riot of Foreigners at Rhein, Sask., 8 June 1916.
17 "Prayers for Safety of Empire Offered in Regina Churches," *Leader* (Regina), 10 August 1914.
18 "Impressive Service for the Troops," *Leader* (Regina), 17 August 1914.
19 "Impressive Camp Service," *Leader* (Regina), 24 August 1914.
20 "Prayers for Safety of Empire Offered in Regina Churches," *Leader* (Regina), 10 August 1914.
21 Philip Buckner writes that the emergence of British identity "owed a great deal to the strong sense of Protestantism shared by the majority of the population in England, Wales and Scotland and the minority in Ireland and to the prolonged wars against Catholic France from 1689 to 1815." Buckner, "Whatever Happened to the British Empire?" 12.
22 "Sang National Anthem as Legislature Voted for $750,000 for War Purposes," *Leader* (Regina), 24 September 1914.
23 Ibid.
24 Ibid.

25 Miller, *Our Glory and Our Grief*, 32.
26 "Regina Farewells Overseas Contingent at Patriotic Concert in Auditorium Rink," *Leader* (Regina), 21 August 1914.
27 Ibid.
28 Brennan, "Political History," 214.
29 Hopkins, ed., *Canadian Annual Review of Public Affairs, 1914*, 631–32.
30 CORA, COR-5, File 2196, Finance: Canadian Expeditionary Force, 1914, City Clerk to J.F.L. Embury, 27 October 1914.
31 Ibid., COR-5, file 2555, Finance: Canadian Expeditionary Force, 1916, portion of a special committee report as adopted by council at its meeting held on 4 April 1916.
32 Ibid., COR-1, Volume 11 (2), City Council Minutes, 20 July 1915.
33 Morton, *When Your Number's Up*, 3–4.
34 Ibid., 8.
35 Ibid., 8–9.
36 "Saskatchewan Frontiersmen Will Go to War," *Leader* (Regina), 8 August 1914.
37 "Total Contingent of About 250 Men," *Leader* (Regina), 11 August 1914.
38 "Nearly 300 Men and Officers to Camp Tonight," *Leader* (Regina), 15 August 1914.
39 "Grant $1000 To Contingent for Foreign Service," *Leader* (Regina), 18 August 1914.
40 "Quiet Sunday at Military Camp," *Leader* (Regina), 17 August 1914.
41 "Men as Keen as Mustard, Says Drill Sergeant," *Leader* (Regina), 19 August 1914.
42 "Regina Farewells Overseas Contingent at Patriotic Concert in Auditorium Rink," *Leader* (Regina), 21 August 1914.
43 "Thousands See Regina's First Contingent Start for the Front," *Leader* (Regina), 24 August 1914.
44 "A Call to Duty," *Leader* (Regina), 26 August 1914.
45 "Two Hundred Participate in Manoeuvres," *Leader* (Regina), 28 September 1914.
46 "Many Recruits Need Assistance," *Leader* (Regina), 17 October 1914.
47 Letter to the editor from T.D. Brown, *Leader* (Regina), 23 October 1914.
48 "Find Temporary Employment for Several Recruits," *Leader* (Regina), 19 October 1914.
49 Robert Brown and Donald Loveridge, "Unrequited Faith: Recruiting the CEF 1914–18," *Revue Internationale d'Histoire Militaire* (1982): 57.
50 Ibid. Since some occupations are difficult to classify, categories are rough-and-ready rather than precise. For example, without additional information, it is hard to know where to place a "civil servant" or a "merchant." The detailed occupational listing for the Ninety-Fifth Rifles' contribution to the second contingent is as follows: accountants, 4; bank clerks, 9; bricklayer, 1;

boilermaker, 1; building inspector, 1; bookkeepers, 4; barbers, 2; butchers, 2; carpenters, 13; clerks, 39; cooks, 4; civil servant, 1; customs officer, 1; coachman, 1; chauffeur, 1; decorator, 1; engineers, 14; electricians, 4; farmers, 45; firemen, 3; gardener, 1; grocer, 1; harness maker, 1; janitor, 1; lawyer, 1; labourers, 41; law students, 4; linemen, 1; lumber agent, 1; merchants, 1; miner, 1; messenger, 1; miller, 1; musician, 1; plumbers, 3; plasterers, 2; rancher, 1; soap maker, 1; students, 8; surveyors, 3; ship joiner, 1; salesmen, 6; shoemaker, 1; stereotyper, 2; shipper, 1; telegraph operators, 2; tinsmiths, 2; teamsters, 4; tailors, 2; veterinary surgeon, 1; waiters, 3.

51 "Patriotic Demonstration of Unprecedented Character Marks Departure of Second Contingent," *Leader* (Regina), 2 November 1914.
52 "'It's a Long, Long Way to Tipperary' Famous Song of British Troops Thrills Great Regina Audience," *Leader* (Regina), 25 September 1914.
53 "Patriotic Demonstration of Unprecedented Character Marks Departure of Second Contingent," *Leader* (Regina), 2 November 1914.
54 "Regina Rugby Champions Return Home; In Good Spirits After Big Game," *Leader* (Regina), 3 November 1914.
55 "Regina Citizens Form Home Guard Similar to 1885," *Evening Province and Standard* (Regina), 14 August 1915.
56 "Good Turnout At First Drill Of Business Men," *Leader* (Regina), 15 October 1914; "Over 120 Members of Business Men's Co.," *Leader* (Regina), 31 October 1914.
57 Letter to the editor from Herbert W. Taylor, *Leader* (Regina), 3 November 1914.
58 "Regina Women Want Military Training Now," *Leader* (Regina), 30 November 1914.
59 "Large Scale War Map at the Public Library," *Leader* (Regina), 8 August 1914.
60 "The Leader Passes 20,000 Mark," *Leader* (Regina), 5 December 1914.
61 "Local Branch of Red Cross Assn. Formed," *Leader* (Regina), 17 Sept. 1914.
62 "We Don't Talk War," *Leader* (Regina), 10 October 1914.
63 "War Pictures Most Realistic," *Leader* (Regina), 29 December 1914.
64 "Highlanders! Fix Bayonets!" advertisement, *Leader* (Regina), 5 July 1915.
65 "Patriotic Scene at Glasgow House," *Leader* (Regina), 27 October 1914.
66 "Daughters of Empire Expect to Raise $2000," *Leader* (Regina), 7 August 1914.
67 "Hold Patriotic Concert Friday to Raise Funds," *Leader* (Regina), 12 August 1914.
68 "Hebrew Ladies Raise Funds for Hospital Ship," *Leader* (Regina), 12 August 1914.
69 "Ladies Collect Nearly $1,200 on Tag Day In Regina," *Leader* (Regina), 17 August 1914.
70 "Monies Received For Hospital Ship in Regina," *Leader* (Regina), 31 August 1914.

71 "Local Branch of Red Cross Assn. Formed," *Leader* (Regina), 17 September 1914.
72 "Campaign of Red Cross Society Is Launched in City," *Leader* (Regina), 29 October 1914.
73 "Regina Branch of Red Cross Society," *Leader* (Regina), 28 September 1914.
74 "Appeal for Relief Belgian People Brings Ready Response," *Leader* (Regina), 12 October 1914.
75 "Flags of the Allies Form Decorations," *Leader* (Regina), 14 November 1914; "Realized $616 On Belgian Day," *Leader* (Regina), 17 November 1914.
76 "Sunday Concerts," *Leader* (Regina), 16 November 1914.
77 "Fine Tableaux Were a Feature," *Leader* (Regina), 23 December 1914.
78 "Regina Farewells Overseas Contingent at Patriotic Concert in Auditorium Rink," *Leader* (Regina), 21 August 1914.
79 Desmond Morton, *Fight or Pay: Soldiers' Families in the Great War* (Vancouver: University of British Columbia Press, 2004), 29.
80 Ibid., 30.
81 Ibid., 32.
82 Ibid., 49.
83 Ibid., 65.
84 Ibid., 66.
85 "For Those Left Behind," *Leader* (Regina), 15 September 1914.
86 "Strong Local Committee Is Appointed for Regina Branch of Patriotic Fund," *Leader* (Regina), 15 September 1914.
87 "Members of Provincial Cabinet to Give Ten Per Cent of Salaries to Canadian Patriotic Fund," *Leader* (Regina), 16 September 1914.
88 "Whirlwind Campaign for Patriotic Fund Starts in Regina This Morning," *Leader* (Regina), 22 September 1914.
89 "Socialist Talks on Causes of War," *Leader* (Regina), 3 August 1914.
90 "Will Pay Dues of Printers Who Go to the Front," *Leader* (Regina), 10 August 1914.
91 "Smoker in Honor of Street Railway Men Going to War," *Leader* (Regina), 18 August 1914.
92 "Established Fine Record in Service," *Leader* (Regina), 12 October 1914.
93 Melnycky, "Internment of Ukrainians," 1.
94 The phrase comes from Howard Palmer, *Patterns of Prejudice: A History of Nativism in Alberta* (Toronto: McClelland and Stewart, 1982).
95 J.S. Woodsworth cited in Katie Pickles, *Female Imperialism and National Identity: Imperial Order Daughters of the Empire* (Manchester: Manchester University Press, 2002), 38.
96 Rutherdale, *Hometown Horizons*, 119.
97 Ibid., 124.
98 Although most enemy aliens in Canada came from Germany or Austria-Hungary, a smaller number originated in Turkey and Bulgaria, who also fought on the side of the Central Powers.

99 Peter Melnycky states that approximately 80,000 enemy aliens were registered during the war. Bohdan Kordan places the total number of enemy aliens (both registered and unregistered) at about 120,000. Assuming these figures are correct, close to 40,000 enemy aliens did not formally register, as the law required them to do. Melnycky, "Internment of Ukrainians," 1; Bohdan Kordan, *Prisoners of War: Internment in Canada During the Great War* (Montreal and Kingston: McGill-Queen's University Press, 2002), 5.
100 Canada, Department of the Secretary of State, *Copies of Proclamations, Orders in Council and Documents Relating to the European War* (Ottawa, 1915), cited in *Ukrainians in Canada During the Great War*, ed. Swyripa and Thompson, 171.
101 Melnycky, "Internment of Ukrainians," 2.
102 For a map showing the names and locations of all the camps, see Lubomyr Luciuk, *Without Just Cause: Canada's First National Internment Operations and Ukrainian Canadians 1914–20* (Kingston: Kashtan Press, 2006), 5.
103 Rutherdale, *Hometown Horizons*, 120.
104 Donald Avery, "Ethnic and Class Relations in Western Canada During the First World War: A Case Study of European Immigrants and Anglo-Canadian Nativism," in *Canada and the First World War: Essays in Honour of Robert Craig Brown*, ed. David MacKenzie (Toronto: University of Toronto Press, 2005), 276.
105 Kordan, *Prisoners of War*, 18.
106 Melnycky, "Internment of Ukrainians," 6.
107 Most Ukrainians who came from Galicia were Byzantine or Eastern Rite Catholics, also referred to as "Uniates" or "Greek Catholics." See Stella Hryniuk, "Pioneer Bishop, Pioneer Times: Nykyta Budka in Canada," in *Prophets, Priests and Prodigals: Readings in Canadian Religious History, 1608 to Present*, ed. Mark G. McGowan and David B. Marshall (Toronto: McGraw-Hill Ryerson, 1992), 162–63.
108 Ibid., 157.
109 Ibid.
110 Stella Hryniuk, "The Bishop Budka Controversy: A New Perspective," *Canadian Slavonic Papers* 23, 2 (1981): 158–65.
111 Desmond Morton, "Sir William Otter and Internment Operations in Canada During the First World War," *Canadian Historical Review* 55, 1 (1974): 37.
112 Luciuk, *Without Just Cause*, 3.
113 The story is told in Bill Waiser, *Park Prisoners: The Untold Story of Western Canada's National Parks, 1915–46* (Saskatoon and Calgary: Fifth House, 1995).
114 "Majority Of Alien Enemies Approved," *Leader* (Regina), 3 December 1914.
115 "Worthless Husband Will Be Interned," *Leader* (Regina), 14 December 1914.
116 It is not altogether clear what contemporaries meant by the term "Galician." According to Elizabeth Mitchell, it was "a vague word, tinged with contempt,

that lumps together Ruthenians, Roumanians, Slovenians, and South-Eastern Europeans generally." Mitchell, *Western Canada Before the War*, 11.
117 "800 Aliens Registered at the Regina Office," *Leader* (Regina), 23 December 1914.
118 "Alien Enemies Must Register or Suffer," *Leader* (Regina), 9 January 1915.
119 "Registration of Alien Enemies Nearly Finished," *Leader* (Regina), 14 January 1915.
120 *Der Courier*, 12 August 1914, cited in Luttmer, "The German Experience in Regina," 41.
121 Luttmer, "The German Experience in Regina," 42.
122 Saskatchewan Archives Board, Walter Scott Papers, M I IV.160, World War I: German Canadians, 1914–1915, A.B. Perry to Walter Scott, 15 October 1914, 59570.
123 Luttmer, "The German Experience in Regina," 41.
124 Ibid., 44.
125 Ibid., 49.
126 Elwyn B. Robinon, *History of North Dakota* (Fargo: North Dakota State University Institute for Regional Studies, 2003), 354.
127 "Can Good Come Out of Evil?" *Leader* (Regina), 24 December 1914.
128 "Ideal Weather for New Year's," *Leader* (Regina), 2 January 1915.

Chapter 2

1 Brennan, *Regina*, 195.
2 Ibid., 91.
3 "Eleven Strong Men Wanted," *Leader* (Regina), 18 November 1914.
4 Brennan, *Regina*, 99.
5 "To the Ratepayers of the City of Regina," *Leader* (Regina), 23 November 1914.
6 "An Inaugural Address by Mayor Balfour," *Leader* (Regina), 5 January 1915.
7 Brennan, *Regina*, 65.
8 "New and Views of Labor," *Leader* (Regina), 17 October 1914.
9 Waiser, *Park Prisoners*, 5. See also David Schulze, "The Industrial Workers of the World and the Unemployed in Edmonton and Calgary in the Depression of 1913-1915." *Labour/Le Travail* 25 (1990), 52.
10 "Unemployment in Regina Subject of Big Conference," *Leader* (Regina), 9 January 1915.
11 "Work of the Bureau of Public Welfare," *Leader* (Regina), 14 January 1915.
12 "Provincial Government to Help Unemployed," *Leader* (Regina), 18 January 1915.
13 "700 Unemployed Are Now Registered," *Leader* (Regina), 15 January 1915.
14 "To Inaugurate Campaign," *Leader* (Regina), 20 February 1915.
15 "Ministerial Association to Assist," *Leader* (Regina), 17 February 1915.

16 "Unemployed and Spring Work: A Possible Solution," *Leader* (Regina), 18 February 1915.
17 "Canvass Will Start Monday," *Leader* (Regina), 27 February 1915.
18 "News and Views of Labor," *Leader* (Regina), 3 April 1915.
19 "Bureau Public Welfare Hold Annual Meeting," *Leader* (Regina), 24 November 1915.
20 "Unique Scheme Adopted by the Bureau of Public Welfare," *Leader* (Regina), 2 November 1914.
21 "News and Views of Labor," *Leader* (Regina), 6 February 1915.
22 "Welfare Bureau Shelter Condemned by Labormen: A Strong Denunciation," *Leader* (Regina), 9 February 1915.
23 "To Interview Prov. Health Authorities," *Leader* (Regina), 23 February 1915.
24 Letter from W.E. Cocks, *Leader* (Regina), 10 February 1915.
25 "Unemployed to Wait on Mayor with Petition Asking for Work," *Leader* (Regina), 26 April 1915.
26 "Death of Capt. Lewis Rounding," *Leader* (Regina), 18 May 1916.
27 Ibid.
28 "Mayor Returns with a Million," *Leader* (Regina), 17 May 1915.
29 "Premier Scott Made a Strong Appeal to Prevent Financial Exhaustion," *Leader* (Regina), 24 June 1915.
30 Hopkins, ed., *Canadian Annual Review of Public Affairs, 1915*, 664.
31 "'Out of Work' Has Become Profession," *Leader* (Regina), 30 March 1915.
32 "Unemployed Problem and Agriculture," *Leader* (Regina), 22 February 1915.
33 David Jones, "'There Is Some Power About the Land: The Western Agrarian Press and Country Life Ideology,'" in *The Prairie West: Historical Readings*, ed. R. Douglas Francis and Howard Palmer (Edmonton: Pica Pica Press, 1992), 456.
34 Ibid., 459.
35 Ibid., 460–61. For further discussion of the rural myth, see David Jones, "The Zeitgeist of Western Settlement: Education and the Myth of the Land," in *Schooling and Society in Twentieth Century British Columbia*, ed. J. Donald Wilson and David C. Jones (Calgary: Detselig, 1980), 71–89.
36 "News and Views of Labor," *Leader* (Regina), 5 June 1915.
37 "News and Views of Labor," *Leader* (Regina), 3 April 1915.
38 "News and Views of Labor," *Leader* (Regina), 5 June 1915.
39 "News and Views of Labor," *Leader* (Regina), 30 January 1915.
40 Ibid.
41 "Regina and the Unemployed: First Article," *Leader* (Regina), 19 February 1915.
42 "Unemployment: Third Article," *Leader* (Regina), 2 March 1915.
43 See Chapter 10.
44 "P. McAra, Jr. Resigns from Board of Trade Council," *Leader* (Regina), 30 March 1915.

45 "Regina Made Western Distributing Point for Mail Order Business of Robert Simpson Co. of Toronto," *Leader* (Regina), 19 July 1915.
46 Waiser, *Saskatchewan*, 210.
47 "City Releases Half Street Cleaning Staff to Work in Harvest Fields," *Evening Province and Standard* (Regina), 11 August 1915.
48 "Out-of-Works Who Won't Work," *Leader* (Regina), 19 August 1915.
49 "Tax Sale Being Held in City Hall Tomorrow," *Leader* (Regina), 27 October 1915.
50 Ibid.
51 "Regina Collects $50,000 Arrears Taxes in One Day," *Leader* (Regina), 28 October 1915.
52 "Will Hold Tax Sale During the Evenings," *Leader* (Regina), 6 November 1915.
53 "To Renew the Real Estate Movement We Will Give Away $5000," *Leader* (Regina), 9 October 1915.
54 "Regina Nearly Clears Up Taxes Owing for 1914," *Leader* (Regina), 9 November 1915.
55 "Building Permits in Regina This Year," *Leader* (Regina), 23 December 1915.
56 "All Able-Bodied Men in City Are Working, Report," *Evening Province and Standard* (Regina), 4 November 1915.
57 "Packed Theatres Indicate Better Local Conditions," *Evening Province and Standard* (Regina), 4 November 1915.
58 "Financial Conditions Improving," *Leader* (Regina), 11 December 1915.
59 "Saskatchewan Boys At Valcartier," *Leader* (Regina), 2 September 1914.
60 Ibid.
61 Morton, *When Your Number's Up*, 17.
62 Ibid.
63 "With the Troops at Valcartier," *Leader* (Regina), 3 October 1914.
64 Ibid.
65 Morton, *Fight or Pay*, 29.
66 "With the Troops at Valcartier," *Leader* (Regina), 3 October 1914.
67 Morton, *When Your Number's Up*, 14–15 and 20.
68 Ibid., 20.
69 Ibid., 21.
70 Ibid., 27.
71 "Officers and Boots Are Weak," *Leader* (Regina), 4 January 1915.
72 Morton, *When Your Number's Up*, 32.
73 Ibid., 37.
74 "'Art' Chatwin Writes of Life at the Front," *Leader* (Regina), 22 March 1915.
75 "Regina Boys Under Fire," *Leader* (Regina), 25 March 1915.
76 "Letters from the Front," *Leader* (Regina), 31 March 1915.
77 "Wanted—A Smoke," *Leader* (Regina), 3 April 1915.

78 "The Morning Leader Tobacco Fund," advertisement, *Leader* (Regina), 3 April 1915.
79 "'Smokes' for Our Soldiers," *Leader* (Regina), 14 April 1915.
80 Cook, *Clio's Warriors*, 14.
81 Morton, *When Your Number's Up*, 42.
82 Ibid., 43.
83 Ibid.
84 Morton and Granatstein, *Marching to Armageddon*, 63.
85 Morton, *When Your Number's Up*, 44.
86 "Letters from the Front," *Leader* (Regina), 5 June 1915.
87 Ibid.
88 Ibid.
89 "Letters Written by Regina Boys During the Greatest Battle of the War," *Leader* (Regina), 20 May 1915.
90 Ibid.
91 "Barracks Full of Wounded Bombarded by the Germans," *Leader* (Regina), 1 June 1915.
92 "Describes Fight Between French and German Planes," *Leader* (Regina), 29 May 1915.
93 "Letters from the Front," *Leader* (Regina), 8 June 1915.
94 "Local Boy Killed in Fighting," *Leader* (Regina), 10 May 1915.
95 "Last Letter from Joseph Hilsenteger," *Leader* (Regina), 24 May 1915.
96 "Regina Man Tells of Horrors of the War," *Leader* (Regina), 1 June 1915.
97 Ibid.
98 "Lieutenant Graham Writes of 'The Realities of War,'" *Leader* (Regina), 3 June 1915.
99 "Regina Man Tells of Horrors of the War," *Leader* (Regina), 1 June 1915.
100 "From the Front," *Leader* (Regina), 3 July 1915.
101 "From the Front," *Leader* (Regina), 12 June 1915.
102 "We Are Still on the Big Job," *Leader* (Regina), 2 June 1915.
103 "Canadians Are Always in the Thick of Fight," *Leader* (Regina), 19 July 1915.
104 Annette Becker, *War and Faith: The Religious Imagination in France 1914–1930*, trans. Helen McPhail (New York: Berg, 1998), 16–17. For efforts to establish the veracity of the story, see Desmond Morton, *Silent Battle: Canadian Prisoners of War in Germany, 1914–19* (Toronto: Lester, 1992), 1–4.
105 "Canada Was There," *Leader* (Regina), 26 April 1915.
106 Ibid.
107 "The Patriotic Fund Appeal," *Leader* (Regina), 11 May 1915.
108 Ibid.
109 "Canada's Duty," *Leader* (Regina), 3 July 1915.
110 "Our Young Men and the War," *Leader* (Regina), 6 August 1915.
111 Ibid.
112 "Wind Helped in Destruction of the Armada," *Leader* (Regina), 10 May 1915.

113 Ibid.
114 Ibid.
115 "Four Hundred Volunteers Now Encamped in Winter Fair Building: Two Units," *Leader* (Regina), 4 February 1915; "Troops Inspected at the Winter Fair Building by Major General Steele," *Leader* (Regina), 8 March 1915.
116 "Saskatchewan Authorized to Raise Two New Infantry Battalions for Overseas," *Leader* (Regina), 29 June 1915.
117 "Your King and Country Need You," *Leader*, 30 June 1915.
118 "Don the Khaki," *Leader* (Regina), 8 July 1915.
119 "The Call Has Come," *Leader* (Regina), 10 July 1915.
120 "The Unmarried Man's Responsibility," *Leader* (Regina), 9 September 1915.
121 "Four Passed Examinations Yesterday," *Leader* (Regina), 17 July 1915.
122 "Government Should Lead," *Leader* (Regina), 14 July 1915.
123 "No Longer is a Man Prevented from Enlisting if Wife Objects; Parents No Power to Stop Minors," *Evening Province and Standard* (Regina), 9 August 1915.
124 "Everybody Must Do Their Part," *Leader* (Regina), 23 July 1915.
125 "Rev. Walter Western Makes Strong Plea to Young Men to Respond to Call of King and Country," *Leader* (Regina), 19 July 1915.
126 "Recruiting Officers Hear Many Excuses," *Evening Province and Standard* (Regina), 5 January 1916.
127 "Eighteen Men Joined Yesterday," *Leader* (Regina), 31 July 1915.
128 "Travellers' Parade Created a Sensation in City, Friday," *Leader* (Regina), 31 July 1915.
129 "Patriotic Film at Rose; Also Million Dollar," *Leader* (Regina), 20 March 1915.
130 "Soccer Football Items That Will Interest You," *Leader* (Regina), 26 July 1915.
131 "Four More Footballers Going to Battlefields," *Leader* (Regina), 11 August 1915.
132 Ibid.
133 "Here's a Chance for Athletes to Enlist," *Leader* (Regina), 8 September 1915.
134 "Athletes Are Prominent in Recruiting Soldiers," *Leader* (Regina), 11 September 1915.
135 "One-Third of Thirty-Six Members of Local Force Have Enlisted," *Leader* (Regina), 17 September 1915.
136 "Leader Job Men Presented with Wrist Watches," *Leader* (Regina), 18 September 1915.
137 "Seven Members of Department of Agriculture Enlisted Yesterday for Defence of the Empire," *Leader* (Regina), 10 August 1915.
138 "Presentation Was Made to Capt. Mantle," *Leader* (Regina), 18 September 1915.
139 "Anniversary of War Was Celebrated by Regina Citizens at Mass Meeting; Patriotic Resolution Passed Unanimously," *Leader* (Regina), 5 August 1915.
140 Ibid.

141 "Jimmie Balfour Arrives Today on a Furlough," *Leader* (Regina), 22 February 1918.
142 "Anniversary of War Was Celebrated by Regina Citizens at Mass Meeting; Patriotic Resolution Passed Unanimously," *Leader* (Regina), 5 August 1915.

Chapter 3

1 John Thompson notes that many non-British voters in western Canada (with the notable exception of French Canadians) voted for prohibition in wartime referenda. He writes: "But many of these people saw the prohibition referendum as a kind of loyalty test, through which they could prove that they were good Canadian citizens, even during this time of crisis." John Thompson, "'The Beginning of Our Regeneration': The Great War and Western Canadian Reform Movements," *Historical Papers* (1972): 233.
I would phrase this slightly differently, placing more emphasis on the atmosphere of intimidation and coercion in which the dominant British group was able impose its version of "good Canadian citizenship" on the rest of the population.
2 Joseph R. Gusfield, *Symbolic Crusade: Status Politics and the American Temperance Movement* (Urbana: University of Illinois Press, 1963), 5.
3 Cheryl Krasnick Warsh, "'John Barleycorn Must Die': An Introduction to the Social History of Alcohol," in *Drink in Canada: Historical Essays*, ed. Cheryl Krasnick Warsh (Montreal and Kingston: McGill-Queen's University Press, 1993), 11.
4 Nancy M. Sheehan, "The WCTU on the Prairies, 1886–1930: An Alberta–Saskatchewan Comparison," *Prairie Forum* 6, 1 (1981): 17.
5 Erhard Pinno, "Temperance and Prohibition," MA thesis, University of Regina, 1993, p. 11–12.
6 Ibid., 25.
7 Ibid., 26–27.
8 Brennan, *Regina*, 67.
9 Warsh, "'John Barleycorn Must Die,'" 6–8.
10 Luttmer, "The German Experience," 37.
11 Pinno, "Temperance and Prohibition in Saskatchewan," 31 and 34.
12 Hopkins, ed., *Canadian Annual Review of Public Affairs, 1913*, 580.
13 Brennan, "A Political History of Saskatchewan," 250–51.
14 Pinno, "Temperance and Prohibition in Saskatchewan," 20–21, quoted in Warsh, "'John Barleycorn Must Die,'" 22.
15 Erhard Pinno, "Temperance and Prohibition in Saskatchewan," 42.
16 C.E. Eymann to J.A. Calder, March 1915, published in *Evening Province* (Regina), 31 May 1916.
17 Pinno, "Temperance and Prohibition in Saskatchewan," 51.
18 Ibid., 52.

19 Hopkins, ed., *Canadian Annual Review of Public Affairs, 1915*, 683.
20 "Temperance Rally Well Attended," *Leader* (Regina), 24 February 1915.
21 Ibid.
22 Pinno, "Temperance and Prohibition in Saskatchewan," 58.
23 "What Prominent Public Men Think of Temperance Proposals of Government," *Leader* (Regina), 19 March 1915.
24 "Telegrams of Congratulations Pour into Premier's Office; Many Prominent People Give Opinions," *Leader* (Regina), 20 March 1915.
25 Ibid.
26 "Packed Audience Heard Pastor of Knox Presbyterian Church Favor Temperance Proposals," *Leader* (Regina), 29 March 1915.
27 "Scott's Policy Wins General Approval," *Leader* (Regina), 20 March 1915.
28 "Principal Lloyd Addressed Mass Meeting of Temperance People of the City Yesterday," *Leader* (Regina), 31 May 1915.
29 Pinno, "Temperance and Prohibition in Saskatchewan," 70–71.
30 Hopkins, ed., *Canadian Annual Review of Public Affairs, 1915*, 671.
31 Pinno, "Temperance and Prohibition in Saskatchewan," 75.
32 Gusfield, *Symbolic Crusade*, 3.
33 Pickles, *Female Imperialism*, 2.
34 Ibid., 42.
35 For discussion of the strains of nativism and racism in prohibitionism, see M.G. Decarie, "Paved with Good Intentions: The Prohibitionists' Road to Racism in Ontario," *Ontario History* 66 (1974): 15–22.
36 "Searchlight of War on Home Conditions," *Leader* (Regina), 12 April 1915.
37 Thompson, "'The Beginning of Our Regeneration,'" 232. See also Craig Heron, *Booze: A Distilled History* (Toronto: Between the Lines, 2003), 178.
38 Ibid., 96.
39 "A Memorable Session," *Leader* (Regina), 25 June 1915.
40 "Drunkenness is Disappearing," *Leader* (Regina), 9 October 1915.
41 "Drunkenness Has Decreased Fully Seventy-Five Per Cent According to Official Figures," *Leader* (Regina), 2 December 1915.
42 *Leader* (Regina), 3 December 1915, cited in Pinno, "Temperance and Prohibition in Saskatchewan," 106.
43 "The Banished Bar and the Drunkard's Horse," *Evening Province and Standard* (Regina), 31 July 1915.
44 "Banish the Bar Forces Conclude with a Rousing Mass Meeting," *Leader* (Regina), 29 July 1915.
45 "The Liquor Stores as Sources of Revenue," *Leader* (Regina), 25 July 1915.
46 "The Friendless Dispensary," *Evening Province and Standard* (Regina), 6 January 1916.
47 "Seven Liquor Districts Voting," *Leader* (Regina), 4 December 1915.
48 "A Red Letter Anniversary," *Leader* (Regina), 18 March 1916.
49 Pinno, "Temperance and Prohibition in Saskatchewan," 111.
50 "The Referendum Ballot," *Leader* (Regina), 11 December 1916.

51 "Registration of Voters," *Leader* (Regina), 1 September 1916.
52 "Prepare to Register," *Leader* (Regina), 26 August 1916.
53 "Drank Up Liquor Secured for East End Celebration," *Leader* (Regina), 4 November 1916.
54 "Stabbing Affray Outcome of Row in the East End," *Leader* (Regina), 15 November 1916.
55 "Rumanian Soldier Jumped on by Gang at East End Dance," *Leader* (Regina), 22 November 1916.
56 "Regina Pastors Direct Attacks on 'Wets' Sunday," *Leader* (Regina), 7 December 1916.
57 "Helps to Abolish the Liquor Dispensaries by a Huge Majority," *Leader* (Regina), 12 December 1916.
58 "Women Working Well in Getting Out Vote on Liquor Referendum," *Daily Post* (Regina), 11 December 1916.
59 "Result by Polls in Aldermanic Vote and on the Referendum," *Leader* (Regina), 12 December 1916.
60 Pinno, "Temperance and Prohibition in Saskatchewan," 121.
61 Brennan, "A Political History of Saskatchewan," 401–402.
62 Wendy Mitchinson, "The WCTU: 'For God, Home and Native Land': A Study of Nineteenth-Century Feminism," in *A Not Unreasonable Claim: Women and Reform in Canada, 1980s–1920s*, ed. Linda Kealey (Toronto: Women's Press, 1979), 193.
63 Ibid., 196–97.
64 Catherine L. Cleverdon, *The Woman Suffrage Movement in Canada* (Toronto: University of Toronto Press, 1974), 119.
65 Thompson, *Harvests of War*, 107.
66 Carol Lee Bacchi, *Liberation Deferred? The Ideas of the English-Canadian Suffragists, 1877–1918* (Toronto: University of Toronto Press, 1983), 149.
67 "Women Are Now Earning Right to Vote," *Leader* (Regina), 26 November 1915.
68 Pickles, *Female Imperialism*, 1.
69 Ibid., 16–17.
70 Ibid., 26.
71 "Forget IODE Annual Meeting and Elections," *Leader* (Regina), 7 January 1916.
72 "Municipal Chapter Has Worked Well," *Leader* (Regina), 14 March 1916.
73 "Women of West-End Form Patriotic Club," *Leader* (Regina), 23 June 1915.
74 "Municipal Chapter Has Worked Well," *Leader* (Regina), 14 March 1916.
75 Nadine Small notes that the number of IODE chapters in the prairie provinces increased from forty-nine at the end of 1913 to 220 at the end of 1918, with an estimated membership of 40,000. Nadine Small, "Stand by the Union Jack: The Imperial Order Daughters of the Empire in the

Prairie Provinces During the Great War 1914–18," MA thesis, University of Saskatchewan, 1988, p. 44.
76 "Provincial Chapter Daughters of Empire Conclude Convention," *Leader* (Regina), 30 June 1915.
77 Ibid.
78 "The Provincial President Reviews IODE Work of Last Year—Forecast Future," *Leader* (Regina), 13 April 1916.
79 "Municipal Chapter Has Worked Well," *Leader* (Regina), 14 March 1916.
80 "Salisbury Chapter Gets Letters from Men of 28th, France," *Leader* (Regina), 29 March 1916.
81 "Another Pair of Letters from the Front to IODE," *Leader* (Regina), 30 March 1916.
82 "Red Cross Starts New Year Well," *Leader* (Regina), 2 November 1915.
83 "Regina Red Cross Society Has Raised Nearly $9,800—Retiring President's Summary of Year," *Leader* (Regina), 2 November 1915.
84 "Drop in and Visit the Red Cross Women," *Leader* (Regina), 26 November 1915.
85 "Regina Red Cross Society Has Raised Nearly $9,800—Retiring President's Summary of Year," *Leader* (Regina), 2 November 1915.
86 "Red Cross Will Benefit by One Thousand Dollars as Result of RNWMP Fete," *Leader* (Regina), 22 July 1915.
87 Ibid.
88 "$2,171 Goes From Here to Red Cross," *Leader* (Regina), 22 October 1915.
89 "Peter Pan's Pipes," *Leader* (Regina), 31 July 1916.
90 "Peter Pan's Pipes," *Leader* (Regina), 8 May 1916.
91 "Peter Pan's Pipes," *Leader* (Regina), 15 May 1916.
92 "Peter Pan's Pipes," *Leader* (Regina), 22 March 1916.
93 "Earliest Steps Taken to Form an Auxiliary to 195th," *Leader* (Regina), 21 March 1916.
94 "Colors for 68th to be Presented This Afternoon," *Leader* (Regina), 20 April 1916.
95 "Colors Given 68th in View of Big Crowd," *Leader* (Regina), 21 April 1916.
96 "Regina Nurse to Represent Saskatchewan," *Leader* (Regina), 9 March 1915.
97 "Purse for Red Cross Nurse," *Evening Province and Standard* (Regina), 18 March 1915.
98 "Nurse Dale Gets Word to Report for Duty Soon," *Leader* (Regina), 19 April 1915.
99 "Local Nurse Will Be Sent to Front," *Leader* (Regina), 22 April 1915.
100 "Hearty Send-Off Given the Nurses Leaving for Front," *Daily Post* (Regina), 26 October 1916.
101 "Miss Creswell for 24 Hours War Prisoner," *Leader* (Regina), 7 September 1918.
102 "Regina Nurse Writes Friend from Cliveden," *Evening Province and Standard* (Regina), 23 October 1915.

Notes

103 "Miss E. Chatwin Passes Test as Transport Driver," *Leader* (Regina), 7 September 1918.
104 "Peter Pan's Pipes," *Leader* (Regina), 18 October 1918.
105 "Peter Pan's Pipes," *Leader* (Regina), 25 December 1915.
106 Elizabeth Ann Kalmakoff, "Woman Suffrage in Saskatchewan." MA Thesis, University of Regina, 1993, 73–76.
107 Ibid., 87–88.
108 "Women's Suffrage," *Evening Province and Standard* (Regina), 18 January 1916.
109 Ibid.
110 June Menzies, "Votes for Saskatchewan Women," in *Politics in Saskatchewan*, ed. Norman War and Duff Spafford. (Don Mills: Longmans, 1968), 81.
111 Kalmakoff, "Woman Suffrage in Saskatchewan," 89–91 and 94.
112 Ibid., 93–94.
113 Ibid., 95–96.
114 Ibid., 96.
115 "Home Guard Wants a Thousand Men," *Evening Province* (Regina), 11 April 1916.
116 "Women Are Now Earning Right to Vote," *Leader* (Regina), 26 November 1915.
117 James M. Pitsula, *An Act of Faith: The Early Years of Regina College* (Regina: Canadian Plains Research Center, 1988), 49.
118 "Women Are Now Earning Right to Vote," *Leader* (Regina), 26 November 1915.
119 "Women's Rights Strengthened By This War," *Leader* (Regina), 13 November 1915.
120 "Woman and Her Relation to War," *Leader* (Regina), 12 May 1915.
121 "1,200 Women Sign Petition for Franchise," *Evening Province and Standard* (Regina), 12 February 1916.
122 "Women Receive the Vote From Scott Government at Memorable St. Valentine's Day Assembly," *Leader* (Regina), 15 February 1916.
123 Ibid.
124 Ibid.
125 Ibid.
126 Ibid.
127 Brennan, "A Political History of Saskatchewan," 327.
128 "Women Receive the Vote From Scott Government at Memorable St. Valentine's Day Assembly," *Leader* (Regina), 15 February 1916.
129 "Miss Stinson Shows Complete Mastery of Air," *Leader* (Regina), 25 July 1916.
130 "Big Fair Closes with Sensational Drop by Aviatrix," *Leader* (Regina), 29 July 1916.
131 "Peter Pan's Pipes," *Leader* (Regina), 28 July 1916.
132 "University Women Organize Club with 16 Charter Members," *Leader* (Regina), 19 November 1915. The sixteen charter members had earned

university degrees as follows: Victoria College, University of Toronto, 5; Queen's, Kingston, 3; University of Toronto, 2; University of Manitoba, 1; Albion College, Michigan, 1; Otago College, New Zealand, 1; Mount Allison University, 1; Acadia, Nova Scotia, 1; University of Missouri, 1.
133 "Peter Pan's Pipes," *Leader* (Regina), 4 February 1916.
134 "Peter Pan's Pipes," *Leader* (Regina), 17 May 1916.
135 "Women Receive the Vote from Scott Government at Memorable St. Valentine's Day Assembly," *Leader* (Regina), 15 February 1916.

Chapter 4

1 McLaren, *Our Own Master Race*, 47.
2 Buckner, "Whatever Happened to the British Empire?" 28.
3 Saskatchewan, *Department of Education Annual Report*, 1913, 70. W.S. Cram, quoted in Marilyn Barber, "Canadianization Through the Schools of the Prairie Provinces Before World War I: The Attitudes and Aims of the English-Speaking Majority," in *Ethnic Canadians: Culture and Education*, ed. Martin L. Kovacs (Regina: Canadian Plains Research Center, 1978), 283.
4 Waiser, *Saskatchewan*, 9–10.
5 Ibid., 10.
6 *Evening Province* (Regina), 26 May 1915, cited in Brennan, "A Political History of Saskatchewan," 288.
7 "Both Parties Oppose Bilingualism," *Leader* (Regina), 3 June 1915.
8 Ibid.
9 Ibid.
10 Ibid.
11 Ibid.
12 "An Anti-British Policy," *Leader* (Regina), 3 June 1915.
13 "A Call to Service," *Leader* (Regina), 23 June 1915.
14 "On Education," *Evening Province and Standard* (Regina), 4 October 1915.
15 "Educational Association is Formed," *Leader* (Regina), 28 July 1915.
16 "Convention of Prominent Citizens Yesterday Demonstrated Necessity of Reforms in Public School System of Instruction in Saskatchewan," *Leader* (Regina), 23 September 1915.
17 "The Meaning of This Campaign," *Leader* (Regina), 22 September 1915.
18 "Democracy, Education and Public Interest," *Leader* (Regina), 19 February 1916.
19 "Many Instructive Addresses Were Delivered on 'Better Schools Day' at Different Points in Saskatchewan; People of Province Interested," *Leader* (Regina), 8 July 1916.
20 Ibid.
21 Harold Foght, *A Survey of Education in the Province of Saskatchewan.* (Regina: King's Printer, 1918) , 41.
22 Ibid., 42.
23 Ibid., 44.

24 Ibid.
25 David C. Jones, "Better School Day in Saskatchewan and the Perils of Educational Reform," *Journal of Educational Thought* 14, 2 (1980): 128.
26 "Many Instructive Addresses Were Delivered on 'Better Schools Day' at Different Points in Saskatchewan; People of Province Interested," *Leader* (Regina), 8 July 1916.
27 Ibid.
28 "Principal Lloyd to Premier Scott," *Leader* (Regina), 23 October 1915.
29 Jones, "Better School Day in Saskatchewan," 127.
30 "What Our Education Department is Doing," *Leader* (Regina), 27 November 1915.
31 "Educational Agriculture," *Leader* (Regina), 16 October 1915.
32 Ibid.
33 "Farmers Pledge Aid to Better Schools," *Evening Province and Standard* (Regina), 25 September 1915.
34 Foght, *A Survey of Education in the Province of Saskatchewan*, 10.
35 Ibid., 19.
36 Ibid.
37 "Many Instructive Addresses Were Delivered on 'Better Schools Day' at Different Points in Saskatchewan; People of Province Interested," *Leader* (Regina), 8 July 1916.
38 Hopkins, ed., *Canadian Annual Review of Public Affairs, 1914*, 630.
39 "Interpreting the School Law," *Evening Province and Standard* (Regina), 13 September 1915.
40 Hopkins, ed., *Canadian Annual Review of Public Affairs, 1914*, 630.
41 Ibid., 631.
42 Hopkins, ed., *Canadian Annual Review of Public Affairs, 1916*, 712.
43 Hopkins, ed., *Canadian Annual Review of Public Affairs, 1914*, 631.
44 Hopkins, ed., *Canadian Annual Review of Public Affairs, 1913*, 618–19.
45 Hopkins, ed., *Canadian Annual Review of Public Affairs, 1914*, 620.
46 Adolf Ens, "The Public School Crisis Among Mennonites in Saskatchewan 1916–25," in *Mennonite Images: Historical, Cultural and Literary Essays Dealing with Mennonite Issues*, ed. Harry Loewen (Winnipeg: Hyperion Press, 1980), 75.
47 Foght, *A Survey of Education in the Province of Saskatchewan*, 145–47.
48 "Convention of Prominent Citizens Yesterday Demonstrated Necessity of Reforms in Public School System of Instruction in Saskatchewan," *Leader* (Regina), 23 September 1915.
49 Ibid.
50 Hopkins, ed., *Canadian Annual Review of Public Affairs, 1915*, 679.
51 "Inspector J.T.M. Anderson at Metropolitan on Education of Non-English Speaking Citizen," *Leader* (Regina), 8 November 1915.
52 Ibid.

53 Ibid.
54 Ibid.
55 "J.T.M. Anderson, Inspector of Schools for Yorkton District, Delivers a Striking Address, 'Education of the New Canadian,'" *Leader* (Regina), 22 February 1918.
56 Mariana Valverde, *The Age of Light, Soap and Water: Moral Reform in English Canada, 1885–1925* (Toronto: McClelland and Stewart, 1991), 123.
57 "A Policy of Friendliness," *Leader* (Regina), 4 December 1915.
58 Ibid.
59 "A Policy of Friendliness," *Leader*, (Regina), 27 November 1915.
60 "A Policy of Friendliness," *Leader* (Regina), 4 December 1915.
61 "A Policy of Friendliness," *Leader* (Regina), 27 November 1915.
62 "The Language Question," *Leader* (Regina), 11 March 1916.

Chapter 5

1 Barnhart, *"Peace, Progress and Prosperity,"* 19–20.
2 Ibid., 78.
3 Ibid., 16.
4 Smith, *Prairie Liberalism*, 23.
5 Ibid., 38.
6 Ibid.
7 Hopkins, ed., *Canadian Annual Review of Public Affairs, 1913*, 583.
8 Scott wrote: "What my rights and standing in Presbyterian Church courts may be I am not sure—I have always been and am an adherent and supporter but not a communicant—I purpose finding out." "I Charge You with Flagrant and Willful False Witness," *Leader* (Regina), 13 January 1916.
9 Barnhart, *"Peace, Progress and Prosperity,"* 9–13.
10 Ibid., 22–23.
11 Queen's University Archives (QUA), MacKinnon Family Fonds, 3023.1, Box 1, "General Information," "The MacKinnon Brothers of Lake Ainslie," written by Rev. Dr. Murdoch MacKinnon, Edmonton, 1951.
12 United Church of Canada/Victoria University Archives (UCC/VUA), Biographical Files Collection, MacKinnon, Murdoch Archibald (Rev.), Biography (1871–1954), clipping from *Observer*, 1 September 1954.
13 Grant's role as public intellectual is discussed in Carl Berger, *The Sense of Power: Studies in the Ideas of Canadian Imperialism 1867–1914* (Toronto: University of Toronto Press, 1970), especially 23–33. His importance to Queen's University is dealt with in Hilda Neatby, *To Strive, To Seek, To Find and Not To Yield, Queen's University, Vol. 1, 1841–1917* (Montreal and Kingston: McGill-Queen's University Press, 1978).
14 Neatby, *To Strive, To Seek*, 238–40.
15 Lilian Vaux MacKinnon, *Miriam of Queen's* (Toronto: McClelland and Stewart, 1921), 99.

16 Ibid., 230.
17 Raymond Huel, "Pastor vs. Politician: The Reverend Murdoch MacKinnon and Premier Walter Scott's Amendment to the School Act," *Saskatchewan History* 32, 2 (1979): 62.
18 Ibid., 62–63.
19 Patrick Kyba, "J.T.M. Anderson," in *Saskatchewan Premiers of the Twentieth Century*, ed. Gordon L. Barnhart (Regina: Canadian Plains Research Center, 2004), 124–25.
20 Huel, "Pastor vs. Politician," 63.
21 Ibid., 64.
22 Ibid., 65.
23 Harold Foght noted in 1918: "With only 19 separate school districts out of over 4,000, the problem can hardly be considered an acute one." Foght, *A Survey of Education in the Province of Saskatchewan*, 143.
24 "Rev. M.A. MacKinnon Deals with Saskatchewan School Question in Sunday Evening Sermon," *Leader* (Regina), 27 December 1915.
25 For a discussion of the pro-British mindset of English-speaking Canadians in western Canada in this period, see Barber, "Canadianization Through the Schools"; and Raymond Huel, "The Public School as a Guardian of Anglo-Saxon Traditions: The Saskatchewan Experience, 1913–1918," in *Ethnic Canadians: Culture and Education*, ed. Martin L. Kovacs (Regina: Canadian Plains Research Center, 1978).
26 "Rev. M.A. MacKinnon Deals with Saskatchewan School Question in Sunday Evening Sermon," *Leader* (Regina), 27 December 1915.
27 Ibid.
28 Ibid.
29 Ibid.
30 Saskatchewan Archives Board (SAB), Walter Scott Papers, M 1, VI 6, J.A. Allan to Walter Scott, 18 July 1918, 78396-7.
31 "Rev. M.A. MacKinnon Deals with Saskatchewan School Question in Sunday Evening Sermon," *Leader* (Regina), 27 December 1915.
32 "An Open Letter to Mr. MacKinnon from the Premier," *Leader* (Regina), 27 December 1915.
33 "Rev. Mr. MacKinnon and the Leader," *Leader* (Regina), 28 December 1915.
34 "Profaning a Pulpit," *Evening Province and Standard* (Regina), 29 December 1915.
35 "Rev. Murdoch MacKinnon's Reply," *Leader* (Regina), 30 December 1915.
36 "Premier Scott Presents Separate School Facts," *Leader* (Regina), 1 January 1916.
37 "Rev. M.A. MacKinnon Replies to Premier Scott," *Leader* (Regina), 8 January 1916.
38 Ibid.
39 "I Charge You with Flagrant and Willful False Witness," *Leader* (Regina), 13 January 1916.

40 "Citizenship and the Crime of its Coercion, or Freedom in its Religious, Educational and Social Development," *Leader* (Regina), 24 January 1916.
41 Brennan, "A Political History of Saskatchewan," 293.
42 Ibid., 295–96.
43 Ibid., 297.
44 "Premier Scott to Speak on School Law," *Leader* (Regina), 23 February 1916.
45 "Frank Admission by Judge McLorg That Former Supreme Court Decisions Must Stand," *Leader* (Regina), 25 February 1916.
46 "Judge McLorg Wires Letter to the Press," *Leader* (Regina), 26 February 1916.
47 "Frank Admission by Judge McLorg That Former Supreme Court Decisions Must Stand," *Leader* (Regina), 25 February 1916.
48 Ibid.
49 "Commends MacKinnon—Condemns Scott," *Leader* (Regina), 26 February 1916.
50 "Splendid Tribute Paid to Rev. Murdoch MacKinnon by the Scotch Presbyterian Liberals," *Evening Province and Standard* (Regina), 28 February 1916.
51 SAB, Walter Scott Papers, M 1, VI 6, Walter Scott to "Certain Members of Knox Church Session," 23 September 1918, 78540.
52 "Probably we may take it that the Presbyterian church in Canada is shy one adherent, while stronger in the service of one minister who must feel the renewed confidence in himself through the fact that his church is not lacking in appreciation of good work well performed." "Rev. Murdoch MacKinnon, M.A., D.D.," *Evening Province* (Regina), 4 April 1916.
53 "Regina Presbytery Replies to the Cowardly Attack on Rev. Murdoch MacKinnon," *Evening Province and Standard* (Regina), 2 March 1916.
54 "Condemns the Scott Attack on MacKinnon," *Evening Province and Standard* (Regina), 2 March 1916.
55 Angus A. Graham, "Saskatchewan Separate School Situation, *The Presbyterian*, 27 April 1916, 392.
56 "Still Another Answer to the Attack on Rev. MacKinnon," *Evening Province and Standard* (Regina), 7 March 1916.
57 Letter from "Presbyterian Liberal, Politically Mad," *Evening Province and Standard* (Regina), 10 January 1916.
58 Ibid.
59 Letter from "Daylight's Dad," "Prostituting Principles of Liberalism," *Evening Province and Standard* (Regina), 19 January 1916.
60 Ibid.
61 Ibid.
62 "Obnoxious Clauses to be Deleted," *Evening Province and Standard* (Regina), 22 January 1916.
63 Smith, *Prairie Liberalism*, 51.
64 "Believe Scott Has Handed in a Resignation," *Evening Province and Standard* (Regina), 18 March 1916.

65 *Census of Prairie Provinces, 1916.*
66 Barnhart, *"Peace, Progress and Prosperity,"* 107–108.
67 Ibid., 123.
68 Ibid., 115.
69 Public Archives of Canada, Wilfrid Laurier Papers, W. Scott to Laurier, 2 March 1916, pp. 191281–82, cited in Brennan, "A Political History of Saskatchewan," 307.
70 "Premier Scott's Absence," *Leader* (Regina), 28 February 1916.
71 "Walter Thomas Scott Was Afraid to Face the Music," *Evening Province* (Regina), 28 February 1916.
72 Barnhart, *"Peace, Progress and Prosperity,"* 141.
73 SAB, Walter Scott Papers, M 1, VI 6, Robert Sinton to Walter Scott, 30 September 1918, 78596.
74 Angus A. Graham, "Saskatchewan Separate School Situation, *The Presbyterian*, 27 April 1916, 392.
75 Ibid.
76 SAB, Walter Scott Papers, M 1, VI 6, Walter Scott to Angus Graham, 1 September 1918, 78506.
77 Ibid., W.R. Motherwell to Walter Scott, 13 September 1918, 78531.
78 Ibid., 78532.
79 Ibid., Walter Scott to Angus Graham, 1 September 1918, 78507.
80 "'Restless Partisans' and 'Sick Slackers,'" *Moose Jaw Times,* 21 December 1918.
81 Barnhart, "Peace, Progress and Prosperity," 143.
82 SAB, Walter Scott Papers, M 1, VI 6, Walter Scott to J.A. Allan, 4 July 1918, 78376.
83 Huel, "Pastor vs. Politician," 68.
84 "Rev. MacKinnon Resigns From Knox Church," *Leader* (Regina), 14 August 1918.
85 "Apologies Are Due" (letter to the editor), *Leader* (Regina), 16 August 1918.
86 "Apologies Are Due" (letter to the editor), *Leader* (Regina), 21 August 1918.
87 SAB, Walter Scott Papers, M 1, VI 6, Walter Scott to J.A. Allan, 4 July 1918, 78380.
88 Ibid., J.A. Allan to Walter Scott, 18 July 1918, 78395.
89 Ibid.
90 Ibid., James Balfour to Walter Scott, 30 October 1918, 78650–1.
91 Ibid., James Balfour to Walter Scott, 30 October 1918, 78655–56.
92 "Rev. M.A. MacKinnon Deals with Saskatchewan School Question in Sunday Evening Sermon," *Leader* (Regina), 27 December 1915.
93 Brennan, "A Political History of Saskatchewan," 322–23 and 327; Hopkins, ed., *Canadian Annual Review of Public Affairs, 1916,* 710.
94 Barnhart, *"Peace, Progress and Prosperity,"* 142.
95 SAB, Walter Scott Papers, M 1, VI 6, Walter Scott to George Langley, 5 September 1918, 78422.

Chapter 6

1. "Girls Appreciate Best Gifts from Boys at Front," *Leader* (Regina), 23 December 1916.
2. "Rats as Big as Bulldogs in Trenches," *Leader* (Regina), 18 December 1915.
3. "Letters Received at St. Chad's College from Boys at Front," *Leader* (Regina), 10 November 1915.
4. "Pte. Williams Returns from the Front," *Leader* (Regina), 26 November 1915.
5. "Pte. Williams Was Guest of Honor," *Leader* (Regina), 29 November 1915.
6. "Pte. Williams Returns from the Front," *Leader* (Regina), 26 November 1915.
7. "Sergeant Hall 7th Batt. Relates War Experiences," *Leader* (Regina), 7 January 1916.
8. Ibid.
9. Ibid.
10. "Intimate Description of Soldiers' Work at the Front, by Private Kay Just Returned Home," *Leader* (Regina), 31 December 1915.
11. "Rats as Big as Bulldogs in Trenches," *Leader* (Regina), 18 December 1915.
12. "Sergeant Ensor Who Has Been in Trenches for Over Year Writes," *Leader* (Regina), 23 October 1915.
13. "Pte. J.V. Preece Writes Letter to a Friend Here," *Leader* (Regina), 29 November 1915.
14. "Germans Inquire About 'Banish the Bar' Here," *Leader* (Regina), 29 October 1915.
15. "Driving Transport with Rations for Men in Trenches," *Leader* (Regina), 24 February 1916.
16. "Hun Sniper Killed Major A.F. Mantle," *Leader* (Regina), 24 October 1916.
17. "Major Mantle, Regina Officer, Dies at Front," *Leader* (Regina), 4 October 1916.
18. "Impressive Memorial Service to Late Major Mantle Was Held at Westminster Church Yesterday," *Leader* (Regina), 9 October 1916.
19. Ibid.
20. LAC, RG 150 Acc 92-93/166, Box 5907-2, Mantle, Alfred Frank.
21. "Captain Cullum Regina Doctor, Dies of Wounds," *Leader* (Regina), 13 November 1916.
22. "Capt. J.A. Cullum Dies of Wounds in the Somme Action," *Daily Post* (Regina), 13 November 1916.
23. "Col. Laird Tells of Talking with Captain Cullum," *Daily Post* (Regina), 13 November 1916.
24. Donald George Scott Calder, *The History of the 28th (Northwest) Battalion, C.E.F. (October 1914–June 1919)* From the Memoirs of Brigadier General Alexancer Ross (Regina: Regina Rifle Regiment, 1961), 107.
25. "Touching Service Held at St. Paul's for Dead Heroes," *Daily Post* (Regina), 20 November 1916.
26. "Cressie is Glad to be in Regina," *Leader* (Regina), 25 December 1916.

Notes

27 "'Come On, You Regina Boys,' Yelled 'Cressy,'" *Leader* (Regina), 4 November 1916.
28 Calder, *The History of the 28th (Northwest) Battalion*, 12.
29 "Lieutenant 'Hick' Abbott Decorated with Military Cross for His Bravery," *Leader* (Regina), 10 July 1917.
30 LAC, RG 150 Acc 1992-3/166, Box 4–28, Abbott, Edward Lyman.
31 "Two Well-Known Local Boys Killed," *Leader* (Regina), 22 August 1918.
32 LAC, RG 150 Acc 1992-3/166, Box 4–28, Abbott, Edward Lyman.
33 "Charlie Otton Writes Breezy Letter on War," *Leader* (Regina), 17 February 1917.
34 LAC, RG 150, Acc 92-93/166, Box 7507–66, Otton, Charles Edward.
35 Calder, *History of the 28th (Northwest) Battalion*, 12.
36 "Shocked Beyond Measure Were Friends of Bob," *Leader* (Regina), 30 March 1917.
37 "In Memoriam: Robert Boucher," *Leader* (Regina), 30 March 1917.
38 "Fred McCulloch Recommended for the Military Cross for his Conspicuous Gallantry," *Leader* (Regina), 21 March 1917.
39 "Clarrie Dale Meets Death at the Front," *Leader* (Regina), 10 August 1917.
40 "Regina Boys in Thick of All Fighting," *Leader* (Regina), 12 July 1917.
41 "Clarrie Dale Met His Death While Leading His Men," *Leader* (Regina), 4 September 1917.
42 "One of City's Finest Young Men Called," *Leader* (Regina), 28 April 1917.
43 "H. Longworthy Gives His Life on Battlefield," *Leader* (Regina), 28 April 1917.
44 LAC, RG 150, Acc 92-93/166 Box 5315, Laird, Homer Waring.
45 "Letters Relate How Lieut. Laird Met His Death," *Leader* (Regina), 8 November 1917.
46 SAB, Taylor Papers, Neil (Piffles) and Merril Samuel, R-2930, Neil Taylor to Mother, 2 December 1918.
47 Ibid., Neil Taylor to Sam Taylor, 11 December 1917.
48 Morton, *Silent Battle*, ix, 43, and 71–73.
49 SAB, Taylor Papers, Neil (Piffles) and Merril Samuel, R-2930, Neil Taylor to Mother, 2 December 1918.
50 Ibid.
51 Ibid., Neil Taylor diary, 10 January 1918.
52 Ibid., Sam Taylor to mother, 26 August 1917.
53 Ibid., Neil Taylor to mother, 17 December 1918.
54 Ibid., Major J.W. Andrews to Mr. Taylor, 10 July 1918.
55 Ibid., Neil Taylor to mother, 17 December 1918.
56 "Lieut W.M. Scanlan, Regina One of the Gallant Canadians to Pay Cost of Vimy Ridge," *Leader* (Regina), 16 April 1917.
57 "Former Leader Employee Wins Military Medal," *Leader* (Regina), 18 November 1916.
58 LAC, RG 150, Acc 1992-93/166 Box 8684-48, Scanlan, William Maunsell.

59 "Lieut W.M. Scanlan, Regina One of the Gallant Canadians to Pay Cost of Vimy Ridge," *Leader* (Regina), 16 April 1917.
60 "How Lieut. Scanlan Met His Death," *Leader* (Regina), 12 May 1917.
61 "Poem Written by Late Lieut. W.M. Scanlan," *Leader* (Regina), 5 May 1917.
62 Morton, *When Your Number's Up*, 50.
63 "68th Start Recruiting Campaign," *Leader* (Regina), 5 January 1916.
64 "Ninety Recruits from Campaign of Yesterday," *Leader* (Regina), 6 January 1916.
65 "Recruiting Address at Sherwoods," *Leader* (Regina), 8 January 1916.
66 "Recruiting is Going Strong," *Leader* (Regina), 7 January 1916.
67 "Excuses Offered by Physically Fit Young Men in Regina for Not Enlisting for Overseas Service," *Leader* (Regina), 18 December 1915.
68 Ibid.
69 "Peter Pan's Pipes," *Leader* (Regina), 17 May 1916.
70 Ibid.
71 "Sergeant Roach Makes a Hit at Recruiting," *Leader* (Regina), 30 March 1916.
72 Ibid.
73 "68th Battalion Was Given a Great Send-Off," *Leader* (Regina), 24 April 1916.
74 Robert Craig Brown and Donald Loveridge, "Unrequited Faith: Recruiting the CEF 1914–18," *Revue Internationale d'Histoire Militaire* (1982): 59.
75 "Regina Citizens Recruiting League Formed at Huge Mass Meeting City Hall Last Night," *Leader* (Regina), 4 March 1916.
76 "Lt.-Col. Garner Will Command 195th Battalion," *Leader* (Regina), 3 February 1916.
77 "Recruiting for 195th Battalion Starts Today," *Leader* (Regina), 10 February 1916.
78 "Oppose Mere Boys Enlisting," *Leader* (Regina), 29 February 1916.
79 Pitsula, *An Act of Faith*, 36.
80 "Privileges Given to Students Who Join the Colors," *Leader* (Regina), 15 February 1916.
81 "A Duty to Our Children," *Evening Province and Standard* (Regina), 15 September 1915.
82 "Splendid Concert at Regina Theatre For 195th Recruiting," *Leader* (Regina), 27 March 1916.
83 "Regina Citizens Recruiting League Formed at Huge Mass Meeting City Hall Last Night," *Leader* (Regina), 4 March 1916.
84 "Prominent Men Identified With 195th Recruiting," *Leader* (Regina), 26 February 1916.
85 "Census Indicates Very Few Eligible Soldiers Left Here," *Leader* (Regina), 24 March 1916.
86 "Eighteen More Men Join Ranks of 195th Battalion," *Leader* (Regina), 24 March 1916.
87 "195th Battalion Now Past Half Total Strength," *Leader* (Regina), 31 March 1916.

88 "City of Regina Battalion Goes Over 600 Mark," *Leader* (Regina), 3 April 1916.
89 "Funds of the 195th," letter to the editor from A.C. Garner, *Leader* (Regina), 8 April 1916.
90 Ibid.; "Military Notes and News," *Leader* (Regina), 13 May 1916.
91 "Over 900 Men Are Now with 195th Battalion," *Leader* (Regina), 24 April 1916.
92 "Twenty-One Joined the 195th Yesterday," *Leader* (Regina), 11 April 1916.
93 "Battle Cry of Peace Comes to Rose Monday," *Leader* (Regina), 22 April 1916.
94 Paul Litt, "Canada Invaded! The Great War, Mass Culture and Canadian Cultural Nationalism." in *Canada and the First World War: Essays in Honour of Robert Craig Brown*, ed. David Mackenzie. (Toronto: University of Toronto Press, 2005), 338–40.
95 "Battle Cry of Peace," *Leader* (Regina), 24 April 1916.
96 "Leader Will Produce Proof That Britain is Prepared," *Leader* (Regina), 2 May 1916.
97 "Britain Prepared," *Leader* (Regina), 3 May 1916.
98 "Canon Hill's Stirring Call to Men of Canada," *Leader* (Regina), 17 May 1916.
99 "School Children Saw 'Britain Prepared,'" *Leader* (Regina), 18 May 1916.
100 Ibid.
101 "Boy of Nine Asked to Enlist So He Can See 'Daddy,'" *Evening Province* (Regina), 22 June 1916.
102 "195th Battalion Reached Eight Hundred Mark," *Leader* (Regina), 15 April 1916.
103 "195th Battalion An Integral Part of Life of City of Regina; Whole Battalion Raised in Three Months," *Leader* (Regina), 3 June 1916.
104 Ibid.
105 "Thousand Guests Accept Invitation of 60th Battery," *Leader* (Regina), 15 May 1916.
106 Ibid.
107 "Sixtieth Battery Prepare for Camp After Residence of Little Over Two Months in Regina City," *Leader* (Regina), 27 May 1916.
108 "60th Battery Left the City," *Leader* (Regina), 29 May 1916.
109 "Military Notes and News," *Leader* (Regina), 24 May 1916.
110 "Draft of 77th Battery Left the City Yesterday," *Leader* (Regina), 10 August 1916.
111 "Trenches to Be Dug Here to Show War," *Daily Post* (Regina), 22 November 1916.
112 "Bombs Break Even Frozen Regina Mud," *Daily Post* (Regina), 22 December 1916.
113 Ibid.
114 Morton, *When Your Number's Up*, 62.
115 Ibid., 53.

116 "Splendid Recruiting Record Was Made by 249th Battalion Under Lieut.-Col. Keenleyside," *Leader* (Regina), 19 May 1917.
117 "You are Wanted!" *Leader* (Regina), 18 January 1917.
118 "The Hun Declares for Unrestricted Murder on the High Seas," *Leader* (Regina), 2 February 1917.
119 "This is the Fiend Whose Orgy of Murder Must be Ended," *Leader* (Regina), 24 February 1917.
120 "Win the War Week," *Leader* (Regina), 10 March 1917.
121 "'Win-The-War Week' Opens with Stirring Appeals for Recruits from Pulpits of City Churches," *Leader* (Regina), 19 March 1917.
122 "Regina Lad of German and Austrian Parents Joins British Ranks," *Leader* (Regina), 30 October 1915.
123 "Ruthenians Ready for Home Service," *Leader* (Regina), 1 December 1916.
124 "Rumanians Hear a Naval Appeal from Mayor and P. McAra," *Leader* (Regina), 20 February 1917.
125 "Officers Warned to Investigate Alien Recruits," *Daily Post* (Regina), 31 October 1916.
126 "East End Barred to Local Troops," *Evening Province and Standard* (Regina), 22 May 1915.
127 "Recruiting Campaign Starts in Earnest Today To Gain 200 More Men For 249th Batt.," *Leader* (Regina), 20 March 1917.
128 Ibid.
129 "Women to Work for Men Scheme Not a Success," *Leader* (Regina), 29 March 1917.
130 "Make Men Enlist or Put Them in Skirts, She Says," *Leader* (Regina), 24 March 1917.
131 "Recruiting Campaign Starts in Earnest Today to Gain 200 More Men For 249th Batt.," *Leader* (Regina), 20 March 1917.
132 "Finding Excuses More Plentiful Than Recruits," *Leader* (Regina), 21 March 1917.
133 "All is Ready for Big Parade This Afternoon," *Leader* (Regina), 22 March 1917.
134 "Regina Scored for Apathy in War Interest," *Leader* (Regina), 23 March 1917.
135 "Slackers and Shirkers," *Leader* (Regina), 23 March 1917.
136 Ibid.
137 Brown and Loveridge, "Unrequited Faith," 62.
138 "Military Notes and News," *Leader* (Regina), 9 May 1916; "217th Battalion Was Raised in Little Over a Year From Regina and Points East," *Leader* (Regina), 2 April 1917; "Military Notes and News," *Leader* (Regina), 10 June 1916; "Military Notes and News," *Leader* (Regina), 6 July 1916; "Military Notes and News," *Leader* (Regina), 13 July 1916; "Recruiting Starts in Regina for 253rd Highland Battalion," *Leader* (Regina), 27 December 1916; "Recruiting to Start Here Today for the 152nd," *Leader* (Regina), 3 May 1916; "Military Notes and News," *Leader* (Regina), 13 July 1916; "Military Notes and News," *Leader*

(Regina), 27 July 1916; "Saskatchewan Naval Recruiting League was Formed in Regina Yesterday; Committee Formed," *Leader* (Regina), 26 October 1916; "Scandinavian Battalion is Recruiting Here," *Leader* (Regina), 4 March 1916; "Battalion No. 203 Recruiting Here," *Leader* (Regina), 17 March 1916; "Battalion of Americans to Recruit Here," *Leader* (Regina), 18 March 1916; "Recruiting Here for the American Legion Progresses," *Leader* (Regina), 6 April 1916; "Recruiting Brisk for Universities Battalion No. 196," *Leader* (Regina), 23 March 1916; "Forestry Battalion Recruiting in Regina," *Leader* (Regina), 28 March 1916.
139 Morton, *When Your Number's Up*, 63.
140 "All Troops in Future Cross Over as Drafts," *Daily Post* (Regina), 27 December 1916.
141 "A Serious Situation," *Leader* (Regina), 28 April 1917.
142 "Organize the Dominion," *Leader* (Regina), 29 March 1916.
143 "Is This Right? Is it Fair?" *Leader* (Regina), 14 December 1916.

Chapter 7

1 LAC, "A Guide to Sources Relating to Units of the Canadian Expeditionary Force, Infantry Battalions," prepared by Barbara Wilson.
2 Ibid.
3 Ibid.
4 LAC, RG9 III D 1, vol. 4964, folder 55, file 1, Historical Record.
5 LAC, RG 150, Acc 92-93/166, Box 2901-32, Embury John Fletcher Leopold.
6 Calder, *History of the 28th (Northwest) Battalion*, 16.
7 Ibid., 19–20.
8 Ibid., 19.
9 Ibid., 24.
10 Ibid., 25.
11 LAC, RG 9 II B 5, vol. 5, CEF: 18th, 19th–22nd, 24th–27th Bns., Abridged Annual Report Upon 28th Battalion, CEF, Inspected at Winnipeg on 7 and 8 April 1915, H.Q. 64-82-2, signed by H.B.B. Ketchen, Colonel, Commdg 6th Inf. Bde. CEF, Inspecting Officer.
12 Ibid.
13 LAC, RG9 III D 1, vol. 4964, folder 55, file 1, Historical Record, Story of the 28th North West Battalion, 6th Infantry Brigade, by G.E. Hewitt.
14 Calder, *History of the 28th (Northwest) Battalion*, 26.
15 Ibid., 22.
16 LAC, "A Guide to Sources Relating to Units of the Canadian Expeditionary Force, Infantry Battalions," prepared by Barbara Wilson.
17 LAC, RG9 III D 1, vol. 4964, folder 55, file 1, Historical Record.
18 Calder, *History of the 28th (Northwest) Battalion*, 30.
19 Ibid., 35.

20 Ibid., 41.
21 Ibid., 41–42.
22 Ibid., 50.
23 Ibid., 52.
24 LAC, RG9 III D 1, vol. 4964, folder 55, file 1, Historical Record, Story of the 28th North West Battalion, 6th Infantry Brigade, by G.E. Hewitt.
25 Ibid.
26 Calder, *History of the 28th (Northwest) Battalion*, 64.
27 Ibid.
28 Ibid., 70.
29 Ibid., 66.
30 Ibid., 66–67 and 71.
31 Ibid., 72.
32 Ibid., 85.
33 Ibid., 82.
34 Ibid., 83.
35 Ibid., 85.
36 Ibid., 87.
37 It inspired William Scanlan's poem, quoted in the previous chapter.
38 Calder, *History of the 28th (Northwest) Battalion*, 90.
39 LAC, RG9 III D 1, vol. 4964, folder 55, file 9, Operations. Narrative of man in B Coy 28th Bn. of his company's operations during the attack on 15 Sept. 1916.
40 Ibid.
41 Ibid.
42 LAC, RG9 III D 1, vol. 4964, folder 55, file 1, Historical Record, Story of the 28th North West Battalion, 6th Infantry Brigade, by G.E. Hewitt.
43 Calder, *History of the 28th (Northwest) Battalion*, 91.
44 Ibid., 89.
45 Ibid., 3.
46 Ibid., 92.
47 Ibid., 101.
48 Ibid., 106.
49 Ibid.
50 Ibid., 111.
51 Ibid.
52 LAC, RG9 III D 1, vol. 4964, folder 55, file 1, Historical Record, Story of the 28th North West Battalion, 6th Infantry Brigade, by G.E. Hewitt.
53 Calder, *History of the 28th (Northwest) Battalion*, 119.
54 Ibid., 125.
55 Ibid.
56 Ibid.
57 Ibid.
58 "E. Sneath Writes a Breezy Letter of Vimy Ridge," *Leader* (Regina), 9 June 1917.

Notes

59 Calder, *History of the 28th (Northwest) Battalion*, 127.
60 LAC, RG9 III D 1, vol. 4964, folder 55, file 1, Historical Record, Story of the 28th North West Battalion, 6th Infantry Brigade, by G.E. Hewitt.
61 "Thrilling Tale of the Capture of Vimy Ridge by the Canadians as Related by Capt. Rev. Earp," *Leader* (Regina), 12 September 1917.
62 Michael Valpy, "Vimy Ridge: The Making of a Myth," *Globe and Mail* (Toronto), 7 April 2007.
63 "After Three Years," *Leader* (Regina), 4 August 1917.
64 Ross, "Preface," in Calder, *History of the 28th (Northwest) Battalion*, viii.
65 Geoffrey Hayes, Andrew Iarocci, Mike Bechthold, eds., *Vimy Ridge: A Canadian Reassessment* (Waterloo: Laurier Centre for Military and Disarmament Studies and Wilfrid Laurier University Press, 2007), 1.
66 Jonathan Vance, "Battle Verse: Poetry and Nationalism After Vimy Ridge," in *Vimy Ridge*, ed. Hayes, Iarocci, and Bechthold, 267–71.
67 Calder, *History of the 28th (Northwest) Battalion*, 144.
68 LAC, RG9 III D 1, vol. 4964, folder 55, file 1, Historical Record, Story of the 28th North West Battalion, 6th Infantry Brigade, by G.E. Hewitt.
69 Ibid.
70 Calder, *History of the 28th (Northwest) Battalion*, 152.
71 Ibid., 153.
72 Ibid.
73 Ibid., 157.
74 Ibid.
75 Ibid., 161–62.
76 Ibid., 162.
77 Ibid., 163.
78 Ibid., 164.
79 Ibid., 159.
80 Ibid., 171.
81 Ibid.
82 Ibid., 175.
83 Ibid., 176.
84 Ibid., 178.
85 Ibid., 181.
86 Ibid., 183.
87 Ibid., 193.
88 Ibid., 198.

Chapter 8

1 J.L. Granatstein, "Conscription in the Great War." in *Canada and the First World War: Essays in Honour of Robert Craig Brown*, ed. David Maclenziee. (Toronto: University of Toronto Press, 2005), 67.

2   SAB, Taylor Papers: Neil (Piffles) and Merril Samuel, R-2930, Neil Taylor to father, 6 June 1917.
3   Granatstein, "Conscription in the Great War," 68.
4   Martin Robin, "Registration, Conscription and Independent Labour Politics, 1916–17," in *Conscription 1917*, ed. Ramsay Cook, Craig Brown, and Carl Berger (Toronto: University of Toronto Press, n.d.), 62.
5   "Premier Borden, Hon. J.A. Calder and R.B Bennett Address a Big Gathering in the Interests of National Service," *Leader* (Regina), 20 December 1916.
6   "National Service Cards," *Leader* (Regina), 28 December 1916.
7   "Regina Labor Men Decline to Sign Registration Cards and Call on Dominion Government to Resign," *Leader* (Regina), 4 January 1917.
8   Ibid.
9   "R.B. Bennett Tells Regina Labor Men They Are Defying the Law of Country in Which They Are Living," *Leader* (Regina), 23 January 1917.
10 Robin, "Registration, Conscription and Independent Labour Politics," 68.
11 Ibid., 69–70.
12 Ibid., 68.
13 "Soldiers Control Meeting Called of Working People of Regina in the Labor Temple," *Leader* (Regina), 1 June 1917.
14 Ibid.
15 Ibid.
16 Ibid.
17 Ramsay Cook, "Dafoe, Laurier, and the Formation of Union Government," *Canadian Historical Review* 42, 3 (1961): 26–27.
18 Ibid., 33.
19 "Meeting Passes Resolution for a National Government and a Union Candidate," *Leader* (Regina), 14 September 1917.
20 "Canada's Two Wars," *Leader* (Regina), 13 October 1917.
21 Ibid.
22 Hopkins, ed., *Canadian Annual Review of Public Affairs, 1912*, 533.
23 Allan R. Turner, ed., "Reminiscences of the Hon. J.A. Calder," *Saskatchewan History* 25 (1972): 55–62.
24 "Regina Gives a Cordial Reception to Ministers of Union Government," *Leader* (Regina), 24 October 1917.
25 Ibid.
26 Ibid.
27 Ibid.
28 "Mr. Calder's Announcement," *Leader* (Regina), 29 October 1917.
29 "Candidate is Imbued With Union Spirit," *Leader* (Regina), 13 November 1917.
30 "Union Government Convention Names Dr. W.D. Cowan to Carry Win-the-War Banner in Pending Dominion Election," *Leader* (Regina), 13 November 1917.

31 "Ald. M'Beth is Liberal-Labor Choice for Seat," *Leader* (Regina), 16 November 1917.
32 "How Would the Kaiser Vote?" *Leader* (Regina), 26 November 1917.
33 Ibid.
34 "Points for Union Government Are Made in Sermon," *Leader* (Regina), 10 December 1917.
35 "Father Daly States Views on Election," *Leader* (Regina), 10 December 1917.
36 Luttmer, "The German Experience in Regina," 55.
37 "Union Government Meeting Under Auspices of the Great War Veterans a Big Success," *Leader* (Regina), 14 December 1917.
38 Ibid.
39 "Union Campaign Concluded at Meeting Addressed by Hon. J.A. Calder and Others," *Leader* (Regina), 17 December 1917.
40 "Official Count Shows Cowan's Majority 5, 196," *Leader* (Regina), 28 December 1917.
41 John English, *The Decline of Politics: The Conservatives and the Party System, 1901–1920* (Toronto: University of Toronto Press, 1977), 195.
42 Thompson, *Harvests of War*, 122.
43 Morton, *When Your Number's Up*, 65.
44 "Privileges and Penalties," *Leader* (Regina), 5 November 1917.
45 Morton, *When Your Number's Up*, 66.
46 Ibid.
47 "Where the Regina City Exemption Tribunals Are to Hold Forth," *Leader* (Regina), 24 September 1917.
48 "District Court Judge Hannon Names Men Chosen by Him to Act on Boards of Exemption," *Leader* (Regina), 18 September 1917.
49 "Camp Exhibition is Getting Ready for Conscripts," *Leader* (Regina), 19 September 1917.
50 "Military Enquiry Starts This Morning into the Fire Which Destroyed Barracks," *Leader* (Regina), 19 December 1917.
51 "More Witnesses Heard Regarding Winter Fair Fire," *Leader* (Regina), 29 December 1917.
52 "Headquarters of District 12 and Troops to Stay," *Leader* (Regina), 27 December 1917.
53 "Having the District Military Headquarters Worth About $4,500,000 Yearly to Regina," *Leader* (Regina), 10 November 1917.
54 CORA, City Council Minutes, COR-1, volume 14, Committee Reports re: Sherwood Building for Troops, 6 January 1918.
55 "Soldiers Taking Over Sherwood's Block This Week," *Leader* (Regina), 24 December 1917.
56 "Allies', Canada's and Saskatchewan's Share in the Great War Form Theme of Addresses at Annual Meeting of the Canadian Club," *Leader* (Regina), 23 February 1918.
57 Ibid.

58 "The Exemption Tribunals," *Leader* (Regina), 26 November 1917.
59 Ibid.
60 "Complaint that Bona Fide Farmers Have Been Refused Exemption Answered by Referring Stated Cases to T.M. Molloy," *Leader* (Regina), 14 February 1918.
61 "Farmers Now in Depot Battalion May Get Release," *Leader* (Regina), 15 February 1918.
62 "Many Farmers Given Exemption by Judge Hannon," *Leader* (Regina), 10 January 1918.
63 "More Exemptions than Soldiers in this Big List," *Leader* (Regina), 22 January 1918.
64 "'Farmers' Letter," *Leader* (Regina), 13 June 1918.
65 "Latest Call for Soldiers Bound to Hurt Farmers," *Leader* (Regina), 29 April 1918.
66 "Repeal the Wartime Elections Act and Conscript the Naturalized Aliens," *Leader* (Regina), 19 April 1918.
67 Morton, *When Your Number's Up*, 70.
68 For a defence of conscription, see Granatstein, "Conscription in the Great War," 62–75.
69 "Funds Diminish While Urgency for Relief Grows," *Leader* (Regina), 8 May 1915.
70 "Patriotic Fund Subscriptions," *Leader* (Regina), 21 November 1914.
71 "Funds Diminish While Urgency for Relief Grows," *Leader* (Regina), 8 May 1915.
72 "Regina Citizens Have Paid Over $55,000 to Patriotic Fund in Less Than a Year," *Leader* (Regina), 14 August 1915.
73 "Appeal for Further Contributions to Patriotic Fund," *Leader* (Regina), 5 October 1915.
74 "City Makes Grant of $40 Per Month to Patriotic Fund," *Leader* (Regina), 29 October 1915.
75 "Campaign for Second Year of Regina Patriotic Fund Starts With Enthusiastic Meeting," *Leader* (Regina), 26 November 1915.
76 "The Case Against Government Control of the Patriotic Fund," *Leader* (Regina), 4 December 1916.
77 "Campaign for Second Year of Regina Patriotic Fund Starts with Enthusiastic Meeting," *Leader* (Regina), 26 November 1915. For insight into the political patronage machine, see Smith, *Prairie Liberalism*, Chapter 2.
78 "Campaign for Second Year of Regina Patriotic Fund Starts with Enthusiastic Meeting," *Leader* (Regina), 26 November 1915.
79 Hopkins, ed., *Canadian Annual Review of Public Affairs, 1916*, 718.
80 "Raise Patriotic Fund by Taxation," *Leader* (Regina), 2 February 1916.
81 "Levy Taxes to Maintain Patriotic Fund," *Leader* (Regina), 2 February 1916.
82 "The Patriotic Fund" (letter to the editor), *Leader* (Regina), 28 November 1916.
83 "Want Patriotic Fund Raised by Taxation," *Leader* (Regina), 9 January 1917.

Notes

84 "The Case Against Government Control of the Patriotic Fund," *Daily Post* (Regina), 1 December 1916.
85 "Premier Martin Urges Support for Patriotic Fund Campaign in Address at the Canadian Club," *Leader* (Regina), 23 November 1916.
86 Philip H. Morris, ed., *The Canadian Patriotic Fund: A Record of its Activities from 1914 to 1919* (N.p., 1920), 257 and 259.
87 Ibid.
88 "Monthly Subscriptions of $2 and $5 to the Patriotic Fund Plan Outlined by Committee," *Leader* (Regina), 25 November 1916.
89 "Regina Patriotic Fund Work During Year is Reviewed and Board of Officers Elected," *Leader* (Regina), 16 February 1917.
90 "Santa Claus Comes Down Chimney at Theatre in Full View of 460 Boys and Girls," *Leader* (Regina), 31 December 1915.
91 "Regina Patriotic Fund Work During Year is Reviewed and Board of Officers Elected," *Leader* (Regina), 16 February 1917.
92 "Regina Receives Many Requests for Exemption," *Leader* (Regina), 10 August 1917.
93 Morris, ed., *Canadian Patriotic Fund*, 261.
94 "Regina Branch of the Patriotic Fund Association Holds its Annual Meeting and Reviews Work Done During Year," *Leader* (Regina), 21 November 1917.
95 "The Patriotic Fund," *Leader* (Regina), 30 June 1916.
96 Rutherdale, *Hometown Horizons*, 111–12.
97 "First Steps Taken Towards Forming Soldiers' Wives Club," *Leader* (Regina), 10 November 1916.
98 "Lonely Women with Husbands at Front Band Together to Relieve Tedium of Waiting and Distress," *Daily Post* (Regina), 9 November 1916.
99 "Soldiers' Wives' Club Has Completed Profitable Year," *Leader* (Regina), 6 December 1917.
100 "Regina District Organized for Victory Loan Campaign to be Launched November 12," *Leader* (Regina), 26 October 1917; "Regina—'Carry On,'" *Leader* (Regina), 22 November 1917.
101 "Regina District Organized for Victory Loan Campaign to be Launched November 12," *Leader* (Regina), 26 October 1917.
102 "Boys and Girls All Have a Duty to Victory Loan," *Leader* (Regina), 10 November 1917.
103 "Splendid Parade Stirs Patriotic Spirit in the City," *Leader* (Regina), 16 November 1917.
104 "Victory Loan Drive Netted $21,752,250 in Saskatchewan Final Figures Are Reported," *Leader* (Regina), 11 December 1917.
105 Ibid.
106 "Plan for Obviating Over-Lapping Among the Patriotic and Charitable Organizations," *Leader* (Regina), 25 April 1916.
107 "Approval Committee Handles Big Bunch of Proposed Schemes," *Leader* (Regina), 29 April 1916.

108 "Committee Considers Means of Securing Patriotic Funds," *Leader* (Regina), 23 June 1916.
109 "Pair of Tagging Committees Likely to Conflict Badly," *Leader* (Regina), 5 July 1917.
110 "Illegal to Hold Tag Day Without a Proper Permit," *Leader* (Regina), 17 August 1917.
111 "Tag Day and All Requests Are Held Up," *Leader* (Regina), 22 January 1918.
112 "Council Wants Approval Board to Act Again," *Leader* (Regina), 12 March 1918.
113 "Tag Days Will Be Kept Within 14-Day Bounds," *Leader* (Regina), 5 April 1918.
114 "Tag Days May Happen Every Week After All," *Leader* (Regina), 13 April 1918.
115 "Rotarians Are Asked to Aid War Chest Idea," *Leader* (Regina), 4 September 1918.
116 "War Relief Funds," *Leader* (Regina), 13 September 1918.
117 James M. Pitsula, *Helping Families Through Life: A History of Family Service Regina* (Regina: Family Service Regina, 2001), 64.
118 "The Future of the Patriotic Fund," *Leader* (Regina), 9 October 1917.
119 For the history of the welfare state in Canada, see Dennis Guest, *The Emergence of Social Security in Canada*. (Vancouver: University of British Columbia Press, 1997); and James Struthers, *No Fault of Their Own: Unemployed and the Canadian Welfare State, 1914–1941*. (Toronto: University of Toronto Press, 1994).

Chapter 9

1 Brennan, "A Political History of Saskatchewan," 218.
2 Saskatchewan in 1914 had 5,348,300 acres planted in wheat; in 1919 the wheat acreage had risen to 10,587,000. Hopkins, ed., *Canadian Annual Review of Public Affairs, 1915*, 686; Saskatchewan Department of Agriculture, *Agricultural Statistics, 1975*, 36.
3 Thompson, *Harvests of War*, 70.
4 Ibid., 69.
5 Ibid., 46.
6 "The Census Figures," *Leader* (Regina), 18 October 1916.
7 "Regina Census Investigation Will Be Held," *Leader* (Regina), 31 October 1916.
8 "Oil Refining Plant to Be Located Here," *Leader* (Regina), 5 January 1916.
9 "Recent Census Shows Regina's Population to Be 26,105; Only City in the West with Decrease," *Leader* (Regina), 18 October 1916.
10 "House Building Shows a Marked Activity in City," *Leader* (Regina), 7 June 1917.
11 "Activity in All Building Trades in Province," *Leader* (Regina), 7 July 1917.

Notes

12 "Regina People Have Plenty of Money for Holiday Gifts Says Business Men of City," *Leader* (Regina), 14 December 1916.
13 "Regina Stores All Report Big Holiday Trade," *Leader* (Regina), 27 December 1916.
14 "Regina Has 1,423 Autos, Licenses Issued Indicate," *Leader* (Regina), 1 September 1917.
15 "Opening of Provincial Legislature Attended by the Usual Ceremonies: Dr. R.M. Mitchell is Elected Speaker," *Leader* (Regina), 14 November 1917.
16 "Debate on Address in Reply to Speech from Throne is Concluded in Legislature," *Leader* (Regina), 16 November 1917.
17 "Budget Speech by Provincial Treasurer in Legislature Replete with Interesting Figures; Per Capita Debt Still Lowest," *Leader* (Regina), 14 December 1917.
18 "Bennett Speaks Before Members of Legislature," *Leader* (Regina), 2 March 1917.
19 "Greater Denial and Economy is Necessary," *Leader* (Regina), 24 October 1917.
20 Brennan, "The Public Career of Charles Avery Dunning," 42.
21 "First Popular Appeal to People of Province to Provide Funds to Increase Food Production," *Leader* (Regina), 19 September 1917.
22 "Privileges for Collegiate Boys Helping on Farms," *Leader* (Regina), 8 May 1917.
23 "Seventy Students of Regina Collegiate Take Advantage of 'Farm Labor Regulations,'" *Leader* (Regina), 10 May 1917.
24 "Collegiate Girl Proves Big Help with Farm Work," *Leader* (Regina), 1 November 1917.
25 "Women Needed More for Indoor Work Than Anything Else," *Leader* (Regina), 10 August 1916.
26 "Farmers Finding it Difficult to Get Right Men," *Leader* (Regina), 18 June 1917.
27 "The Domestic Help Problem," *Leader* (Regina), 14 April 1916.
28 "Town Women Asked to Let Their Maids Help Farmer's Wife," *Leader* (Regina), 11 August 1916.
29 "Women Working on the Section for CPR Here," *Leader* (Regina), 3 September 1917.
30 "Exhaustive and Interesting Report Presented at Annual Meeting of Board of Trade," *Leader* (Regina), 2 February 1917.
31 Jim Warren and Kathleen Carlisle, *On the Side of the People: A History of Labour in Saskatchewan* (Regina: Coteau Books, 2006), 58.
32 "Alien Enemies Arrive to Help Out on Farms," *Leader* (Regina), 16 May 1917.
33 "Austrians Must Take Pay Offered or Go to Prison," *Leader* (Regina), 23 August 1917.
34 "Regina No Place for Austrians to Dictate Wages," *Leader* (Regina), 22 August 1917.

35 "Austrians Must Take Pay Offered Or Go To Prison," *Leader* (Regina), 23 August 1917.
36 "Labor Protest Against Arrest of Harvesters," *Leader* (Regina), 28 August 1917.
37 "Alien Hired Men on Farms Show a Greedy Spirit," *Leader* (Regina), 26 September 1918.
38 "T.M. Molloy Informs Delegates What is Being Done in Solving Question of Labor for the Farms," *Leader* (Regina), 8 March 1918.
39 "A Call to the Cities," *Leader* (Regina), 25 February 1918.
40 "Regina Citizens Organize to Campaign City Properly for Farm Help Assistance," *Leader* (Regina), 21 March 1918.
41 "Lining Up Man Power of City for Farm Work," *Leader* (Regina), 22 March 1918.
42 "Need of Helping Farmers and of Growing Vegetables on City Lots Emphasized," *Leader* (Regina), 30 March 1918.
43 "Citizens to Aid Farmers in the Wheat Fields," *Leader* (Regina), 2 September 1918.
44 "L.E. McCormick to Place Boys on the Farms," *Leader* (Regina), 27 February 1918.
45 "Soldiers of Soil to Come Largely from the Schools, Colleges and City Offices," *Leader* (Regina), 5 March 1918.
46 "Saskatchewan's Call to Service," *Leader* (Regina), 16 March 1918.
47 "'Soldiers of Soil' Enlistment Week Inaugurated with Several Addresses to Boys at City Hall," *Leader* (Regina), 18 March 1918.
48 "Many Boys Ready to Go Out and Help on Farms," *Leader* (Regina), 20 March 1918.
49 "Soldiers of Soil Badges Arrive at Headquarters," *Leader* (Regina), 13 July 1918.
50 "Acute Boy Scarcity is Feature of Regina's Commercial Life; Good Wages Going A-Begging," *Daily Post* (Regina), 20 October 1916.
51 "Labor Movement in Regina is Only Ten Years Old But it is a Healthy Youngster," *Leader* (Regina), 1 September 1917.
52 "Splendid Appearance Made by Labor Unions in Their Annual Parade Through City Streets," *Leader* (Regina), 4 September 1917.
53 Walter J.C. Cherwinski, "The Formative Years of the Trade Union Movement in Saskatchewan, 1905–1920," MA thesis, University of Saskatchewan, 1966, p. 140.
54 "Carpenters Set Scale at 55 Cents and 9-Hour Day," *Leader* (Regina), 16 March 1917.
55 Brennan, "Political History of Saskatchewan," 398.
56 "Carpenters Get Their Increase," *Leader* (Regina), 2 May 1917.
57 "Strike Lasts But Few Hours; Power House Employees Get Increase and Resume Work," *Leader* (Regina), 24 February 1917.

58 "Threats to Kill Are Alleged by Civic Teamsters," *Leader* (Regina), 10 November 1916.
59 Cherwinski, "The Formative Years," 140.
60 Ibid., 141.
61 Ibid., 145.
62 Warren and Carlisle, *On The Side of the People*, 60.
63 Brennan, "The Public Career of Charles Avery Dunning," 44.
64 Ibid., 45.
65 "No More Idlers," *Leader* (Regina), 8 April 1918.
66 Ibid.
67 "Many 'Loafers' Being Rounded Up These Days," *Leader* (Regina), 23 May 1918.
68 Cherwinski, "The Formative Years," 138.
69 "Only One Legitimate Kind of Strike," *Leader* (Regina), 23 October 1918.
70 "Another Call to Canada," *Leader* (Regina), 23 April 1917.
71 "The Duty of the Hour," *Leader* (Regina), 3 May 1917.
72 "Movement Has Added Much to Beautify the City," *Leader* (Regina), 29 September 1917.
73 "Five Years Old Movement is a Lusty Youngster," *Leader* (Regina), 29 September 1917.
74 "Estimated Value of Between $20,000 and $25,000 on Vacant Lot Garden Produce for Year," *Leader* (Regina), 29 September 1917.
75 Ibid.
76 Ibid.
77 Ibid.
78 Ibid.
79 "Movement Has Added Much to Beautify the City," *Leader* (Regina), 29 September 1917.
80 "Flowers in War Time," *Leader* (Regina), 21 March 1918.
81 Ibid.
82 "Form Regina Food Production Association to Take the Place of Old Vacant Lot Garden Body," *Leader* (Regina), 22 February 1918.
83 "Gardens and Vacant Lots of Regina Will Aid Greatly in Solving Food Problem," *Leader* (Regina), 1 March 1918.
84 "'Watch Reginans Grow' is the New Slogan," *Leader* (Regina), 23 March 1918.
85 "The War Gardens of 1918," *Leader* (Regina), 9 April 1918.
86 "Jolly Rotarians Prove Experts in Operating Tractors and Open Production Campaign Properly," *Leader* (Regina), 12 April 1918.
87 "Raise a Pig and Save a Life in France; Every Farmer Called on to Increase Pork Production," *Leader* (Regina), 1 December 1917.
88 CORA, COR-080, file 00393, Bylaw Relating to Public Health: Bylaw No. 393, 5 June 1907.

89 "Unwise to Keep Pigs in City, Thinks M.H.O.," *Leader* (Regina), 28 December 1917.
90 CORA, City Council Minutes, COR-1, volume 14, George Beach, City Clerk, re: Greater Pork Production, 2 January 1918.
91 "Some Glaring Instances of Profiteering Show Why Living is High in Regina," *Leader* (Regina), 31 August 1917.
92 Ibid.
93 Ibid.
94 "Peter Pan's Pipes," *Leader* (Regina), 31 August 1917.
95 United Church of Canada/Victoria University Archives, Hugh Dobson Collection, 3384, Box A3—Child Welfare, Venereal Diseases, Health and Food, File R Food, Regina Civic Food Committee Minute Book 1918, microfilm reel #9, 18 September 1917.
96 Robert Craig Brown, and Ramsay Cook, *Canada 1896–1921: A Nation Transformed* (Toronto: McClelland and Stewart, 1974), 238.
97 "Promulgation of Orders Without Due Consideration by Central Food Board Has Caused Considerable Dissatisfaction," *Leader* (Regina), 25 June 1918.
98 "Dr. James W. Robertson Hears Some Very Frank Criticism of Food Controller's Office," *Leader* (Regina), 12 October 1917.
99 "Promulgation of Orders Without Due Consideration by Central Food Board Has Caused Considerable Dissatisfaction," *Leader* (Regina), 25 June 1918.
100 "Waste of Food was Discussed in Paper Read by Miss Twiss," *Leader* (Regina), 12 November 1917.
101 "Women's Local Council to Ask All its Societies to Stop Serving Refreshments," *Leader* (Regina), 23 January 1918.
102 "Food is Wasted Said Mr. Rook by a Fourth Meal," *Leader* (Regina), 31 January 1918.
103 "Federal Government Called on by the Local Council of Women to Pass Legislation for Enforcing Food Conservation in Canada," *Leader* (Regina), 31 January 1918.
104 "Glasgow House Windows Ask All to Save Food," *Leader* (Regina), 26 January 1918.
105 "Regina Citizens More Economical with Their Food," *Leader* (Regina), 4 October 1917. It is likely that Regina's population was higher in 1912 than it was in 1917, because of the impact of the 1913 recession.
106 "Federal Government Called on by the Local Council of Women to Pass Legislation for Enforcing Food Conservation in Canada," *Leader* (Regina), 31 January 1918.
107 Ibid.
108 Ibid.
109 "Regina Women Recognize Food Controller's Demand to End All Food Waste is Serious," *Leader* (Regina), 30 June 1917.

Chapter 10

1. Thompson, "'The Beginning of Our Regeneration,'" 227.
2. Richard Allen, *The Social Passion: Religion and Social Reform in Canada 1914–28.* (Toronto: University of Toronto Press, 1973), 4. For more on the social gospel, see Ramsay Cook, *The Regenerators: Social Criticism in Late Victorian English Canada* (Toronto: University of Toronto Press, 1985); David B. Marshall, *Secularizing the Faith: Canadian Protestant Clergy and the Crisis of Belief, 1850–1940* (Toronto: University of Toronto Press, 1992); Brian Fraser, *The Social Uplifters: Presbyterian Progressives and the Social Gospel* (Waterloo: Wilfrid Laurier University Press, 1988); Phyllis D. Airhart, *Serving the Present: Revivalism, Progressivism and the Methodist Tradition in Canada* (Montreal and Kingston: McGill-Queen's University Press, 1992); and Nancy Christie and Michael Gauvreau, *Full-Orbed Christianity: The Protestant Churches and Social Welfare in Canada, 1900–1940* (Montreal and Kingston: McGill-Queen's University Press, 1996).
3. Allen, *Social Passion*, 8.
4. George Thomas Daly, *Catholic Problems in Western Canada* (Toronto: Macmillan, 1921), 83.
5. Joseph Ratzinger (Pope Benedict XVI), *Jesus of Nazareth: From the Baptism in the Jordan to the Transfiguration*, trans. Adrian J. Walker (New York: Doubleday, 2007), 54.
6. Quoted in Michael McGerr, *A Fierce Discontent: The Rise and Fall of the Progressive Movement in America* (New York: Oxford University Press, 2003), 66.
7. Ibid.
8. Allen, *Social Passion*, 35.
9. Quoted in Bliss, "The Methodist Church and World War I," 216.
10. Ibid., 231.
11. Allen, *Social Passion*, 4–5.
12. Ibid., 10.
13. "Church Must Take a Hand in Social Regeneration if it Would Continue to Be Force," *Leader* (Regina), 12 November 1917.
14. Ibid.
15. Ibid.
16. Ibid.
17. "Thrilling Tales Fresh from War Zone by Rev. Dr. Chown at Canadian Club Luncheon," *Leader* (Regina), 18 October 1917.
18. Ibid.
19. "Rev. Dr. Gordon Preaches Strong Sermon at Knox," *Leader* (Regina), 5 November 1917.
20. "Thrilling Tales Fresh from War Zone by Rev. Dr. Chown at Canadian Club Luncheon," *Leader* (Regina), 18 October 1917.
21. "'We're Only Worth Sacrifice if We Straighten Up' Says C. Brown at Anniversary," *Leader* (Regina), 13 December 1915.

22　Ibid.
23　Ibid.
24　Ibid.
25　"Allies', Canada's and Saskatchewan's Share in the Great War Form Theme of Addresses at Annual Meeting of the Canadian Club," *Leader* (Regina), 23 February 1918.
26　Ibid.
27　"Sunday Forum Starts Sunday Afternoon Next," *Leader* (Regina), 26 December 1917.
28　"Some of the Changes Which Re-Organization Will Work," *Leader* (Regina), 27 March 1916.
29　Ibid.
30　Ibid.
31　United Church of Canada/Victoria University Archives, Finding Aid 168, Hugh Wesley Dobson, 1879–1956.
32　"Snapshots at the Congress (By a Delegate)," *Leader* (Regina), 29 November 1916.
33　Allen, *Social Passion*, 13.
34　"Snapshots at the Congress (By a Delegate)," *Leader* (Regina), 29 November 1916.
35　"Saskatchewan Social Service Congress Opens Under Favorable Auspices at Metropolitan Church," *Leader* (Regina), 28 November 1916.
36　Ibid.
37　Ibid.
38　Ibid.
39　"Saskatchewan Parliament of Social Service Deals with Wide Range of Topics of Interest to All Canada," *Leader* (Regina), 29 November 1916.
40　Ibid.
41　Ibid.
42　Ibid.
43　Ibid.
44　Ibid.
45　Ibid.
46　Ibid.
47　Ibid.
48　Ibid.
49　Ibid.
50　Ibid.
51　"Important Resolutions of National Significance Passed in Closing Hours of Social Service Congress," *Leader* (Regina), 30 November 1916.
52　Ibid.
53　Ibid.
54　Ibid.

55 Ibid.
56 "Resolutions Adopted by the Social Service Congress," *Leader* (Regina), 30 November 1916.
57 "Saskatchewan Parliament of Social Service Deals with Wide Range of Topics of Interest to All Canada," *Leader* (Regina), 29 November 1916.
58 Ibid.
59 Hugh Dobson, "A Win-the-War Platform for a United Canadian People," *Leader* (Regina), 6 August 1917.
60 Ibid.
61 Ibid.
62 Ibid.
63 Ibid.
64 Ibid.
65 "Social Service Council of Saskatchewan Issues Stirring Appeal to People of Canada," *Leader* (Regina), 6 August 1917.
66 Ibid.
67 United Church of Canada/Victoria University Archives, Hugh Dobson Collection, 3384, Box A4—General Correspondence, 1917–1920, File A General Correspondence, May 1917–June 1919, Regina Social Service Council, microfilm reel #9, Memo to J.A. Calder, 23 October 1917.
68 "Re-organization for Year's Work by Saskatchewan Social Service; Strong Resolutions Are Passed," *Leader* (Regina), 12 February 1918.
69 "Social Service Council Plans Season's Work," *Leader* (Regina), 21 February 1918.
70 "Grant of $1,500 By Government," *Leader* (Regina), 5 April 1918.
71 Gertrude S. Telford, "The First Child Welfare Conferences in Saskatchewan," *Saskatchewan History* 4: 57.
72 "'Conservation of Childhood'—Hugh Dobson," *Leader* (Regina), 26 June 1916.
73 Telford, "First Child Welfare Conferences," 58.
74 "Babies Conference Has Been Splendidly Successful Feature," *Leader* (Regina), 28 July 1916.
75 Morton, *When Your Number's Up*, 200.
76 Jeffrey Keshen, *Propaganda and Censorship During Canada's Great War* (Edmonton: University of Alberta Press, 1996), 182.
77 Morton, *When Your Number's Up*, 267.
78 Saskatchewan, Bureau of Health, *Annual Report of the Bureau of Public Health for the Province of Saskatchewan, 1919–20*, 18–19.
79 United Church of Canada/Victoria University Archives, Hugh Dobson Collection, 3384, Box A4—General Correspondence, 1917–1920, File A General Correspondence, May 1917–June 1919, Regina Social Service Council, circular letter, 28 December 1917.
80 Ibid., microfilm reel no. 9, re: *Damaged Goods* film.
81 United Church of Canada/Victoria University Archives, Hugh Dobson Collection, 3384, microfilm reel no. 9, Box A4—General Correspondence,

1917–1920, File H, General Correspondence September 1917–January 1920, J.R.C. Honeyman to Dobson, 25 May 1918.
82   "All Venereal Diseases Placed in Contagious and Infectious Class and Must be Reported," *Leader* (Regina), 4 January 1918.
83   United Church of Canada/Victoria University Archives, Hugh Dobson Collection, 3384, microfilm reel no. 15, Box A5—General Correspondence 1917–1921 (N–Z), File Pb, Premier of Sask. Correspondence (W.M. Martin) November 1917–May 1921, Hugh Dobson to Premier Martin, 4 January 1918.
84   "Miss Maclachlan Magistrate for Juvenile Court," *Leader* (Regina), 31 August 1917.
85   Kimberley Anne Marschall, "Raising Juvenile Delinquents: The Development of Saskatchewan's Child Welfare Laws 1905–1930," MA thesis, University of Saskatchewan, 2003, p. 41.
86   "Paying Pensions to Indigent Mothers Heartily Approved," *Leader* (Regina), 28 November 1917.
87   United Church of Canada/Victoria University Archives, Hugh Dobson Collection, 3384, microfilm reel no. 10, Box A4—General Correspondence 1917–1920, File P General Correspondence October 1917–June 1919, Hugh Dobson to Miss A.E. Patterson, 19 December 1917.
88   "The Evolution of a Policy," *Leader* (Regina), 16 October 1915.
89   "The Honor of the Soldier," *Leader* (Regina), 27 June 1918.
90   Ibid.
91   "Playing Cards in Parcels from Wesley Ladies," *Leader* (Regina), 7 November 1917.
92   "Great Scope for Social Service in Saskatchewan," *Leader* (Regina), 8 April 1918.
93   Ibid.
94   Ibid.
95   "Citizens' League Advocated by Social Service Council to Preserve Public Morals," *Leader* (Regina), 8 July 1918.
96   Ibid.
97   "Peter Pan's Pipes," *Leader* (Regina), 5 January 1918.
98   "Safeguarding of Young Girls in Town Was Given Thought," *Leader* (Regina), 28 February 1917.
99   "Peter Pan's Pipes," *Leader* (Regina), 10 January 1918.
100 "Citizens' League Advocated by Social Service Council to Preserve Public Morals," *Leader* (Regina), 8 July 1918.
101 "Issue Today in Canada is Between Autocracy and Democracy, Says Rev. Dr. Milliken at Metropolitan," *Leader* (Regina), 17 September 1917.
102 Ibid.
103 Ibid.
104 Quoted in Michael A. Lerner, *Dry Manhattan: Prohibition in New York City* (Cambridge MA: Harvard University Press, 2007), 1.

Chapter 11

1. Desmond Morton and Glenn Wright, *Winning the Second Battle: Canadian Veterans and the Return to Civilian Life, 1915–1930* (Toronto: University of Toronto Press, 1987), 7–8.
2. Morton, *When Your Number's Up*, 256.
3. Ibid., 256.
4. Ibid., 258–59.
5. Ibid., 272–74.
6. "Personnel of the Provincial Commission Formed to Aid Disabled Canadian Soldiers," *Leader* (Regina), 6 November 1915.
7. "Sask. Hospital Commission Tells of Duty of Individuals to Men Returning from War," *Leader* (Regina), 20 November 1915.
8. Ibid.
9. Ibid.
10. "Returned Soldiers Welcome and Aid League Meeting," *Leader* (Regina), 10 December 1915.
11. "Welcome League Will Complete Organization," *Leader* (Regina), 16 December 1915.
12. "Preparing for Occupation of Soldiers' Home," *Leader* (Regina), 7 January 1916.
13. "Official Opening of Convalescent Soldiers Home," *Leader* (Regina), 10 April 1916.
14. "Vocational Officer Has Been Appointed for Saskatchewan," *Leader* (Regina), 23 May 1916; "Supervisor Hewitt Tells of Work Being Done in Way of Training Disabled Soldiers for Vocations," *Leader* (Regina), 18 November 1916.
15. "Supervisor Hewitt Tells of Work Being Done in Way of Training Disabled Soldiers for Vocations," *Leader* (Regina), 18 November 1916.
16. "St. Chad's Home Offers Training in Agriculture," *Leader* (Regina), 19 December 1916.
17. Morton and Wright, *Winning the Second Battle*, 40; "Returned Men Being Trained at University," *Leader* (Regina), 14 June 1917.
18. "Deal With Plans for Re-Education of Returned Men," *Leader* (Regina), 28 June 1917.
19. "Work of Military Hospitals Commission for Saskatchewan," *Leader* (Regina), 14 July 1917. Under the *Soldier Settlement Act*, passed in 1917 and greatly expanded in 1918, veterans could apply for land and 5 percent loans. By 1930, almost half of the 24,907 soldier-settlers had abandoned their farms. See Morton, *When Your Number's Up*, 271.
20. "Splendid Work in Assisting Soldiers Regain Health at St. Chad's Convalescent Home," *Leader* (Regina), 6 October 1917.
21. Morton, *When Your Number's Up*, 257.
22. "Director of Military Hospitals Issues Statement in Regard to Refusal of Benson School Offer," *Leader* (Regina), 7 March 1917.

23 SAB, W.M. Martin Papers M4 I 16, Armed Forces: Re-establishment, 1916–1919, 10036–10038, An Act to incorporate the Saskatchewan Returned Soldiers' Employment Commission, assented to 10 March 1917.
24 SAB, 9924-9928, Minutes of the Executive Committee of the Saskatchewan Returned Soldiers' Employment Commission, 27 February 1918, appended report.
25 SAB, W.M. Martin Papers M4 I 16, Armed Forces: Re-establishment, 1916–1919, 9937, Memo for Mr. Reynolds, 21 March 1918.
26 "First Session of the Fourth Legislature Prorogued by Lieut.-Governor Saturday," *Leader* (Regina), 17 December 1917.
27 Ibid.
28 "Wounded Heroes Get Cold Welcome on Their Return," *Leader* (Regina), 28 August 1916.
29 "Indignant Over Treatment to Returned Soldiers," *Leader* (Regina), 29 August 1916.
30 "Reception to Returned Soldiers," *Leader* (Regina), 4 September 1916.
31 "To Meet All Soldiers Who Return Here," *Leader* (Regina), 27 October 1916.
32 "Hearty Welcome Given Party of Returned Heroes," *Leader* (Regina), 26 March 1917.
33 "Cordial Welcome Home Given Party of Returned Soldiers Who Reached City Yesterday," *Leader* (Regina), 2 April 1917.
34 "Returned Soldiers Given a Rousing Welcome Home Sunday by Thousands of Regina Citizens," *Leader* (Regina), 9 July 1917.
35 Ibid.
36 "Returned Soldiers Given an Elaborate at Home by League," *Leader* (Regina), 15 December 1916.
37 "28th Battalion Returned Men Gather Around Festive Board in Their First Annual Re-Union," *Leader* (Regina), 1 November 1917.
38 "Menu of the 28th Battalion Banquet is Neatly Worded," *Leader* (Regina), 1 November 1917.
39 "28th Battalion Returned Men Gather Around Festive Board in Their First Annual Re-Union," *Leader* (Regina), 1 November 1917.
40 Ibid.
41 Morton, *When Your Number's Up*, 264–65.
42 "Army and Navy Veterans League Organized Here," *Leader* (Regina), 13 September 1916.
43 "Politics Causes Split in Ranks of the Veterans," *Leader* (Regina), 15 May 1917.
44 Morton and Wright, *Winning the Second Battle*, 70.
45 "Regina Branch of Great War Veterans' Assn.," *Leader* (Regina), 8 June 1917.
46 "D.J. Wylie Objects Long and Noisily But Argument is Weak Against Giving Soldiers Seats," *Leader* (Regina), 9 March 1917.
47 Ibid.

48 "Veterans Oppose Soldiers Getting Their Members," *Leader* (Regina), 27 February 1917.
49 "D.J. Wylie Objects Long and Noisily But Argument is Weak Against Giving Soldiers Seats," *Leader* (Regina), 9 March 1917.
50 Brennan, "Political History," 368.
51 Ibid., 371.
52 Ibid., 372.
53 "Enormous Popular Majority for Saskatchewan Liberals Revealed by Official Figures of Voting," *Leader* (Regina), 6 October 1917.
54 "Great War Veterans Are Opposed to Appointment of Lt.-Col. M'Vean as Commander of Depot Battalion," *Leader* (Regina), 2 November 1917.
55 SAB, W.M. Martin Papers, M4 I 10 (4) Armed Forces, 1916–1922, 8314, Martin's address to the GWVA, 2 November 1917.
56 SAB, W.M. Martin Papers, M4 I 10 (3) Armed Forces, 1916–1922, 8251, James McAra, President, Saskatchewan Branch of Great War Veterans Association of Canada, to Premier Martin, 22 Nov 1917.
57 Ibid.
58 Ibid., 8256, Premier Martin to Major James McAra, 22 December 1917; 9036, J. Cameron to Premier Martin, 9 January 1920.
59 "Annual Convention of Great War Veterans of Province Has Opened in Saskatoon," *Leader* (Regina), 2 July 1918.
60 Morton, *When Your Number's Up*, 269–70.
61 SAB, W.M. Martin Papers, M4 I 10 (4) Armed Forces, 1916–1922, 8836, Premier Martin to J.R. Renton, 5 June 1919.
62 Ibid., 8453–8455, Resolutions GWVA, 1–3 July 1918.
63 Ibid., 8456, Premier Martin to C.G. MacNeil, 5 August 1918.
64 "Veterans Sending a Delegation to Prussia, Sask.," *Leader* (Regina), 14 September 1917; "Prussia Streets Named by CPR Deputation Told," *Leader* (Regina), 15 September 1917.
65 "Leader is Name Chosen to Take Prussia's Place," *Leader* (Regina), 1 October 1917.
66 "Veterans Found Prussia People Most Cordial," *Leader* (Regina), 22 September 1917.
67 SAB, W.M. Martin Papers, M4 I 10 (4) Armed Forces, 1916–1922, 8453, Resolutions GWVA, 1–3 July 1918.
68 Ibid., 8456, Premier Martin to C.G. MacNeil, 5 August 1918.
69 "Lieut. J.L. Bryant Spending Furlough with Brother Here," *Leader* (Regina), 27 February 1918.
70 "J.F. Bryant Injects Strong Political Tinge into Address Before the School Teachers," *Leader* (Regina), 12 April 1917.
71 "Convention Expresses Strong Disapproval of J.F. Bryant's Attack on the Government," *Leader* (Regina), 12 April 1917.

72 "J.F. Bryant's Political Speech Will Not Be Published in Annual Report of Provincial Education Association," *Leader* (Regina), 13 April 1917.
73 Smith, *Prairie Liberalism*, 58–59.
74 "Meeting in Interests of General Embury is Addressed by Leader of Opposition and Other Speakers," *Leader* (Regina), 12 June 1917.
75 Brennan, "Political History," 361
76 "Regina Branch of the National British League," *Leader* (Regina), 3 May 1917.
77 "Splendid Addresses on Educational Topics by Premier, Judge Hannon, and Presidents of University and College," *Leader* (Regina), 30 October 1917.
78 Ibid.
79 "Farmers Are Needed to Produce But No Slackers Can Hide Behind Them, Molloy Tells Veterans," *Leader* (Regina), 15 February 1918.
80 "Grain Growers Reaffirm Position of Two years Ago on the Language Question," *Leader* (Regina), 16 February 1918.
81 Ibid.
82 Ibid.
83 "Convention Declares Armistice For Day on Contentious Matters So That It Can Settle Itself," *Leader* (Regina), 21 February 1918.
84 "Convention Approves Making English Sole Language of Tuition," *Leader* (Regina), 22 February 1918.
85 Ibid.
86 Ibid.
87 Ibid.
88 Ibid.
89 Brennan, "Political History," 393.
90 Ibid., 392.
91 "Trustees Thank Government for New Regulation," *Leader* (Regina), 27 March 1918.
92 "Important Amendments Are Introduced Into the School Regulations of Province," *Leader* (Regina), 17 June 1918.
93 Ens, "Public School Crisis," 78–79.
94 "Father Orders Son Off Place For Enlisting," *Leader* (Regina), 25 April 1918.
95 "Many Foreign-Speaking Communities Now Helping Canadian Patriotic Fund," *Evening Province* (Regina), 13 May 1916.
96 "Residents of East End Will Aid Red Cross," *Leader* (Regina), 7 June 1918.
97 "East End is Enthusiastic For Red Cross," *Leader* (Regina), 12 June 1918.
98 Queen's University Archives, C.A. Dunning Papers, 2121, J.A. Calder to C.A. Dunning, 14 January 1919.
99 "Explanation is Given by the Editor," *Leader* (Regina), 5 September 1918.
100 "Alien Enemy Language Papers," *Leader* (Regina), 10 October 1918.
101 "*Courier* Makes Appearance as English Paper," *Leader* (Regina), 10 September 1918.
102 "Language in Our Schools," *Leader* (Regina), 18 December 1918.
103 Ibid.

Notes

104 Ibid.
105 "Language Question is Debated by Leaders in Legislative Assembly," *Leader* (Regina), 19 December 1918.
106 SAB, Regina Rifles Regiment Collection, R-647, V3, "CEF Casualties—Province of Saskatchewan."

Chapter 12

1 "Easter Music and Profusion of Flowers at the Services in City Churches Yesterday," *Leader* (Regina), 1 April 1918.
2 "Dr. Murray Shows that Christianity Has Not Failed," *Sheaf* (University of Saskatchewan) 4, 2 (November 1915).
3 "First Death from Spanish Grippe Here," *Leader* (Regina), 7 October 1918.
4 Gina Kolata, *Flu: The Story of the Great Influenza Pandemic of 1918 and the Search for the Virus that Caused It* (New York: Simon and Schuster, 2001), 4.
5 Ibid., 7.
6 Ibid., 27.
7 Ibid., 8.
8 Ibid., 9.
9 Ibid., 12.
10 Ibid., 7.
11 Ibid.
12 Ibid., 12.
13 Ibid., 5. Saskatchewan followed the common worldwide "age attack" pattern. According to the provincial Bureau of Public Health, there were 5018 deaths over a twenty-month period. Although the age group of twenty to thirty-nine made up only 37 percent of the population, it accounted for 58 percent of fatalities. This might be explained by the fact that most caregivers fell into that group. They were most likely to be exposed to the infection. Fred Burch, "The Spanish Influenza and Canada's Criminal Justice System: Lessons for Pandemic Planners," Scholars Series, Saskatchewan Institute of Public Policy, 24–25.
14 "No Need for Any Panic Opinion of Medical Men," *Leader* (Regina), 8 October 1918.
15 "More Cases of Grippe Reported," *Leader* (Regina), 12 October 1918.
16 "Rev. Fr. A. Suffa, After 15 Years' Service is Dead," *Leader* (Regina), 14 October 1918.
17 "Ten New Cases of Influenza in City Yesterday," *Leader* (Regina), 14 October 1918.
18 "Hospitals Full; 15 New Cases of Influenza Here," *Leader* (Regina), 15 October 1918.
19 "Council is Agitated at the Epidemic," *Leader* (Regina), 16 October 1918.
20 "Influenza Tightens Hold Here," *Leader* (Regina), 16 October 1918.

21 "Epidemic is Gaining Ground; Sixty New Cases Reported or Known Yesterday," *Leader* (Regina), 17 October 1918.
22 "Dr. Bow, MHO, Issues Request to Cease Public Assemblies," *Leader* (Regina), 17 October 1918.
23 "Public Library is to Remain Open as Antidote for Dull," *Leader* (Regina), 19 October 1918.
24 Ibid.
25 "No Street Cars on Sunday Until Churches Reopen," *Leader* (Regina), 19 October 1918.
26 "St. Mary's School is Offered as Hospital; 270 Cases in City Now," *Leader* (Regina), 18 October 1918.
27 "Influenza Epidemic is Still Spreading Here," *Leader* (Regina), 19 October 1918.
28 Ibid.
29 Ibid.
30 "Wearing Mask in Street Not Best Methods, Say Drs.," *Leader* (Regina), 31 October 1918.
31 Brennan, "Political History," 402.
32 "Regina College Voluntarily in Quarantine Now," *Leader* (Regina), 19 October 1918.
33 "Collegiate Will Close at Request of Regina MHO," *Leader* (Regina), 21 October 1918.
34 "Attendance Away Below Normal Now," *Leader* (Regina), 23 October 1918.
35 "Strong Action Being Taken to Cope with the Epidemic Here," *Leader* (Regina), 25 October 1918.
36 "Influenza Death List Now 31; City Total 450 Cases," *Leader* (Regina), 21 October 1918.
37 "Influenza is Still Raging in the City," *Leader* (Regina), 28 October 1918.
38 "An Appeal for More Voluntary Workers," *Leader* (Regina), 1 November 1918.
39 "Selfishness of Some Women is Much Discussed," *Leader* (Regina), 11 November 1918.
40 "Teacher Nurses Are to be Given a Deserved Rest," *Leader* (Regina), 9 November 1918.
41 "Peter Pan's Pipes," *Leader* (Regina), 29 October 1918.
42 "The City Hall Must Act," *Leader* (Regina), 29 October 1918.
43 "Wearing Mask in Street Not Best Methods, Say Drs.," *Leader* (Regina), 31 October 1918.
44 "Forty Public Spirited Men Answer Call," *Leader* (Regina), 31 October 1918.
45 Ibid.
46 "2,000 People Suffer From Epidemic," *Leader* (Regina), 31 October 1918.
47 "Ten Deaths in City Yesterday; Total is Now 144," *Leader* (Regina), 2 November 1918.
48 "Influenza Takes Toll of Twenty Lives Yesterday," *Leader* (Regina), 30 October 1918.

49 "Nine More Dead in Regina Yesterday," *Leader* (Regina), 29 October 1918.
50 "The City Hall Must Act," *Leader* (Regina), 29 October 1918.
51 "Thirteen Died from Epidemic Here Yesterday," *Leader* (Regina), 5 November 1918.
52 "Teacher Nurses Are to Be Given a Deserved Rest," *Leader* (Regina), 9 November 1918.
53 "3,070 Cases of Influenza Cared For, Miss Cooper," *Leader* (Regina), 11 November 1918.
54 "Thirteen Died From Epidemic Here Yesterday," *Leader* (Regina), 5 November 1918.
55 "Epidemic Shows a Decided Change for the Better," *Leader* (Regina), 13 November 1918.
56 "Last Patient is Discharged from St. Joseph's School," *Leader* (Regina), 28 November 1918.
57 "'Flu' Figures Go to Show Young Men Succumbed," *Leader* (Regina), 25 November 1918.
58 The figure is for the period between October 1918 and March 1920. Burch, "The Spanish Influenza," 7–8.
59 "Large Number of Worshippers at City Churches," *Leader* (Regina), 25 November 1918.
60 "Regina Resumes Normal Life at Six P.M. Today," *Leader* (Regina), 28 November 1918.
61 Calder, *History of the 28th (Northwest) Battalion*, 203.
62 Ibid., 204.
63 Ibid., 205.
64 Ibid., 209.
65 Ibid., 211.
66 Ibid., 215.
67 Ibid., 220.
68 Ibid., 221–22.
69 Ibid., 223.
70 Ibid., 226.
71 Ibid., 227.
72 Ibid.
73 Ibid., 230.
74 Ibid., 234.
75 Major Gord Goddard, Director, Saskatchewan Military Museum, Personal Papers, "Private George Lawrence Price, Last Man Killed in World War I."
76 "Peter Pan's Pipes," *Leader* (Regina), 12 November 1918.
77 "Alarms Keep Fire Brigade on Run," *Leader* (Regina), 12 November 1918.
78 "Regina Celebrates in Royal Fashion," *Leader* (Regina), 12 November 1918.
79 Miller, *Our Glory and Our Grief*, 44.
80 "Regina Celebrates in Royal Fashion," *Leader* (Regina), 12 November 1918.

81 Ibid.
82 "Citizens Give Thanks to God For Victory," *Leader* (Regina), 2 December 1918.
83 Ibid.
84 Ibid.
85 Ibid.

Epilogue

1   "Peter Pan's Pipes," *Leader* (Regina), 14 November 1918.
2   Donald E. Graves, "The Proposed Saskatchewan War Memorial Museum, 1919–1926," *Organization of Military Museums of Canada Journal* 7 (1978–79): 14.
3   Ibid., 14.
4   SAB, RE-962,"Soldiers Cemetery," Regina,
5   "The Cross of Sacrifice," *Leader* (Regina), 24 June 1922.
6   "Civil Service to Observe Armistice Day at Buildings," *Leader* (Regina), 11 November 1919.
7   "Armistice Day is Celebrated by Veterans of City; Throng Crowds Association Rooms," *Leader* (Regina), 12 November 1920.
8   "Veterans Want Armistice Day on November 11," *Leader* (Regina), 10 November 1921.
9   Vance, *Death So Noble*, 213.
10 "Ball is Given by United Services," *Leader* (Regina), 11 November 1921.
11 "Anticipate Large Sale of Poppies," *Leader* (Regina), 9 November 1921.
12 "Poppies to Be Sold on Streets Today," *Leader* (Regina), 11 November 1922.
13 "Poppies of Flanders Extolled in Essays Written by Children," *Leader*, 10 November 1923.
14 Ibid.
15 "Crowds Flock to Worship on Armistice Day," *Leader* (Regina), 12 November 1923.
16 "Program Ready for Service on Armistice Day," *Leader* (Regina), 8 November 1923.
17 "Crowds Flock to Worship on Armistice Day," *Leader* (Regina), 12 November 1923.
18 Ibid.
19 "Regina to Pay Tribute to Men Who Gave Lives," *Leader* (Regina), 10 November 1923.
20 Jonathan Vance discusses the tension between the two impulses. Vance, *Death So Noble*, 204–05.
21 CORA, Wascana Park Improvement File, COR-18-284, Report of Sub-Committee Re: War Memorial, 19 December 1923.
22 "Fix Conditions for Plans for City Cenotaph," *Leader* (Regina), 6 November 1925.

Notes

23 CORA, City Council Minutes, COR-1-(21) (1), 17 March 1925.
24 "Notice! City of Regina Voting on Bylaws," *Leader* (Regina), 22 April 1925.
25 "Bylaw Voting Was Shock to War Veterans," *Leader* (Regina), 9 May 1925.
26 Ibid.
27 "Ald. Taylor to Take Up Matter in the Council," *Regina Post*, 11 May 1925.
28 CORA, City Council Minutes, COR-1-(21) (1), 2 June 1925.
29 "Cenotaph for Regina Voted by Citizens," *Leader* (Regina), 18 July 1925.
30 "City Fathers Agree on Wascana Park as Site of Civic War Memorial," *Leader* (Regina), 16 October 1925.
31 "Cenotaph to Be Placed in Center of Victoria Park is Latest Decree," *Leader* (Regina), 21 October 1925.
32 See <http://www.bbc.co.uk/religion/remembrance/history/cenotaph.shtml>.
33 CORA, City Council Minutes, COR-1-(21) (2), 17 November 1925.
34 Maquettes of Frederick Chapman Clemesha's St. Julien Memorial were placed in the legislative building in Regina. They are above the Grand Staircase and in alcoves on either side of the bottom of the stairs. Barnhart, *Building for the Future*, 47.
35 CORA, City Council Minutes, COR-1-(22) (1), 8 February 1926.
36 CORA, City Council Minutes, COR-1-(22) (1), 1 June 1926.
37 CORA, City Council Minutes, COR-1-(22) (1), 16 February 1926.
38 "Silence Reigns as Union Jack on War Memorial Flutters to Ground Revealing Tribute to Soldier Dead," *Leader* (Regina), 12 November 1926.
39 Regina Public Library, Local History Collection, Program of the Unveiling of the War Memorial Erected in Victory Park by the City of Regina, 11 November 1926.
40 "Silence Reigns as Union Jack on War Memorial Flutters to Ground Revealing Tribute to Soldier Dead," *Leader* (Regina), 12 November 1926.
41 Regina Public Library, Local History Collection, Program of the Unveiling of the War Memorial Erected in Victory Park by the City of Regina, 11 November 1926.
42 "Silence Reigns as Union Jack on War Memorial Flutters to Ground Revealing Tribute to Soldier Dead," *Leader* (Regina), 12 November 1926.
43 "Simple Legend on Memorial to Regina War Dead," *Leader* (Regina), 12 November 1926.
44 "Silence Reigns as Union Jack on War Memorial Flutters to Ground Revealing Tribute to Soldier Dead," *Leader* (Regina), 12 November 1926.
45 Ibid.
46 "Regina Again Pays Honor to Her War Dead," *Leader* (Regina), 12 November 1927.
47 "The Cenotaph Unveiling Today," *Leader* (Regina), 11 November 1926.
48 Ibid.
49 "Regina Children Do Themselves and Instructors Much Credit by Presentation of 'The Beaver,'" *Leader* (Regina), 2 June 1917.
50 Ibid.

51 "Dr. Salem Bland Appeals for a United Canada Built Up of the Best from All People Here," *Leader* (Regina), 17 July 1918.
52 "The Canadian Club," *Leader* (Regina), 25 February 1918.
53 "Allies', Canada's and Saskatchewan's Share in the Great War Form Theme of Addresses at Annual Meeting of the Canadian Club," *Leader* (Regina), 23 February 1918.
54 "What is a Canadian?" *Leader* (Regina), 11 July 1917.
55 Alex Ross, "Preface" to D.E. Macintyre, *Canada at Vimy* (Toronto: Peter Martin, 1967), viii.
56 "Land Settlement After the War," *Leader* (Regina), 23 May 1916.
57 "Second Life for Sheaf After Public Backlash," *Leader-Post* (Regina), 18 December 2007. See also Michael Jackson, "Take a Scythe to the Sheaf," *Leader-Post* (Regina), 19 December 2007.
58 Becker, *War and Faith*, 26.
59 SAB, Taylor Papers, Neil (Piffles) and Merril Samuel, R-2930, Neil Taylor to mother, 2 December 1918.

Bibliography

Primary Sources

Archival Documents
City of Regina Archives

City Clerk's Office Files, 1914–1926.
City Council Minutes and Agendas, 1914–1926.
City Manager's Records, 1914–1926.

Library and Archives of Canada

28th Canadian Infantry Battalion (RG 9 III C3, vol. 4139; RG 9 III D1, vol. 4964; RG 9 II B5, vol. 5).
195th Canadian Infantry Battalion (RG 9 III D1, vol. 4703).
Military District N. 12 (RG 9 II B5, vol. 5).
Service Records, Canadian Expeditionary Force, World War I (RG 150, Acc 92-93/166).

Private Papers

Major Gord Goddard Personal Papers

Regina Public Library

Local History Collection

Queen's University Archives

C.A. Dunning Papers
MacKinnon Family Fonds

Saskatchewan Archives Board

W.M. Martin Papers

Walter Scott Papers
Regina Rifles Regiment Collection
Neil (Piffles) and Merril Samuel Taylor Papers

United Church of Canada/Victoria University Archives

Biographical Files Collection
Hugh Dobson Papers

Newspapers

Daily Post (Regina). 1916–1918.
Evening Province (Regina). 1916.
Evening Province and Standard (Regina). 1914–1916.
Leader (Regina). 1914–1926.
Moose Jaw Times. 1918–1919.
Phoenix (Saskatoon). 1914.
The Presbyterian, Journal of the Presbyterian Church in Canada. 1916.
Sheaf (University of Saskatchewan). 1914–1919.

Printed Matter

Beach, George. *Municipal Manual, City of Regina*. Regina: City of Regina, 1919.

Department of Temperance and Moral Reform of the Methodist Church and the Board of Social Service and Evangelism of the Presbyterian Church. *Report of a Preliminary and General Social Survey of Regina*. September 1913.

Foght, Harold F. *A Survey of Education in the Province of Saskatchewan: A Report to the Government of the Province of Saskatchewan*. Regina: King's Printer, 1918.

Government of Canada, *1911 Census of Canada*. Ottawa: Dominion Bureau of Statistics, 1911.

—. *Census of Prairie Provinces, 1916: Population and Agriculture.* Ottawa: Dominion Bureau of Statistics, 1916.

Government of Saskatchewan, *Budget Speeches.* Hon. C.A. Dunning, 27 January 1920.

Hopkins, J. Castell, ed. *Canadian Annual Review of Public Affairs.* Toronto: Canadian Annual Review Ltd., 1912–1918.

Saskatchewan Bureau of Health. *Annual Report of the Bureau of Public Health for the Province of Saskatchewan, 1919–1920.* Regina: King's Printer, 1921.

Saskatchewan Department of Agriculture, *Agricultural Statistics, 1975.* Regina: Saskatchewan Department of Agriculture, 1975.

Secondary Sources

Books

Airhart, Phyllis D. *Serving the Present: Revivalism, Progressivism and the Methodist Tradition in Canada.* Montreal and Kingston: McGill-Queen's University Press, 1992.

Allen, Richard. *The Social Passion: Religion and Social Reform in Canada, 1914–28.* Toronto: University of Toronto Press, 1973.

Anderson, J.T.M. *The Education of the New Canadians: A Treatise on Canada's Greatest Educational Problem.* Toronto: J.M. Dent and Sons, 1918.

Avery, Donald. *"Dangerous Foreigners": European Immigrant Workers and Labour Radicalism in Canada, 1896–1932.* Toronto: McClelland and Stewart, 1979.

Bacchi, Carol Lee. *Liberation Deferred? The Ideas of the English-Canadian Suffragists, 1877–1918.* Toronto: University of Toronto Press, 1983.

Barnhart, Gordon L. *Building for the Future: A Photo Journal of Saskatchewan's Legislative Building.* Regina: Canadian Plains Research Center, 2002.

—. *"Peace, Progress and Prosperity": A Biography of Saskatchewan's First Premier, T. Walter Scott*. Regina: Canadian Plains Research Center, 2000.

Barry, John M. *The Great Influenza: The Story of the Deadliest Pandemic in History*. New York: Penguin, 2005.

Becker, Annette. *War and Faith: The Religious Imagination in France, 1914–1930*. Trans. Helen McPhail. New York: Berg, 1998.

Berger, Carl. *The Sense of Power: Studies in the Ideas of Canadian Imperialism 1867–1914*. Toronto: University of Toronto Press, 1970.

Blanchard, Jim. *Winnipeg 1912*. Winnipeg: University of Manitoba Press, 2005.

Bland, Salem. *The New Christianity*. Toronto: University of Toronto Press, 1973. First published 1920 by McClelland and Stewart.

Boyer, Paul. *Urban Masses and Moral Order in America, 1820–1920*. Cambridge, MA: Harvard University Press, 1978.

Brennan, J. William. *Regina: An Illustrated History*. Toronto: James Lorimer and Co. and Canadian Museum of Civilization, 1989.

Brown, David S. *Richard Hofstadter: An Intellectual Biography*. Chicago: University of Chicago Press, 2006.

Brown, Robert Craig. *Robert Laird Borden: A Biography*. 2 vols. Toronto: Macmillan, 1975. Reprint, 1980.

Brown, Robert Craig, and Ramsay Cook. *Canada 1896–1921: A Nation Transformed*. Toronto: McClelland and Stewart, 1974.

Buckner, Phillip, and R. Douglas Francis, eds. *Canada and the British World: Culture, Migration and Identity*. Vancouver: University of British Columbia Press, 2006.

Buitenhuis, Peter. *The Great War of Words: British, American and Canadian Propaganda and Fiction, 1914–1933*. Vancouver: University of British Columbia Press, 1987.

Calder, Donald George Scott. *The History of the 28th (Northwest) Battalion, CEF (October 1914–June 1919) From the Memoirs of Brigadier General Alexander Ross*. Regina: Regina Rifle Regiment, 1961.

Christie, Nancy, and Michael Gauvreau. *A Full-Orbed Christianity: The Protestant Churches and Social Welfare in Canada, 1900–1940*. Montreal and Kingston: McGill-Queen's University Press, 1996.

Cleverdon, Catherine L. *The Woman Suffrage Movement in Canada*. Toronto: University of Toronto Press, 1974. First published 1950.

Cook, Ramsay. *The Regenerators: Social Criticism in Late Victorian English Canada*. Toronto: University of Toronto Press, 1985.

—. *The Politics of John W. Dafoe and the Free Press*. Toronto: University of Toronto Press, 1963.

Cook, Tim. *Clio's Warriors: Canadian Historians and the Writing of the World Wars*. Vancouver: University of British Columbia Press, 2006.

Craig, Grace Morris. *But This Is Our War*. Toronto: University of Toronto Press, 1981.

Crerar, Duff. *Padres in No Man's Land*. Montreal and Kingston: McGill-Queen's University Press, 1995.

Crosby, Alfred W. *America's Forgotten Pandemic: The Influenza of 1918*. New York: Cambridge University Press, 2003.

Daly, George Thomas, CSSR. *Catholic Problems in Western Canada*. Toronto: Macmillan, 1921.

Danbom, David B. *The World of Hope: Progressives and the Struggle for an Ethical Public Life*. Philadelphia: Temple University Press, 1987.

Danysk, Cecilia. *Hired Hands: Labour and the Development of Prairie Agriculture, 1880–1930*. Toronto: McClelland and Stewart, 1995.

Dawley, Alan. *Changing the World: American Progressives in War and Revolution*. Princeton: Princeton University Press, 2003.

Dawson, Graham: *Soldier Heroes: British Adventure, Empire and the Imagining of Masculinities*. London: Routledge, 1994.

Eisler, Dale. *False Expectations: Politics and the Pursuit of the Saskatchewan Myth*. Regina: Canadian Plains Research Center, 2006.

Eksteins, Modris. *Rites of Spring: The Great War and the Birth of the Modern Age*. Toronto: Lester and Orpen Dennys, 1989.

English, John. *The Decline of Politics: The Conservatives and the Party System, 1901–1920.* Toronto: University of Toronto Press, 1977.

Falconer, R.A. *The German Tragedy and Its Meaning for Canada.* Toronto: University of Toronto Press, 1915.

Fowke, Vernon C. *The National Policy and the Wheat Economy.* Toronto: University of Toronto Press, 1957.

Frantzen, Allen J. *Bloody Good: Chivalry, Sacrifice, and the Great War.* Chicago: University of Chicago Press, 2004.

Fraser, Brian. *The Social Uplifters: Presbyterian Progressives and the Social Gospel.* Waterloo: Wilfrid Laurier University Press, 1988.

Fussell, Paul. *The Great War and Modern Memory.* New York: Oxford University Press, 1975.

Granatstein, J.L. *Hell's Corner: An Illustrated History of Canada's Great War, 1914–1918.* Vancouver: Douglas and McIntyre, 2004.

—, and J.M. Hitsman. *Broken Promises: A History of Conscription in Canada.* Toronto: Oxford University Press, 1977.

Guest, Dennis. *The Emergence of Social Security in Canada.* Vancouver: University of British Columbia Press, 1997.

Gusfield, Joseph R. *Symbolic Crusade: Status Politics and the American Temperance Movement.* Urbana: University of Illinois Press, 1963.

Gwyn, Sandra. *Tapestry of War: A Private View of Canadians in the Great War.* Toronto: HarperCollins, 1992.

Heron, Craig. *Booze: A Distilled History.* Toronto: Between the Lines, 2003.

Hofstadter, Richard. *The Age of Reform: From Bryan to F.D.R.* New York: Alfred A. Knopf, 1956.

Jones, Esyllt W. *Influenza 1918: Disease, Death and Struggle in Winnipeg.* Toronto: University of Toronto Press, 2007.

Kennedy, David. *Over Here: The First World War and American Society.* New York: Oxford University Press, 1964.

Keshen, Jeffrey. *Propaganda and Censorship During Canada's Great War.* Edmonton: University of Alberta Press, 1996.

Knight, Louise W. *Citizen: Jane Addams and the Struggle for Democracy*. Chicago: University of Chicago Press, 2005.

Kolata, Gina. *Flu: The Story of the Great Influenza Pandemic of 1918 and the Search for the Virus that Caused It*. New York: Simon and Schuster, 2001.

Kordan, S. Bohdan. *Prisoners of War: Internment in Canada During the Great War*. Montreal and Kingston: McGill-Queen's University Press, 2002.

Lerner, Michael A. *Dry Manhattan: Prohibition in New York City*. Cambridge, MA: Harvard University Press, 2007.

Luciuk, Lubomyr Y. *Without Just Cause: Canada's First National Internment Operations and Ukrainian Canadians, 1914–20*. Kingston: Kashtan Press, 2006.

MacDonald, Robert H. *Sons of the Empire: The Frontier and the Boy Scout Movement, 1890–1918*. Toronto: University of Toronto Press, 1993.

MacIntyre, D.E. *Canada at Vimy*. Toronto: Peter Martin, 1967.

MacKenzie, John M. *Propaganda and Empire: The Manipulation of British Public Opinion, 1880–1960*. Manchester: Manchester University Press, 1985.

MacKinnon, Lilian Vaux. *Miriam of Queen's*. Toronto: McClelland and Stewart, 1921.

Macleod, David I. *Building Character in the American Boy: The Boy Scouts, YMCA and their Forerunners, 1870–1920*. Madison: University of Wisconsin Press, 1983.

Mansfield, Harvey C. *Manliness*. New Haven: Yale University Press, 2006.

Marshall, David B. *Secularizing the Faith: Canadian Protestant Clergy and the Crisis of Belief, 1850–1940*. Toronto: University of Toronto Press, 1992.

McClung, Nellie. *In Times Like These*. Toronto: University of Toronto Press, 1972. First published 1915 by McLeod and Allen.

McCormack, A. Ross. *Reformers, Rebels and Revolutionaries: The Western Canadian Radical Movement 1899–1919.* Toronto: University of Toronto Press, 1977.

McGerr, Michael. *A Fierce Discontent: The Rise and Fall of the Progressive Movement in America.* New York: Oxford University Press, 2003.

McLaren, Angus. *Our Own Master Race: Eugenics in Canada, 1885–1945.* Toronto: McClelland and Stewart, 1990.

Miller, Ian. *Our Glory and Our Grief: Torontonians and the Great War.* Toronto: University of Toronto Press, 2002.

Miller, J.O. *The New Era in Canada: Essays Dealing with the Upbringing of the Canadian Commonwealth.* Toronto: J.M. Dent, 1917.

Mitchell, Elizabeth B. *Western Canada Before the War.* Saskatoon: Western Producer Prairie Books, 1981. First published 1915 by John Murray, London.

Morris, Philip H., ed. *The Canadian Patriotic Fund: A Record of its Activities From 1914 to 1919.* N.p., 1920.

Morton, Desmond. *When Your Number's Up: The Canadian Soldier in the First World War.* Toronto: Random House, 1993.

—. *A Military History of Canada.* Toronto: McClelland and Stewart, 2007.

—. *Fight or Pay: Soldiers' Families in the Great War.* Vancouver: University of British Columbia Press, 2004.

—. *Silent Battle: Canadian Prisoners of War in Germany, 1914–19.* Toronto: Lester, 1992.

—, and J.L. Granatstein. *Marching to Armageddon: Canadians and the Great War 1914–1919.* Toronto: Lester and Orpen Dennys, 1989.

—, and Glenn Wright. *Winning the Second Battle: Canadian Veterans and the Return to Civilian Life, 1915–1930.* Toronto: University of Toronto Press, 1987.

Neatby, Hilda. *To Strive, To Seek, To Find and Not To Yield, Queen's University, Vol. I, 1841–1917.* Montreal and Kingston: McGill-Queen's University Press, 1978.

Nye, Russel B. *Midwestern Progressive Politics: A Historical Study of its Origins and Development 1870–1958*. East Lansing: Michigan State University Press, 1959.

Palmer, Howard. *Patterns of Prejudice: A History of Nativism in Alberta*. Toronto: McClelland and Stewart, 1982.

Pettigrew, Eileen. *The Silent Enemy: Canada and the Deadly Flu of 1918*. Saskatoon: Western Producer Prairie Books, 1983.

Pickles, Katie. *Female Imperialism and National Identity: Imperial Order Daughters of the Empire*. Manchester: Manchester University Press, 2002.

Pitsula, James M. *An Act of Faith: The Early Years of Regina College*. Regina: Canadian Plains Research Center, 1988.

—. *Helping Families Through Life: A History of Family Service Regina*. Regina: Family Service Regina, 2001.

Ratzinger, Joseph (Pope Benedict XVI). *Jesus of Nazareth: From the Baptism in the Jordan to the Transfiguration*. Trans. Adrian J. Walker. New York: Doubleday, 2007.

Read, Daphne, ed. *The Great War and Canadian Society*. Toronto: New Hogtown Press, 1978.

Robinson, Elwyn B. *History of North Dakota*. Fargo: North Dakota State University Institute for Regional Studies, 2003.

Rutherdale, Robert. *Hometown Horizons: Local Responses to Canada's Great War*. Vancouver: University of British Columbia Press, 2004.

Shipley, Robert. *To Mark Our Place: A History of Canadian War Memorials*. Toronto: NC Press, 1987.

Smith, David E. *Prairie Liberalism: The Liberal Party in Saskatchewan 1905–71*. Toronto: University of Toronto Press, 1976.

Socknat, Thomas P. *Witness Against War: Pacifism in Canada, 1900–1945*. Toronto: University of Toronto Press, 1987.

Strachan, Hew. *The First World War*. New York: Viking, 2004.

Struthers, James. *No Fault of Their Own: Unemployment and the Canadian Welfare State, 1914–1941*. Toronto: University of Toronto Press, 1994.

Thompson, John Herd. *The Harvests of War: The Prairie West 1914–18*. Toronto: McClelland and Stewart, 1978.

Valverde, Mariana. *The Age of Light, Soap and Water: Moral Reform in English Canada, 1885–1925*. Toronto: McClelland and Stewart, 1991.

Vance, Jonathan. *Death So Noble: Memory, Meaning, and the First World War*. Vancouver: University of British Columbia Press, 1997.

Waiser, Bill. *Saskatchewan: A New History*. Calgary: Fifth House, 2005.

—. *Park Prisoners: The Untold Story of Western Canada's National Parks, 1915–46*. Saskatoon and Calgary: Fifth House, 1995.

Warren, Jim, and Kathleen Carlisle. *On the Side of the People: A History of Labour in Saskatchewan*. Regina: Coteau Books, 2006.

Wilson, A.N. *After the Victorians: The Decline of Britain in the World*. New York: Farrar, Straus, and Giroux, 2005.

Wilson, Barbara. *Ontario and the First World War*. Toronto: Champlain Society, 1977.

Winter, Jay, Geoffrey Parker, and Mary R. Habeck, eds. *The Great War and the Twentieth Century*. New Haven: Yale University Press, 2000.

Wise, S.F. *Canadian Airmen and the First World War: The Official History of the Royal Canadian Air Force*. Vol. 1. Toronto: University of Toronto Press, 1980.

Articles

Allen, Richard. "The Social Gospel as the Religion of Agrarian Revolt." In *The West and the Nation: Essays in Honour of W.L. Morton*, ed. Carl Berger and Ramsay Cook. Toronto: McClelland and Stewart, 1976.

Artibise, Alan F.J. "Boosterism and the Development of Prairie Cities, 1871–1913." In *The Prairie West: Historical Readings*, ed. R. Douglas Francis and Howard Palmer. Edmonton: Pica Pica Press, Textbook Division of University of Alberta Press, 1992.

Avery, Donald. "Ethnic and Class Relations in Western Canada During the First World War: A Case Study of European Immigrants and Anglo-

Canadian Nativism." In *Canada and the First World War: Essays in Honour of Robert Craig Brown*, ed. David MacKenzie. Toronto: University of Toronto Press, 2005.

Barber, Marilyn. "Nationalism, Nativism and the Social Gospel." In *The Social Gospel in Canada: Papers of the Interdisciplinary Conference on the Social Gospel in Canada*, ed. Richard Allen. Ottawa: National Museums of Canada, 1973.

—. "Canadianization Through the Schools of the Prairie Provinces Before World War I: The Attitudes and Aims of the English-Speaking Majority." In *Ethnic Canadians: Culture and Education*, ed. Martin L. Kovacs. Regina: Canadian Plains Research Center, 1978.

Barnhart, Gordon L. "Walter Scott." In *Saskatchewan Premiers of the Twentieth Century*, ed. Gordon L. Barnhart. Regina: Canadian Plains Research Center, 2004.

Bliss, J.M. "The Methodist Church and World War I." *Canadian Historical Review* 49, 3 (1968).

Bourdon, David. "Sportsmen's Patriotic Response to the First World War: The Calgary Experience." In *Proceedings of the 5th Canadian Symposium on the History of Sport and Physical Education*. Toronto: University of Toronto, 1982.

Bray, Robert Matthew. "Fighting as an Ally: The English-Canadian Patriotic Response to the Great War." *Canadian Historical Review* 61, 2 (1980).

Brown, Robert Craig, and Donald Loveridge. "Unrequited Faith: Recruiting the CEF 1914–18." *Revue Internatonale d'Histoire Militaire* (1982).

Buckner, Phillip. "Whatever Happened to the British Empire?" *Journal of the Canadian Historical Association* 4 (1993).

Burch, Fred. "The Spanish Influenza and Canada's Criminal Justice System: Lessons for Pandemic Planners." Scholars Series, Saskatchewan Institute of Public Policy (2007).

Cook, Ramsay. "Dafoe, Laurier and the Formation of Union Government." *Canadian Historical Review* 42, 3 (1961).

Decarie, M.G. "Paved with Good Intentions: The Prohibitionists' Road to Racism in Ontario." *Ontario History* 66 (1974).

English, John. "Political Leadership in the First World War." In *Canada and the First World War: Essays in Honour of Robert Craig Brown*, ed. David MacKenzie. Toronto: University of Toronto Press, 2005.

Ens, Adolf. "The Public School Crisis Among Mennonites in Saskatchewan 1916–25." In *Mennonite Images: Historical, Cultural and Literary Essays Dealing with Mennonite Issues*, ed. Harry Loewen. Winnipeg: Hyperion Press, 1980.

Granatstein, J.L. "Conscription in the Great War." In *Canada and the First World War: Essays in Honour of Robert Craig Brown*, ed. David MacKenzie. Toronto: University of Toronto Press, 2005.

Graves, Donald E. "The Proposed Saskatchewan War Memorial Museum, 1919–1926." *Organization of Military Museums of Canada Journal* 7 (1978–79).

Hayden, Michael. "Why Are All Those Names on the Walls? The University of Saskatchewan and World War I." *Saskatchewan History* 58, 2 (2006).

Hryniuk, Stella. "Pioneer Bishop, Pioneer Times: Nykyta Budka in Canada." In *Prophets, Priests and Prodigals: Readings in Canadian Religious History, 1608 to Present*, ed. Mark G. McGowan and David B. Marshall. Toronto: McGraw-Hill Ryerson, 1992.

—. "The Bishop Budka Controversy: A New Perspective." *Canadian Slavonic Papers* 23, 2 (1981).

Huel, Raymond. "Pastor vs Politician: The Reverend Murdoch MacKinnon and Premier Walter Scott's Amendment to the School Act." *Saskatchewan History* 32, 2 (1979).

—. "The Public School as a Guardian of Anglo-Saxon Traditions: The Saskatchewan Experience, 1913–1918." In *Ethnic Canadians: Culture and Education*, ed. Martin L. Kovacs. Regina: Canadian Plains Research Center, 1978.

Jones, David. C. "'There is Some Power About the Land': The Western Agrarian Press and Country Life Ideology." In *The Prairie West: Historical*

Readings, ed. R. Douglas Francis and Howard Palmer. Edmonton: Pica Pica Press, Textbook Division of University of Alberta Press, 1992.

—. "The Zeitgeist of Western Settlement: Education and the Myth of the Land." In *Schooling and Society in Twentieth Century British Columbia*, ed. J. Donald Wilson and David C. Jones. Calgary: Detselig Enterprises, 1980.

—. "Better School Day in Saskatchewan and the Perils of Educational Reform." *The Journal of Educational Thought* 14, 2 (1980).

Kealey, Gregory. "State Repression of Labour and the Left in Canada, 1914–1920: The Impact of the First World War." *Canadian Historical Review* 73 (1992).

—. "1919: The Canadian Labor Revolt." *Labour/Le Travail* 13 (1984).

Kyba, Patrick. "J.T.M. Anderson." In *Saskatchewan Premiers of the Twentieth Century*, ed. Gordon L. Barnhart. Regina: Canadian Plains Research Center, 2004.

Litt, Paul. "Canada Invaded! The Great War, Mass Culture and Canadian Cultural Nationalism." In *Canada and the First World War: Essays in Honour of Robert Craig Brown*, ed. David MacKenzie. Toronto: University of Toronto Press, 2005.

Lux, Maureen K. "'The Bitter Flats': The 1918 Influenza Epidemic in Saskatchewan." *Saskatchewan History* 49, 1 (1997).

Maroney, Paul. "'The Great Adventure': The Context and Ideology of Recruiting in Ontario, 1916–17." *Canadian Historical Review* 77 (1996).

Melnycky, Peter. "The Internment of Ukrainians in Canada." In *Loyalties in Conflict: Ukrainians in Canada During the Great War*, ed. Frances Swyripa and John Herd Thompson. Edmonton: Canadian Institute of Ukrainian Studies, 1983.

Menzies, June. "Votes for Saskatchewan Women." In *Politics in Saskatchewan*, ed. Norman Ward and Duff Spafford. Don Mills: Longmans, 1968.

Mitchinson, Wendy. "The WCTU: 'For God, Home and Native Land': A Study of Nineteenth Century Feminism." In *A Not Unreasonable Claim:*

Women and Reform in Canada, 1880s–1920s, ed. Linda Kealey. Toronto: Women's Press, 1979.

Morton, Desmond. "Sir William Otter and Internment Operations in Canada During the First World War." *Canadian Historical Review* 55, 1 (1974).

—. "Polling the Soldier Vote: The Overseas Campaign in the Canadian General Election of 1917." *Journal of Canadian Studies* 10, 4 (1975).

Mott, Morris. "One Solution to the Urban Crisis: Manly Sports and Winnipeggers, 1900–1914." *Urban History Review* 12, 2 (1983).

O'Brien, Mike. "Manhood and the Militia Myth: Masculinity, Class and Militarism in Ontario, 1902–1914." *Labour/Le Travail* 42 (1998).

Ramkhalawansingh, Ceta. "Women During the Great War." In *Women at Work: Ontario, 1850–1930*, ed. Janice Acton. Toronto: Women's Press, 1974.

Regehr, Ted. "William M. Martin." In *Saskatchewan Premiers of the Twentieth Century*, ed. Gordon L. Barnhart. Regina: Canadian Plains Research Center, 2004.

Robertson, Peter. "Canadian Photojournalism During the First World War." *History of Photography* 2 (1978).

Robin, Martin. "Registration, Conscription and Independent Labour Politics, 1916–17." In *Conscription 1917*, ed. Ramsay Cook, Craig Brown, and Carl Berger. Toronto: University of Toronto Press, n.d.

Sangster, Joan. "Mobilizing Women for War." In *Canada and the First World War: Essays in Honour of Robert Craig Brown*, ed. David MacKenzie. Toronto: University of Toronto Press, 2005.

Schulze, David, "The Industrial Workers of the World and the Unemployed in Edmonton and Calgary in the Depression of 1913–15." *Labour/Le Travail* 25 (1990).

Sheehan, Nancy M. "The WCTU on the Prairies, 1886–1930: An Alberta-Saskatchewan Comparison." *Prairie Forum* 6, 1 (1981).

—. "Philosophy, Pedagogy and Practice: The IODE and the Schools in Canada, 1900–1945." *Historical Studies in Education* 2, 2 (1990).

Siemiatycki, Myer. "Munitions and Labour Militancy: The 1916 Hamilton Machinists' Strike." In *Canadian Labour History*, ed. David Bercuson. Toronto: Copp Clark, 1987.

Stacey, C.P. "Nationality: The Experience of Canada." *Historical Papers* (1968).

Telford, Gertrude S. "The First Child Welfare Conferences in Saskatchewan." *Saskatchewan History* 4.

Thompson, John H. "'The Beginning of Our Regeneration': The Great War and Western Canadian Reform Movements." *Historical Papers* (1972).

Travers, Tim. "Canadian Film and the First World War." In *The First World War and Popular Cinema: 1914 to the Present*, ed. Michael Paris. New Brunswick, NJ: Rutgers University Press, 2000.

Turner, Allan R, ed. "Reminiscences of the Hon. J.A. Calder." *Saskatchewan History* 25 (1972).

Vance, Jonathan. "Battle Verse: Poetry and Nationalism After Vimy Ridge." In *Vimy Ridge: A Canadian Reassessment*, ed. Geoffrey Hayes, Andrew Iarocci, and Mike Bechthold. Waterloo: Laurier Centre for Military and Disarmament Studies and Wilfrid Laurier University Press, 2007.

Voisey, Paul. "The Urbanization of the Canadian Prairies, 1871–1916." *Histoire Sociale/Social History* 8, 15 (1975).

Warsh, Cheryl Krasnick. "'John Barleycorn Must Die': An Introduction to the Social History of Alcohol." In *Drink In Canada: Historical Essays*, ed. Cheryl Krasnick Warsh. Montreal and Kingston: McGill-Queen's University Press, 1993.

Young, Alan R. "'We Throw the Torch': Canadian Memorials of the Great War and the Mythology of Heroic Sacrifice." *Journal of Canadian Studies* 24 (1989–90).

Honours Papers and Theses

Boudreau, J.A. "The Enemy Alien Problem in Canada, 1914–1921." PhD thesis, University of California, 1965.

Brennan, J. William. "A Political History of Saskatchewan, 1905–1929." PhD thesis, University of Alberta, 1976.

—. "The Public Career of Charles Avery Dunning in Saskatchewan." MA thesis, University of Saskatchewan, Regina Campus, 1968.

Cherwinski, Walter J.C. "The Formative Years of the Trade Union Movement in Saskatchewan, 1905–1920." MA thesis, University of Saskatchewan, 1966.

Dahl, Ken. "Public Attitudes Toward the Liquor Question in Saskatchewan, 1880–1925." MA thesis, University of Saskatchewan, 1999.

Kalmakoff, Elizabeth Ann. "Woman Suffrage in Saskatchewan." MA thesis, University of Regina, 1993.

Luttmer, Katherine. "The German Experience in Regina to the End of World War I." BA honours paper, University of Regina, 1986.

Marschall, Kimberley Anne. "Raising Juvenile Delinquents: The Development of Saskatchewan's Child Welfare Laws, 1905–1930." MA thesis, University of Saskatchewan, 2003.

Pinno, Erhard. "Temperance and Prohibition in Saskatchewan." MA thesis, University of Saskatchewan, Regina Campus, 1971.

Small, Nadine. "Stand By the Union Jack: The Imperial Order Daughters of the Empire in the Prairie Provinces During the Great War 1914–18." MA thesis, University of Saskatchewan, 1988.

Index

A

Abbott, Edward L., 138
agriculture: after war, 266, 278–79, 320n2; and Big Interests, 11; and conscription, 182–84; as king in Saskatchewan, 3, 9–10; labour for, 198–99, 200–202, 205; pre-war growth of, 7–8, 320n2; and school reform, 103–5, 198; and soldiers' employment after war, 235, 330n19; urban people used in, 12–13, 50–51, 51–52, 201–2; during war, 12–13, 51, 195, 197–98, 210. *See also* rural myth
Alexandra Club, 35
Algerians, 57
Allan, J. A., 127–28, 186, 217
Allan, James, 132
Allan, Miss, 189, 190
Amiens, Battle of, 257–58
Anderson, J. T. M., 6, 109–10, 220
Andrews, Jonathan, 251
Andrews, Mrs. W. W., 91
Andrews, W. W., 218
anti-loafing law, 204–5
ANV. *See* Army and Navy Veterans (ANV)
Armistice Day memorials, 267–70, 273–76
Army and Navy Veterans (ANV), 238, 239, 240, 242, 262, 270
Arnett, J. H., 261, 262
L'Association Franco-Canadien of Saskatchewan, 107–8
Atcheson, J. L., 245–46
Austria-Hungary, 21–22, 25, 39, 243

B

Bacchi, Carol Lee, 80
Bagshaw, Frederick, 61–62
Balfour, James: and charity, 86; deals with unemployment, 46–47, 49–50; and MacKinnon-Scott dispute, 122, 128; and war, 68, 181, 237; wins mayoralty race, 46
Balfour, Jimmy, 68, 140
Balfour, John, 46–47, 48, 51, 52–53
Ball, A. H., 108, 151–52, 186
Ban-the-Bar crusade, 71–76, 100, 129
Ban-the-Bar Crusader, 72
Bartz case, 127
The Battle Cry of Peace (film), 148
Bawden, Reg, 56
Becker, Annette, 280
Bee, Thomas M., 37

Belcher, Inspector, 41–42
Belgian Relief Fund, 3, 35, 82, 186, 188
Belgium, 4, 22, 260
Bell, A. H., 259
Bell, George, 26, 68, 236
Benedict XVI, Pope, 214
Bennett, Richard B., 174, 175, 197–98
Bergl, J. J., 247
Best, Miss, 87
Besta, Martin, 203
Betts, W., 67
Bidniuk, John, 78
Big Interests: and coalition government, 176–77; as farmer's nemesis, 11; focus of social reform movement, 217–18, 221–22, 226, 230–31; link to rural myth, 279; role in 1917 election, 180; and war contracts, 12, 196
Bigelow, Sadie, 94
bilingualism, 6, 96–99, 105
Black, Norman F., 100, 101, 110–11, 252, 253
Bland, Salem, 215–16, 277
Bliss, J. M., 215
Bloomfield, Reginald, 267
Board of Trade, 191, 204, 252
Board to Regulate Public Contributions, 192
Bocz, Rudolf, 152
Bole, J. F., 76
Bollert, Miss, 90
Bolster, E., 86
Bond, G. F. D., 259
Boomhower, Elmer, 60
Borden, Robert, 11, 143, 168, 174–75, 176, 184
Boucher, Bob, 139
Bow, Malcolm, 207, 251–52, 253, 256
Bradshaw, George, 181
Bradshaw, J. E., 88, 98, 122, 129
Britain Prepared (film), 148–49
British Empire: Canadian belief in, 4, 277, 278; and IODE, 80, 82–83; patriotism toward, 35–36; and prohibition, 75
British heritage: Canada pulling away from, 6–7, 277–78; and control of schools, 82, 95–96; and English only schools movement, 244, 246; and MacKinnon-Scott dispute, 119; pride in, at outbreak of war, 23, 24, 31; and prohibition, 75–76; in Regina politics, 4–6, 47, 113; in school curriculum, 98, 109–10
British War Office, 55
Brown, C. W., 216–17
Brown, George W., 27, 29, 37

355

Brown, Milton, 149
Bruton, Martin J., 181
Bryant, James F., 117, 243, 245
Buckner, Philip, 5, 95, 287n21
Budden, Alfred, 38
Budka, Nykyta, 40–41, 152
Bureau of Public Welfare, 30, 41, 46–48
Burgess, Cecil S., 272, 273
Burrows, Claude, 183
Burton, Jack, 56
business: charity from, 81; elites, 11, 12, 15; and social reform, 221–22; and Spanish flu, 253, 255; and unions, 203; and war advertising, 34; and war economy, 53, 196–97, 208, 209–10; and war profit, 174–75, 180, 217–18; and war-time labour, 199–200, 201, 202; and war unemployment, 46, 51. *See also* Big Interests
Byng, Lord, 267

C

Cairns, H. G., 220
Calder, D. G. Scott, 171
Calder, J. A., 71, 177–78, 279
Callander, Robert, 250
Canada: declaration of war, 3–4; prohibition, 77; sense of nationhood, 1, 64, 168–69, 277–78; war recruitment, 28, 155
Canada, Government of: and agriculture tariffs, 11; bans publications in enemy languages, 247; calls for a welfare state, 193–94; and care of returning soldiers, 233, 235, 242; and censorship, 19; and conscription, 174, 180–81, 184; control of charities, 192; and food conservation, 209; and internment camps, 40; and labour action, 204; and naturalization of immigrants, 39–40; and pensions, 233–34; and recruitment, 65, 143, 146, 155; school policy, 97; social reform proposals for, 225–26; Unionist coalition, 176–77; and war contracts, 12
Canadian Club, 277
Canadian Pacific Railway, 199
Canadian Patriotic Fund, 37. *See also* Patriotic Fund
Canadian Trades and Labour Congress, 175
Carruthers, G. F., 239
Catholic Church: attitude toward war, 26, 262; and immigration, 15; in MacKinnon-Scott dispute, 117–19, 120; and prohibition, 71; and schools, 107; and social gospel, 214, 224
Cavell, Edith, 151
Cawthorpe, C. H., 129
cenotaph, 270–73, 273–76
censorship, 19–20, 34, 148, 227–28
Chapman, Percy, 256

charity work: and enforced donations, 38; fundraising, 35–38, 84–85, 148, 149, 186–88, 247; government organization of, 185, 187–88, 191–93; and moral code, 229, 230; by Patriotic Fund, 185–90; by Victory Loan campaigns, 190–91; by women, 3, 35–36, 80–83, 83–86, 189–90. *See also* Imperial Order Daughters of the Empire (IODE); Patriotic Fund; Red Cross
Chatwin, Art, 55–56
Chatwin, Elsie, 87–88
Chauvin, F. X., 102
children: and essay-writing, 268–69; and social reform, 219, 220, 226, 227, 228
Chown, Samuel D., 13, 72–73, 215, 216
Christie, H. D., 186–87
churches. *See* religion
Citizens' Recruiting Committee, 151–53, 154
City of Regina Battalion (195th), 146–49, 157
Clemesha, Frederick, 272, 337n34
Clink, William, 183
Cochrane, Mrs., 87
Cocks, A. W., 104
Committee of One Hundred, 71, 100, 109
Connaught, Duke of, 159
conscription, 173, 174–76, 179, 180–84, 205, 241
Conservative Party: charges of corruption against Liberals, 122, 125; media of, 19; and 1917 election, 240–41; pro-British policy of, 5, 6, 113; and prohibition, 74; and schools policy, 95–96, 97, 98
convalescent homes, 235–36
Cook, Harry W., 268
Cooper, Nurse, 253–54, 256, 280
Corbett, F. A., 219
Cornwell, K., 202
Courcelette, Battle of, 137–38, 142, 163–65
Cowan, Walter D., 34, 152, 178, 179–80, 204, 206, 208
Creswell, Austin, 67, 87, 137–38
Creswell, Catherine, 87, 280
criminal law, 220–21, 228
Cripps, W. T. H., 163
Cross, J. A., 261
Cullum, John A., 136–37, 280
Cunning, Sergeant, 148

D

Daily Post, 19, 150, 187, 202
Dale, Clarence R., 139–40
Dale, Nurse, 86
Daly, George T., 15, 178–79, 214
Damaged Goods (film), 227–28
Daughters and Maids of England, 35
Davidson, Arthur, 183

Davidson, G. F., 262–63
Davidson, Mrs. C. O., 90, 92, 94, 222–23
Denmark, 103
Der Courier: and conscription, 176, 179; on German used in schools, 107; and Liberal support, 5; pledges loyalty to Canada, 42; on prohibition, 70–71, 74; suspends publication, 247; and war outbreak, 25
Der Staats-Anzeiger, 43
Derling, Reverend, 26
Devline, E. H., 93, 129
Dickie, Constable, 42
Dishorn, Joseph, 200
Dix, Arthur J., 83
Dobson, Hugh: and food prices, 208; and loose morals, 229; on school reform, 101; and social reform, 218, 220, 221, 224–25, 226–28; and Spanish flu, 254; on unemployment, 51
Doner, A. L., 170
Dorie, George, 223
Doughty, A. G., 266
Doyle, J. A., 220
Drummond, Gertrude, 179
Duff, Lyman, 180
Dunning, Charles, 10, 50, 136, 197, 198, 204, 240
Dusanko, Jack, 203
Dyonski, John, 200

E

Earl Grey School, 149, 150
Earp, E. C., 167–68
Edgar, Norman S., 152
education. *See* schools
Elliott, C., 87
Elwood, E. L., 234
Ely, Richard T., 214
Embury, J. F. L.: as civilian, 158, 241, 274; as soldier, 32, 161, 162, 165, 280
employment: of 1914-1915, 45, 46–53; and Saskatchewan government, 198, 236–37; of soldiers after war, 234, 235, 236–37; of women, 53, 198–200, 201, 223, 252–53
England, 55, 87
Ens, Gerhard, 106
Ensor, W. J. A., 134
entertainment: and moral policing, 229–30; for soldiers, 54–55, 58, 163, 166, 172, 229, 238; and Spanish flu, 251–52, 257; before the war, 16–18; in war-time, 53, 84, 85, 148–49, 188, 218
Equal Franchise League, 89
essay-writing contest, 268–69
Evening Province, 19
Evening Province and Standard: history, 19; and MacKinnon-Scott dispute, 119, 126;

and prohibition, 76; on recruitment and militarism, 146–47; and schools policy, 97–98, 99–100; on suffrage, 89
Eymann, C. E., 71–72

F

Fargo *Courier News,* 43
Farmer, S. J., 25–26, 122
Ferguson, Robert, 59–60
Fifteenth Canadian Reserve Battalion, 157
Fifth Battalion, 157
Fifth Brigade, 163
Fifty-First Scottish Division, 259
Fillmore, Frank, 183
First Depot Battalion, 155, 181–82, 190
Fisher, Alice, 268
Fisher, D. W., 53
Foght, Harold, 105
food: conservation, 209–10, 211, 225; high prices for, 208, 211, 225
Foote, W. H., 163
foreigners. *See* immigrants/immigration
Forty-Sixth Battalion, 80
Forty-Third Battalion, 138
Fourth Brigade, 163
Frame, J. F., 217
Frampton, Edward, 275
France, 22, 55, 57
Francophones, 107–8, 111
French language rights, 246, 247–48

G

Gage, H. L., 149
Galbraith, Miss, 189
Galicia/Galicians, 40, 42, 291n116
gardening, 205–7
Gardiner, J. G., 27, 274–75
Gardiner, Leslie, 253
Garner, A. C., 146, 271
gas attacks, 57, 58, 59, 61–62, 258
German-Canadian Alliance, 106–7, 243
German immigration: and anti-German feeling, 24–25, 39, 42–43, 98, 243–44; and language in schools, 106–7, 245; Liberal support of, 5; and prohibition, 70–71, 74; in Regina, 16, 18
Germantown: attitude towards war, 25; description, 18; ethnic tension in, 42–43; fundraising in, 247; and prohibition, 70, 78, 79; and Spanish flu, 255–56; during war-time, 152, 176, 205, 241
Germany: anticipated offensives of, 171, 183–84; in children's essays, 268, 269; claims of atrocities by, 61–62, 62–63, 74, 151, 215; demonized by church, 13, 63–64, 215,

219–20; and end of war, 262; feelings toward, at outbreak of war, 25–27; and gas attacks, 57, 58, 59, 61–62, 258; at Second Ypres, 57–61; and start of war, 4, 22, 43; and trench warfare, 56, 57, 134, 135; against Twenty-Eighth Battalion, 161–62, 164–65, 170–71, 258–59, 260; at Versailles, 247–48; views on, during war, 62–64, 89, 99, 147
Gibson, Albert, 67
Glenn, Joseph, 89
Graham, Angus A., 117, 126, 220
Graham, Major, 182
Graham, Wilson M., 61
Grant, Don, 59
Grant, George, 115
Gravetch, Joseph, 200
Great Britain, 4, 22, 24–28, 148–49, 164. *See also* British Empire; British heritage; England
Great War Veterans' Association (GWVA): anti-immigrant motions, 242–43; and conscription, 175–76; and end of war, 262; and English only schools, 246; essay-writing contest, 268–69; formation and early growth of, 238, 239–40, 241–42; and labour unrest, 204, 205; and memorials, 267, 270, 271; and national anthems, 7; and 1917 election, 179, 240
Green, F. W., 10
Gusfield, Joseph, 75
GWVA. *See* Great War Veterans' Association (GWVA)

H

Habkirk, James, 181
Haight, Zoa, 91
Hall, F. L., 133–34
Hamilton, Edward, 34
Hamilton, Roy, 67
Hanna, W. J., 209
Hannon, Judge, 183
Harding, Bishop, 26
Harton, S. L. W., 222
Haultain, Frederick, 147, 237
Hawthorne, E. H., 67
Hayish, John, 204
Hayward, James W., 254
Hazell, Albert, 60, 132, 134
health care, 225, 227–28
Heffernan, J. H., 181, 200
Henry, E. H., 70
Hepburn, A. C., 287n16
Heughan, R. G., 272–73
Hewitt, W. P., 235
Hill, George, 137, 148–49, 154
Hillman, Mrs. H. M., 35

Hilsenteger, Joseph, 60, 275, 280
Hilsenteger, Mrs. A., 275
Hilton, J. H., 244–45
Hodson, Lt. Col., 261
Hofstadter, Richard, 7
Hogarth, B. D., 183
Holmes, W. Stanley, 183
home front: anti-German feeling, 62–63; eagerness for news, 33–34; pleasures of, 44; pride in soldiers, 45, 62–63; and unemployment, 45
Home Guard, 33
Honeyman, J. R. C., 228, 252
Houston, Lieutenant, 148
Hughes, Sam, 28, 55, 155

I

immigrants/immigration: Canadianization of, 95–96, 106, 108, 110; disenfranchisement of, 176, 184; employment during war, 45, 48–49; and English only schools, 242–48; and ethnic tension, 3, 6, 24–25, 39, 242, 246–47; internment of, 40–41; and language instruction in schools, 106–11; and Liberal policy, 5, 18, 242, 243; lifestyles of, 18; naturalization of, 39–40, 41–42; and 1917 election, 241; and prohibition movement, 70–71, 78; and religion, 15, 245–46; schools of, 102–3; and separate schools tax question, 128, 129; serving in army, 152, 179; slurs against, 243, 245, 248; and social reform, 220; socio-economic position, 5; and Spanish flu, 255–56; and W. Scott's downfall, 113–14; and war-time labour, 199, 200, 204–5. *See also* German immigration; Ukrainian immigration
Imperial Oil Company, 196
Imperial Order Daughters of the Empire (IODE): charity work, 35, 80–83, 86, 188, 299n75; and memorials, 266, 267; moral code of, 230; support of war, 2, 148, 150
industry, 12, 196
infant mortality, 227
internment camps, 40, 41, 42, 200
IODE. *See* Imperial Order Daughters of the Empire (IODE)
Iwuy, 259

J

Japp, Elsie, 268
Jeffs, Wilfred A., 60–61

Index

K

Kearney, Father, 271
Keenleyside, C. B., 71, 150–51
Kemmel sector, 159–60
Kemp, Edward, 155
Kerr, W. F., 19
Keshen, Jeffrey, 19
Ketchen, H. B. B., 158–59, 166–67
Kipling, Rudyard, 4
Kirk, Ernest C., 175
Kit, Joseph, 204
Knox Church, 122–24, 126, 127–28
Kokogauzuk, Bill, 78
Kosowski, Mike, 204
Kusch, F. X., 247

L

labour: strikes, 203–5; war-time, 198–202, 204–5. *See also* employment; Trades and Labour Council; unions
Labour Bureau, 47
LaDrue, A. B., 181
Laird, Homer W., 137, 140
Lajoe, Steve, 204
Lake, R. S., 224, 261, 267
land market, 9, 20, 52
Langley, George, 10, 26–27, 98, 136
Last Post fund, 268
Latta, S. J., 217
Laubach, F., 277
Laurier, Wilfrid, 11, 97, 125, 176, 178
Lawton, Alice, 91, 92–93
Ledster, W. J., 183
Legion of Frontiersmen, 28
Legislative Building, 9
Lewis, A. S., 262
Lewis, Harry T., 26, 75, 219
Liberal Party: charges of corruption against, 122, 125, 129; and coalition government, 176–78; and 1917 election, 178–80, 240–41; and 1912 election, 11–12; pro-British policy of, 6, 113; pro-immigrant policy of, 5, 18; and prohibition, 71–72; and Regina *Leader*, 19; and schools policy, 95–96; and social reform, 14, 213, 279. *See also* Martin, William; Scott, Walter
livestock, 195, 207, 219
Lloyd, George E., 71, 72, 73, 74, 103–4
Local Council of Women, 35, 91–92, 153, 191, 209, 210, 230
Longworthy, Howie, 140
Lovering, H. S., 106
Lukon, Joseph, 200
Lusitania, 63, 151
Lutyens, Edwin, 272

Lysck, John, 204

M

MacBeth, Andrew, 178
Macdonald, John A., 11
MacKay, John, 221, 223
MacKenzie, Norman, 188
MacKinnon, Alderman, 251
MacKinnon, Eleanor, 268–69
MacKinnon, Lilian Vaux, 115
MacKinnon, Murdoch: background, 115; dispute with W. Scott, 113–14, 116–25, 126, 128, 130; on prohibition, 73–74; resigns from Knox Church, 127; and school laws, 116–21, 244; and war, 63–64, 179, 237
MacLachlan, Ethel, 228
MacLean, J. J., 271–72
Mantle, A. Frank, 2–3, 67, 135–36
Martin, Billy, 140
Martin, Harold, 135
Martin, Mrs. William, 35–36, 82
Martin, William: and agriculture, 10; and anti-immigrant motions, 242, 243; and employment for veterans, 236–37; and English only schools movement, 244; fundraising campaign, 188, 190; and 1917 election, 240, 241; and social reform, 207, 226–27, 228; support of veterans, 241, 242; and war, 68, 267
Mason, Mayor, 273, 274
Mathieu, O. E., 71, 224, 262
McAra, James, 33, 241, 266
McAughey, Eric, 269
McCarthy, John, 255–56
McCormick, L. E., 201
McDonald, L. T., 50, 196, 252–53
McDonald, Mrs., 189–90
McInnis, Alderman, 271
McIntosh, A. W., 124, 219
McIsaac, J. J., 183
McKay, J. F., 258
McKinnon, John, 29
McLaren, Angus, 5
McLennan, D., 61
McLeod, J. J., 255
McLorg, E. A. C., 116, 122–23
McNabb, Archie, 266
McNaughton, Mrs. John, 223
McNeil, Jimmy, 59
McPhail, A. J., 67
McRoberts, Mr., 202
McTavish, R. L., 220–21
Mee, Mr., 36
Melnycky, Peter, 291n99

memorials: Armistice Day, 267–70, 273–76; City Cenotaph, 270–76; Regina cemetery, 266–67; war museum, 266
Mennonites, 108, 244, 246
Methodist church: attitude toward war, 13–14, 26; and prohibition, 72–73, 75; and social reform, 15, 214, 215, 218–24
Mile of Pennies, 80–81
Military District 12, 182
Military Hospitals Commission, 188, 233–34, 235
Military Service Act, 180–81
Miller, Ian, 4
Miller, Mrs. A. D., 89–90, 234
Milliken, Robert, 13–14, 230, 262
Milne, Stan, 33
Miriam of Queen's (MacKinnon), 115–16
Mitchell, Elizabeth, 8
Mitchell, Silas W., 125
Mokah, Karl, 200
Molloy, Thomas, 183, 201, 222
Monteith, Oswald, 61
Moore, S. R., 129
Moore, T. Albert, 223
Moral and Social Reform Council of Canada, 219–24
Morgan, Grace, 90
Morton, Desmond, 239
Mothers' Pensions Act (Saskatchewan), 228
Motherwell, W. R., 10, 126, 136, 207, 221–22
Mumford, George, 140
Murphy, Gerald D., 161
Murphy, Tommy, 33
Murray, Walter, 25, 37, 73, 249
Musselman, J. B., 105

N

National British Citizenship League, 244
National Service Board, 174
Naylor, I. B., 271
Neuville-Vitasse, 258
New Zealand nurses, 89–90
Newcombe, Mrs. F., 243–44
Newnham, Bishop, 224
newspapers: and censorship, 19–20; eagerness for war news in, 33–34; and recruitment, 151; and social reform, 226; and Vimy Ridge, 168; before the war, 19–20; war letters in, 2. *See also Der Courier; Evening Province and Standard; Regina Leader*
Nicholak family, 41
Nicol, John H., 220
Nineteenth Battalion, 161
Ninety-Fifth Rifles, 24, 30, 32, 146, 288n50
Nobles, H. R., 269
Noonan, J. D., 38

North Dakota, 43
nursing, 86–88, 253–56, 280
Nye, Russel, 11

O

Oliver, E. H., 73, 108–9
Oman, Mrs., 210
195th Battalion, 146–49, 157
102nd Battalion, 157
179th Battalion, 240
O'Phelan, James, 139
Otton, Charles E., 67, 138–39

P

Pander, Rev., 107, 245
Parker, F. H., 254
Parlee, Medley K., 83
Passchendaele, 169–71
Patriotic Fund, 3, 37–38, 82, 185–90, 189–90, 242
Patriotic Revenues Act (Saskatchewan), 187–88
patriotism: and charity, 35–36, 186; in essay-writing contest, 268–69; at the front, 133; on home front, 62–63; and 1916 recruitment drive, 145–46; at outbreak of war, 23–25. *See also* British Empire; British heritage; Canada
Paulsen, Mr., 53
pensions, 228, 233–34
People's Forum, 218, 227
Perrett, T. E., 64
Perry, A. B., 37, 42
Perry, Harry, 91
Perry, Mrs. A. B., 84
Petrov, Miladin, 78
Piccaninnies, 169
Pidgeon, George C., 222
Pierce, H. C., 129
Polish immigrants, 107
poppies, 268, 269
Potts, Joe, 137
Preece, J. V., 134–35
Price, George L., 260
prisoner-of-war camps, 141
Progressivism, 13, 14–15, 217–18, 279, 280
prohibition: at the front, 135; goes into effect, 76–79; link to war, 14; momentum towards, 70–74, 297n1; referendums, 77–79; and school reform, 100, 102; and social reform, 220; and Spanish flu, 253; as symbolic crusade, 75–76
propaganda, 34, 66, 148–49, 151, 209–10
Protich, Bud, 24
Provincial Equal Franchise Board, 89
Prussia, Saskatchewan, 242

Index

Q

Quance, F. M., 183
Quebec, 23, 176, 179

R

raffles, 85
Raise a Pig campaign, 207
Rasorabowicz, Michael, 110
Rauschenbusch, Walter, 214
recreation. *See* entertainment
Red Cross: fundraising for, 188, 192, 247; Regina chapter founded, 35; women's work for, 3, 81, 82, 83–88
Reekie, W. P., 104, 223
Regina: history, 8–9; population, 3, 24, 196, 324n105; pre-war description of, 4–5, 16–19; pre-war economy, 8–9, 20, 30, 46–53; reaction to outbreak of war, 22–23, 24–26; recruitment, 2, 28–31, 32. *See also* Regina, City of
Regina, City of: and charities, 185, 191–93; memorial project, 270–73; and social reform, 230; and Spanish flu, 251, 255, 256; support for war, 28, 207, 208; and unemployment, 46–47, 49–50, 51–52; and unions, 203–4
Regina Citizens' War Economy Board, 266
Regina College, 16, 90, 94–95, 146, 188, 253, 261
Regina Collegiate Institute, 146
Regina Food Production Association, 206
Regina *Leader*: on agriculture, 9–10, 50–51, 201; and Canadian identity, 277–78; and censorship, 19–20; on charity work, 85, 188, 189, 193, 247; circulation during war, 33–34; and city census, 196; on coalition government, 176–77, 178; and conscription law, 184; on end of war, 260–61; and gardening, 206–7; and German atrocities, 62; and immigrant patriotism, 25; and labour unrest, 204, 205; links to the front, 53, 56, 67, 132; and MacKinnon-Scott dispute, 119, 121, 126, 127, 130; and memorials, 267, 269–70, 275–76; on national sentiment, 6–7; on nature of sacrifice, 37–38, 43–44; politics of, 19, 114; and prohibition, 76, 77–78; and protection of French language rights, 247–48; as recruitment booster, 65, 66, 145–46, 152, 154–55, 156; and school reform, 100–101; as site of war news, 22, 23; and social reform, 229; and Spanish flu, 255; on trench warfare, 56–57; tributes to soldiers, 139, 140; and Vimy Ridge, 168; war boosting, 12, 30, 62–63, 280; on women's war work, 85, 88, 93, 198

Regina Patriotic Fund, 37–38. *See also* Patriotic Fund
Regina Returned Soldiers' Welcome and Aid League, 234–35, 237, 238, 239
Regina Rifle Regiment, 274
Regina Royal Rifles, 32
Regina Trades and Labor Council, 187
Reid, Margaret C., 87
religion: and anti-German rhetoric, 63–64; and conscription, 179; and end of war, 262–63; at the front, 166; and immigrants, 15, 245–46; and MacKinnon-Scott dispute, 116–21, 122–25; and memorials, 271, 275; and moral policing, 229–30; and 1917 election, 178–79; number of churches, 16; and patriotic concerts, 36; and prohibition, 70, 71, 72–74, 75, 78; and recruitment, 66, 152; in school curriculum, 107, 108, 119; and schools, 13, 96–97, 116–20, 127, 128; stand on war, 25–26; and suffrage movement, 80; war oratory, 214–17, 249–50. *See also* social gospel
Renton, J. R., 238
Resoski, John, 204
Retail Merchants' Association, 208
Ridgeway, W. F., 254
RNWMP (Royal North West Mounted Police), 37, 38, 84, 190
Roach, Sergeant-Major, 145
Robbins, Raymond, 219–20
Robinson, Mrs. George, 81
Robson, Mrs. Charles, 91–92
Rose, John A., 251
Ross, Alexander: at Battle of Amiens, 257, 258; on Cambrai, 259; on Canadian identity, 278; delays order, 280; on esprit de corps, 165, 166, 169, 170, 172; on Iwuy, 259; on Neuville-Vitasse, 258; on Ross rifle, 162; and shell holes, 164; signs up, 158; takes command of Sixth Brigade, 259; takes command of 28th, 165; and trenches, 159–60, 170; on Vimy Ridge, 167, 168; on Ypres, 160, 169; at Ypres-Menin, 161, 162
Ross, James Hamilton, 114, 126–27, 130
Ross, James M., 254
Ross rifle, 57, 162
Rotary Club, 192, 207, 271
Rounding, Lewis, 49
Row, G. Wall, 58–59
Royal Commission on corruption allegations, 122, 125, 129
Royal North West Mounted Police (RNWMP), 37, 38, 84, 190
Rumanian Hall protest, 48–49
Rumanians, 152
rural myth: after WWI, 278–79; of agriculture as moulder of character, 50; defined, 7;

361

manifestation of, 9–13; and school reform, 103–5; during war-time, 210
Russia, 21–22, 43

S

Salmon, H. L. N., 170
Sampson, H. E., 181, 223
Saskatchewan: pre-war growth of, 7–8; war-time economy of, 195–98
Saskatchewan, Government of: charges of corruption against, 122, 129; and control of Patriotic Fund, 185, 187–88; and employment, 47, 50, 198, 236–37; financial support for war, 27, 37–38; and 1917 election, 240–41; and prohibition, 70, 71, 76; school reform, 99–100, 105, 108, 247; and social reform, 14, 116, 226–27, 228, 279; and suffrage, 88; support of veterans, 241, 242; ties to SGGA, 10, 198; war memorial museum, 266
Saskatchewan Deutsches Volksverein, 107
Saskatchewan Grain Growers' Association (SGGA), 10, 89, 183, 198, 244–45
Saskatchewan Greater Production Loan program, 198
Saskatchewan Public Education League, 100, 105
Saskatchewan Returned Soldiers' Employment Commission, 236–37
Saskatchewan School Trustees' Association, 245–46
Saskatchewan Social and Moral Reform Council, 70
Saskatchewan Social Service Council, 14, 224–28, 229
Scanlan, William, 53, 54, 55, 142–43
schools: and agriculture, 103–5, 198; battle over bilingualism in, 6, 96–99, 105; as centre of Britishness, 82, 95–96; English only movement, 242–48; language of instruction debate, 106–11; and MacKinnon-Scott dispute, 116–21; and memorials, 268–69; in pre-war Regina, 16; reform of, 99–103, 106–11; role of Canadianizing immigrants, 106, 108, 110; separate school tax question, 116–20, 127, 128; and social reform, 101–3, 226; and Spanish flu, 252, 253–54, 257; and war work, 150, 190–91, 235
Scott, Mrs. Walter, 35
Scott, Walter: background, 114–15; and bilingualism in schools, 97, 98–99; charges of corruption against, 122, 125; dispute with M. MacKinnon, 113–14, 116–21, 122–25, 129, 130; and ethnic tensions, 25, 42; and financial support of soldiers, 36–37; health problems, 125–27; and J. A. Calder,
177; and Knox Church, 122–24, 127–28; legacy of, 129–30; "moral leper" speech and reaction, 123–25; and 1912 election, 11–12; on outbreak of war, 27; and prohibition, 71, 72, 73, 74, 77; and Regina *Leader*, 19; resigns office, 127, 129, 130; on Saskatchewan's promise, 8, 9; and school reform, 99–100, 103; and SGGA, 10; and suffrage, 88, 89, 92; and unemployment, 50; and unions, 14
Scythes, W. G. F., 53
Second Canadian Machine Gun Battalion, 172
Second Ypres, Battle of, 45, 57, 58–61, 63–64, 138
separate school tax question, 116–20, 127, 128
Serbia, 21–22
Seventy-Ninth Cameron Highlanders, 67, 152
Seventy-Seventh Battery, 150, 181
sewing circles, 81–82, 190, 214
SGGA (Saskatchewan Grain Growers' Association), 10, 89, 183, 198, 244–45
Shamrock, Mr., 202
Shannon, Elsie, 86–87
Sheppard, J. A., 129
Sifton, Clifford, 97
Simpson, A. F., 258
Sinton, Mrs. Robert, 76
Sixth Canadian Infantry Brigade: at Amiens, 258; at Courcelette, 163–64; formation, 159; and J. F. Embury, 162; in reserve, 169; at St. Eloi, 161; supporting the line, 171–72; at Vimy Ridge, 167
Sixtieth Battery Canadian Field Artillery, 150
Sixty-Eighth Battalion: broken up, 157; and charity work, 85–86; filling ranks of 28th, 162; formation, 64; at the front, 135, 138, 139–40; recruitment for, 65, 66–67, 143–46, 149; returning, 235
Smith, H. G., 181
Smith, J. C., 67
Smith, J. W., 181
Smith, Mrs. A. D., 86
Sneath, Edwin, 167
snipers, 162–63
social gospel: and government action, 230–31; link to war, 215–16, 280; and moral policing, 229–31; and People's Forum, 218; premise of, 213–14; and Social Service Congress, 219–24; and support for war, 13; and unemployment, 51
social reform: and Big Interests, 217–18, 221–22, 226, 230–31; and criminal law, 220–21, 228; and health care, 225, 227–28; and Liberal Party, 14, 213, 279; platform of Saskatchewan Social Service Council, 224–28; and religion, 13–14, 15, 51, 213–14; roots of, 213; by Saskatchewan government, 14–15, 116, 226–27, 228, 279; and schools,

Index

101–3, 226; and soldiers, 229; and unions, 14, 222
Social Service Congress, 219–24
Social Service Council of Canada, 219
Society for the Prevention of Cruelty to Animals (SPCA), 191–92
Soldier Settlement Act, 330n19
soldiers: in convalescence, 235–36; departing Regina, 31–32, 53–54; dispersed into different battalions, 32, 157; entertainment, 54–55, 58, 163, 166, 172, 229, 238; experiences at the front, 132–37, 137–43, 159–60, 165, 170; finances, 30, 36–38; first action, 45; flying corps, 140–42; and gas attacks, 57, 58, 59, 61–62, 258; gifts sent home, 131; kit of, 54, 162; letters, 2, 56, 60, 83, 110, 134–35, 144; medical care after war, 233–34; as prisoners, 141; recruitment, 28–31, 64–67, 143–52; return to Canada, 233–38, 242; shell shock, 132–33, 135; and social reform, 229; training, 54, 55, 158, 159, 171; voluntary recruitment dries up, 151–56, 174; wounded, 2, 137–43, 165, 167–68, 173, 233, 237. *See also* conscription; Twenty-Eighth Battalion
Soldiers of the Soil campaign, 201–2, 206
Somme, 163–65
Spanish flu, 204, 250–57, 262, 333n13
SPCA (Society for the Prevention of Cruelty to Animals), 191–92
St. Chad's College, 235–36, 253
St. Peter's Bote, 71, 74
Stacey, Charles, 1, 6
Stapleford, Ernest W., 179, 188
Stapleford, Maude, 80, 90
Stapleford, Mrs, 209, 210
Stewart, Fraser, 67
Stewart, W. J., 71
Stinson, Katherine, 93
Storey, Jack, 201–2
strikes, labour, 203–5
Stuart, Herbert, 34
Styles, A. G. "Tiny," 32–33, 161, 269
Styles, W. G., 181
Suffa, A., 251
suffrage movement, 14, 79–80, 88–93
Surman, Will, 274
Sveinbjoinson, Louise, 268
Swartz, Henry, 287n16

T

tag days, 84–85, 192
Tallet, Corporal, 238
Tate, F. C., 26
Taylor, Herbert W., 33
Taylor, Neil J. "Piffles," 140–41, 142, 173, 281
Taylor, Sam, 141–42
Telegraph Hill, 258
temperance societies, 69–70, 71–76, 100. *See also* prohibition; Women's Christian Temperance Union (WCTU)
Tenth Battalion, 132
Thackeray, Mrs, 190
Thirty-First Battalion, 161
Thirty-Second Reserve Battalion, 157
Thom, D. J., 151
Thompson, H. N., 67
Thornton, L. A., 272
Thornton, Major, 153
Todd, Archibald, 183
Trades and Labour Council, 48, 91, 200, 202, 204, 205, 237
Trafalgar Day, 82
Turner, Harris, 236–37
Turner, R. E. W., 162
Twain, Mark, 231
Twenty-Eighth Infantry Battalion, 157–72; and Battle of Amiens, 257–58; and Battle of Courcelette, 163–65; at Cambrai, 258–59; formation, 32, 157–58; at the front, 135–36, 136–37; at Iwuy, 259; at Lens, 169; march to Mons, 260; and Neuville-Vitasse, 258; at Passchendaele, 169–71; reunion, 238; secret offensive, 172; shipped out, 159; supporting the line, 171–72; training, 158–59; trench warfare, 159–60; in Valenciennes, 260; at Vimy Ridge, 165–69; at Ypres-Menin Road, 161–62
Twenty-First Battalion, 162
Twenty-Ninth Battalion, 161, 258
Twenty-Seventh Battalion, 159, 161
Twiss, Fannie, 209
249th Battalion, 151–52, 155, 157
217th Battalion, 149, 240

U

Ukrainian immigration, 15, 40–41, 48–49, 108–9, 152
Unionist government, 177, 178–80
unions: and conscription, 174–75; growth of, 202–5; and 1917 election, 178; as part of social reform, 14, 222; support for war, 38, 187, 196
United Services Institute, 267, 270
United States, 43, 101, 198, 215
University Women's Club, 93, 301n132
urban development, 8–9

V

vacant lot gardening, 205–7
Valcartier, 32, 54, 55

Valenciennes, 260
Van Egmond, W. G., 272
venereal disease, 227–28
veterans' organizations, 2, 238–42. *See also* Army and Navy Veterans (ANV); Great War Veterans' Association (GWVA)
Victoria Park monument, 270–73
Victory Loan campaigns, 190–91
Ville-sur-Haine, 260
Vimy Ridge, 140, 142, 165–69

W

Waldron, Branch W., 67
Wancourt, 258
Ward, J. W., 136
Wartime Elections Act, 176, 184
Wascana Park, 271
Wass, R. E., 87
Watson, Blanche, 198
Watson, T., 187
Watters, James, 175
WCTU (Women's Christian Temperance Union), 35, 70, 78, 79, 89, 91, 229
Weed, E. N., 255
welfare state, 193–94, 224–28
West, E. A., 62
Western, Walter, 66, 221
Westgate, R. J., 52
Wetmore, J. A., 181
WGGA (Women's Grain Growers' Association), 89
wheat, 51, 195, 210, 266, 320n2
Whigham, F. C. "Bubbles," 163
White, A. H., 137
Wigtiuk, John, 78
Williams, F. McIvor, 132
Williams, J. K. R., 53, 208
Williams, R. H., 86
Willners, Henry, 246–47
Willoughby, Wellington B., 74, 98, 234, 241, 248
Win the War Week, 151–53, 154
Winter, Jay, 4
women: charity work, 3, 35–36, 80–86, 189–90; employment, 53, 198–200, 201, 223, 252–53; fight for equal rights, 93–94; and food conservation, 209, 210, 211; in Home Guard, 33; as nurses, 86–88, 253–56, 280; and prohibition, 70, 78; and recruitment, 65–66, 153, 154; and returning soldiers, 234, 237–38; and social reform, 223; and Spanish flu, 252–53, 255, 256; on strike, 204; and suffrage movement, 14, 79–80, 88–93; and Wartime Elections Act, 176. *See also* Local Council of Women; Women's Christian Temperance Union (WCTU)
Women's Christian Temperance Union (WCTU), 35, 70, 78, 79, 89, 91, 229
Women's Educational Club, 90
Women's Grain Growers' Association (WGGA), 89
Wood, Charles A., 67
Woodsworth, J. S., 13, 17–18, 20
World War I: ends, 260–63, 265; explanation of how it occurred, 4, 21–22; seen as "holy war," 63–64. *See also* soldiers; Twenty-Eighth Battalion *and specific units*
Wylie, Barbara, 89
Wylie, D. J., 89, 98, 240

Y

YMCA (Young Men's Christian Association), 29, 80, 255
Youmans, Letitia, 70, 79
Ypres, Battle of Second, 45, 57, 58–61, 63–64, 138
Ypres Salient, 160, 169–70

Z

Zarona, Pete, 203
Zimmer, H., 247